Regulating Content – European Regulatory Framework for the Media and Related Creative Sectors

EUROPEAN MONOGRAPHS

Editor-in-Chief Professor David O'Keeffe

In this series *European Monographs* this book *Regulating Content – European Regulatory Framework for the Media and Related Creative Sectors* is the fifty-third title.

The titles published in this series are listed at the end of this volume.

EUROPEAN MONOGRAPHS

Regulating Content – European Regulatory Framework for the Media and Related Creative Sectors

**Michael Holoubek/Dragana Damjanovic/
Matthias Traimer**

KLUWER LAW
INTERNATIONAL

Published by:
Kluwer Law International
P.O. Box 316
2400 AH Alphen aan den Rijn
The Netherlands
E-mail: sales@kluwerlaw.com
Website: http://www.kluwerlaw.com

Sold and distributed in North, Central and South America by:
Aspen Publishers, Inc.
7201 Mc Kinney Circle
Frederick, MD 21704
United States of America

Sold and distributed in all other countries by:
Turpin Distribution Services Ltd.
Stratton Business Park
Pegasus Drive, Biggleswade
Bedfordshire SG18 8TQ
United Kingdom

ISBN 90-411-2597-3

List of Contributors

Christoph Bezemek, Assistant at the Institute for Austrian and European Public Law, Vienna University of Economics and Business Administration

Dragana Damjanovic, Assistant at the Institute for Austrian and European Public Law, Vienna University of Economics and Business Administration

Matthias Hofstätter, Assistant at the Institute for Austrian and International Tax Law, Vienna University of Economics and Business Administration

Michael Holoubek, Professor at the Institute for Austrian and European Public Law, Vienna University of Economics and Business Administration

Margit Nemetz, Assistant at the Institute of Civil, Commercial and Securities Law, Department of Information Technology Law and Intellectual Property Law, Vienna University of Economics and Business Administration

Mathias Neubauer, Assistant at the Institute of Civil Commercial and Securities Law, Department of Information Technology Law and Intellectual Property Law, Vienna University of Economics and Business Administration

Gregor Ribarov, Assistant at the Institute for Austrian and European Public Law, Vienna University of Economics and Business Administration

Michaela Seifert, Assistant at the Europainstitut, Vienna University of Economics and Business Administration

Peter Thyri, Assistant at the Department for Labour, Economic, and European Law, University Salzburg

Andreas Wiebe, Professor at the Institute of Civil, Commercial and Securities Law, Department of Information Technology Law and Intellectual Property Law, Vienna University of Economics and Business Administration

Foreword

Within the European Union the content and creative economy has an important role to play, in particular with a view to future economic growth and the development of a competitive business environment in Europe. At Community level a wide variety of measures have been taken to promote this branch of industry, especially in fields in which new and innovative digital technologies are used to enhance the market potential of content, creative products and services. A closer look at the legal implementation of the individual initiatives and programmes in the field of content shows a wide range of legal instruments used to regulate the content and creative economy. These include general regulatory instruments as well as measures specifically attuned to the needs of individual aspects related to the production and distribution of content.

European Content regulation, however, is only one part of the content regulation network of Europe, regulation by Member States being the other. Regarding the fact that content in a European context is not only of economic but equally of vital cultural importance, the interrelationship and balance between culture and commerce is a focal point in regulating content.

Starting from the bird's eye perspective with a systematic overview of the legal bases of European Content regulation this book attempts to systematize regulatory interventions in the content industry under Community law. This leads to a closer insight in the functioning of the European legal framework for the content industry, its guiding principles, its explicit and sometimes more hidden agenda *vis-à-vis* policy areas falling largely into Member States competences. In this aspect the book can also be read as an analysis of the impact of the cooperation between European and Member State regulation when economic as well as social, democratic and cultural policy goals are at stake.

The basis of this book was a research project commissioned by the Austrian Federal Chancellery in preparation for a Seminar entitled 'Content for Competitiveness - Strengthening the European Creative Industries in the Light of the i2010 Strategy' organized by the Federal Chancellery and supported by the European Commission in connection with Austria's European Presidency in the first half of 2006.

To acknowledge and document the decisive initiative and the profound professional advice provided to the research process by the experts within the Federal Chancellery, Matthias Traimer co-edits in representation. Special acknowledgement and expression of gratitude have to be given nonetheless to Kathrin Kneissel, without her enormous efforts and dedication the project would not exist, and to Patrick Segalla, whose outstanding expertise and whose organizational and social skills kept the project going. Andreas Ulrich provided important support in establishing the factual basis for the legal research and wrote an overview about trends in the individual branches of the content industry for the study presented at the above mentioned Seminar. As usual, however, the scientific responsibility especially for all errors and mistakes lies with the authors of the individual chapters of the book and the first two of the editors alone.

These editors are further indebted to David O'Keeffe, who suggested many improvements, to Emin T. Balic for the graphics, to Ursula Cordt and her team for the translation of the study presented at the seminar and to Elisabeth Koller for her professional technical assistance. We also like to thank Karel van der Linde and Femke Koenraads from Kluwer Law International with whom it was a pleasure to work.

Michael Holoubek/Dragana Damjanovic/Matthias Traimer

Contents

PART THREE SYSTEMATIZATION, EVALUATION AND CONCLUSION – A STRUCTURAL ANALYSIS 213

Part One
The Legal Aspects of European Content Regulation – Purpose and Scope of the Study

Chapter 1

Objective of the Book: A Horizontal Approach to European Content Regulation

Michael Holoubek/Dragana Damjanovic

I. THE BACKGROUND – CONTENT AS PART OF EUROPE'S CULTURE

In Europe, the production of content has a long tradition, which in many ways is bound up with European history. Content is part of Europe's culture and thus part of its multi-faceted cultural heritage. In line with the European Union's objective expressed in its Lisbon Strategy to 'make the Union the most competitive and dynamic knowledge-based area', the content industry has always played a key role.

The content industry is not only a central factor for the further development of the information and technology sector and thus for the digital economy as a whole, but also has a distinct value of its own in that it forms part of the European cultural sphere. It is an essential component of European integration and significantly contributes to the success and viability of the European model of society.

As part of the creative – and thus cultural – economy, the content industry is defined, in manifold ways, by the typically European heritage of cultural diversity – including, at least to a considerable extent, the diversity of languages. In this respect, it is the traditional cultural roots that determine the inherent laws governing the European content industry and make for its specific strengths. At the same time, however, the content industry is – in an almost exemplary way – subject to the overall prevailing conditions of globalization, particularly with regard to the transmission of audiovisual and other contents offered online, i.e. eContent. The new multiplatforms, and especially the Internet, are increasingly globalizing the content markets, and accordingly, all fields of activity of the content industry (including the European one).

M. Holoubek, D. Damjanovic and M. Traimer (eds), *Regulating Content – European Regulatory Framework for the Media and Related Creative Sectors*, pp. 3–5

A successful implementation of the strategic objectives of Lisbon regarding the content industry might well serve as a key model for keeping European traditions and culture competitive and viable in the face of the requirements of a globalized economy and society, and not only to prevent them from being overwhelmed by the process of globalization but actually enabling them to make a special, essentially European contribution to it.

II. A SYSTEMATIC REVIEW AND ANALYSIS OF EUROPEAN CONTENT REGULATION ON A HORIZONTAL BASIS

In spite of the content industry's importance for the European society, in economic as well as in cultural terms, there is no such thing as an uniform European 'content policy', as this is, e.g., the case with environmental protection or the postal sector, to name just a few. Much rather, the content industry as a cross-sectional subject matter falls within the terms of various political and regulatory efforts. In addition to numerous funding programmes for the content industry established under the Community policies, special mention must here be made of the EC Treaty which contains essential guidelines for the content industry, as the fundamental freedoms and in particular also the culture exemption clause, the EC general competition rules, tax law measures, the law of copyrights and related rights and finally sector-specific provisions that have been developed at EC level, on the one hand, for the electronic communication infrastructures which are necessary to deliver eContent and, on the other hand, for the eContent itself. Latter provisions are mainly laid down in the TWF Directive[1] and the E-Commerce Directive.[2]

This book sets about reviewing and systematically presenting all these different interventions under Community law in the content industry, which is defined for the purposes of this book in a narrow way, comprising the media and related creative sectors. The review is thereby conducted in a horizontal way, meaning that the analysis focuses on the entire content industry rather than on its individual branches – the printing and publishing, music, cinema, radio/TV and the online sector – and that it is broken down according to the aforementioned individual areas of Community rules governing the content industry – the EC Treaty, Competition Law, Sector-Specific Market Rules at infrastructural and content level, Intellectual Property Rights and Tax Measures. The analysis of these individual regulatory areas, in turn, is structured according to the various objectives pursued by the European interventions in the media and related creative sectors: to ensure functioning market structures and in particular the maintenance of the single market, the protection of third

1. Directive 97/36/EC, OJ 1997 L 202/60.
2. Directive 2000/31/EC, OJ 2000 L 178/1.

party and other general interests as well as the direct promotion of the production and distribution of content.

The analysis on European content regulation is structured in this particular way, firstly, to make apparent, to what extent the relevant rules take into consideration, on the one hand, economic and, on the other hand, social, cultural and democratic policy aspects of the media and related creative sectors. Secondly it provides the basis for pointing out what kind of regulatory instruments are used to pursue each of these objectives. This, in turn, makes it possible to spotlight the relationship between the various regulatory instruments used and at the same time to highlight cross-links and interactions between the various objectives pursued by these instruments.

On this basis the analysis will show the general basic principles governing the regulation of the content industry under Community law, and it will make the structures underlying these regulations transparent. From this, finally, problematic aspects of the individual rules as well as of the overall concept of the European content regulation will be addressed and the ongoing discussion at the European level in this context reflected.

This systematic review and analysis of the regulatory instruments and measures used at Community level with regard to the media and related creative sectors, in short the content industry, may serve as a usefull basis for developing an integrated overall concept and a coherent regulatory framework for the European content industry, as it is pursued within the Lisbon Strategy.

Chapter 2
Structure and Methods

Michael Holoubek/Dragana Damjanovic

I. DEFINITION OF THE SUBJECT UNDER INVESTIGATION

The analysis starts with a definition of the subject under investigation, the content industry, and an explanation of the specific legal terminology developed at Community level with regard to this industry.[1] The definition used in this book is a narrow one, focusing on the core segments of the content industry, the media and related creative sectors, which comprise the following types of content: published content, games, audio/music, video/cinema and broadcast content (TV and radio programmes).

In order to establish a basis for the horizontal analysis of the regulatory interventions into these complex markets, the content industry is categorized in the offline content market, comprising the traditional activities of the media and related creative sectors and the online content market, which is characterized by the fact that eContent (published content, games, audio/music and video/film in digitalized form) is distributed via the three digital multiplatforms: the PC broadband platform, the digital TV platform and the mobile platform.

II. ANALYSIS OF THE INDIVIDUAL REGULATORY AREAS OF EUROPEAN COMMUNITY LAW GOVERNING THE CONTENT INDUSTRY

Part Two of the book contains six individual analyses on the various regulatory areas governing, at the level of Community law, the content industry. Regarding the book's horizontal approach to European content regulation and in order to allow for a systematic review and evaluation of these provisions, the individual

---

1. *See* Part One Chapter 3.

M. Holoubek, D. Damjanovic and M. Traimer (eds), *Regulating Content – European Regulatory Framework for the Media and Related Creative Sectors*, pp. 7–14

analyses follow a basic pattern, insofar as they are all structured according to the various objectives pursued by the European interventions into the media and related creative sectors. These objectives comprise:

- the safeguarding of functioning market structures, i.e. essentially of a system of free competition within the content industry;
- the maintenance of a single market, in particular by way of harmonization and coordination of the Member States' interventions into the content industry;
- the protection of third-party and other general interests, i.e. the realization of certain social, cultural and democratic policy aspects within the content industry or in short, of other than economic policy aspects (as pursued by the two aforementioned objectives) and finally;
- the direct promotion of the production and distribution of content.

The only contribution which does not follow this structural pattern is the one on the 'Fundamentals of Community Law and Policies', where a separate discussion of the individual objectives did not appear appropriate in view of the fact that, in particular, at the level of the EC's primary law these individual objectives are closely interconnected with each other.

In particular, the individual analyses comprise the following:

1. 'Fundamentals of Community law and policies (including funding programmes) governing the content industry': This chapter, conducted by *Michaela Seifert*, looks at the competences of the EC with regard to the content industry and in particular with regard to its social, democratic and cultural policy aspects. In this context Article 151 EC, which provides that the Community has only a complementary competence limited specifically to funding measures, explicitly excluding any harmonization of the legal and administrative provisions of the Member States in cultural matters and thus delegating the pursuit of cultural and socio-political objectives in the content industry to a great extent to the Member States, is carefully examined. The application of the fundamental freedoms to the content industry – of which primarily the free movement of goods and the freedom to provide services are relevant – forms another major subject area within this part. These treaty provisions aim at establishing and maintaining a single market for the content industry, based on an open market economy with free competition, by prohibiting any discriminatory or otherwise restraining interventions in the content industry by the Member States. Deviations from these general rules of the EC treaty, which enable the consideration of other than economic policy aspects with regard to the content industry by the Member States, are only allowed for the protection of certain imperative requirements in the general interests. The EC recognized the maintenance of a certain level of programme quality, the safeguarding

of diversity of programmes, as well as the protection of consumers from excessive commercial advertising as 'content-specific' reasons which can justify restrictions of the fundamental freedoms. Within the context of the fundamental freedoms and the EC's harmonization and coordination measures deriving from there, *Michaela Seifert* also addresses the heavily disputed planned Service Directive[2] and its relevance for the content industry as a horizontal measure as well as its relation to other sector-specific harmonization measures in this field, in particular the planned Audiovisual Media Service Directive.[3] Finally she gives a review on the multitude of funding and action programmes at EC level, which are of specific relevance for the content industry. These include the Culture 2000 Programme (and its successor, Culture 2007) which deals with the fostering of cultural projects with a Community-wide dimension; the MEDIA Plus programme and MEDIA Training, which are to be consolidated into a single instrument – the new MEDIA 2007 programme – in the future and which serve the purpose of strengthening the competitiveness of the European audiovisual industry, as well as the various programmes established in connection with and within the framework of the i2010 Initiative for the creation of a European information society for growth and employment. Of particular importance for the content industry are the funding programme eContentplus, which is to facilitate access to digital content and its use and exploitation in Europe, and the programme 'Safer Internet plus', which aims to promote the safer use of the Internet and new online technologies, as well as the numerous measures within the framework of the third pillar of i2010, which are to establish an 'inclusive' information society (eInclusion).

2. The examination of the application of the EC general competition rules to the content industry by *Peter Thyri* contains an in-depth analysis on both, the EC antitrust rules (the competition rules that deal with the activities of the private entities), and the competition rules that deal with the activities of the Member States within the content industry. The former include the cartel prohibition according to Art. 81 EC, the merger control under the Merger Regulation and the prohibition on the abuse of a dominant market position pursuant to Art. 82 EC; the latter the state aid control under Art. 81 EC and the control of public undertakings – within the content industry these are primarily the public service broadcasters – under Art. 86 EC. After a brief insight to the particularities on the definition of the relevant markets within the content industry, i.e. the media and related creative sectors, *Thyri* moves on, by referring to numerous case studies in this area, to assess the relevance of the EC antitrust rules to the content industry. In this context he places special emphasis on

2. *See* the Proposal for a directive on services in the internal market, COM (2006) 160 final.
3. *See* the Proposal for a directive amending the Television without Frontiers Directive 89/552/EEC, COM (2005) 646 final.

exclusive agreements concerning the purchase or sale of content rights for the creation of a media product, as these are common practice in the content markets, in particular when it comes to sports content. Such agreements are to be assessed in the light of Art. 81 EC and to be prohibited if they do have particular negative competitive effects (e.g. they cause considerable foreclosure problems *vis-à-vis* downstream markets or result in the coordination of the pricing policy). If such agreements are made with market players who have a dominant position and lead, for example, by the refusal to grant a licence to the denial of market entry, Art. 82 EC also plays a role. In the context of the merger control, which – in difference to Art. 81 and 82 EC – is aimed at preserving ex ante distortions of effective competition in the common market, various joint venture cases in the media sector, both with a horizontal (e.g. the recent Sony/BMG case) and with a vertical effect (e.g. the RTL/Veronica/Endemol case) are mentioned. With regard to the competition rules dealing with the activities of the Member States in the content industry, *Thyri* focuses on the EC state aid control framework, in particular referring to the financing systems of the public service broadcasters which recently have also been in the focus of the Commission's state aid policy.

3. Chapter 3 on 'Sector specific regulation at infrastructural level', conducted by *Dragana Damjanovic*, deals with the infrastructure related sector specific rules relevant for the content industry. The subject matter of these rules is not the content itself, but the electronic communications infrastructures. Nevertheless, as the electronic communications infrastructures form a necessary precondition for the provision of eContent, they play a vital role for the content industry, more precisely the online content market, as well. The analysis first sets out to examine those sector-specific instruments, whose main purpose is to guarantee functioning market structures in the communications markets, the most important ones to be the market entry and the access regime. Subsequently their special relevance for the content industry is discussed. As to the market entry regime, this can be deduced from an exemption clause which allows also for media and cultural policy criteria to be taken into consideration when allocating resources used for the distribution of television and radio broadcasts, and not only for economical criteria as this is normally the case within this regime. The access regime is in general of importance for the content industry as it forms the basis on which eContent providers may demand access to electronic networks in order to be able to offer their services to their customers. The analysis then moves on to the instruments of this sector-specific regime which primarily aim at safeguarding public interests in the content industry. This is, in particular, to ensure a basic supply of the population with content to prevent the emergence of a digital divide in the information society. At the level of sector specific infrastructure market regulation this objective is guaranteed by the concept of open access for everyone to electronic communications

infrastructures and thus also to the content that is transmitted through them. It is implemented by various regulatory approaches: (a) by the universal service regime and the must-carry provisions according to the Universal Service Directive[4] (b) by the provisions on the broadcasting of major events according to the TWF Directive[5] and (c) by the provisions on the special role and importance of the public service broadcasters laid down in the EC treaty. Finally, the author looks at the various standardization activities in the content industry that are to guarantee interoperability which, in turn, plays a central role not only for the maintenance of the single market in the media and related sectors but also for the development of a large selection of content and with it the guarantee of media pluralism and freedom of information.

4. As distinct from Chapter 3 this chapter conducted by *Christoph Bezemek* and *Gregor Ribarov* explores the kind of sector specific regulations which aim at the content itself, in other words at the act of producing and distributing content. The legal foundation for such provisions can be found in various community directives, one being the TWF Directive[6] for content broadcast via television. Regulations for so-called 'information society services' are enclosed in the E-Commerce Directive.[7] In addition, Community Law also features a few individual product-related regulations which, due to the specific characteristics of the product in question or the impact it may have, also standardize advertisement in connection with this product inasmuch as they contain subject-matter regulations governing the performance of content and are therefore to be considered in the given framework, as for example the Tobacco Directive.[8] After delivering a short insight to the presently at EC level conducted and highly debated revision of the TWF directive – the central provision within the EC sector-specific regulatory framework at content level – the authors start their analysis by looking at the relevant provisions first from the angle of their objective to protect third parties and public interests. In this context the text analyzes regulatory measures for the protection of human dignity, and of other fundamental values of a democratic society as well as for the protection of minors, health, consumers and personal rights. Another objective of sector specific regulation at content level is the promotion of production and distribution of content. Especially indirect promotion by limiting regulatory possibilities – Art. 10 ECHR being the most relevant provision in this context – is described and discussed here. Naturally, maintaining the single market by harmonizing Member States' sector-specific rules at content level plays an important role as

4. Directive 2002/22/EC, OJ 2002 L 108/51.
5. Directive 97/36/EC, OJ 1997 L 202/60.
6. Directive 97/36/EG, OJ 1997 L 202/60.
7. Directive 2000/31/EC, OJ 2000 L 178/01.
8. Directive 2003/33/EG, OJ 2003 L 152/16.

well. The final remarks therefore deal in particular with those provisions at EC level of European sector specific regulation at content level whose objective is to directly and constitutively harmonize the content industry. In this context the various principles developed for the harmonization of the Member States' sector-specific rules for the content industry like the affected market principle and the country-of-origin principle, laid down in the TWF Directive and the E-Commerce Directive, are addressed.

5. The chapter on 'copyright and related rights' written by *Margit Nemetz, Mathias Neubauer and Andreas Wiebe,* contains a critical account on copyright law and the related rights as a protective system for the production and distribution of content. The authors start out by giving an overview of the protection available to the producers and distributors of content and thereby concentrate on the Information Society Directive[9] as the major legal instrument to adapt the existing rules for the 'digital age'. With regard to this directive the broad definition of the exploitation rights and the merely optional character of the limitations provisions from these rights as well as the lack of clarity regarding the exact scope of these limitations are addressed. Furthermore the different application of the country-of-origin principle to copyright protection with regard to content distributed online, resulting from the exclusion of this area from the E-Commerce Directive,[10] is questioned. The necessity to coordinate the cross-border activities performed by the collecting societies with the use of digital rights management systems is also discussed in this context. The second part contains a critical account on the debate, inherent in every intellectual property rights protection system, how to ensure an adequate balance between the interest to provide by this system market incentives to produce content, on the one hand, and to protect the interest of the general public to have access to content, on the other hand. Here the authors argue that the limits provided by the Information Society Directive to safeguard the interest of the general public are too narrow in some areas. This is in particular the case for the purpose of protecting libraries, teaching and research, where a precise and mandatory enforcement regulation system seems to be required in order not to jeopardize the adequate balance of interests.
6. The last chapter in this part, written by *Matthias Hofstätter*, finally shows how the development of the content industry is influenced and governed by tax measures in Europe. Direct tax instruments, which traditionally play a central role as means for the promotion of the production and distribution of content, are at Community level only of minor importance compared to the funding by the Member States, because of the Community's limited competences in this field. The author thus concentrates on the instruments within the field of indirect taxation, which are contained

9. Directive 2001/29/EC, OJ 2001 L 167/10.
10. Directive 2000/31/EC, OJ 2000 L 178/1.

in the sixth VAT directive.[11] On the one hand, these regulations provide for a system according to which the Member States are allowed to apply a reduced tax rate to certain supplies of goods or services within the content industry, as for example the supply of books, the reception of radio and television broadcasting services and the supply of certain services of writers, composers and performing artists. On the other hand, they oblige the Member States to exclude the activities of public radio and television broadcasting organizations from the value added tax.

III. CONCLUSION AND EVALUATION

Based upon the individual analyses contained in Part Two, Part Three sets about to summarize and evaluate the provisions of the various regulatory areas in a cross-sectional approach. As within the scope of these regulatory areas efforts to strengthen the European content industry are essentially made in two directions – first, via the safeguarding of functioning market structures and secondly, by enforcing certain cultural, democratic and social policy concerns – the provisions are broken down in the following categories:

- Regulations safeguarding functioning market structures in the content industry, which can be divided again in regulations dealing with the activities of the market players (the EC antitrust rules and the sector specific market rules) and regulations dealing with the activities of the Member States and public enterprises, as well as other state-sponsored bodies. The latter covers the application of the fundamental freedoms, in particular the free movement of goods and services to the content markets, the control of 'state aids' and the control of public enterprises and other state-sponsored bodies. The harmonization measures of the EC in the field of intellectual property rights or the audiovisual media sector, implemented in first instance to maintain a functioning single market, also fall in this category.
- Regulations serving to ensure the realization of certain social, democratic and cultural policy concerns within the content industry. They include measures which aim at, a) the direct support of the production and distribution of European content in order to foster European identity, b) the guarantee of a basic supply of the population with content (and with communications infrastructures required for the transmission of content) and, c) the safeguarding of certain third-party interests in these markets, such as, in particular, the protection of human dignity, consumers and minors.

11. Directive 77/799/EEC, OJ 1977 L 336/15.

While the regulations which aim at safeguarding functioning market structures are in general formulated as 'hard law measures', the cultural, democratic and social interventions at EC level are primarily realized by 'soft law measures', i.e. direct and indirect funding instruments, or via specific exemption clauses from the economic market structure regulation within which the Member States may become active in order to realize these socio-political and cultural aims.

Part Three closes with some conclusions drawn from the results of this systematic review and evaluation of European content regulation and with some recommendations as to the future development of this regulatory complex. Basically, the argument is that there is no such thing as 'a super legislator' for all aspects of the content industry, that only a network system of various regulatory areas, as it presently exists at the EC level with regard to the European content industry, can cope with the complex cross-sectional matter content effectively. The central task of European content regulation therefore is 'network coordination', which needs common guiding principles at EC level to establish, on the one hand, a 'mission' for the European content policy (e.g. 'common diversity for a multi-cultural community') and to define criteria for an appropriate balance between economic and cultural aspects within the content industry, on the other hand. This, in turn, requires – as the 'culture article' (Art. 151 EC) in its present form does not appear to live up to this challenge – the equipment of the Community with the necessary regulatory competences in the field of cultural policy. These concluding recommendations should serve as an impulse for the ongoing discussion at EC level which is essential to find solutions for the challenges of the future European content regulation.

Chapter 3
The European Content Industry – Categorization and Definitions

Michael Holoubek/Dragana Damjanovic

I. THE SUBJECT UNDER INVESTIGATION

A very broad field of activities can be associated with the term 'content' and thus also with the term 'content industry'. This field certainly includes printing and publishing, TV and radio broadcasters, the music, video and cinema sectors as well as the online content market. While these sectors may be summarized under the heading of the 'core content industries' (meaning the media and related creative sectors), content is also produced and/or distributed by all those who produce art, i.e. painters, architects, actors, musicians and photographers, as well as by cultural institutions such as theatres, concert halls and museums, by players in the market whose function is to deliver certain types of information (such as stock exchange prices), by governmental institutions that provide information important to the public (for instance in the fields of culture, education and health), and, last but not least, by the consumers themselves, e.g. by participating in Internet fora or by providing content via weblogs which are publicly accessable. It is obvious that there is no single or uniform criterion to be applied to the entire range of individuals, institutions and activities that produce and/or distribute content in some way.

Even if we concentrate exclusively on the core sectors, the media and related creative sectors, the rapid changes they have been undergoing due to digital technologies make it anything but easy to draw a clear picture of the content industry in its present form. New distribution channels – multiplatforms for digital video broadcasting (DVB) and the third generation of mobile phone networks (UMTS) – have given rise to many new products and services and have changed consumer behaviour. This, in turn, has had significant implications for traditional business plans and practices in these sectors, blurred the traditional

M. Holoubek, D. Damjanovic and M. Traimer (eds), *Regulating Content – European Regulatory Framework for the Media and Related Creative Sectors*, pp. 15–21

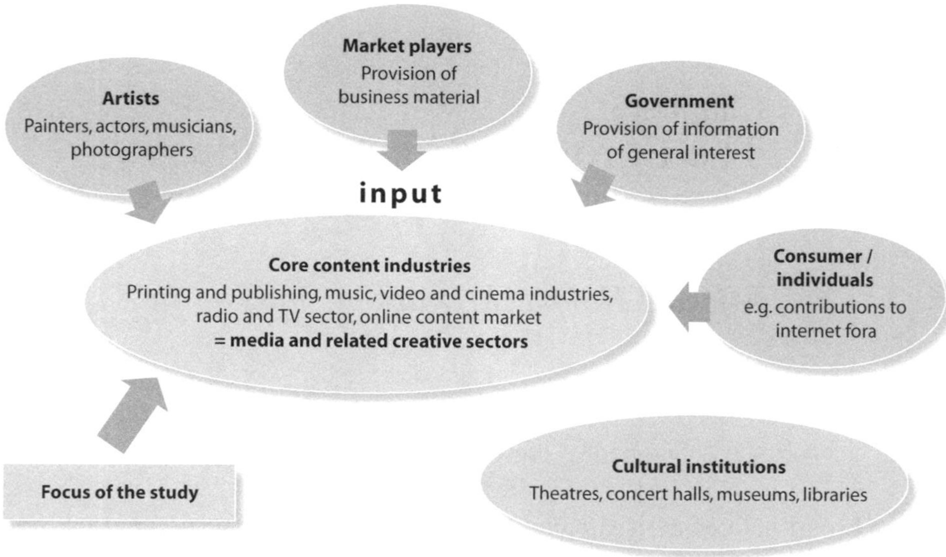

Figure 1: Focus of the Study

lines of separation between the individual areas and resulted in the emergence of new markets.

Figure 1 is thus merely intended as a simplified presentation of the complex matter 'content' which shall help to systematize our approach to the European regulation in this area and to define the focus of our analysis: the core segments of the content industry – printing and publishing, TV and radio, music, video and cinema on the one hand and the online industry on the other, or in short: the media and related creative sectors.

II. CATEGORIZATION OF THE CONTENT INDUSTRY

The content industry as defined for our purposes comprises the production and distribution of content. It is traditionally broken down into the categories: published content, games, audio/music, video/cinema and broadcast content (TV and radio programmes).[1]

---

1. The chapter is based on the following studies recently undertaken at EC level: *Publishing Market Watch Final Report,* prepared by Turku School of Economics and Business Administration and Rightscom Ltd, submitted to the DG Enterprise, European Commission, 27 January 2005; *Impact Study of Measures (Community and National) Concerning the Promotion of Distribution and Production of TV Programmes Provided for Under Article 25(a) of the TV Without Frontiers Directive – Final Report,* prepared by David Graham and Associated Limited for the Audiovisual, Media and Internet Unit Directorate-General

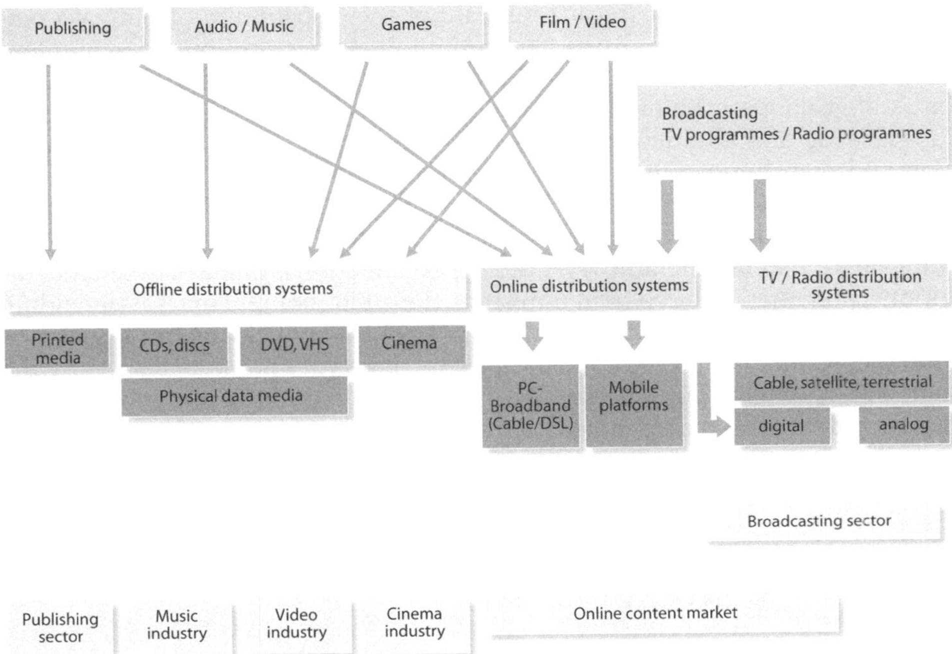

Figure 2: Branches of the content industry broken down according to content category and distribution system

In the past, it was possible to link these content categories fairly clearly to certain distribution channels and consequently to classify and distinguish the different players in these categories. Thus, published content (basically content comprising text and images or a combination thereof) was traditionally made available to the end user via the distribution channel of printed media (newspapers, magazines, books and directories) so that it was possible to distinguish printing and publishing from the other content sectors by virtue of its particular distribution channel 'printed media'. To give another example, music content used to be distributed via physical data media such as CDs whose production, marketing and distribution was in the hands of the music industry. The video industry was in charge of the distribution of games and films via physical data

Information Society and Media European Commission, 24 May 2005. *European Information Technology Observatory 2005* (Mainz, Eggebrecht-Presse KG, 2005); OECD (Working Party on the Information Economy), Digital Broadband Content: Digital Content Strategies and Policies, DSTI/ICCP/IE(2005)3, 1 June 2005; OECD (Working Party on the Information Economy), Digital Broadband Content: Mobile Content – New Content for new Platforms, DSTI/ICCP/IE(2004)14/FINAL, 3 May 2005. Most of these studies use the categories also embedded in this chapter.

media, while the cinema sector took care of the distribution of films via cinemas. Radio and TV are distinct from the foregoing traditional core content industries in that their content, which consists of edited, clearly defined audio or audiovisual programmes, is distributed electronically.

The use of digital technologies in these media branches (both in production and distribution) has made it possible to disseminate all these content categories now online as well. This has complicated matters, but if we are ready to accept some degree of fuzziness it is still possible to distinguish the individual branches of the content industry. Usually, a distinction is made between the traditional activities of the content industry – the offline content market (including analog broadcasting, but also the digital distribution of classic braodcast programmes) – and the online content market.[2] The latter is characterized by the fact that eContent (published content, games, audio/music and video/film in digitalized form) is disseminated via the three digital multiplatforms – the PC broadband platform, the digital TV platform and the mobile platform.[3]

III. LEGAL DEFINITIONS RELATING TO THE CONTENT INDUSTRY

While there is no specific legal terminology at community level concerning the offline content market, community law has developed specific legal concepts for the online content market, in which it intervenes in the form of sector-specific provisions.

The definition which has been of central significance to the content industry to date is the one given in the TWF Directive[4] for television broadcasting, which stipulates that 'television broadcasting means the initial transmission by wire or over the air, including that by satellite in unencoded or encoded form, of television programmes intended for reception by the public'. This definition, which comes from the world of analog television, is to be replaced, within the scope of a revision of the TWF Directive,[5] by a new definition that takes the aspects of digital television into account.

In the interest of developing an integrated overall concept for all forms of electronic distribution of audiovisual contents, the idea is to take the concept of audiovisual media services as the point of departure, and to define these as services, in line with the EC Treaty (Arts 49 and 50), which serve the distribution of moving pictures, with or without sound, destined for the general public and transmitted via electronic networks. In this way the subject matter regulated by the TWF Directive, which will according to these processes be renamed

2. This distinction underlies all the studies on which this chapter is based. Cf. fn. 1.
3. Cf. EITO [2005] pp. 92 *et seq.*
4. Directive 97/36/EC, OJ 1997 L 202/60.
5. For more details on this revision process, *see* Part Two, Chapter 4.I.B.

Directive on 'Audiovisual Media Services', is to be extended from television broadcasting alone to all forms of audiovisual content.[6]

This extension of the scope of application of Community law provisions in the audiovisual field is intended to create a uniform concept for all forms of audiovisual content (games, films, video clips and classic television programmes)[7] irrespective of the distribution platforms used (analog and digital TV, PC broadband or mobile online distribution systems). This is to be the basis for a coherent and consistent regulatory framework capable of adequately reacting to current and future developments in the audiovisual content markets. Within the scope of this concept, television programmes will – on the basis of their specific characteristics, in particular with regard to their impact on society as mass media – continue to be treated specially by the distinction between linear and non-linear audiovisual media services. Linear audiovisual media services would comprise content traditionally known as television programmes. This is content which contains of edited programmes with a fixed daily schedule, as e.g. classic TV programmes, webcasting, streaming as well as video broadcasts with individual starting times specified by the service provider.[8] Non-linear audiovisual content services, on the other hand, would include all 'on demand services', i.e. content (e.g. games, films, individual video clips etc.) which can be individually accessed, or in other words, where the user decides upon the transmission time.[9]

Community law has already established a definition for these non-linear audiovisual media services, as they can be subsumed under the so called 'information society services', for which the E-Commerce Directive[10] has laid down specific rules. They are defined in a very broad way as 'any service, normally provided for remuneration, at a distance, by electronic means and at the individual request of a recipient of services'. This includes not only audiovisual content which can be individually accessed – i.e. non-linear audiovisual media services – but also, in particular, published content provided on demand by electronic means (e.g. online information services, online data bases) as well as individually accessible audio content (e.g. online music stores). In addition, the term 'information society services' also includes a number of electronic services

6. *See* the proposal for a directive amending the Television without Frontiers Directive 89/552/EEC, COM (2005) 646 final.
7. The express limitation to the distribution of 'moving pictures with or without sound' excludes from the definition 'audiovisual media services', however, electronically transmitted published content, i.e. content essentially based on text and pictures or a combination thereof (e.g, especially online editions of newspapers), as well as mere audio content (music and radio programmes).
8. Cf. Article 1 lit c proposal for a directive amending the Television without Frontiers Directive 89/552/EEC, COM (2005) 646 final.
9. Cf. Article 1 lit e proposal for a directive amending the Television without Frontiers Directive 89/552/EEC, COM (2005) 646 final.
10. Directive 2000/31/EC, OJ 2000 L 178/1.

other than content, in particular all services provided in the context with the online sale of goods.

Finally, Community law uses the terms eContent and audiovisual works, but only in the context of funding programmes, i.e. at the 'soft law' level. The term eContent (in the context of the eContentplus programme)[11] covers any content provided via digital distribution platforms. In the Media Plus Programme[12] the term 'audiovisual works' is used broadly for contents composed of moving pictures with or without sound irrespective of the form of distribution. This includes both cinema and TV productions as well as other audiovisual works (such as works distributed via DVD).[13]

At the infrastructural level, i.e. in respect of the markets upstream of the content industry which are relevant for the electronic distribution of content, the package of measures for electronic communication markets[14] has introduced the terms 'electronic communication networks' and 'electronic communication services'. In the interest of a uniform regulation of all electronic communication networks irrespective of the technology used, 'electronic communication networks' are defined – in brief – as transmission systems that enable the electronic transmission of signals.[15] 'Electronic communication services' are defined as services which consist entirely or mainly in the transmission of signals on electronic communication networks.[16] These definitions, thus, cover in particular also the distribution platforms used for the electronic transmission of content – the multiplatforms for digital television (DTV), digital radio (DTB), the digital broadband network and the latest generation of mobile phone systems (UMTS) – as well as the content-relevant transport services, such as, in the field of digital TV, conditional access systems or multiplexing.[17]

The definitions covering the content industry at the legal level may be represented graphically as Shown in Figure 3.

11. Cf. Decision 456/2005/EC, OJ 2005 L 79/1.
12. Cf. Decision 846/2004/EC, OJ 2004 L 157/4.
13. As a rule, cinema film productions are treated as a category of audiovisual works in its own right. *See*, e.g., the Communication on cinema film aid, OJ 2002 C 43/6.
14. The measures are for download available http://europa.eu.int/information_society/policy/ecomm/index_en.htm, 23 June 2006. Cf. Part Two, Chapter 3, Section II.
15. Article 2 lit a Framework Directive 2002/21/EC, OJ 2002 L 108/33.
16. Article 2 lit c Framework Directive 2002/21/EC, OJ 2002 L 108/33.
17. For a definition of these services cf. Part Two, Chapter 3, Section II.C.3.

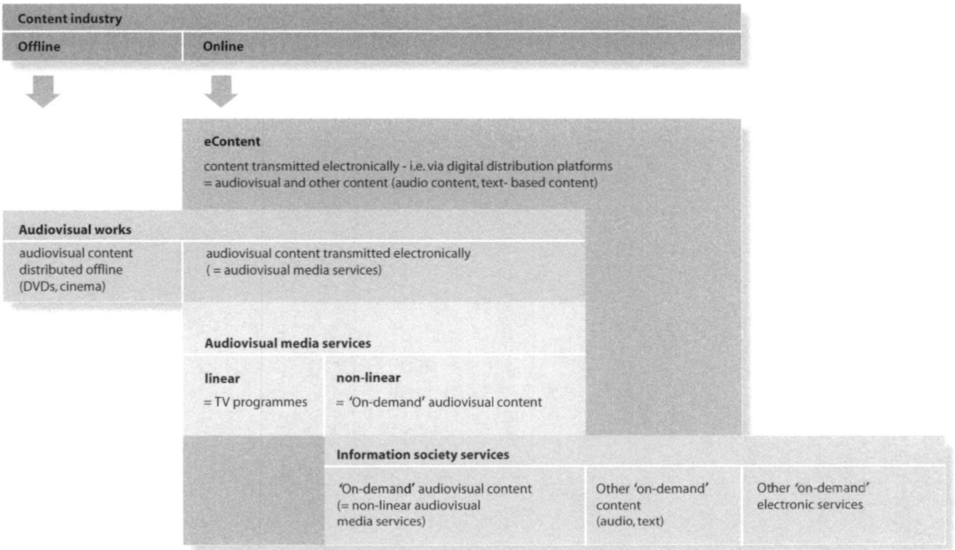

Figure 3: Legal definitions related to the content industry

Part Two
The Individual Regulatory Fields – an Analysis of the Different European Provisions for the Content Industry

Chapter 1

Fundamentals of Community Law and Policies (Including Funding Programmes) Governing the Content Industry

Michaela Seifert

I. PRELIMINARY REMARKS

Both the provisions of the Treaty establishing the European Community and legislative instruments adopted by the European institutions pursuant to the provisions of the treaties (secondary legislation) constitute the basis of the regulatory framework of Community law relevant to the content industry. The fundamental freedoms under the Treaties and the case-law of the European Court of Justice represent the starting point of this paper as they guarantee the smooth operation of the internal market by prohibiting discriminatory as well as restrictive national measures in the area of the content industry. The provisions governing the free movement of goods ensure the free circulation of physical content products such as DVDs, CDs, CD-ROMs, video games, video tapes, whereas the freedom to provide services pertains *inter alia* to the vast area of cross-border broadcasting services. In this paper some leading cases relating to these freedoms are presented as well as those national measures that may, in exceptional circumstances, restrict them for protecting imperative requirements in the general interest as specified in the EC Treaty and the case-law of the European Court of Justice.

Actively promoting the creation and distribution of content, however, is primarily the aim of targeted measures of the Community's secondary legislation, namely specific funding and action programmes, which are subsequently dealt with, as well as those relevant legal provisions which represent their legal basis. To give a full picture, also those provisions of primary law are portrayed

M. Holoubek, D. Damjanovic and M. Traimer (eds), *Regulating Content – European Regulatory Framework for the Media and Related Creative Sectors*, pp. 25–60

that are not covered by special contributions of this Study,[1] such as Article 6 of the Treaty on European Union regarding the application of fundamental rights in Community law, the 1997 Protocol on Public Broadcasting ('Amsterdam Protocol') or the exemption clause for state aid aimed at promoting culture, as in particular the latter legal provisions lay down principles that must be observed in the context of actively promoting the creation and distribution of content. Moreover, the contested Commission's proposal for a directive on services in the internal market is outlined, as this reform is also to apply to certain services in the content industry.[2]

II. FUNDAMENTALS OF PRIMARY LAW

A. THE FUNDAMENTAL FREEDOMS – TREATY ESTABLISHING THE EUROPEAN COMMUNITY AND CASE-LAW OF THE EUROPEAN COURT OF JUSTICE

The provisions of the EC Treaty and the case-law of the ECJ relating to the four fundamental freedoms may be regarded as the 'framework rules' regulating the content industry for the following reasons. Firstly, they have the purpose of promoting the single market by prohibiting any discriminatory and restrictive national measures and secondly, these provisions constitute the basis for certain sector-specific measures of secondary-law.[3] Moreover, the judgments of the European Court of Justice relating to the four fundamental freedoms exemplify which categories of national measures may, in exceptional cases, be justified if they serve public-interest aims.

As physical media the products of the content industry may be subject to the rules on the free movement of goods but also – as in the case of broadcasting – to the freedom to provide services. Moreover, the rules governing the freedom of movement for workers may be of relevance for the content industry in cases where EU citizens work in another Member State.[4] Similarly, if persons regularly work on a self-employed basis and/or businesses or branches are set

---

1. As regards the relevant European competition rules relating to the content industry as well as the provisions regarding taxes and copyright, please refer to the respective chapters of this Study.
2. *See* IV.B. *below*.
3. The main goal of Directive 89/552/EEC on the coordination of certain provisions concerning the pursuit of television broadcasting activities ('Television Without Frontiers'), OJ L 1997 202/60, for example, is to specify the provisions of the Treaty establishing the European Economic Community regarding the freedom of movement for services by establishing specific rules for television broadcasting. *See also* Case C-412/93, *Leclerc-Siplec*, [1995] ECR I-179.
4. Pursuant to Article 39 *et seq.* of the EC Treaty and Council Regulation 1612/68 on freedom of movement for workers within the Community, OJ L 1968 257/12, any discrimination based on nationality between workers of the Member States is prohibited.

up in other Member States, the rules on the freedom of establishment may be applicable.[5] However, this paper focuses on the free movement of goods and the freedom to provide services as these two fundamental freedoms are of primary interest to the distribution of content products and services.[6] The provisions of the Treaties and the case law of the ECJ are particularly relevant to those sectors of the content industry for which, so far, no harmonization measures have been taken at Community level.

The ECJ has gradually adopted a common approach to the four freedoms by prohibiting not only discriminatory national measures but also restrictive indistinctly applicable rules. In 1995, in *Gebhard*, the ECJ explicitly held for all four freedoms in a uniform way that any national measures liable to hinder or make less attractive the exercise of fundamental freedoms guaranteed by the Treaty may only be invoked in exceptional circumstances if they fulfil four conditions: 1) they must be applied in a non-discriminatory manner; 2) they must be justified by imperative requirements in the general interest; 3) they must be suitable for securing the attainment of the objective which they pursue; 4) and they must not go beyond what is necessary in order to attain it.[7]

Initial problems regarding the boundary lines between the provisions of the free movement of goods and the freedom to provide services in the audiovisual area were solved by the ECJ stating that the transmission of television signals comes, as such, within the rules of the Treaty relating to services, whereas trade in material is subject to the rules relating to freedom of movement for goods.[8] Moreover, according to the jurisprudence the transmission of signals by cable television falls within the scope of the rules relating to services.[9] However, where

5. In order to make the work of self-employed persons easier, a number of directives were issued on the basis of the rules governing the internal market, obliging Member States to mutually recognize foreign professional diplomas. Only recently these directives were consolidated in, and partly also amended by, Directive 2005/36/EC on the recognition of diplomas, OJ L 2005 255/22. For more details on the recognition of professional qualifications *see* M. Seifert, 'Rechtliche Grundlagen des Bologna-Prozesses und der Lissabon-Strategie – Europaweite Vereinheitlichung der Studienstrukturen und Maßnahmen zur Erleichterung der Anerkennung von Diplomen', *Working Paper of the Europainstitut No. 56*, Vienna 2004, <www.fgr.wu-wien.ac.at/institut/ef/wplist.html>, 16 June 2006.
6. A detailed description of all four fundamental freedoms, in particular the comprehensive and complex case-law of the European Court of Justice relating to the freedom of establishment would exceed the scope of this Study. As regards the issues of establishing agencies and/or cross-border transfer of companies registered offices, *see especially* Case C-212/97, *Centros*, [1999] ECR I-1459, Case C-208/00, *Überseering*, [2002] ECR I-9919 as well as Case C-9/02, *Lasteyrie du Saillant*, [2004] ECR I-2409.
7. *See* Case C-55/94, *Gebhard*, [1995] ECR I-4165, para. 37. As regards the implications of this judgment also *see* E. Spaventa, 'From Gebhard to Carpenter: Towards a (non-)economic European Constitution', (2004) 41 *Common Market Law Review*, 743 as well as P. Craig/G. de Burca (eds) *EU-Law – Text, Cases and Materials*, (3rd edn, Oxford, 2003), 784 *et seq.* Nevertheless, this view is not uncontested in literature.
8. Case 155/73, *Sacchi*, [1974], ECR 428.
9. Case 52/7, *Debauve*, [1980] ECR 833, Case C- 11/95, *Commission v. Belgium*, [1996] ECR I-4115.

a national measure affects both the freedom to provide services and the free movement of goods, as in the *Omega* case, the Court in principle, examines it in relation to just one of those two fundamental freedoms if it 'is clear that, in the circumstances of the case, one of those freedoms is entirely secondary in relation to the other and may be attached to it'.[10]

1. Free Movement of Goods

Article 28 EC which is relevant to the free movement of goods and thus to physical content products (CDs, DVDs, CD-ROMs, video games, video tapes, etc.) prohibits all quantitative restrictions on imports and all measures having equivalent effect between Member States.[11]

As the EC Treaty does not further specify the term 'measures having equivalent effect', the case-law of the ECJ is essential for the interpretation of that term. Initially, the ECJ ruled that all trading rules enacted by Member States which are capable of hindering, directly or indirectly, actually or potentially, intra-community trade are to be considered as measures having an effect equivalent to quantitative restrictions.[12] As the *Dassonville* case concerned a provision relating specifically to imported goods,[13] opinions varied after this judgment as to whether this formula should only apply to discriminatory measures, that is, directly targeting at imported goods, or also to measures that were 'indistinctly applicable', that is, measures which are equally applicable to domestic and imported products. For this reason the ECJ extended its interpretation further in the *Cassis-de-Dijon* case and explicitly stated that also indistinctly applicable national measures fall within this definition.[14]

In the *Keck* case, the ECJ – not least due to massive criticism in literature concerning its extensive interpretation[15] – modified the scope of its 'Cassis de

10. Case C-36/02, *Omega Spielhallen- und Automatenaufstellungs-GmbH*, [2004] ECR I-9609, para. 26.
11. Similarly, Article 29 EC provides that all quantitative restrictions on exports and all measures having equivalent effect are prohibited between Member States.
12. Case 8/74, *Dassonville*, [1974] ECR 837, para. 5.
13. More specifically, this case concerned a Belgian provision according to which certain goods could only be imported if accompanied by a certificate of origin issued by the government of the exporting country as proof of quality. The Belgian Dassonville brothers, who duly acquired a consignment of Scotch whisky already in free circulation in France and imported it into Belgium, were not in possession of a certificate of origin from the British customs authorities, thereby infringing Belgian rules.
14. Case 120/78, *Cassis de Dijon*, [1979] ECR 649. This case dealt with a German provision according to which the marketing of fruit liqueurs was conditional upon a minimum alcohol content of 25%. The German authority prohibited the import and sale of the French black currant liqueur 'Cassis de Dijon' liqueur reasoning that it only had an alcohol content between 15% and 20%. For a critical review of the interpretation of Article 28 EC, *see, for example*, J. Steiner, 'Drawing the Line: Uses and Abuses of Article 30 EEC' (1992) 29 *Common Market Law Review*, 749.
15. For further details on the development of the case-law of the ECJ and a review *see Craig/de Burca* [2003] 641 *et seq.*

Dijon' formula, stating that 'certain selling arrangements' are not measures having equivalent effect within the meaning of Article 28 of the EC Treaty 'so long as those provisions apply to all relevant traders operating within the national territory and so long as they affect in the same manner, in law and in fact, the marketing of domestic products and of those from other Member States.'[16] Thus selling arrangements were excluded from the ambit of Article 28 EC and were only subject to a test of discrimination.[17]

More recent rulings are again characterized by a shift in direction: The ECJ now tends to withdraw the privileges extended to selling arrangements by increasingly focusing on the aspect of market access.[18] Accordingly, also selling rules may be characterized as measures having equivalent effect if they are of such a kind as to prevent or impede access to the market by products from another Member State.[19] The ECJ decided in the *Gourmet* case that the Swedish 'prohibition of all advertising directed at consumers in the form of advertisements in the press, on the radio and on television, the direct mailing of unsolicited material or the placing of posters on the public highway is liable to impede access to the market by products from other Member States more than it impedes access by domestic products, with which consumers are instantly more familiar'.[20]

In the *Doc Morris* case the ECJ confirmed this approach by ruling that a prohibition of the mail-order sale of medicines over the internet is more of an obstacle to pharmacies outside Germany than to those within it. 'Although there is little doubt that as a result of the prohibition, pharmacies in Germany cannot use the extra or alternative method of gaining access to the German market consisting of end consumers of medicinal products, they are still able to sell the products in their dispensaries. However, for pharmacies not established in Germany, the internet provides a more significant way to gain direct access to the German market. A prohibition which has a greater impact on pharmacies established outside German territory could impede access to the market for products from other Member States more than it impedes access for domestic products.' [21]

---

16. Cases C-267 and 268/91, *Keck and Mithouard*, [1993] ECR I-6097, para. 16.
17. Also *see* S. Weatherill, 'After Keck: Some Thoughts on how to Clarify the Clarification' (1996) 33 *Common Market Law Review*, 885 or P. Koutrakos, 'On Groceries, Alcohol, and Olive Oil: More on Free Movement of Goods after Keck?' (2001) 26 *European Law Review*, 391.
18. For a critical review of the Keck judgment, in particular any uncertainties associated with the term 'selling arrangements' *see Craig/de Burca* [2003] 650 *et seq.*
19. Strictly speaking, the more recent judgments of the ECJ with a stronger focus on the criterion of market access may be interpreted as merely an accentuation of the second requirement of the Keck formula 'so long as they [these provisions] affect in the same manner, in law and in fact, the marketing of domestic products and of those from other Member States'; *see* Joined Cases C-267/91 and 268/91, *Keck and Mithouard*, [1993] ECR I-6097, para. 16.
20. Case 405/98, *Gourmet*, [2001] ECR I-1795, para. 21.
21. Case 322/01, *DocMorris*, [2003] ECR I-14887.

If the ECJ finds that a national measure basically constitutes a 'measure having equivalent effect' prohibited under the EC Treaty this does not mean that such a measure necessarily is contrary to EC-law. For discriminatory rules, i.e. measures resulting in an unfair treatment of foreign goods, Article 30 of the Treaty gives an exhaustive list of public interest grounds which Member States can use to justify national measures.[22] These requirements as expressly provided for in Article 30 EC are the following:

- Public morality, public policy or public security;
- Protection of health and life of humans, animals or plants;
- Protection of national treasures possessing artistic, historic or archaeological value as well as;
- Protection of industrial and commercial property.

Moreover, since the *Cassis-de-Dijon* case the ECJ has established the 'rule of reason' list of mandatory requirements to justify indistinctly applicable restrictions, i.e. measures which are equally applicable to domestic and imported products and has expanded this list continuously in subsequent rulings.[23] Among these mandatory requirements justifying restrictive rules which are indistinctly applicable are the following:

- Effectiveness of fiscal supervision;
- Protection of public health;
- Fairness of commercial transactions;
- Protection of consumers;
- Improving the living and working environment;
- Protection of the environment;
- Protection of diversity of the media.

Generally speaking one can say that any national measures explicitly discriminating against goods from other Member States can only be justified on those grounds listed in Article 30 EC as such measures strike at the very heart of what the EC Treaty wants to prevent – discrimination on grounds of nationality. As regards indistinctly applicable restrictions, on the other hand, the whole range of mandatory requirements is applicable. However, the distinction

22. Any protective measures within the scope of Article 30 EC are, however, only allowed as long as harmonization of national rules has not taken place in the respective policy area. If a harmonization of rules has already taken place at European level, the Member States may only maintain and/or introduce more restrictive national measures by meeting those strict requirements as specified in Articles 95(4) and 5 EC.
23. These mandatory requirements are not identical with the grounds listed in Article 30 EC. On the comprehensive case-law of the ECJ on these public-interest grounds *see Craig/de Burca* [2003] 661 *et seq.* Nevertheless, a measure which restricts intra-Community trade cannot be justified by a Member State's wish to safeguard the survival of an undertaking, *see* Case C-324/93, *Evans Medical Ltd*, [1995] ECR I-563, para. 26.

between the grounds for justifying discriminatory measures provided for in Article 30 EC and the rule of reason exceptions to Cassis is not always precisely drawn by the ECJ.[24]

The *Gourmet* and *Doc Morris* cases serve as good examples illustrating mandatory requirements for indistinctly applicable rules. In the *Gourmet* case the ECJ held that a prohibition of all advertisements in the press, on the radio and on television, the direct mailing of unsolicited material or the placing of posters on the public highway constitutes an obstacle to trade between Member States. Nevertheless the ECJ concluded in this case that the national ban was justified and proportionate as such rules restricting the advertising of alcoholic beverages in order to combat alcohol abuse reflect public health concerns.[25] In the *Doc Morris* case, where a national prohibition regarding the selling of medicinal products via mail-order was contested, however, the ECJ made a distinction between medicinal products subject to medical prescription and medicinal products not subject to medical prescription and ruled that only in the first case a prohibition on mail-order sales was necessary and proportionate for protecting consumers.[26]

As regards those cases that are of relevance to the content industry, the issue of fixing the retail selling price of books was of crucial importance as its permissibility was long disputed.[27] In the *Leclerc* case, the ECJ considered such a national measure as a measure equivalent in effect to a quantitative restriction on imports as specified in Article 28 EC. In that regard two different situations had to be considered: firstly, that of books published in another Member State and imported into the Member State concerned, and, secondly, that of books published in the Member State concerned and re-imported, following exportation to another Member State.[28] The argument put forward by the French government that French legislation on the price of books served imperative requirements of consumer protection was not accepted by the ECJ reasoning that Article 30 EC must be interpreted strictly and neither the safeguarding of consumers' interests nor the protection of creativity and cultural diversity in the realm of publishing is mentioned therein.[29] According to the ECJ a national

24. For a critical review *see Craig/de Burca* [2003] 634 *et seq.* For this reason the authors argue in favour of applying the same grounds of justification for discriminatory and indistinctly applicable rules.
25. Case C-405/98, *Gourmet*, [2001] ECR I-1795, para. 27.
26. Case C-322/01, *Doc Morris*, paras 74 and 119. The German government, however, anticipated this judgment by liberalizing the entire mail-order sale of medicines.
27. Due to inadequacies resulting from the application of Article 30 EC, other issues relating to the protection of cultural objects are now the subject of secondary legislation. In this connection mention should be made of Council Regulation (EEC) No 3911/92 on the export of cultural goods, OJ L 1992 395/1, which provides for an export licence for the cultural objects specified in the Annex as well as Council Directive 93/7/ECC on the return of cultural objects unlawfully removed from the territory of a Member State, OJ L 1993 74/74.
28. Case 229/83, *Leclerc*, [1985] ECR 1, paras 23 and 24.
29. Case 229/83, *Leclerc*, [1985] ECR 1, para. 30.

measure that does not distinguish between domestic and imported books and hence is an indistinctly applicable rule constitutes a measure equivalent in effect to a quantitative restriction on imports unless it is established that the books in question were exported for the sole purpose of re-importation in order to circumvent legislation of the type at issue.[30] The ECJ, however, in the case at hand did not verify whether the measure might serve the Cassis criteria[31] but only focused on Article 30 EC.

Community policy subsequently took a change of approach for the protection of the book as a cultural object insofar as in 2001 the Council invited the Commission in a Resolution 'when applying competition rules [. . .], to take account of the specific value of the book as a cultural object and the importance of books in promoting cultural diversity, and of the cross-border dimension of the book market'.[32] In practice, the Commission since then has not taken any measures against such rules enacted by the Member States, such as in the case of Austria where the '*Bundesgesetz über die Preisbindung bei Büchern*' (Federal Act on the Fixing of Book Prices) which applies to all forms of distribution with the exception of cross-border Internet sale was passed in 2000.[33]

2. Freedom to Provide Services

Article 49 *et seq.* EC relating to the freedom to provide services are residual in the sense that they apply only insofar as the provisions relating to freedom of movement for goods, capital and persons do not apply.[34] As far as the dividing line between the right of establishment and the freedom to provide services is concerned, the 'temporary nature' of activities pursued in another Member State is of central importance.[35] However, the freedom to provide services is only granted to a natural or legal person already established in the territory of the Community. In its famous *Gebhard* ruling the ECJ defined the factors for determining whether the activity comes under the provision of the freedom to provide services or the right of establishment. According to the ECJ the temporary nature of the activites has to be assessed 'in the light, not only of the duration of the provision of the service, but also of its regularity, periodicity or continuity. The fact that the provision of services is temporary does not mean that the provider of services within the meaning of the Treaty may not equip himself with some form of infrastructure in the host Member State (including

30. Case 229/83, *Leclerc*, [1985] ECR 1, para. 27.
31. *See* II.A.1.
32. Council Resolution on the application of national fixed book-price systems, OJ 2001 C 73/5.
33. A similar book price fixing act was passed in Germany in 2002. Also *see* G. Ress/J. Ukrow, 'Article 151 EC' in *Das Recht der Europäischen Union*, E. Grabitz/M. Hilf (eds) (München, 2000), margin No. 85.
34. For an outline of the new service directive *see* Section IV.B.
35. Article 50 EC.

an office, chambers or consulting rooms) in so far as such infrastructure is necessary for the purpose of performing the services in question'.[36]

The ECJ ruled that, due to this temporary nature of activities pursued, requirements applying to the right of establishment, such as the criteria of residence and/or the setting up of an establishment, are as a rule incompatible with Community law as regards the freedom to provide services. In any event a Member State 'may not make the provision of services in its territory subject to compliance with all the conditions required for establishment and thereby deprive of all practical effectiveness the provisions whose object is to guarantee the freedom to provide services'.[37] On the other hand it is inadmissable to use the freedom to provide services to circumvent the rules of freedom of establishment if the true intention is to pursue activities on a self-employed basis.[38] In such cases the person may be treated as being established in that Member State.[39]

The freedom to provide services may take various forms: The freedom to provide services in another Member State (as explicitly provided for in Art 49 EC), the freedom for the recipient of a service to move in another Member State[40] and cases where neither the provider nor the recipient of the service move across the border but only the service itself. The latter form e.g. applies to the field of broadcasting, where services – as an exception – may also be provided on a permanent basis. Thus the freedom to provide services ensures that also new forms of technology having developed in the course of time are covered by the provisions on the internal market. As the case-law in the field of the freedom to provide services has become very complex and manifold, the following outline focuses on the comprehensive rulings of the ECJ relating to broadcasting.[41]

As regards the freedom to provide services, both discriminatory and indistinctly applicable national restrictions are covered by Community law. As in the area of free movement of goods, the ECJ has gradually extended the scope of Article 49 EC by explicitly stating that also non-discriminatory restrictions are prohibited.[42] Pursuant to Article 55 EC which refers to Articles 45 to 48 EC discriminations on grounds of public policy, public security or public health are permitted. Starting with the *Van Binsenberg* case – the ECJ further developed the list of imperative requirements – similarly to the area of free movement of

36. Case C-55/94, *Gebhard*, [1995] ECR I-4165, para. 27.
37. *See e.g.* Case C-43/93, *Raymond Vander Elst*, [1994] ECR I-3803, para. 17.
38. *See*, Case 33/74, *Van Binsenberg*, [1974] ECR I-1299, Case C-148/91, *Veronica*, [1993] ECR I-487, or Case C-23/93, *TV10*, [1994] ECR I-4795 where the Court held that national measures that were designed to prevent such circumvention are justified.
39. Case 33/74, *Van Binsenberg*, [1974] ECR I-1299, para. 13.
40. Case 286/82 and 26/83, *Luisi and Carbone*, [1984] ECR 377.
41. For further reading on the development of the case-law in relation to services by practical examples *see Craig/de Burca* [2003] 800 *et seq.* or V. Hatzopoulos, 'Recent Developments of the Case Law of the ECJ in the Field of Services', (2000) 37 *Common Market Law Review* 2000, 43 as well as ibid. et al. 'The Case Law of the ECJ Concerning the Free Provision of Services: 2000–2005,' (2006) 43 *Common Market Law Review*, 923–991.
42. *See e.g.* Case C-384/93, *Alpine Investments BV*, [1995] ECR I-1141.

goods – that may justify restrictive national measures provided they stand a test of proportionality.[43] A decisive criterion of such a test is whether the host Member State imposes on the service provider a condition which results in a 'duplication' of the requirements which were already satisfied in the state of establishment.[44] According to the case-law of the ECJ it represents, for example, a violation of the Treaty to impose additional authorization requirements in the host Member State for the broadcasting of cable television programmes transmitted by a service provider established in another Member State.[45]

In the following cases which primarily concern the area of broadcasting the ECJ accepted a series of imperative requirements that may be invoked in order to justify a restriction of the freedom to provide services. In the *Bacardi France* case it was contested whether French rules prohibiting indirect television advertising for alcoholic beverages during bi-national sporting events taking place in other Member States were justified or not.[46] The ECJ interpreted the national measure in question (loi evin) as a measure having equivalent effect as it entails a restriction on freedom to provide advertising services 'in so far as the owners of the advertising hoardings must refuse, as a preventive measure, any advertising for alcoholic beverages if the sporting event is likely to be retransmitted in France'. These rules also impede the provision of broadcasting services for television programmes as bi-national sporting events allowing indirect advertising for alcoholic beverages in another Member State may not be broadcast in France.[47]

However, regarding the proportionality of the measure the ECJ held that these rules are proportionate to the objective pursued due to the fact that the prohibition is limited to indirect advertising broadcasts during the retransmission of bi-national sporting events which specifically target a French audience.[48] Multinational sporting events which do not specifically target a French audience are, however, exempt from the prohibition of advertising. The French government put forward, and the ECJ recognized, the protection of public health to justify measures restricting the advertising of alcoholic beverages in order to combat alcohol abuse.[49] The ECJ furthermore emphasized that, in the absence of Community harmonization measures, it is for the Member States to decide on the degree of protection which they wish to afford to public health and on

43. For further details *see* the cases of the ECJ, described below, in the field of the freedom to provide services.
44. *See, for example,* the tourist guide cases Case C-154/89, *Commission v. France*, [1991] ECR I-659 and Case C-180/89, [1991] ECR 709 where the ECJ ruled that licence requirements as a rule are disproportionate except for reasons of the conservation of the national historical and artistic heritage.
45. Case C- 11/95, *Commission v. Belgium*, [1996] ECR I-4115.
46. Case C-262/02, *Commission v. France*, ECR I-6569 as well as Case C-429/02, *Bacardi France*, [2004] ECR I-6613.
47. Case C-262/02, *Commission v. France*, para. 26.
48. Case C-262/02, *Commission v. France*, para. 35.
49. Case C-262/02, *Commission v. France*, para. 30.

the way in which that protection is to be achieved. They may do so, however, only within the limits set by the Treaty and must, in particular, observe the principle of proportionality.[50]

In the *Omega* case, the ECJ held that a restriction of the freedom to provide services was justified due to an infringement of the fundamental right of human dignity. More precisely, the Bonn police authority (Oberbürgermeisterin der Stadt Bonn) issued an order against Omega prohibiting it from facilitating or allowing in its establishment games for entertainment with simulated killing actions by using sub-machine-gun-type laser targeting devices and sensory tags fixed either in the firing corridors or to jackets worn by players.[51] In this case the ECJ refered to the significance of the fundamental rights in Community law and justified the restriction by arguing that the activity concerned constituted a danger to public policy, specifically the disregard of human dignity, as 'the Community legal order undeniably strives to ensure respect for human dignity as a general principle of law'.[52] It should also be noted that, by prohibiting only the variant of the laser game the object of which is to fire on human targets and thus 'play at killing' people but not the game the object of which is to fire on sensors fixed in firing corridors, the ECJ affirmed the proportionality of the measure.[53]

In the *RTL* case the question referred to the Court was whether films which have been made for television and which provide, from their conception, for breaks for the insertion of advertising come within the meaning of 'films made for television' in Article 11(3) of the Television Without Frontiers Directive and should be subject to stricter standards than so-called 'series'. The ECJ rejected the argument put forward by RTL that the protection of the artistic value of audiovisual works cannot be extended to films which have been produced specifically for television and designed from the outset to provide breaks for the insertion of advertising spots.[54] Such a construction conflicts with both the wording of Article 11(3) of the Directive and its history. This provision is intended to establish a 'balanced protection of the financial interests of the television broadcasters and advertisers, on the one hand, and the interests of the rights holders, namely the writers and producers, and of consumers as television viewers, on the other'.[55] The Court concluded that the restriction by the Member State implementing the Television Without Frontiers Directive was proportionate from the point of view of the protection of consumers against abuses of advertising or, as an aim of cultural policy, the maintenance of a certain level of programme quality. This also justified the restriction on the

50. Case C-429/02, *Bacardi France*, para. 33.
51. Case C-36/02, *Omega Spielhallen- und Automatenaufstellungs-GmbH*, [2004] ECR I-9609.
52. Case C-36/02, *Omega Spielhallen- und Automatenaufstellungs-GmbH*, para. 34.
53. Case C-36/02, *Omega Spielhallen- und Automatenaufstellungs-GmbH*, para. 39.
54. Case C-245/01, *RTL*, 2003 [2003] ECR I-12489.
55. Case C-245/01, *RTL*, 2003, paras 58, 62.

freedom of expression as enshrined in Article 10(1) of the ECHR as put forward by RTL.[56]

With regard to the protection of consumers and maintaining the diversity of programmes, the ECJ, in the *ARD* case, allowed a Member State to provide for television broadcasters under their jurisdiction the net principle for advertisements which may be inserted during programmes.[57] According to this principle, the duration of the advertisements is not included in determining the number of advertising interruptions allowed, thereby – contrary to the gross principle provided for in the Television Without Frontiers Directive governing the transmission of broadcasts across frontiers – more strictly restricting the broadcast of advertisements.

The protection of consumers from excessive advertising or, in the context of a cultural policy, maintaining a certain level of programme quality as public-interest aims had already been recognized by the ECJ in the *Mediawet I* and *Mediawet II* cases. In these judgments the maintenance of a radio and television system which secures pluralism was, in principle, recognized as an imperative requirement for safeguarding the freedom of expression of the various social, cultural, religious and philosophical components of society.[58] In the *Veronica* case, the ECJ accepted a national rule of the Mediawet according to which a broadcasting organization established in the Netherlands is prohibited from investing in a broadcasting company established or to be established in another Member State and providing a bank guarantee or drawing up a business plan and giving legal advice to a television company to be set up in another Member State. This provision, in particular, provides that the financial resources available to the national broadcasting organizations to enable them to ensure pluralism in the audio-visual sector must not be diverted from that purpose and used for purely commercial ends.[59]

The argument of safeguarding the freedom of expression in the audiovisual sector of the various components, in particular social, cultural, religious and philosophical ones, was upheld by the ECJ also in the *TV 10* case. The disputed question in this case was a national legal provision treating as a domestic

56. Case C-245/01, *RTL*, 2003, paras 71 *et seq.*
57. Case C-6/98, *Arbeitsgemeinschaft Deutscher Rundfunkanstalten (ARD)*, [1999] ECR I-7599, paras 49 *et seq.*
58. Case C-288/89, *Stichting Collectieve Antennevoorziening Gouda and others v. Commissariaat voor de Media ('Mediawet I')*, [1991] ECR I-4007. In the specific case, the ECJ ruled that the national measures at issue are not justified as they affect only advertising intended specifically for the public in the Member State in question since they are designed to restrict the competition to which a national body with a monopoly over the broadcasting of such advertising may be exposed from foreign operators, para. 28. Also *see* the *'Mediawet II'* case, Case C-353/89, *Commission of the European Communities v. Kingdom of the Netherlands ('Mediawet II')*, [1991] ECR I-4069. Moreover, the measure relating to the structure of foreign broadcasting bodies was not accepted by the ECJ stating that there is no necessary connection between such a cultural policy and the conditions relating to the structure of foreign broadcasting bodies; Case C-288/89, paras 23, 24.
59. Case C-148/91, *Veronica*, [1993] ECR I-487, para. 11.

broadcaster a broadcasting body constituted under the law of another Member State and established in that State whose activities are wholly or principally directed towards the territory of the first Member State and which was established there in order to enable it to avoid the rules which would be applicable to it if it were established within the first State. Such obligations designed to maintain the pluralist and non-commercial character of programmes must be observed.[60]

In this connection it should be pointed out that, according to the case-law of the ECJ, where a television broadcaster has more than one establishment, this broadcaster is subject to the jurisdiction and supervision of the Member State in which the broadcaster has the centre of his activities and decisions concerning programme policy are taken and the programmes to be broadcast are finally put together.[61] It is solely for the Member State from which television broadcasts emanate to ensure compliance with the Television Without Frontiers Directive, and, the receiving Member State is not authorized to exercise its own control in that regard.[62]

In the *De Agostini* case concerning a provision of the Swedish broadcasting law which provides that advertisements broadcast during commercial breaks on television must not be designed to attract the attention of children under twelve years of age the ECJ did not allow the argument of the protection of minors. The reasons given by the ECJ were that Articles 16 to 22 of the Television Without Frontiers Directive bring about a partial harmonization with regard to the protection of minors. As regards domestic television broadcasters it is, however, permissible to apply the stricter Swedish provision.[63]

B. THE RELEVANCE OF FUNDAMENTAL RIGHTS IN COMMUNITY LAW

As the above mentioned judgments regarding the free movement of services touch upon the issue of fundamental rights, the relevant foundations of Community law are to be illustrated in the following.

Article 6(2) of the Treaty on European Union clearly states that the Union shall 'respect fundamental rights, as guaranteed by the European Convention for the Protection of Human Rights and Fundamental Freedoms signed in Rome on 4 November 1950 and as they result from the constitutional traditions common to the Member States, as general principles of Community law'. Even before the Treaty on European Union was established in 1993, the Court consistently held that fundamental rights form an integral part of the general principles of law.[64]

---

60. Case C-23/93, *TV10*, [1994] ECR I-4795, 17 *et seq.*
61. Case C-56/96, *VT4 Ltd*, [1997] ECR I-3143, 19. *See* also Case C-222/94, *Commission v. Great Britain*, [1996] ECR I-4025 or Case C-14/96, *Denuit*, [1997] ECR I-2785.
62. Case C-11/95, *Commission v. Belgium*, [1996] ECR I-4115, paras 34 and 86.
63. Cases C-34/95, C-35/95 and C-36/95, *De Agostini*, [1997] ECR I-3843, paras 55 *et seq.*
64. Case C-23/93, *TV10*, [1994] ECR I-4795, para. 24, Case C-260/89, *ERT*, [1991] ECR I-2925, Case C-353/89, *Commission/Netherlands*, [1991] ECR I-4069.

By inserting this provision into the Treaty those fundamental rights relevant to the content industry, such as Article 10 ECHR, have become the yardstick to which restrictive measures are to be compared. Article 10(1) ECHR, for example, provides as follows:

> 'Everyone has the right to freedom of expression. This right shall include freedom to hold opinions and to receive and impart information and ideas without interference by public authority and regardless of frontiers. This article shall not prevent States from requiring the licensing of broadcasting, television or cinema enterprises.'

Article 10(2) ECHR, however, provides for certain possible restrictions of the freedom of opinion:

> 'The exercise of these freedoms, since it carries with it duties and responsibilities, may be subject to such formalities, conditions, restrictions or penalties as are prescribed by law and are necessary in a democratic society, in the interests of national security, territorial integrity or public safety, for the prevention of disorder or crime, for the protection of health or morals, for the protection of the reputation or rights of others, for preventing the disclosure of information received in confidence, or for maintaining the authority and impartiality of the judiciary.'

Some experts have interpreted Article 10 ECHR to include a mandate for pluralism in the sense of an obligation to secure a pluralism of programmes.[65] In numerous judgments, the ECJ had to balance the protection of the interests of television broadcasters and advertisers invoking the freedom of expression under Article 10(1) ECHR for protecting the broadcast of advertising on the one hand, and the interests of consumers against excessive advertising on the other hand.[66] Accordingly, a restriction of the freedom of expression as enshrined in Article 10(2) ECHR is justified if it pursues a legitimate aim involving 'the protection of the ... rights of others within the meaning of that provision, namely the protection of consumers as television viewers, as well as their interest in having access to quality programmes. Those objectives may justify national measures against excessive advertising'.[67]

---

65. T. Oppermann, *Europarecht* (3rd edn, München 2005), § 26, margin No. 27.
66. Case C-245/01, *RTL*, paras 39 *et seq.* and 64 *et seq.*
67. Case C-245/01, *RTL*, paras 68 *et seq.* In addition, the Court undermined this result restricting advertisers also by invoking earlier judgments relating to the freedom to provide services and held that the 'protection of consumers against abuses of advertising or, as an aim of cultural policy, the maintenance of a certain level of programme quality are objectives which may justify restrictions by the Member States on freedom to provide services in relation to television advertising'. *See* Case C-245/01, *RTL*, para. 71 with reference to the judgments in Case C-288/89, *Collectieve Antennevoorziening Gouda*, para. 27 and Case C-6/98, *ARD*, para. 50.

C. The Amsterdam Protocol on Public Broadcasting and the Exemption Clause for State Aid Aimed at Promoting Culture and Cultural Heritage

The Protocol on Public Broadcasting added to the EC Treaty in Amsterdam sets the regulatory boundaries of EC control as regards the funding of broadcasting by providing that the 'provisions of the Treaty establishing the European Community shall be without prejudice to the competence of Member States to provide for the funding of public service broadcasting insofar as such funding is granted to broadcasting organizations for the fulfilment of the public service remit as conferred, defined and organized by each Member State, and insofar as such funding does not affect trading conditions and competition in the Community to an extent which would be contrary to the common interest, while the realization of the remit of that public service shall be taken into account.'[68]

In laying-down this provision, the ambiguity that had so far existed between the broadcasting sovereignty of the Member States as part of their national and cultural identities, on the one hand, and competition rules provided for in Community law, on the other hand, was lessened. Thus, the conceptualization of the programmes must be regarded as part of the national identities of the Member States respected by the Union pursuant to Article 6(3) of the EU Treaty.[69]

Similarly, the exemption clause to promote culture and heritage conservation, which was inserted into the EC Treaty in Maastricht, reflects the division of competences between the EC and the Member States in the field of cultural activites as provided for under the Treaty. Basically, the policies of Member States to promote the production and distribution of content is subject to European state aid law for the purpose of protecting the internal market against national measures distorting competition.[70] As regards a vital part of the content industry, namely promoting culture and maintaining the cultural heritage, the EC Treaty defines an exception in Article 87(3)(d) EC, which has far-reaching implications in practice, in particular for the funding of films.[71]

68. On the role of public broadcasting in the European Community also *see* Chapter 3, Section III.E *below*.
69. Oppermann [2005] § 26, 30.
70. On the framework of state aid for the content industry also *see* Chapter 2, Section V *below*.
71. As regards public service broadcasters it must be noted that Article 87(3)(d) only refers to State aid that goes beyond the scope of application of the Amsterdam Protocol. For more details please refer to Communication public service broadcasting and state aid, OJ 2001 C 320/5. In its state aid action plan, the Commission has also announced a revision of this legal framework, *see* State Aid Action Plan – Less and better targeted state aid: a roadmap for state aid reform 2005–2009 (Consultation document). 17 *et seq.*, <http://europa.eu.int/comm/competition/state_aid/others/action_plan/saap_en.pdf>, 16 June 2006.

Pursuant to this provision, the Commission may consider 'aid to promote culture and heritage conservation where such aid does not affect trading conditions and competition in the Community to an extent that is contrary to the common interest . . . to be compatible with the common market'. This particular exception to state aid may thus be considered a special expression of Article 151(4) EC, which states that the Community 'shall take cultural aspects into account in its action under other provisions of this Treaty, in particular in order to respect and to promote the diversity of its cultures'.[72]

To specify this exception to state aid and to minimize the distortion of competition, the Commission has, in its Communication on certain legal aspects relating to cinematographic and other audiovisual works, established criteria used by the European Commission to assess the compatibility with the EC Treaty of aid schemes for cinema and TV production.[73] The reason why these criteria were set up were proceedings against France in which the French rules on the funding of cinematographic works were reviewed.

The Commission as a fundamental rule examines whether the conditions for granting state aid infringe the basic treaty provisions such as the principle of non-discrimination of Article 12 EC and the provisions on the free movement of goods, services and the right to establishment. As regards the specific requirements for granting the state aid the Commission outlined four criteria:

First of all the Member State must ensure that the content of the aided production is cultural in its nature according to verifiable national criteria. Second, the producer must as a rule be free to spend at least 20 per cent of the film budget in other Member States without suffering any reduction in the aid provided for under the scheme. In other words, the Commission accepts a territorialization in terms of expenditure of up to 80 per cent of the production budget of an aided film or TV work. Third, aid intensity must in principle be limited to 50 per cent of the production budget, with difficult and low budget films being excluded from this limit.[74] Fourth, aid supplements for specific filmmaking activities (e.g. post-production) are not allowed.[75] This Communication of the Commission, which also lays down the aims of improving the competitiveness and cultural diversity in the audiovisual sector, was confirmed by a Council Resolution.[76]

---

72. On more details regarding Article 151 EC *see below*.
73. Communication from the Commission on certain legal aspects relating to cinematographic and other audiovisual works, COM(2001) 534 final, OJ 2002 C 43/6.
74. In this Communication cinematographic and other audiovisual works, the Commission considers that, under the subsidiarity principle, it is up to each Member State to establish a definition of difficult and low budget film according to national parameters, *see* Communication, 8.
75. Communication cinematographic and other audiovisual works, 7 *et seq.*
76. Council Resolution of 21 January 2002 on the development of the audiovisual sector, OJ 2002 C 32/4.

Due to the positive reaction during the broad consultation process which was organized by the Commission, the validity of the specific compatibility criteria for aid to cinema and TV programme production was extended until June 2007.[77] However, the Commission recalled its concerns over certain territoriality requirements, i.e. the 'territorialization' clauses of certain aid schemes which impose on producers an obligation to spend a certain amount of the film budget in a particular Member State as an eligibility condition for receiving the full aid amount. This may be one of the reasons why in its comprehensive State aid action plan, the Commission has announced its intention to revise the current legal framework and possibly propose to the Council a specific block exemption.[78]

D. The Division of Competences Between the EC and the Member States in Cultural Affairs

1. Preliminary Remarks on the Concept of Culture Enshrined in the EC Treaty

Due to the central significance and the close interconnection between the terms 'content'[79] and 'culture' the following will focus on the meticulous distribution of competences between the EC and the Member States in cultural affairs. Such a description is indispensable as it serves to illustrate the potential and limits of a European cultural policy. The complexity of the matter is shown by the fact that the term 'culture' is disputed, both in terms of substance and scope, on a national as well as at Community level. There is no generally accepted definition. The task of finding a definition can best be coped with by way of enumeration which should help to clarify the scope of the term. From a legal perspective, for example, the following areas of cultural law may be identified: protection of cultural property in the narrow sense, funding of cultural activities, media law, protection of industrial property of artists, professional law for persons active in the cultural field, rules on the professional training for artists, etc.

2. The Concept of Division of Competences Between the EC and the Member States

While on national level very often the terms education, science and culture are combined in the term 'administration of culture',[80] these aspects have to be

77. On the extension of the criteria *see* Communication from the Commission on the follow-up to the Commission communication on certain legal aspects relating to cinematographic and other audiovisual works, COM(2004) 171 final, 1, OJ 2004 C 123/1.
78. *See* the State Aid Action Plan – Less and better targeted state aid: a roadmap for state aid reform 2005–2009, 17 *et seq.*
79. For a definition of the term 'content' *see* Part One, Chapter 3.
80. Oppermann, Europarecht, § 28, margin No. 52.

carefully differentiated on Community level. The reason for that is the complex system of the distribution of competences between the EC and the Member States, which differs in the various areas of policy. Thus, on Community level a distinction between the following competences has to be made: 1) areas where the Union has exclusive competence; 2) shared competences, which means that in principle the Member States and the Union have powers to legislate in a specific area, the Member States exercising their powers in so far as the Union has not exercised, or has decided to stop exercising its competence; 3) in certain areas specified in the EC Treaty, the Union has competences to carry out actions to support, coordinate or complement the actions of the Member States, which basically remain competent for these areas.

As the EC Treaty contains no general definition of these three types of competence, each individual provision of the Treaty must be checked as regards its respective type of competence.[81] With regard to a European cultural policy (Article 151 EC), European educational policy (Articles 149 *et seq.* EC) but also industrial policy (Article 157 EC), the Treaty provides only for a complementary competence. The reason for this being that these areas of policy are considered as the core of national identities and sovereignty, and so far the Member States have been unwilling to give up their authority in these areas. The distinction which was carefully made by the EC Treaty of the various areas of policy points to the fact that the concept of culture enshrined in Article 151 EC must be interpreted strictly. If a Community measure taken in the field of culture also concerns aspects of education, research or industry, the case law of the ECJ provides that the Community act must be founded on the legal basis relating to the main or predominant purpose or component.[82] This is also the reason why relevant funding programmes of the Community are founded on different legal bases depending on their predominant purpose or component.

3. The Cultural Policy of the Community Pursuant to Article 151 EC

The specific and limited conferral of competences to take complementary measures in the field of cultural policy was only incorporated into the EC Treaty in Maastricht in 1993. This explains why prior to this date all Community measures of cultural relevance were primarily based on provisions regarding the promotion of the internal market.[83]

The wording of Article 151(1) EC which states that the Community 'shall contribute to the flowering of the cultures of the Member States, while

81. Articles I-12 *et seq.* of the Treaty establishing a Constitution for Europe, however, make fundamental statements relating to the various types of competences and the areas covered.
82. Case C-491/01, *British American Tobacco*, [2002] ECR I-11453, para. 94.
83. Specifically the provisions concerning the four fundamental freedoms and/or Article 95 EC, which provides for a general competence to approximate laws for the promotion of the internal market.

respecting their national and regional diversity and at the same time bringing the common cultural heritage to the fore', on the one hand refers to the Community's mandate to promote culture, on the other hand to the Member States' right to self-determination in cultural affairs.[84] This complementary function is explained in greater detail in Article 151(2) EC, which determines that action by the Community shall be aimed at encouraging cooperation between Member States and, if necessary, supporting and supplementing their action. This 'complementary competence' in cultural affairs is considered by some as a separate sphere of activity,[85] in general, however, not affecting the competence of the Member States.[86] This is also undermined by the restriction contained in Article 151(5) EC, which specifically determines that the Community shall adopt incentive measures excluding any harmonization of the laws and regulations of the Member States. Moreover, the criterion in Article 151(2) EC that the Community measure has to be *necessary* can be considered as a reference to the application of the principle of subsidiarity.[87]

Possible action by the Community is furthermore limited to specific areas. Article 151(2) EC contains the following exhaustive catalogue of areas of Community action: improvement of the knowledge and dissemination of the culture and history of the European peoples; conservation and safeguarding of cultural heritage of European significance; non-commercial cultural exchanges as well as the artistic and literary creation, including the audiovisual sector.

It is interesting to note that the audiovisual sector is not listed as a separate area but only in connection with artistic and literary creation. Accordingly, broadcasting *per se*, for example, does not qualify for Community support under Article 151(2) EC but only if it brings about artistic and literary creation. This is the reason why the Community may only support television channels which – like the cultural channel ARTE – pursue certain cultural objectives. Moreover, it is contrary to EC-law to promote the development of new technologies within the scope of Article 151(2) EC.[88] Furthermore, programming – as explicitly laid down in the Amsterdam Protocol on Public Broadcasting – falls within the responsibility of the Member States.

Article 151(4) EC moreover contains a so-called horizontal clause providing that the Community shall take cultural aspects into account in its action

84. For more details on Article 151 *see* G. Ress/J. Ukrow, 'Article 151 EC' in *Das Recht der Europäischen Union*, E. Grabitz/M. Hilf (eds) (München, 2000), margin No. 85; H.-J. Blanke, Article '151 EG' in *Kommentar zu EU-Vertrag und EG-Vertrag*, C. Calliess/ H.-J. Ruffert (eds) (Neuwied 2002); J. Sparr, 'Article 151' in *EU-Kommentar*, J. Schwarze (eds) (Baden-Baden 2000).
85. *Blanke*, in Calliess/Ruffert (eds.) [2002] margin No. 5. Affirmative *Oppermann* [2005] § 28, margin No. 56.
86. *Blanke*, in Calliess/Ruffert (eds.) [2002] margin No. 14.
87. *Ress/Ukrow*, in Grabitz/Hilf (eds.) [2000] margin No. 16.
88. *Ress/Ukrow*, in Grabitz/Hilf (eds.) [2000] margin No. 56.

under other provisions of the Treaty, in particular in order to respect and to promote the diversity of its cultures. This clause implies that cultural measures have to be taken into consideration within the scope of other Community measures, such as decisions on the jusitification of state aid.

4. European Cultural Policy in an International Context

Article 151(3) EC puts European cultural policy into an international context by providing that the Community and the Member States 'shall foster cooperation with third countries and the competent international organizations in the sphere of culture, in particular the Council of Europe'. The restrictions of European cultural competencies as outlined above, however, also apply to the area of external relations. This is the reason why international treaties are, as a rule, signed as mixed agreements even if further relevant competences under the Treaty are used as a basis for action of the Community in external relations.

Negotiations on liberalizing trade in services, which in some sectors now have reached a deadlock, are of particular importance for European cultural policy. Physical content products (CDs, films, magazines, etc.) are also governed by the General Agreement on Tariffs and Trade (GATT), which will not be discussed further in this paper as the negotiations about the liberalization of the content sector primarily affect the GATS Agreement.

The ongoing process of liberalizing services is of a very complex nature as the GATS agreement distinguishes four modes of supply for the delivery of services in cross-border trade: from the territory of one Member into the territory of any other Member (mode 1), in the territory of one Member to the service consumer of any other Member (mode 2), by a service supplier of one Member, through commercial presence in the territory of any other Member (mode 3), by a service supplier of one Member, through presence of natural persons of a Member in the territory of any other Member (mode 4).[89]

Moreover, GATS provides for different types of obligations, namely those that apply horizontally to all sectors (most-favoured-nation principle) but allow for exemptions[90] and those that apply only to those sectors where governments have made specific commitments as regards market access and national treatment.[91]

The situation with regard to the obligations undertaken in the content sector within the Doha round of negotiations on liberalizing trade in services is a very complex one. So far, the EU has not managed to speak with one voice at the GATS negotiations as exemptions and/or commitments

89. *See* Article I GATS.
90. Article II GATS (Most-Favoured-Nation Treatment).
91. Article XVI GATS (Market Access) as well as Article XVII GATS (National Treatment).

for individual service sectors vary from Member State to Member State.[92] In this connection mention should also be made of the UNESCO Convention adopted in October 2005 which will possibly have implications on further GATS negotiations.[93]

III. SECONDARY LEGISLATION OF THE EU FOR PROMOTING THE CONTENT INDUSTRY

A. THE LISBON STRATEGY – A NEW IMPETUS FOR PROMOTING THE EUROPEAN CONTENT INDUSTRY

In the following, the major impetus for a number of current and future initiatives for promoting the content industry and its objectives is presented.

In 2000 the European Council set out the Lisbon Strategy with the aim to give new impetus to economic growth in Europe by setting the Union the ambitious strategic goal for the next decade: 'to become the most competitive and dynamic knowledge-based economy in the world capable of sustainable economic growth with more and better jobs and greater social cohesion'.[94] The main instruments provided for in the Treaty for promoting economic growth are the Broad Economic Policy Guidelines to be adopted by the Council pursuant to Article 99 EC which are to ensure the convergence of the economies of the Member States. These broad guidelines are only recommendations as the Treaty provides that economic policy is a matter of common concern[95] which is still in the hands of Member States. Similar provisions are contained in Article 128 EC for employment; these Employment Guidelines must, however, be consistent with the Broad Economic Policy Guidelines.[96]

Insufficient progress in implementing the Lisbon Strategy has prompted the Commission to work out a 'New Start for the Lisbon Strategy',[97] which combines these two guidelines into one instrument, the so-called 'integrated guidelines',[98] and is designed to lead to a stronger coherence between

92. For details regarding the EU's liberalization offer during the current negotiations *see* the Commission's Internet site <http://europa.eu.int/comm/trade/issues/sectoral/services/wto_nego/index_en.htm>, 16 June 2006.
93. For more details on the UNESCO Convention *see* Krajewski [2005] 'Auswirkungen des GATS auf Instrumente der Kulturpolitik und Kulturförderung in Deutschland' in particular 18 *et seq.* <www.unesco.de/c_arbeitsgebiete/kkv_gutachten.pdf>, 16 June 2006.
94. Presidency conclusions – European Council, Lisbon, March 2000, para. 5, *see* <http://www.europarl.eu.int/summits/lis1_en.htm>, 16 June 2006.
95. Article 99(1) EC.
96. A detailed description of the instruments and mechanisms of the economic and monetary policy with all its particularities and economic aims would exceed the scope of this Study; therefore only brief mention is made of the major political framework instruments.
97. Also *see* Commission Staff Working Paper – Working together for growth and jobs – next steps in implementing the revised Lisbon strategy, SEC(2005) 622/2.
98. Integrated Guidelines for Growth and Jobs (2005–2008), COM(2005) 141.

macro-economic, micro-economic and employment policies. This new approach was substantially influenced by the Kok report, a report of the High Level Group on the Lisbon Strategy that was chaired by Wim Kok.[99]

An important objective of these integrated guidelines – as already provided for in the Lisbon Strategy – is to encourage the start-up of new businesses for example by facilitating access to finance and risk capital and strengthening the innovation potential of small and medium-sized enterprises. The Commission, in a Communication, states that small and medium-sized businesses constitute 99 per cent of all enterprises and two thirds of employment.[100]

The creation of an 'information society', in other words the 'shift to a digital, knowledge-based economy, prompted by new goods and services', is expected to be a powerful engine for growth, competitiveness and jobs.[101] For this purpose the Council and the Commission were invited in Lisbon to draw up a 'comprehensive eEurope Action Plan' with the objective to give businesses and citizens access to an inexpensive, world-class communications infrastructure and a wide range of services.[102] This invitation by the European Council may be considered as leveraging a series of subsequent measures in the audiovisual area. In its Communication 'i2010 – A European Information Society for growth and employment' the Commission announced only recently a comprehensive strategy for the dissemination and safe use of information and communication technologies (ICT) which is to ensure completion of the Lisbon Strategy by reforming existing legal acts.[103]

B. General Information on the Funding Programmes of the Content Industry

In contrast to the provisions of primary Community law described above and which primarily have the purpose of regulating and/or curtailing the scope of action of the Member States in cultural affairs (negative integration),[104] the funding programmes of the EC act as a positive incentive for promoting European content industry.

These funding programmes share one common feature: individuals or institutions participating in regular invitations to tender may request financial

99. *See* Facing the Challenge – The Lisbon strategy for growth and employment, Report from the High Level Group chaired by Wim Kok, November 2004, <http://europa.eu.int/grothhandjobs/pdf/kok_report_en.pdf>, 16 June 2006.
100. *See, e.g.* Communication from the Commission: Working together for growth and jobs A new start for the Lisbon Strategy, COM(2005) 24, 15 or the Kok-report, 28 *et seq.*
101. *See* presidency conclusions – European Council, Lisbon, March 2000, para. 8. Also *see* Communication Working together for growth and jobs.
102. Presidency conclusions – European Council, Lisbon, March 2000, para. 9.
103. Communication from the Commission: Regions i2010 – A European Information Society for growth and employment, COM(2005) 229 final [Communication i2010].
104. *Ress/Ukrow*, in Grabitz/Hilf (eds.) [2000] margin No. 5.

assistance (principle of co-funding) for their projects from the European Commission. Those Community co-funding measures form a category *sui generis* and, as a rule, take the form of a Council Decision in order to become legally binding.[105]

The Treaty provides for the adoption of such measures for example in Article 151(5) EC (cultural policy), Article 157(4) EC (industrial policy) as well as Article 150(4) EC (vocational training). 'Culture 2000', the first comprehensive framework programme in support of culture which consolidated earlier measures, was adopted on the basis of Article 151 EC, whereas Funding programmes directly concerning the content industry, such as the MEDIA Plus programme are, in contrast, based on provisions relating to industrial policy or vocational training as was the MEDIA Training programme.[106]

The number of Community programmes aimed at promoting the content industry is constantly increasing. The Commission is of the view that, given the high social impact of the audiovisual media, this sector offers a unique platform for intercultural dialogue[107] and for implementing the concept of citizenship of the Union.[108] The Commission is of the opinion that fostering the mobility of citizens, artists, cultural and audiovisual works and events, helps to create a genuine European identity. Moreover, the audiovisual sector is said to have high potential for growth which – in the opinion of the Commission – is not sufficiently made use of due to its current fragmentation.[109] In 2005 an executive agency for Education, Audiovisual and Culture was set up for the management of certain parts of the EU's programmes in the fields of education, culture and audiovisual.[110]

Due to the broad range of Community funding programmes, only some measures of major importance will be highlighted in the following by way of example.

105. *Blanke*, in Calliess/Ruffert (eds.) [2002] margin No. 17.
106. The proposal for a decision MEDIA 2007, COM(2004) 0470, which determines and consolidates the two relevant current programmes, combines these measures and is therefore based both on Article 157(3) and Article 150(4) EC. What is interesting to note in this connection is that the forerunner programme MEDIA I was adopted for the period 1991–1995 on the legal basis of Article 308 EC (ex Article 235). The MEDIA II programme (1996–2000), however, was based on Article 157(3) EC (ex Article 130[3]).
107. *See* Communication from the Commission: Making citizenship Work: fostering European culture and diversity through programmes for Youth, Culture, Audiovisual and Civic Participation, COM(2004) 0154, 1 *et seq.*
108. In the Maastricht Treaty, the concept of citizenship of the Union was included in Articles 17 *et seq.* of the EC Treaty. This concept has since been used extensively by the European Court of Justice to justify an extension of Community competences, which has been criticized in literature.
109. This was already stated by the Commission in its proposal for a programme in support of the audiovisual industry (MEDIA Plus – 2001–2005) COM(1999) 658.
110. Commission Decision 56/2005/EC setting up the Education, Audiovisual and Culture Executive Agency for the management of Community action in the fields of education, audiovisual and culture in application of Council Regulation (EC) No 58/2003, OJ 2005 L 24/35.

C. Cultural Programmes

The Culture 2000 programme – the first comprehensive programme supporting cultural activites – was originally established for the period from 2000 to 2004 aiming at creating a common cultural area for the peoples of Europe.[111] In 2004 this programme was prolonged until 31 December 2006 and will be replaced by a new programme from 2007 to 2013. Culture 2000 was designed to promote structured, multi-annual cultural actions, between operators of several Member States and those of other States, namely projects from various fields such as music, the performing arts, the plastic and visual arts, literature, books and reading including translation and cultural heritage. Moreover, also trans-sectoral integrated actions, i.e. projects associating several cultural fields by using new media are sponsored. Cultural industries may participate in the programme provided that the projects submitted are not commercial in character.

Specifically Culture 2000 makes a distinction between three types of actions, namely: 1) specific innovative and/or experimental actions provided that operators from at least three States participating in the Culture 2000 programme are involved, 2) integrated actions covered by structured, multi-annual transnational cultural cooperation agreements (co-productions, circulation of works and other cultural events in the European Union, mobility of artists, creators and other cultural operators, further training for professionals in the cultural field, enhancement of cultural sites and monuments within the Community, projects on cultural topics of European importance, use of new technologies, projects aimed at the highlighting of cultural diversity and of multilingualism, promoting mutual awareness of the history, roots, common cultural values of the European peoples and their common cultural heritage, etc.) as well as 3) special cultural events with a European or international dimension (the European Capital of Culture, organizing symposia to study questions of common cultural interest, recognizing and highlighting European artistic talent, etc.).[112] The financial framework for the implementation of the Culture 2000 programme for the period from 2000 to 2004 was originally set at EUR 167 million but was extended to a total of EUR 236.5 million when the programme was prolonged.[113] Community support was limited with 60 per cent of the budget for a specific action. Depending on the action concerned, different upper limits of support are to be set.

In its Proposal for a Decision establishing the Culture 2007 programme (2007–2013) the Commission revealed a number of shortcomings of the current

111. Decision 508/2000/EC establishing the Culture 2000 Programme, OJ 2000 L 63/1 as well as Decision 626/2004/EC amending Decision 508/2004/EC, OJ 2004 L 99/3.
112. As regards the comprehensive catalogue of actions eligible for funding *see* Decision Culture 2000, OJ 2000 L 63/1, Article 1 and Annex 1.
113. Proposal for a Decision of the European Parliament and the Council establishing the Culture 2007 programme (2007–2013), COM(2004) 469.

programme which the new programme is intended to correct as follows: the large number of objectives is to be reduced given the limited financial resources available in order to enhance the effectiveness and 'legibility' of the programme.[114]

The following three aspects are to be given priority support: 1) transnational mobility for people working in the cultural sector, 2) transnational circulation of artistic and cultural works and products and 3) intercultural dialogue.[115] Projects supported by the programme must also be on a sufficient scale and offer maximum added value at the European level; each project must therefore pursue at least two of these objectives. Support is provided for cultural actions, for European organizations active in the field of culture and for analyses and the collection and dissemination of information in the field of cultural cooperation. These new efforts are designed to increase the coherence of the programme.[116] Furthermore, the interim report on the current Culture 2000 programme suggested improvements in the communication and processing strategy of the programme in order to increase the number of applications. Criticism was also raised with regard to the payment system of the Commission, stressing that it would cause cash-flow problems especially to small and medium sized enterprises.[117] Whereas the initial Commission proposal provided for a financial framework of EUR 408 million for the period 2007–2013, the Council reduced the amount to EUR 354 in its political agreement.[118]

D. MEDIA PROGRAMMES

The MEDIA Plus[119] and MEDIA-Training[120] programmes for the programme period 2001 to 2005 were extended until 31 December 2006 by two Council decisions taken in 2004 where at the same time the financial framework was

114. In its proposal the Commission relies on its report Culture 2002 programme in the years 2000 and 2001, COM(2003) 722.
115. For further details *see*, Article 3.2 'The specific objectives of the new programme'.
116. Proposal for a Decision Culture, explanatory memorandum 12, 13.
117. Report from the Commission on the implementation of the Culture 2000 Programme in the years 2000 and 2001, COM(2003) 722, 20 *et seq.*
118. Both amounts are based on 2004 figures and thus subject to technical adjustments according to inflation. For the political agreement *see* Council of the European Union, CULT 40, 8950/06.
119. Council Decision 821/2000/EC on the implementation of a programme to encourage the development, distribution and promotion of European audiovisual works (MEDIA Plus – Development, Distribution and Promotion) (2001–2005), OJ 2000 L 336/82.
120. Decision 163/2001/EC on the implementation of a training programme for professionals in the European audiovisual programme industry (MEDIA-Training) (2001–2005), OJ 2001 L 26/1.

increased from EUR 350 million to EUR 453.6 million for MEDIA Plus and from EUR 52 million to EUR 59.40 million for MEDIA-Training.[121]

The MEDIA Plus programme was established to encourage the development, distribution and promotion of European audiovisual works within and outside the Community for the purpose of strengthening the European audiovisual industry, focusing in particular on the needs and potential of small and medium-sized enterprises (SMEs) operating on the audiovisual market.[122] Community funding is provided for the pre- and post-production of audiovisual measures, in view of the principle of subsidiarity, however, the funding of the actual production of the project remains within the competence of the Member States.[123] Subsequently, the strengthening of distribution (cinema, television, video, DVD, online) of European works outside their production territory is one of the major objectives of the programme, which is also reflected in the allocation of funds for distribution.[124] In its report on the mid-term results of the MEDIA Plus and MEDIA-Training programmes, the Commission, by using the example of cinema, criticized that American works take up to 66 per cent of the market share in Europe, followed by national works, whereas non-national European films come in third with approximately 11 per cent of the market share.[125] In addition to distribution and dissemination measures, this programme also supports the development of production projects (dramas for cinema or television, documentaries, multimedia projects, etc.), aimed at the European and international markets, thereby focusing on production projects that make use of new creation, production and dissemination technologies.[126] The reason for this being that the project development is regarded as essential for the quality and potential to export works. Development spending in Europe, however, accounts for only 2 per cent or 3 per cent of the production

---

121. Decision 846/2004/EC amending Council Decision 2000/821/EC on the implementation of a programme to encourage the development, distribution and promotion of European audiovisual works (MEDIA Plus – Development, Distribution and Promotion) (2001–2005), OJ 2004 L 157/4 as well as Decision 845/2004/EC amending Decision No 163/2001/EC on the implementation of a training programme for professionals in the European audiovisual programme industry (MEDIA-Training) (2001–2005), OJ 2004 L 157/1.
122. Decision 2000/821/EC MEDIA Plus, Recital 21.
123. Communication: Proposal MEDIA Plus – 2001–2005, COM(1999) 658, 38 *et seq.*
124. On the specific objectives of the Programme in the development field *see* Article 3 of Decision 2000/821/EC MEDIA Plus. The funds available for the individual stages of production will be broken down according to the following guideline: development: at least 20%; distribution: at least 57.5%; promotion: approximately 8.5%; pilot projects: approximately 5%; horizontal costs: at least 9%. *See* Annex to Decision 2000/821/EC MEDIA Plus, OJ 2000 L 336/82, 1.5. Breakdown of resources.
125. Report from the Commission Report on the implementation and the mid-term results of the MEDIA Plus and MEDIA Training programmes (2001–2005) and on the results of the preparatory action 'Growth and audiovisual: i2i audiovisual', COM(2003) 725, 6. The average market share for American film distributors is 50%, reaching 80% in the United Kingdom and 70% in Germany.
126. Article 2 of Decision 2000/821/EC MEDIA Plus.

budget, compared to 10 per cent to 12 per cent of the production budgets of the American audiovisual industry.[127]

Moreover, the MEDIA Plus programme was designed to facilitate and encourage the promotion of European audiovisual and cinematographic works at trade shows, fairs and audiovisual festivals in Europe and around the globe and also to promote networking of European operators in the field of promotion.[128] The support of pilot projects was intended to improve access to European audiovisual content and promote the development of new and innovative technologies, including digitalizing new distribution methods. In compliance with the principle of Community co-funding, 50 per cent of project costs, or up to 60 per cent in cases where the enhancement of the diversity of Europe's culture and of multilingualism is of interest are taken over by the Community. The MEDIA Plus programme is supported by the i2i audiovisual initiative, which is financed by the European Investment Bank (EIB) and thus provides new finance and banking instruments to the European audiovisual industry.[129]

The MEDIA-Training programme, on the other hand, put a special focus on promoting competitiveness by improving the vocational training of professionals in the audiovisual field. The programme explicitly mentions the following objectives: training as regards the application of new technologies, and in particular digital technologies, for the production and distribution of audiovisual programmes and the economic, financial and commercial management as well as script-writing techniques and storytelling.[130]

The Commission's proposal for the programme generation 2007–2013 provides for the MEDIA Plus and MEDIA-Training programmes to be consolidated in one legal instrument.[131] This new programme – just as MEDIA Plus and MEDIA-Training – focuses on the pre-production and the post production phases. According to the Commission, the reason why the production phase is not covered by the scope of the programme lies in the application of the principle of subsidiarity, meaning that the funding of productions must continue to remain the responsibility of the Member States.[132]

The Commission also emphasized the importance of revising the present legal instruments in the various areas to create a significant movement towards greater simplicity in the conception and in the operation of Community instruments for the next programme period.[133] With the new MEDIA 2007

127. Report i2i audiovisual, COM(2003) 725, 5.
128. For details *see* Article 4 of Decision 2000/821/EG MEDIA Plus.
129. *See* the Website of the European Investment Bank, <http://www.eib.org/site/index.asp?designation=i2i>, 6 June 2006.
130. Article 2 of Decision 163/2001/EG MEDIA-Training.
131. Proposal for a Decision MEDIA 2007, COM(2004) 470.
132. *See* Proposal for a Decision MEDIA 2007, COM(2004) 470, Recital 2.
133. Communication from the Commission: Making citizenship Work: fostering European culture and diversity through programmes for Youth, Culture, Audiovisual and Civic Participation, COM(2004) 154, 19, emphasizing, among other things, the adequateness and proportionality of verification methods and the applicant's reporting requirements.

programme, the Commission thus intends to increase both the number of actions undertaken and citizens affected.[134] The Commission moreover intends to put measures in place to accompany the changes that digitalization is producing in the audiovisual sector and reduce the imbalances between countries with a high production capacity and countries with low production capacity.[135] The new programme generation will also focus on simplifying the application forms and procedures, transparency in awarding procedures as well as the application of the proportionality principle with regard to the verification of the financial capacity of the applicants and reporting requirements for the beneficiaries.

A significant change as against the 2001–2005 programmes is the amount of aid provided by the EU. In future the financial contribution from MEDIA may amount to up to 75 per cent of the costs for various training activities in connection with the project in the new Member States of the European Union.[136] Moreover, the financial contribution from MEDIA will continue to be up to 60 per cent of the costs to support training activities in countries or regions with low audiovisual production capacity and/or with a restricted linguistic or geographical area and for projects submitted under the sphere of activities of development, distribution/dissemination and promotion which have the merit of highlighting the value of European linguistic and cultural diversity, whereas in the remaing fields the support will amount to 50 per cent. The initial Commission's proposal to set the financial framework to EUR 1.055 million for the period 2007–2013 was reduced by the Council in its political agreement where a sum total of EUR 671 million was fixed.[137]

E. Special Funding Action in the Fields of Information and Communication Technologies (ICT)

Within the scope of the Lisbon Strategy, the creation of an 'information society', in other words the 'shift to a digital, knowledge-based economy, prompted by

134. Specifically the Commission mentions the following targets: action to bring together 1500 audiovisual operators each year, with the potential to reach several millions of citizens; increase the market share of European films distributed outside their country of origin from the current 11% to 20% in 2013; double the number of screens exhibiting European non national films, with particular attention to a young audience; enable 40 European film academies to co-operate for the improvement of skill and the exchanges of know-how at European level; double the number of audiovisual projects supported, with particular attention to coproductions; double the number of European distribution campaigns. *See* Communication Fostering European culture, COM(2004) 0154, 20.
135. Proposal for a Decision MEDIA 2007, COM(2004) 470, Recital 5.
136. Proposal for a Decision MEDIA 2007, COM(2004) 470, Annex Chapter 2: Arrangements for implementation.
137. For the political agreement *see* Council of the European Union, AUDIO 15, 8955/06.

new goods and services, will be a powerful engine for growth, competitiveness and jobs'. The invitation to draw up a 'comprehensive eEurope Action Plan' gave the go-ahead for a number of specific funding programmes relating to the content industry.[138] As already announced in Communication i2010, the internal market should be completed by 2010 in the field of information and communication technologies (ICT).[139] In the following, two examples of the ongoing special funding programmes and in the next chapter the Commission's comprehensive 2010i strategy will be illustrated.

1. The 'eContentplus' Funding Programme

In March 2005 a special programme to make digital content in Europe more accessible, usable and exploitable was established (eContentplus).[140] Thus this programme replaced the eContent programme, which had been set up for the period 2001–2004.[141] This measure is to stimulate access to knowledge for a broad community by increased use of the Internet and broadband communication. Furthermore, improvement of quality and enhancing best practice related to digital content between content providers and users, across sectors, should be facilitated and cooperation between digital content stakeholders and awareness should be reinforced.[142] The focus of activities eligible for co-funding is for example, on the establishment of networks and alliances between stakeholders, encouraging the creation of new services, improving effective cross-border use and exploitation of public sector information between public sector organizations and private companies, fostering the proliferation of open European knowledge pools of digital objects, for education and research communities, as well as the individual and the linking of virtual libraries, etc.[143] The financial framework for the period was set at EUR 149 million. Community funding amounts to 50 per cent of the cost of the project; public sector bodies may be reimbursed on the basis of the additional costs.

---

138. Presidency conclusions – European Council, Lisbon, March 2000, para. 9.
139. Communication i2010, COM(2005) 229.
140. Decision 456/2005/EC of the European Parliament and of the Council establishing a multi-annual Community programme to make digital content in Europe more accessible, usable and exploitable, OJ 2005 L 79/1.
141. Council Decision 2001/48/EC adopting a multi-annual Community programme to stimulate the development and use of European digital content on the global networks and to promote linguistic diversity in the information society, OJ 2001 L 14/32.
142. Decision establishing a Community programme to make digital content more accessible, OJ 2005 L 79/1, Article 1.
143. For further details *see* Decision establishing a Community programme to make digital content more accessible, OJ 2005 L 79/1, Annex I.

2. The 'Safer Internet Plus' Funding Programme

The 'Safer Internet plus' programme was established in May 2005 for the period from 2005–2008.[144] This Community programme is to promote safer use of the Internet and new online technologies, particularly for children, and to fight against illegal content and content unwanted by the end-user. The financial framework for the entire period is set at EUR 45 million. Specifically the fight against illegal content is to be supported by a network of hotlines in all Member States and candidate countries and managed by a coordinating node. In the fight against illegal content, for example, assessing the effectiveness of available filtering technology, exchanges of information and best practices on effective ways of tackling unwanted and harmful content and the take-up of content rating and quality site labels are to be promoted. Furthermore, the development of the 'Safer Internet Forum' is to facilitate discussion and stimulate action relevant to illegal, unwanted and harmful content. Furthermore, so-called awareness-raising nodes will be set up with the objective to devise targeted information campaigns. Community funding for all these measures will normally not exceed 50 per cent of the cost of the project. Public sector bodies may be reimbursed on the basis of the additional costs.

IV. COMMUNITY PROJECTS RELEVANT TO THE CONTENT INDUSTRY

A. Communication from the Commission 'i2010 – A European Information Society for Growth and Employment'

In its 'i2010 Communication' the Commission has presented a comprehensive strategy for the information society and the audiovisual media.[145] This was the Commission's first initiative within the scope of the Lisbon Strategy and in line with the 'Integrated Guidelines'.[146] Due to the significance attributed by the Commission to the information and technology sector for growth and employment, the Commission proposes three priorities for Europe's information society and media policies: 1) the completion of a Single European Information Space which promotes an open and competitive internal market for information society and media, 2) strengthening Innovation and Investment in ICT research to promote growth and more and better jobs, and 3) achieving an

144. Decision No 854/2005/EC of the European Parliament and of the Council establishing a multiannual Community Programme on promoting safer use of the Internet and new online technologies, OJ C 2005 17/6.
145. Communication i2010, COM(2005) 229. Also *see* the relevant Communication on the information society, COM(2005) 757.
146. Communication i2010, COM(2005) 229, 12.

Inclusive European Information Society that promotes growth and jobs in a manner that is consistent with sustainable development.

In order to complete the Single European Information Space the Commission proposes a comprehensive review of regulation, comprising the following:[147]

- Review the electronic communications regulatory framework (2006), including defining an efficient spectrum management strategy (2005)
  - Create a consistent internal market framework for information society and media services by modernizing the legal framework for audio-visual services, starting with a Commission proposal in 2005 for revising the Television Without Frontiers Directive
  - Analysing and making any necessary adaptations to the community acquis affecting information society and media services (2007)
  - Actively promote fast and efficient implementation of the existing and updated acquis governing the information society and media services
- Continued support for the creation and circulation of European content
- Define and implement a strategy for a secure European Information Society (2006)
- Identify and promote targeted actions on interoperability, particularly digital rights management (2006/2007).

B. Proposal for a Directive on Services in the Internal Market and its Implications for the Content Industry

1. General Information

In response to the objective to make the Union the most competitive and dynamic knowledge-based economy in the world set by the European Council in Lisbon, the European Commission submitted in 2000 its Internal Market Strategy for Services[148] which was followed in February 2004 by its disputed Proposal for a Directive on Services in the Internal Market.[149] In its report on the state of the Internal Market for Services the Commission neatly outlined a full range of legal barriers on national level concerning all phases of the provision of services which still exist a decade after the envisaged completion of the Internal Market thus leading to a huge gap between the vision of an

147. Communication i2010, COM(2005) 229, 7.
148. Communication from the Commission: An Internal Market Strategy for Services, COM(2000) 888 of 29 December 2000.
149. Proposal for a Directive of the European Parliament and of the Council on services in the internal market, COM(2004) 2 final/ 2 of 25 February 2004.

integrated EU economy and the reality.[150] Moreoever, it was stated that small and medium-sized enterprises (SMEs) are particularly affected thereby.[151]

The proposal for a service directive had been highly contested right from the beginning in particular as regarded the proposed introduction of the country of origin principle. Due to massive criticism raised by Germany and France the negotiations about the Services Directive temporarily came to a standstill and finally, the negative opinion by the European Parliament on the country of origin principle was the reason for a change of approach.[152] As a consequence, the Commission presented its amended proposal of the directive revising vital parts of its initial version, the most striking amendment being the exclusion of the country of origin principle from the directive.[153]

The Directive is to apply to service providers who provide services in another Member State without being established there, which corresponds to the free movement of services under Article 49 EC, as well as to those cases where an establishment, i.e. an office is set up in another Member State, which falls under Article 43 EC.[154] According to the original proposal of the Commission the provisions of the directive should also apply to the audiovisual sector and supplement existing Community legislation, such as the Television Without Frontiers Directive.[155] As this led to heated debates in the committee responsible in the European Parliament the Commission finally excluded 'audiovisual services, whatever their mode of production, distribution and transmission, including radio broadcasting and the cinema' from the scope of its proposal.[156]

2. The Scope of Application of the Services Directive

In its proposal for a service directive, the Commission chooses the so-called horizontal approach in contrast to the strategy of sector-specific regulation of individual service sectors which had previously been pursued, the reason for this being that many obstacles are common to various service sectors. Due to this horizontal approach those services in the fields of content not being

150. For further details *see* Report from the Commission to the Council and the European Parliament on the State of the Internal Market for Services presented under the first stage of the Internal Market Strategy for Services, COM (2002) 441.
151. Report on the State of the Internal Market for Services, COM(2002) 441, 8.
152. Regarding the negative vote of the Committees *see* already draft report of the Committee on the Internal Market and Consumer Protection, <http://www.europarl.eu.int/meetdocs/2004_2009/documents/PR/568/568225/568225en.pdf>, 16 June 2006, as well as the draft opinion of the Committee on Employment and Social Affairs, <http://www.europarl.eu.int/meetdocs/2004_2009/documents/PA/566/566667/566667en.pdf>, 16 June 2006.
153. Amended Proposal for a Directive on services in the internal market, COM(2006) 160 final.
154. Regarding the factors to distinguish the temporary nature of services from the freedom of establishment, *see* the Gebhard ruling already mentioned above in fn. 36.
155. Proposal for a Directive on Services in the Internal Market, COM(2004) 2 final/2, Recitals 13 and 14
156. Article para. 2 (cd) of the amended proposal COM(2006) 160 final.

covered by the audiovisual exemption clause will come under the new directive if services are provided on a temporary or even constant basis in other Member States.

Nevertheless, for determining whether an individual service sector falls under the directive a closer look must be taken at the provisions regarding the scope of the directive which are highly complex, as there is a wide range of service sectors that are ex-ante excluded from the scope of its application, namely those activities that are listed in Article 2 of the proposal. Determining the scope of the service directive is furthermore made more complicated by the fact that other provisions of the directive additionally list certain policy areas which are not be affected by the directive. For instance, Article 1 of the proposal states that measures taken at Community level or at national level, in conformity with Community law, in order to protect or promote cultural or linguistic diversity or media pluralism as well as labour law shall not be affected. The same applies according to Article 3 of the proposal e.g. in relation to the directive concerning the pursuit of television broadcasting activities, the provisions concerning the recognition of professional qualifications and private international law in the field of consumer protection.

3. Open Questions Regarding the Service Directive

The text of the service directive leaves many questions open. First and most of all, it is not clear whether the amendend version of the text actually will bring about major changes in the application of the freedom to provide services in relation to the legal status quo. The reason for this assumption being that the country of origin principle – the core principle of the initial proposal – had been excluded from the final text. According to this principle service providers would have been subject only to the national provisions of the Member State in which they were established. The application of the country of origin principle would have meant that a service provider who had already obtained an authorization in the Member State of establishment would not have been obliged to obtain an additional authorization in another Member State. Instead of the country of origin principle the relevant provision – Article 16 – now only prohibits direct or indirect non-discriminations as well as restrictive requirements.

As under the current system such restrictions concerning the access to or the exercise of a service activity may be upheld in individual cases by the Member States on condition that they are non-discriminatory, necessary and proportional i.e. justified on grounds of public policy, public security, public health or the protection of the environment. This range of public interest grounds is meant to be an exhaustive list meaning that further imperative requirements as developed by the case law of the ECJ should not be applicable for services which fall under the directive. Nevertheless, as Articles 1 and 3 of the directive expressly state that those provisions e.g. concerning the protection of cultural or linguistic diversity, media pluralism, the exercise of fundamental rights and the rules of private international law in the fields of consumer protection shall not be affected it remains unclear whether those reasons may also be invoked to justify restrictive national measures.[157] In addition, the directive states that in exceptional cases, a Member State may take measures relating to the safety of services.[158] Therefore host Member States will have to decide whether their own national measures are justified in the light of the reasons mentioned above when applying the directive. As the text opens a wide room for interpretation as regards the relationship to other provisions, this will have to be determined – if not clarified by the legislator – by the ECJ on a case-by-case basis.

Apart from this room of discretion regarding the public-interest exceptions which will be left to the Member States, the directive will bring about remarkable progress as regards the simplification of administrative procedures, such as the establishment of points of single contact, which enable the service provider to complete all procedures and formalities needed for access to his service at one single administrative authority. Moreover, easy access to information through these points of single contact as well as the completion of all administrative procedures via electronic means is provided for. In particular, the planned notification process regarding national provisions which might restrict the freedom to provide services and the subsequent screening process by the Commission will help to identify unjustified national measures.

V. CONTENT AS A EUROPEAN CROSS-CUTTING SUBJECT – CONCLUSIONS AND EVALUATION

On the level of European primary law both the provisions of the EC Treaty and the relevant case-law of the ECJ relating to the four fundamental freedoms ensure the smooth operation of the internal market in the field of content. The provisions concerning the movement of goods, for example, generally prohibit all quantitative restrictions on the import and export of goods and all other measures having equivalent effect between the Member States. Similarly, the Treaty and the case-law of the ECJ guarantee the freedom to provide services.

The rather concise provisions of the Treaty were specified and further elaborated by the ECJ in its numerous decisions relating to the free movement of goods, in particular defining the term 'measure having equivalent effect' in the Dassonville, Keck and Gourmet cases. According to the recent case-law, national measures may not prevent access to the market by products from another Member State or impede access any more than they impede the access

157. *See* Article 1 'Subject matter' and Article 3 'Relationship with other provisions of Community law' of the amended proposal COM(2006) 160 final.
158. *See* Article 19 of the amended proposal COM(2006) 160 final.

of domestic products. Similarly the ECJ held that restrictive national measures regarding the freedom to provide services may represent a violation of the Treaty – as was shown by numerous examples. According to this case law, not only discriminatory national measures but also restrictive indistinctly applicable rules, i.e. rules whose effects are equal on domestic goods and services as well as those from other Member States, are prohibited thus ensuring the functioning of the internal market.

In exceptional circumstances, such national measures, however, may be justified for reasons in the general interest provided that these rules are proportionate to the objective pursued. Imperative grounds expressly provided for in the Treaty to justify discriminatory measures directed at foreign goods are grounds of public morality, public policy or public security, grounds of the protection of health and life of humans, animals or plants, grounds of the protection of national treasures possessing artistic, historic or archaeological value as well as grounds of the protection of industrial and commercial property. Moreover, the ECJ recognized mandatory requirements justifying national rules which affect the free movement of goods and are indistinctly applicable such as the effectiveness of fiscal supervision, the protection of public health, the fairness of commercial transactions, the protection of consumers, improving the living and working environment, protection of the environment, the protection of diversity of the media. Similarily, the ECJ gradually developed further the list of public-interest grounds which might be invoked to restrict the freedom to provide services; in cases that are specifically relevant to the content industry the most important grounds put forward were the protection of public health, human dignity, the protection of consumers from excessive advertising, maintaining a certain level of programme quality in the context of a cultural policy, as well as maintaining a radio and television system which secures pluralism.

In addition to guaranteeing the internal market through the relevant provisions in the Treaty on the four fundamental freedoms and the case-law of the ECJ, the active promotion of the creation and distribution of content is primarily the aim of the Community's funding and action programmes based on various provisions of the Treaty such as those relating to cultural policy, industrial policy and vocational training.

The number of funding programmes relevant to the content industry has boomed since the Lisbon summit of the European Council and by way of example in this Study some programmes have been dealt with such as Culture 2000, MEDIA Plus, MEDIA-Training, eContentplus and the Safer Internet plus programmes as well as the follow-up programmes that are to be applied from 2007 onwards. A common feature of these programmes is that individuals or institutions participating in regular invitations to tender may request financial assistance for their projects with the European Commission to obtain co-funding for national content projects with a European context.

The central significance of the content industry for meeting the goals as formulated in the Lisbon strategy is also reflected in the recent 'Communication from the Commission i2010 – A European Information Society for growth and employment'. In this Communication the Commission has announced a comprehensive reform of the relevant legislation with a view to complete the single market in the area of information and communication technologies by removing existing obstacles by 2010.

Chapter 2
The Content Industry and General Competition Law

Peter Thyri

I. ENSURING FUNCTIONING MARKET STRUCTURES

The European Single Market is based on the principles of an open market economy entailing free competition (Articles 4 and 98 EC). Article 3(2)(g) EC provides for a system ensuring that competition in the internal market is not distorted and thus institutionalizes a competitive economy.[1] In addition to protecting and safeguarding economic freedom and equal treatment of the individual, rules on competition ensure functioning market structures as an inherent characteristic of the internal market. In keeping with the structural significance of the rules on competition, the present study on the relevance of general competition law for the European content industry will first focus on how functioning market structures can be ensured.

At the outset, it is important to note that the competition rules of the Treaty neither can nor should safeguard economic success for one specific product or technology. Instead, they are designed to guarantee free competition as a necessary precondition for success on the market.[2] Competition law has a primarily structural function. Whereas various exemptions may aim at directly promoting production and distribution (*see* item E *below*), protecting third parties and the internal market as an institution ultimately serve to safeguard competitive market structures.

---

1. H. Schröter, 'Article 81 to 89' in *Kommentar zum Europäischen Wettbewerbsrecht*, H. Schröter, T. Jakob and W. Mederer (eds) (Baden-Baden, Nomos, 2003), para. 14.
2. *See* P. Lowe, 'Keynote speech: Sector Inquiry New Media (3G)' <http://europa.eu.int/comm/competition/speeches/text/sp2005_007_en.pdf>, 7 July 2006, 3.

M. Holoubek, D. Damjanovic and M. Traimer (eds), *Regulating Content – European Regulatory Framework for the Media and Related Creative Sectors*, pp. 61–89

A. General Applicability of the Competition Rules to the Content Industry

1. Specific Relevance of Competition Rules

Article 81 EC prohibits agreements between two or more undertakings which may affect trade between Member States and which have as their object or effect the prevention, restriction or distortion of competition within the common market. Therefore the production and distribution of content by way of cooperation between undertakings must be judged primarily pursuant to Article 81 EC and any piece of secondary legislation and soft-law instruments relating to it.

Article 82 EC, on the other hand, prohibits any abuse by one or more undertakings of a dominant position within the common market or in a substantial part of it in so far as it may affect trade between Member States. If an undertaking dominates the market for the production or distribution of a product or service, the applicability of Article 82 EC must be assessed.

The *EC Merger Regulation* authorizes the Commission to declare incompatible with the common market any concentration which would significantly impede effective competition in the common market or in a substantial part of it, in particular as a result of the creation or strengthening of a dominant position.[3] This implies that functioning market structures shall be protected ex ante against distortions. In the context of the present study, particular attention is paid to the concentrations in the media sector hitherto reviewed by the Commission.

Article 86(1) EC stipulates that in the case of public undertakings and undertakings to which Member States grant special or exclusive rights, Member States shall neither enact nor maintain in force any measure contrary to the rules contained in the Treaty. To the extent that the production and distribution of content is based on exclusive rights, Article 86(1) EC must be applied. Paragraph 2 of Article 86, however, specifies that undertakings entrusted with the operation of services of general economic interest shall be subject to the rules on competition in so far as the application of such rules does not obstruct the performance, in law or in fact, of the particular tasks assigned to them. If the production and distribution of content are therefore considered services of general economic interest, they can be exempted from the rules on competition according to Article 86(2) EC.

Article 87 EC declares states aids distorting or threatening competition by favouring certain undertakings or the production of certain goods, in so far as they affect trade between Member States, to be incompatible with the common market. Hence, the constant review of state aids by the Commission protects undistorted competition on the markets for the production and distribution of content against direct state intervention.

3. Regulation 139/2004, OJ 2004 L 24/1, Article 2(3).

2. Personal Scope

The rules on competition address undertakings and associations of undertakings. The term undertaking is to be determined functionally, depending on the activity in question. It has been coherently and consistently held by the Commission and the European Court of Justice that economic activity is defined as any activity consisting in offering goods and services on a given market.[4] Accordingly, bodies exclusively social in nature,[5] public bodies in so far as they act as bodies exercising official authority,[6] or bodies not deciding independently upon their own conduct on the market[7] are excluded. As it is the activity and not the legal form that counts, natural persons such as artists[8] and athletes[9] may also constitute undertakings if they offer and provide goods or services on a given market. Creating and distributing content on a commercial basis therefore undoubtedly constitutes an economic activity subject to competition law.

As explained below, economic activities in the content industry at scrutiny for the purposes of this study are carried out at different market stages. The activities of vertically integrated undertakings however, often cover several or all market stages. Most TV stations, for instance, are involved in programme production, the acquisition of programme rights, and the distribution to the final customers (transmission).

---

4. Cf. *Commission v. Italy (customs agents)*, Case No. 118/85 [1987] ECR 2599, para. 7; *Commission v. Italy (customs agents)*, Case No. C-35/96 [1998] ECR I-3851, para. 36; *Pavel Pavlov v. Stichting Pensioenfonds Medische Specialisten*, Case No. C-180/98 to C-184/98 [2000] ECR I-6451, para. 75; *CNSD v. Commission*, Case No. T-513/93 [2000] ECR II-1807, para. 36; *Aéroports de Paris v. Commission*, Case No. T-128/98 [2000] ECR II-3929, para. 107; *Ambulanz Glöckner v. Landkreis Südwestpfalz*, Case No. C-475/99 [2001] ECR I-8089, para. 19; *J. C. J. Wouters et al. v. Algemene Raad van de Nederlandse Orde van Advocaten*, Case No. C-309/99 [2002] ECR I-1577, para. 47; *Ilmailulaitos/Luftfartsverket*, Commission Decision 1999/198/EC, OJ 1999 L 69/24, para. 22; *Eco-Emballages*, Commission Decision 2001/663/EC, OJ 2001 L 233/37, para. 70.
5. *See Poucet and Pistre*, Case No. C-159/91 and C-160/91 [1993] ECR I-637, para. 18.
6. *See Bodson v. SA Pompes funèbres des régions libérées*, Case No. 30/87 [1988] ECR 2479, para. 18; *Aéroports de Paris v. Commission*, Case No. T-128/98 [2000] ECR II-3929, para. 112.
7. Cf. *Imperial Chemical Industries v. Commission*, Case No. 48/69 [1972] ECR 619, paras 132/135; *see BPB Industries v. Commission*, Case No. T-65/89 [1993] ECR II-389, para. 149; *Michelin v. Commission ('Michelin II')*, Case No. T-203/01 [2003] ECR II-4071, para. 290; recently also *Tokai Carbon v. Commission*, Case No. T-236/01 [2004] ECR II-1181, para. 279.
8. *RAI/UNITEL*, Commission Decision 78/516/EEC, OJ 1978 L 157/39, 40.
9. Professional athletes engage in an economic activity, *see Deliège v. Ligue francophone de judo*, Case No. C-51/96 and C-191/97 [2000] ECR I-2549, para. 13.

B. Market Definitions for Media Content

Defining the relevant market in its product and geographic dimension is fundamental to a consistent application of the competition rules. Pursuant to Article 82 EC and the Merger Regulation, the definition of the relevant market provides the analytical basis for appraising a dominant position on a market or its creation through a concentration. Article 81 EC also stipulates that a comprehensive definition of the relevant market is indispensable whenever the effects of an agreement on the market (e.g. market foreclosure) are to be examined. In addition, market definition is essential for assessing an agreement's effect on trade,[10] for the application of many of the block exemption regulations, and for establishing an effect on trade between Member States.[11]

Given the fact that the technological environment is continuously evolving, defining markets for media content is particularly complex.[12] A great number of providers are involved in producing and distributing a variety of products and services. Hence media market definitions will always relate to individual cases and will be valid only for a limited period of time.

In practice, the situation can be roughly sketched as follows: As to the relevant product market, a basic product-related distinction is made between production and acquisition of content (upstream) on the one hand, and distribution to the end customer (downstream) on the other hand, these two levels mutually influencing each other in many ways.[13] With vertically integrated undertakings, for example, their dominant position on the production market will often impact the distribution market as certain premium content products constitute an integral part of the selling offer.[14] The CFI recently held in *M6* that the vertical integration of the EBU and its members, together with its geographical extent, automatically precluded access for all non-member operators.[15]

At the production level, the Commission distinguishes according to the nature of acquired rights in media content. It defines, for example, a separate market for the acquisition and re-sale of football broadcasting rights for

10. Cf. De-minimis notice of the Commission, OJ 2001 C 368/13.
11. Cf. Guidelines on the effect on trade concept, OJ 2004 C 101/81.
12. Cf. L. Garzaniti, *Telecommunications, broadcasting and the Internet – EU Competition Law and Regulation* (2nd edn, London, Sweet & Maxwell, 2003), pp. 452–491; the Commission had its definitions of media markets documented by two comprehensive studies by the Institut für Medienrecht Saarbrücken, *Market Definitions in the Media Sector*, July 2005 and October 2003, <http://ec.europa.eu/comm/competition/publications/publications/>, 7 July 2006.
13. *See* D. Geradin, 'Access to Content by New Media Platforms: A Review of the Competition Law Problems', (2005) 30 *European Law Review*, 68, 73 *et seq.*; *see* e.g. *M6 et al. v. Commission*, Case No. T-185/00, T-216/00, T-299/00 and T-300/00 [2002] ECR II-3805, para. 52.
14. *See Vivendi/Canal+/Seagram*, Commission Decision IV/M.2050, OJ 2000 C 311/3, para. 19.
15. *See M6 et al. v. Commission*, Case No. T-185/00, T-216/00, T-299/00 and T-300/00 [2002] ECR II-3805, para. 67.

events played annually,[16] and distinguishes between a market for broadcasting feature films and programmes produced for television.[17] The Commission at one point also defined a separate market for independently produced Dutch TV programmes (excluding in-house productions).[18] In *Newscorp/Telepiu*[19] the Commission examined the effects of a merger on the markets for exclusive rights to premium films, exclusive rights to football events played annually where national teams participate, exclusive rights to other sports events, and the acquisition of TV channels.[20]

At the distribution level, the Commission distinguishes according to the types of technical broadcasting, such as transmitting audiovisual content to end-users. In the recent *Newscorp/Telepiu* case, for example, a distinction was made between pay-TV, free-to-air TV, cable, and media platforms (in particular 3G mobile telephony).[21] Similarly, the Commission's concluding report on the Sector Inquiry into the provision of sports content via third generation mobile networks suggests that there is insufficient substitution between mobile sports services and TV sports services for these to be considered part of a single relevant market.[22] Moreover, the distinction between sports content and other content, as specified in earlier findings of the Commission, was also confirmed for the 3G sector. The Sector Inquiry showed that point-to-point transmission of individual sports events (in particular football, the Olympics and Formula 1) via 3G technology is aimed at narrow consumer markets that do not compete with other content.[23] Also, the Commissions analysis in the EBU case showed that there seems to exist a yet more specific market for the transmission of major sporting events as opposed to minority sports.[24]

Regarding music distribution, the Commission may, in future, pay greater attention to the role of collecting societies in controlling the use of copyrights by different categories of users. Whereas online providers will profit from the new global licenses that give them access to the worldwide repertoire of all national

16. *Canal+/RTL/GJCD – JV*, Commission Decision Comp/M.2483, Press release of the Commission of 12 November 2001, IP/01/1579.
17. *Vivendi/Canal+/Seagram*, Commission Decision IV/M.2050, OJ 2000 C 311/3; cf. Press release of the Commission of 13 October 2000, IP/00/1162.
18. *RTL/Veronica/Endemol*, Commission Decision 96/649/EG, OJ 1996 L 294/14; confirmed in *Endemol Entertainment Holding v. Commission*, Case No. T-221/95 [1999] ECR II-1299.
19. *Newscorp/Telepiu*, Commission Decision 2004/311/EC, OJ 2004 L 110/73.
20. Cf. D. Geradin, (2005) 30 *European Law Review*, 73.
21. *Newscorp/Telepiu*, Commission Decision 2004/311/EG, OJ 2004 L 110/73.
22. *See* European Commission, *Concluding report on the Sector Inquiry into the provision of sports content over third generation mobile networks*, <http://ec.europa.eu/comm/competition/antitrust/others/sector_inquiries/new_media/3g/final_report. pdf>, 7 July 2006, para. 14; this situation may however change soon due to technolcgical improvements in network quality which offer broadcast-style TV (DVB-H), *see* 'Italians jump ahead in the mobile-TV game', *The Wall Street Journal Europe* (print edition), 1 June 2006, 27.
23. European Commission, *Concluding report sports content* (n. 22 above), paras 19 *et seq.*
24. *See M6 et al. v. Commission*, Case No. T-185/00, T-216/00, T-299/00 and T-300/00 [2002] ECR II-3805, para. 53, 57.

collecting societies and will be able to choose between the individual national societies in a competitive environment, smaller users such as discotheques and cafes will remain tied to their national collecting societies as no such licenses exist for them.[25]

With regard to the geographic scope, national markets or markets that are fairly homogeneous in language are defined according to their differences in culture or language.[26] This does, however, not exclude the effect on trade between Member States of an agreement or unilateral action, required for the applicability of EC competition law. Foreclosing a national market for enterprises from other Member States may certainly have an effect on trade between Member States.[27] As mentioned before, dissolution of the national monopolies for collecting societies seems to result in a first cross-border market definition for online music distribution.[28]

C. COMPETITION RULES CONCERNING THE PRODUCTION LEVEL (UPSTREAM)

The competition rules described in A.1. are principally universally applicable across all relevant market stages. In other words, there is no specific regime in place regulating only the production or only the distribution level. Whenever competition rules concerning production are specifically mentioned in the present context, they refer to production-related cases where the general competition rules have been or could be applied. The term production in its broadest sense used here relates to direct content production as well the compilation of various types of content in order to create a marketable media product.[29] This may imply examining horizontal agreements between companies operating at the same market level or vertical agreements between companies operating at different market levels, as well as the abuse of market power or its *ex-ante* control in the course of merger review.

25. *See IFPI Simulcasting*, Commission Decision 2003/300/EC, OJ 2003 L 107/58; *Santiago Agreement*, COMP/C2/38.126, OJ 2001 C 145/2; *Barcelona Agreement*, COMP/C2/38.377, OJ 2002 C 132/18; *see* A. Capobianco, 'Licensing of Music Rights: Media Convergence, Technological Developments and EV Competition Law', [2004] *European Intellectual Property Review*, 113, 120.
26. *See* D. Geradin, (2005) 30 *European Law Review*, 74 with further reference; J. Faull and A. Nikpay, *The EC Law of Competition*, (Oxford, OUP, 1999), para. 11.66; cf. on geographic market delimitation according to language criteria *Tiercé Ladbroke SA v. Commission ('Ladbroke II')*, Case No. T-504/93 [1997] ECR II-923 (paras 102 *et seq.*); *see M6 et al. v. Commission*, Case No. T-185/00, T-216/00, T-299/00 and T-300/00 [2002] ECR II-3805, para. 53.
27. *See* J. Faull and A. Nikpay, EC Law (n. 26 above), para. 11.62.
28. Cf. A. Capobianco, [2004] *European Intellectual Property Review*, 120 *et seq.*
29. Competitive aspects when selling this media product are treated under 4 *below*.

1. General Cartel Prohibition – Article 81 EC

Content is frequently produced by way of horizontal cooperation between companies operating at the same market level.[30] In 2001, the Commission published its general approach in this context in a Notice on the applicability of Article 81 of the EC Treaty to horizontal cooperation agreements.[31] Although non-binding in nature, this Notice is an important source when assessing agreements relating to the content industry.

Cooperation between several companies may be indispensable for establishing a commercial offer. Hence, the creation of meaningful content in football requires cooperation between individual athletes or clubs. The consumable product, the football match, and in consequence the championship or tournament, requires cooperation between several clubs. And yet, such cooperation does not in principle come under Article 81(1) EC as it does not imply a coordination of the parties' competitive behaviour.[32] The activity covered by the cooperation simply cannot be carried out independently. Agreements concerning such essential cooperation could only come under Article 81(1) EC if the parties possess significant market power[33] and are likely to cause foreclosure problems *vis-à-vis* third parties.[34]

For an operator in the media sector, creating a content product means not only the autonomous production of content but also acquiring the required individual rights and their further processing into consumable programmes, e.g. a sports event.

Pursuant to Article 81 EC, agreements concerning the purchase and sale of content in order to create a media product must be assessed as to the exclusivity of the acquired rights. It is common practice for rights owners to sell these rights in large bundles exclusively to one single purchaser.[35] For example for a feature film, it has in principle been recognized that the owner of a copyright may freely commercialize this right. Conferring exclusive rights must nonetheless always be assessed in the light of Article 81(1) EC and must under the given economic and legal circumstances never lead to a significant restriction of film

30. With regard to aspects of vertical cooperation that impacts exploitation of these products, cf. 4.a. *below*.
31. Guidelines on horizontal cooperation agreements, OJ 2001 C 3/2.
32. Guidelines on horizontal cooperation agreements, OJ 2001 C 3/2, para. 24; also Regulations and rules that are intrinsic to sport and concern the organization of competitions, i.e. the rules of the game, are not considered an economic activity (cf. W. Deselaers, 'Sportverbände und Europäisches Kartellrecht', [1998] *Wirtschaft und Wettbewerb*, 946, 949 *et seq.*; for the Commission's policy in this sector, *see* XXIXth Report on Competition Policy 1999 [2000], paras 139 *et seq.*).
33. Regarding the significance of the determination of the relevant market, *see* 1.c. *above*.
34. Guidelines on horizontal cooperation agreements. OJ 2001 C 3/2, para. 24.
35. *See M6 et al. v. Commission*, Case No. T-185/00, T-216/00, T-299/00 and T-300/00 [2002] ECR II-3805, paras 60 *et seq.*

distribution or a distortion of competition on the cinematographic market.[36] While exclusive agreements may be justified in order to amortize investments in physical assets from the perspective of TV operators,[37] such agreements nevertheless cause considerable foreclosure problems in downstream markets for broadcasting TV programmes.[38] Essential factors in this context are the duration and the scope of the agreement examined. In contrast to the energy sector, where long-term exclusive agreements (up to 15 years)[39] are tolerated because of the high investment involved, in the content industry, much shorter contracts are generally granted (2–3 years).[40] In this context, clauses providing for an automatic extension of exclusive contracts have the same effect as long-term contracts. Their assessment must therefore follow the same criteria.[41]

Regarding sports content, cross-platform bundling has turned out to have particularly negative competitive effects on new products, especially those provided by 3G mobile telephony. Cross-platform bundling refers to practices where a rights owner sells bundled audiovisual rights for various retail platforms to one or a few operators, usually financially powerful operators which subsequently do not exploit the acquired rights of transmission via innovative platforms. As bundling of rights across platforms prevents operators that offer mobile services from purchasing meaningful rights, it limits market access and is therefore a cause for concern within the meaning of Article 81(1) EC.[42]

In the markets studied, exclusive agreements are usually signed between upstream and downstream companies (for the latter *see* item D.1.) below on competition rules relating to distribution). In reference to the upstream market, mention should be made of joint purchasing of media content. In the *Sogecable/Via Digital* case the Commission examined an agreement between two Spanish TV operators on the joint buying and selling of rights to the matches

36. *See Coditel v. Ciné-Vog Films SA (Coditel II)*, Case No. 262/81 [1982] 3381; *see also M6 et al. v. Commission*, Case No. T-185/00, T-216/00, T-299/00 and T-300/00 [2002] ECR II-3805, para. 64.
37. Cf. D. Geradin, (2005) 30 *European Law Review*, 82 *et seq.*, emphasizing that the investment volume in existing technological infrastructure is probably already amortized and hence does not justify a continued exclusive agreement; cf. XXVth Report on Competition Policy 1995 (1996), para. 83.
38. J. Faull and A. Nikpay, EC Law (n. 26 above), para. 11.84; D. Geradin, (2005) 30 *European Law Review*, 70.
39. *Scottish Nuclear*, Commission Decision 91/329/EEC, OJ 1991 L 178/31; Notification under Article 19(3) Regulation 17, *REN/Turbogas*, Case No. IV/E-2/35.485, OJ 1996 C 118/7; Notification under Article 19(3) Regulation 17, *ISAB Energy*, Case No. IV/E-3.35.698, OJ 1996 C 138/3.
40. *UEFA Champions League*, Commission Decision 2003/778/EC, OJ 2003 L 291/25; D. Geradin, (2005) 30 *European Law Review*, 86.
41. *See* H. Ungerer, 'Understanding the TV Rights debate', Speech Barcelona, <http://europa.eu.int/comm/competition/speeches/text/sp2003_024_en.pdf>, 7 July 2006; A. Schaub, 'Sports and Competition: Broadcasting rights for sports events', Speech Madrid, <http://europa.eu.int/comm/competition/speeches/text/sp2002_008_en.pdf>, 7 July 2006; *see* D. Geradin, (2005) 30 *European Law Review*, 68.
42. Cf. European Commission, *Concluding report sports content* (n. 22 above), paras 32 *et seq.*

of the Spanish premier football league.[43] Cooperation was to last for 11 seasons, which was considered far too long a period by the Commission.[44] As explained, long and exclusive exploitation rights may foreclose the market to new entrants. The *Eurovision* case then concerned the joint acquisition of television rights to sporting events and other sports programmes by the European Broadcasting Union (EBU), a non-profit association of radio and TV organizations. In this case, the concerns of the Commission were dispelled by a scheme for sub-licensing that was to ensure third-party access to the Eurovision system.[45] In practice however, the system did not proof to effectively guarantee sufficient opportunities for non-members of the EBU to transmit main sporting events live and the CFI, on complaint of competitors, subsequently annulled the exemption decision of the Commission because of a manifest error of assessment in the application of Articles 81(3)(b) EC.[46]

2. Prohibition to Abuse a Dominant Position – Article 82 EC

As the ECJ holds, a dominant undertaking must be aware of a 'special responsibility' not to abuse this position.[47] Article 82 EC aims in particular at protecting the structure of competition on the merits.[48] Enforcing the ban on abuse of a dominant position may directly protect third parties as well as it may directly promote the production or distribution of content, however generally, such promotion is fostered by safeguarding the structure of competition. A short description of how competition on the merits works shall exemplify how the prohibition to abuse a dominant position promotes production, innovation and development.

The prospect of a particularly strong position on a market is generally a central incentive for entrepreneurial efficiency in a competitive system. Without the prospect of conquering new markets or succeeding in existing markets with new and improved products, enterprises would show little ambition to improve their competitive performance. Following this logic, a dominant position within a market achieved by internal growth through competition on the merits, even

43. Press release by the Commission of 12 April 2000, IP/00/372: 'Commission ready to lift immunity from fines to Telefónica Media and Sogecable in Spanish football rights Case'.
44. In the end, the agreement was not modified and no fine was imposed, as the parties decided on a merger approved by the Commission.
45. *Eurovision*, Commission Decision 2000/400/EC, OJ 2000 L 151/18.
46. *See M6 et al. v. Commission*, Case No. T-185/00, T-216/00, T-299/00 and T-300/00 [2002] ECR II-3805, paras 75 *et seq.*
47. In *RTL/Veronica/Endemol*, Commission Decision 96/649/EC, OJ 1996 L 294/14, the Commission defines a dominant position on the relevant markets according to the value of the programs sold and not according to the sales volume. With a market share exceeding 50 per cent and the existence of further factors (*see* J. Faull and A. Nikpay, EC Law (n. 26 above), para. 11.70 with further reference) this was a case of a dominant market position.
48. *See* T. Eilmansberger, 'How to distinguish good from bad competition under Article 82 EC: In search of clearer and more coherent standards for anti-competitive abuses', (2005) 42 *Common Market Law Review*, 129, 132 *et seq.*

if that position may result in a monopoly, is not prohibited within the meaning of Article 82 EC,[49] but is subject to the code of conduct stipulated in this Article. With reference to the production or creation of goods and services, this implies especially a prohibition of anti-competitive abuses, hindering the competitive performance of competitors. Dominant undertakings may, on account of their very position on the market, engage in anti-competitive conduct and thus limit production in a relevant market.

The special challenge in applying Article 82 lies in weighing the incentives for entrepreneurial efficiency aiming at market domination against the potential for abuse once this position has been acquired. This becomes particularly apparent in cases concerning access to an essential facility. Certain goods or services may be essential for accessing downstream markets, such as intellectual property rights that permit their owner to control products or value chains based on these rights. The owner of a copyright in a film, for instance, may control the downstream levels in the value chain such as showing the film in a cinema, home video selling or rental, TV broadcasting, or distribution via new media platforms, by granting access through licensing.[50] Refusal to grant a license could in very specific situations constitute an abuse of a dominant market position.[51] Forcing access to such an important facility may, however, stifle competition on the merits, which must be considered when assessing whether Article 82 EC can be applied.[52] In conclusion, Article 82 EC can promote the functioning of markets for the production and assembly of content in so far as it aims at a trade-off between undertaking's legitimate striving for market power, which all competition on the merits relies upon, and the resulting strategies in restraint of trade that limit production, which it tries to combat.

The described practice of cross-platform bundling may also lead to an abuse of a dominant position if the acquiring TV operator acquires bundles of new technology transmission rights and subsequently does not exploit these rights.[53] Conduct of that type could come under the category of prevention of a new product within the meaning of the *Magill* decision[54] of the ECJ.[55]

3. Control of Concentrations

Whereas Article 82 EC shall, as mentioned above, prevent the abuse of an already existing dominant position, the Merger Regulation is aimed at ex ante

49. *See* H. Schröter, 'Article 82', in *Kommentar* (n. 1 above), para. 20.
50. D. Geradin, (2005) 30 *European Law Review*, 87.
51. For specifics *see* P. Thyri, 'Immaterialgüterrechte und Zugang zu wesentlichen Einrichtung', [2005] *Wirtschaft und Wettbewerb*, 388, 392.
52. *See* P. Thyri, [2005] *Wirtschaft und Wettbewerb*, 397.
53. The Sector Inquiry Sport-Content confirmed such practices, *see* European Commission, *Concluding report sports content* (n. 22 above), para. 33.
54. *Radio Telefis Eireann (RTE) and Independent Television Publications LTD (ITP) v. Commission ('Magill')*, Case No. C-241/91 P & C-242/91 P, [1995] ECR I-743.
55. *See* T. Eilmansberger, (2005) 42 *Common Market Law Review*, 160.

preventing distortions of effective competition in the common market, in particular as a result of the creation or strengthening of a dominant position. While Articles 81 and 82 EC indirectly protect the competitive structure by prohibiting certain agreements or unilateral actions, the Merger Regulation is an instrument of direct market structure control. Concentrations may take the form of (i) horizontal concentrations between undertakings at the same market level, (ii) vertical concentrations between undertakings at different market levels, and (iii) conglomerate concentrations between undertakings operating in different markets. Horizontal concentrations between undertakings producing and creating content are of particular interest in this context.[56]

When assessing the *Newscorp/Telepiù* case, the Commission saw the danger of a quasi-monopoly position for the acquisition of exclusive film rights[57] and hence for the creation of a specific programming offer on the relevant market. The Commission also paid special attention to so called holdback clauses that aim at keeping the buyers of content rights from selling to certain media platforms. These clauses prevent competitors from entering the market and therefore constitute a barrier to entry. Also in the recent *Sony/BMG* case the Commission assessed the horizontal effects of setting up a joint venture for the joint marketing and sale of recorded music by the parties concerned,[58] but finally abandoned concerns over the emergence of a dominant market position.[59] The CFI however, upon competitors' complaint, annulled the Commission's decision on the basis of inadequate reasoning and a manifest error of assessment in so far as the elements forming the basis of the Decision not to oppose the concentration do not constitute all the relevant data that must be taken into consideration and are not sufficient to support the conclusions that the merger would not create or strengthen a collective dominant position.[60]

In addition to the horizontal effects of concentrations between undertakings at the production level, numerous vertical effects are scrutinized in the

---

56. Relevance of vertical integration for distribution, *see* below.
57. *Newscorp/Telepiu*, Commission Decision 2004/311/EC, OJ 2004 L 110/73, para. 150.
58. *Sony/BMG*, Commission Decision COMP/M.3333 of 19 July 2004.
59. The Commission examined the possible creation of a collective dominant position between the remaining four competitors on the national sound carrier markets. In the case *Time Warner/EMI* in 2000, similar concerns of the Commission had led to a withdrawal of the merger notification by the parties, cf. Commission press release IP/00/1122 of 5 October 2000, 'EMI and Time Warner withdraw their notification to the Commission'. Against the background of clarifying the evidentiary standard required to prove oligopolistic parallel behaviour in *Airtours v. Commission*, Case No. T-342/99 [2002] ECR II-2585, cf. F. Schuhmacher, 'Kollektive Marktbeherrschung und koordinierte Effekte im EG-Wettbewerbsrecht', [2005] *wirtschaftsrechtliche blätter*, 245, and the annulment of two further Commission Decisions on the grounds of insufficient evidence in *Schneider Electric v. Commission*, Case No. T-310/01 [2002] ECR II-4071 and *Tetra Laval v. Commission*, Case No. T-5/02 [2002] ECR II-4381, the Commission decided in *Sony/BMG* that there was not sufficient evidence to prove the possible creation of collective dominance and approved the merger without imposing further conditions.
60. *IMPALA v. Commission*, Case No. T-464/04, judgment of 13 July 2006.

field of merger control (*see* more below). In this context, preventing market foreclosure, in particular by way of restricting availability of content to consumers (restricted choice), may safeguard the interests of third parties (*see* item II. below).

D. Competition Rules Relating to Distribution ('Downstream')

1. General Ban on Cartels – Article 81 EC

Article 81 EC also applies to the distribution of content products. In this context, (i) horizontal cooperation agreements between sales undertakings or agreements for the purpose of distribution (joint selling) and (ii) vertical cooperation agreements between companies operating at the production level and downstream distribution companies are of particular interest. With regard to the latter, the Commission has issued a regulation exempting specific categories of agreements from Article 81(1) EC (Block Exemption Regulation for Vertical Agreements).[61] In keeping with the basic assumption that on balance, vertical agreements generally have a positive effect, this regulation exempts vertical restrictions if the supplier (or the buyer in an exclusive supply arrangement) has a market share of less than 30 per cent (Article 3) on the relevant market and thus does not hold a dominant position. Only those vertical agreements that are held to significantly restrain competition (Article 4) are excluded from this general exemption ('blacklist').[62]

In the content industry, joint selling agreements are very common. Thus, for example, the Commission thoroughly examined an agreement for joint selling of commercial rights to the UEFA Champions League, a competition of European football clubs. The Commission found that these agreements among individual football clubs resulted in coordinating the pricing policy and other commercial conditions on behalf of football clubs participating in the Champions League and hence producing the content.[63]

As will be discussed in more detail in item V.A, these restrictive clauses were exempted according to the specific circumstances stipulated in Article 81(3) EC, as due to these joint selling arrangements, UEFA was able to provide the final consumer with the benefit of centrally distributed competitive media products that otherwise could not be produced and distributed equally efficiently.[64]

In the German Football League (*Deutsche Bundesliga*) case the Commission also dealt with joint selling arrangements of media rights in football.

61. Regulation 2790/1999, OJ L 1999 L 336/21.
62. *See* T. Eilmansberger, G. Herzig, T. Jaeger and P. Thyri, *Materielles Europarecht* (Vienna, LexisNexis, 2005), paras 416 *et seq*.
63. *UEFA Champions League*, Commission Decision, 2003/778/EC, OJ 2003 L 291/25, (1).
64. Cf. *UEFA Champions League*, Commission Decision, 2003/778/EC, OJ 2003 L 291/25, (1).

This agreement had been notified for individual exemption under Regulation 17/62,[65] but was then transferred according to Article 34 of Regulation 1/2003[66] to the new system of legal exemption, which no longer provides for exemption. Accordingly, at the end of the assessment procedure, the Commission did not decide on an exemption to the regulation – as was the case with UEFA – but on a formal commitment submitted by the parties according to Article 9(1) of Regulation 1/2003. Taking the content aspect into consideration, as in the UEFA case, the Commission endeavoured to work towards a transparent system of awarding contracts, a more extensive sharing of the rights packets to TV transmissions and also easier access for internet or mobile network suppliers[67] through formal commitments of the parties involved.

In the field of 3G rights the Commission is of the opinion that these rights should be sold separately by the individual rights holder on condition that joint selling fails. The aim is to ensure maximum exploitation of the present rights of transmission via new media platforms.[68]

In the *Simulcasting* case[69] the Commission examined joint content exploitation based on technology. In parallel to traditional broadcasting media (radio, television) music programmes are now broadcast on the internet ('simulcasting'). Though operators previously were only active on a country- or regional basis and therefore had to deal with only one collecting society, the present case involves a model contract between almost all collecting societies of the EEA as well as numerous other states that provides for the introduction of a global license for all participating countries. The underlying idea is that operators whose signals originate from an EEA state can turn to any single collecting society in the EEA, which then issues an international license ('one-stop-shop'-license) that is valid for the territories of all participating countries and covers the rights of all collecting societies operating in this area. Although this is basically a horizontal restriction of competition within the meaning of Article 81(1) EC, this model contract created competition between the individual collecting societies, as the operator can apply to the collecting society that offers the most favourable prices, including foreign collecting societies. Subject to this undertaking the Commission then also approved the underlying application for individual exemption according to Article 81(3) EC. This example shows that EU competition law is sufficiently flexible to take into account conditions that promote competition.[70]

65. OJ 1962 13/204.
66. OJ 2003 L 1/1.
67. *Deutsche Bundesliga*, Commission Decision COMP/C-2/37.214 of 19 July 2005; *see* S. Wilbert, 'Joint Selling of Bundesliga media rights – first Commission decision pursuant to Article 9 of Regulation 1/2003', [2005] *Competition Policy Newsletter* 2, 44 *et seq*.
68. European Commission, *Concluding report sports content* (n. 22 above), para. 50.
69. *IFPI 'Simulcasting'*, Commission Decision, 2003/300/EC, OJ 2003 L 107/58.
70. *See* A. Heinemann, 'Schutzrechte in der Informationsgesellschaft und ihr Verhältnis zum Kartellrecht', in *Stand und Perspektiven des Schutzes Geistigen Eigentums in Europa*, P. Behrens (Ed.) (Baden-Baden, Nomos, 2004), p. 105, 110 *et seq*.

Similar agreements have been notified by collecting societies concerning (i) rights of public performances of music on the Internet (streaming, webcasting, online music on-demand, etc.) (ii) reproduction rights on the internet and (iii) rights for physical reproduction of music (*Santiago Agreement*, *Barcelona Agreement*, and *Cannes Agreement*).[71] In the first two cases the contracts involved are model contracts according to which the individual national collecting societies are authorized to award nonexclusive licenses on a worldwide basis for public performances or for the reproduction on the internet of music from the repertory of the contracting partners (multi-repertory licenses). Thus content providers gain access to the worldwide repertory of the contracting parties as a package for the purpose of further distribution. As was originally the case in the agreements in *Simulcasting*, the notified *Santiago and Barcelona* Agreements also contain territorial clauses according to which only the collecting society of the country in which the commercial user has its actual and commercial focus is authorized to grant multi-repertory licenses. Due to the monopoly position of the collecting societies in their respective Member States that would mean that each national collecting society would have the exclusive right in its own country to grant multi-territorial multi-repertory licenses. So far, there has been no decision of the Commission on either of these cases. However, in connection with these agreements, the Commission is expected to insist on discarding territory clauses as it did in the case of *Simulcasting*.[72] In the case of the *Santiago Agreement*, a Communication has been issued according to Article 27 (4) of Regulation 1/2003 that clearly shows that in the framework of a consent order according to Article 9 leg cit[73] the parties forego the previously mentioned clause and in this way dispel the concerns of the Commission.[74]

The previously described one-stop-shop license system has also been installed for the administration of mechanical copyright for the reproduction of sound recordings on physical carriers. In 1997, the five major music publishers and 13 mechanical rights collection societies in the EEA and Switzerland concluded the so called *Cannes Agreement* to bring about greater efficiencies in the administration of phono-mechanical rights in the EEA. The Cannes Agreement expired in 2002 and was to be extended in the *Cannes Extension Agreement* notified to the Commission on 1 July 2003 pursuant to Articles 2 and 4 of Regulation 17.[75] The Extension agreement contained *inter alia* new clauses relating (i) to the granting of rebates by collecting societies to record

71. On performance rights cf. *Santiago Agreement*, COMP/C2/38.126, OJ 2001 C 145/2; on internet reproduction rights *see Barcelona Agreement*, COMP/C2/38.377, OJ 2002 C 132/18; on physical reproduction *see Cannes Extension Agreement*, COMP/C2/38.681, OJ 2006 C 122/2.
72. *See* A. Capobianco, [2004] *European Intellectual Property Review*, 119.
73. An individual exemption by the Commission pursuant to Article 81(3) EC is no longer provided for in the new system of legal exceptions.
74. *See* Notice published pursuant to Article 27(4) of Council Regulation 1/2003, *Santiago Agreement*, COMP/C2/38126, OJ 2005 C 200/11, paras 8 *et seq.*
75. *Carlsberg notice*, OJ 2003 C 282/14.

companies in the context of Central Licensing Agreements, which are multi-repertoire one-stop-shop licenses for the whole EEA territory and (ii) relating to the ability of collecting societies to undertake commercial publishing or record producing activities. In a notice pursuant to Article 27(4) of Regulation 1, the Commission stated that the first clause mentioned would require the consent of other collecting societies' members or other collection societies before granting of a rebate and can therefore have the effect of preventing the granting of rebates by a collecting society that negotiates a Central Licensing Agreement with a record company. In addition, the Commission found that the second clause mentioned has the object and may have the effect of crystallizing current market structures and preventing any future potential competition from collecting societies towards music publishers and/or record companies. After the Commission's preliminary assessment, the parties have therefore offered commitments (i) to reformulate the wording of the rebate clause to provide that a collecting society may grant a rebate to a record company, if so decided by the competent body of that society and (ii) to delete the second clause altogether and to not enter in a clause with similar effects for the future. Consequently, the Commission intends, subject to market testing, to adopt a decision under Article 9(1) of Regulation 1/2003 declaring the commitments summarized above to be binding.[76]

Exclusively acquired rights contained in agreements on the purchase or sale of content for producing marketable media products have been dealt with in item C.1. In particular, long-term exclusive supply agreements between production companies and sales- or broadcasting companies raise competition concerns as they may result in massive market foreclosure. In this context, it is immaterial whether exclusive supply agreements were originally concluded to be long-term or contain clauses for automatic renewal.

So-called English clauses may be equally problematic in this context. Such contractual stipulations provide that after the contract has expired, the original customer of e.g. media rights has the option to match the highest bid of an alternative customer after the contracting partner has informed him about the bid. English clauses raise concerns firstly because they can keep a competitor from tendering an attractive competitive bid in the first place and secondly could artificially increase market transparency solely to the advantage of the undertaking dominating the market (which thus obtains a great deal of insight into the offers of its competitors).[77] In the context of the content industry

76. *See* Notice published pursuant to Article 27(4) of Council Regulation 1/2003, *Universal International Music BV/MCPS and other (The Cannes Extension Agreement)*, COMP/C2/38.681, OJ 2006 C 122/2.

77. Cf. *Hoffmann-La Roche v. Commission*, Case No. 85/76 [1979] ECR 461, paras 102 *et seq.*; *Industriegase*, XIXth Report on Competition Policy1989 (1990), para. 62; *IRI/Nielsen*, XXVIth Report on Competition Policy 1996 (1997), para. 64.

English clauses have been held to be equally restrictive of free trade as open-ended renewal agreements.[78]

Another cause for concern in agreements for the sale of content are so-called Most Favoured Nation (MFN) Clauses. Such clauses can usually be found in contracts between the major American film studios and their customers. They provide that if the buyer grants a studio a particular advantage (an advantageous sales condition, an increased share of revenues, etc.) the buyer must also offer this advantage to all other studios. Similar to the English clauses, this practice increases market transparency and tends to harmonize prices and conditions, if it is subject to and reinforced by various control mechanisms. MFN stipulations could firstly come within the scope of Article 81(1) EC as a pricing cartel and secondly, as a restrictive vertical agreement. In the first case, it may be difficult to prove that an agreement has actually been concluded among the studios; in the second case the restrictive effect of the individual agreement may be difficult to establish. However, on the basis of their cumulative anti-competition effect, groups of such agreements may come under Article 81(1) EC with reference to a network of parallel agreements.[79]

2. Prohibition of the Abuse of a Dominant Position – Article 82 EC

Exclusive agreements are yet more problematic if they are concluded with dominant buyers, e.g. large television companies. If a dominant buyer of content enters into an exclusive agreement with the holder of premium content, access to such content is denied for weaker competitors. This consequently impairs their access to the relevant market or may drive such competitors altogether out of the market. Thus, a customer who dominates the market may amortize the high sums spent for acquiring exclusive rights after taking over the market shares of the competitors he succeeded in driving out of the market.[80]

Under Article 82 EC, also exploitative practices have been identified in the area of content distribution. Thus, for example, excessively high broadcasting charges for sports or film rights may infringe Article 82 EC. Indeed, the high costs of content often enable only well established and partly dominant customers to acquire the most exclusive packages of rights. For smaller competitors, especially new or potential entrants, as for example, new media platforms, these costs represent a barrier to entry. According to common practice, the payments that must be made do not follow a system of sales revenue sharing, which would allow market entrants to calculate their costs according

78. Cf. *Sport 7/KNVB*, XXVIIth Report on Competition Policy 1997 (1998), para. 122.
79. *Brasserie de Haecht v. Consorts Wilkin-Janssen*, Case No. 23/67 [1967] ECR 544; *Stergios Delimitis v. Henninger Bräu AG*, Case No. C-234/89 [1991] ECR I-935; on the concept tying contracts recently *Neste Markkinointi Oy v. Yötuuli Ky and Others*, Case No. C-214/99 [2000] ECR I-11121, paras 25 *et seq*.
80. *See* D. Geradin, (2005) 30 *European Law Review*, 82.

to the number of customers, but are calculated on the basis of single payments that are independent of the expected sales revenues. If the holder of the rights has a dominant market position, the mere amount of these charges could constitute an abuse of a dominant position on the part of the rights holder.[81] The need to assume a high financial risk even before a significant market share has been acquired has been held abusive in other cases.[82]

3. Control of Concentrations

With regard to the distribution of content products, the emergence of vertically integrated media companies is being monitored closely. Vertical integration of a production company that already holds a dominant position can strengthen its market dominance. In *RTL/Veronica/Endemol* the Commission examined the planned participation of the Dutch programme producer Endemol in HMG, a joint venture, for the purpose of the shared creation and distribution of television and radio programmes. Additionally, the agreement provided that the new joint-venture company would buy a substantial share of its demand for Dutch television programmes from Endemol. The Commission feared that Endemol could increase its order intake through the structural connection to HMG and thus gain a strong advantage over rivals on the production market. The Commission did not approve this merger and Endemol did not take part in the joint venture.[83] In the case *Sony/BMG*, that also concerned the establishment of a joint venture, the Commission feared that the new unit could discriminate in granting access to content, especially music. Above all, there was concern that Bertelsmann could give *Sony/BMG* preference in access to its distribution infrastructure (radio, TV).[84] The case entailed the danger of strengthening a collective dominant position[85] of the five most important groups on the market for recorded music. In the end, however, the Commission did not find sufficient indication that the planned transaction would lead to a strengthening of an existing collective dominant position.[86]

81. *See* D. Geradin, (2005) 30 *European Law Review*, 80 *et seq.*
82. *BRT v. SABAM I*, Case No. 127/73 [1974] ECR 51, paras 15, 16; *Tetra Pak International SA v. Commission (‚Tetra Pak II')*, Case No. T-83/91 [1994] ECR II-755, para. 122.
83. *RTL/Veronica/Endemol*, Commission Decision 96/649/EC, OJ 1996 L 294/14.
84. Press release of the Commission IP/04/2000: 'Commission opens in-depth investigation into Sony/Bertelsmann recorded music venture'.
85. Cf. comprehensive work on the concept of collective market dominance F. Schuhmacher, [2005] *wirtschaftsrechtliche blätter*, 245.
86. *Sony/BMG*, Commission Decision COMP/M.3333 of 19 July 2004, para. 154; annulled for inadequate reasoning and a manifest error of assessment in *IMPALA v. Commission*, *see* above n. 60.

II. PROTECTING THIRD PARTIES AND SAFEGUARDING GENERAL INTERESTS

Principally, three types of parties can be categorized in observing the effects of third party protection in the EU competition regime. First (i) final consumers, second (ii) competitors and third (iii) trading partners of undertakings possibly engaging in anti-competitive conduct. Previously, mention has been made of third-party protection in this text. At this point, several specific details will be added.

A. PROTECTING THE FINAL CONSUMER

Competition rules guarantee free competition on the internal market and shall thus contribute to the most efficient allocation of available resources in a free market system. Through safeguarding a competitive structure, final consumers are protected in two ways. First, the prohibition of anti-competitive agreements and the rules against the abuse of market power seek to guarantee market participants the maximum possible freedom in setting their prices so that the market law of supply and demand takes effect. Thus final consumer shall be protected from exploitative prices. In addition, a system of competition on the merits shall also guarantee constant innovative efforts on the part of rivals, thus benefiting the final consumer by generating new and improved products or a larger selection of products. The above example concerning the market for sports content shows how the application of Articles 81 and 82 EU not only attempts to protect the final consumer from exploitative prices by means of combating exclusive rights agreements in distribution, but also specifically increases the opportunities for new media platforms to position themselves on the relevant markets against the long-established TV networks, strengthens their position, and thus guarantees conditions of fair competition to the advantage of the consumer of recently-developed technologies.[87]

Measures planned by the Commission against embargo time in awarding sports content are aimed directly at improving the range of programmes offered to the final consumer. With reference to technical limitations and in particular upholding the value of TV rights, awarding transmission rights for sports events presently is very limited in regard to time (only highlights). In light of the very limited substitution between TV broadcasts and 3G services, the Commission considers these limitations to be out-of-scale and therefore problematic from the perspective of competition law. Loosening this present restrictive practise of awarding rights would, on the one hand, increase the value of 3G services and thus facilitate their market entry as well as ensure that consumers gain access to more attractive products.[88]

---

87. Cf. also P. Lowe, 'Keynote speech' (n. 2 *above*), 3.
88. European Commission, *Concluding report sports content* (n. 22 above), paras 40 *et seq.*

B. Protecting Competitors?

European competition law has been accused of protecting smaller competitors that often operate inefficiently instead of protecting the final consumer (e.g. as in the consumer welfare approach found in U.S. anti-trust law).[89] As explained above, the primary goal of Article 81 *et seq.* EC is guaranteeing competition on the merits. Thus rivals are only indirectly protected if their competitive performance is obstructed by way of practices that are considered an anti-competitive abuse under Article 82 EC. It is then incumbent on competition law to restore conditions allowing free competition. These relations are illustrated by the following example from the content industry. The Commission established that access to certain content (premium content) may be essential to downstream markets for the general distribution of audio-visual content.[90] It can be assumed that if a supplier does not have this premium content in its programme, the final consumer will decide against buying this supplier's products. For example, should a vertically integrated rights holder refuse access and thereby exclude all competition on downstream markets from the distribution of content, this may represent an abuse of a dominant market position. As a remedy in such a case the Commission may order access for competitors on the basis of a direct application of Article 82 EC or access to downstream markets may even be enforced by a national court, applying the legal consequences of an obligation to deal. While in such a case it is obvious that the competitor benefits from Article 82 EC as he directly gains access, the scope of the provision, as mentioned, goes beyond the right of the individual, aiming at keeping open downstream markets and value chains.

C. Protecting Trading Partners

Several of the rules listed in Article 82(2)(a-d) EC show that the prohibition of abusive conduct also safeguards trading partners and customers of dominant companies from suffering from the fact that, by definition, dominant companies are subject to only limited forces of competition in establishing their commercial relations.[91] Companies that are only to a limited extent or not at all subject to the pressure of competition have only relatively little incentive to improve their performance and to provide the best-possible offer of goods and services as regards quality and price.

89. Cf. E. Fox, 'We Protect Competition, You Protect Competitors', [2003] *World Competition*, 149, who effectively rebuts this allegation.
90. *Vivendi/Canal+/Seagram*, Commission Decision IV/M.2050, OJ 2000 C 311/3, para. 19.
91. A. Jones and B. Sufrin, *EC Competition Law* (2nd edn, Oxford, OUP, 2004), p. 253–254; J. Faull and A. Nikpay, EC Law (n. 26 above), paras 3.10-3.19; H. Schröter, 'Article 82', in *Kommentar* (n. 1 above), para. 19; H. Schröter, 'Article 82', in *Kommentar zum Vertrag über die Europäische Union und zur Gründung der Europäischen Gemeinschaft*, H.v.d. Groeben and J. Schwarze (eds) (Baden-Baden, Nomos, 2003), para. 18.

Article 82 EC protects customers specifically by banning the abuse of a dominant position resulting from the absence of competition. Following the basic ruling in the *United Brands* case, it must be assessed 'whether the holder of such a position used the resulting options to obtain business advantages that he would otherwise not have obtained had there been normal and sufficiently effective competition'.[92] Companies that dominate the market are thus forced to act as if they were subject to effective competition.[93]

III. PRESERVING THE SINGLE MARKET

In order to understand and interpret the competition rules of the EC-Treaty, it is of essence to look at the integrative function these rules have for the Common Market. Competition law is not only designed to pursue the conventional aims of competition (namely the best possible allocation of resources), but also to ensure that the national internal market barriers that were eliminated by the internal market rules primarily aimed at Member States (the fundamental freedoms and the relevant secondary legislation) are not replaced by measures set up by private undertakings to foreclose the markets.[94] In this sense the competition rules also help preserve the internal market.

Notwithstanding, in the SACEM ruling, territorial monopolies for collecting societies were basically accepted. As the establishment of parallel collecting societies and control systems was considered inefficient, the Court assumed the presence of a natural monopoly.[95] With regard to the *Simulcasting* ruling[96] and the notified *Santiago* und *Barcelona Agreements*[97] presented above, it becomes clear that the situation has changed with advancing technological development. Parallel collecting structures for broadcasting music on the Internet, where problems of control of the physical world become inapplicable, can now clearly be established efficiently. Thus, a separate territorial jurisdiction of national collecting societies is no longer required. In the course of its assessment of the international licences envisaged in *Simulcasting*, the Commission has thus

92. *United Brands v. Commission*, Case No. 27/76 [1978] ECR 207, para. 248.
93. Cf. Ch. Weiser, *Preismissbrauch nach Artikel 86 EWG-Vertrag* (Köln, Heymann, 1987), p. 215–220; H. Schröter, 'Article 82', in *Kommentar* (n. 1 *above*), para. 168; H. Schröter, 'Article 82', in *Kommentar*-Groeben/Schwarze (n. 91 *above*), para. 167; W. Möschel, 'Article 86', in *EG-Wettbewerbsrecht*, U. Immenga and E.-J. Mestmäcker (eds) (Munich, Beck, 1997), para. 123; E.-J. Mestmäcker and H. Schweitzer, *Europäisches Wettbewerbsrecht* (2nd edn, Munich, Beck, 2004), § 15 para. 33; D. Dirksen, 'Article 82', in *Kommentar zum deutschen und europäischen Kartellrecht*, E. Langen and H. Bunte (eds) (Neuwied, Luchterhand, 2001), para. 97.
94. *Italy v. Council and Commission*, Case No. 32/65 [1966] ECR 458, 486.
95. *Ministère Public v. Jean-Louis Tournier (SACEM I)*, Case No. 395/87 [1989] ECR 2521; *Lucazeau v. SACEM (SACEM II)*, Case No. 110/88, 241/88 and 242/88 [1989] ECR 2811.
96. *IFPI 'Simulcasting'*, Commission Decision 2003/300/EC, OJ 2003 L 107/58.
97. *Santiago Agreement*, COMP/C2/38.126, OJ 2001 C 145/2; *Barcelona Agreement*, COMP/C2/38.377, OJ 2002 C 132/18.

not authorized an originally intended customer allocation clause under which one collecting society may only grant a license to broadcasters whose broadcast signals were transmitted from the same territory. The Commission has thus implemented the freedom of choice for broadcasters to contract with collecting societies from any of the Member States. Similar commitments can be expected in the other two cases. Doing-away with these clauses thus cleared the way for the establishment of an internal market for licensing online music.[98]

A direct way of upholding the internal market is also to be seen in the particular effort the Commission makes to limit so-called territorial clauses in state aid schemes of the Member States when granting licenses in the film industry. As a prerequisite for the producer of a film to benefit from full state aid, territorial clauses often require a specified amount of the film budget to be spent in one particular Member State. In this case, the main concern of the Commission is not the amount of the aid, as the purpose of such aid is to promote culture and thus in principle can be approved. Rather, such clauses may impede the freedom of movement of employees as well as the free movement of goods and services in the EC and thus lead to a fragmentation of the internal market and curb its development.[99] The Commission thus clears such clauses only to a limited degree.

IV. INTERACTIONS BETWEEN THE INTENDED AIMS

Within the scope of this paper, the interconnections among the various ways the competition provisions can be applied to the content industry have been outlined where appropriate in the specific factual context. Here it shall suffice to point out once again that general competition law affects the aspects dealt with in I., II., III., and V. to varying degrees. In general, the central concern of competition law is safeguarding functioning market structures. Protecting the customer from being exploited is a specific goal of the prohibition of exploitative abuse according to Article 82 EC. The general ban on allocating markets is not only to be seen to the background of the effect it has, which equals price fixing, but also in light of the internal market end.

Basically, these aims work collectively. For example, the prohibition on territorial customer allocation protects the final consumer from exploitation by local monopolies and also fulfils the purpose of protecting the internal market. In contrast, the previously-mentioned effects can also, among other things, run against one another. Thus, if a dominant undertaking refuses access to an essential facility, such as a licence for the use of the structure of a database,[100]

98. Cf. A. Capobianco, [2004] *European Intellectual Property Review*, 118.
99. Communication on the film industry, COM(2004) 171, OJ 2004 C 123/1, para. 6.
100. Cf. *IMS Health v. NDC Health*, Case No. C-418/01 [2004] ECR I-5039; *see* Ch. Wolff, *Zwangslizenzen im Immaterialgüterrecht* (Göttingen, V & R Unipress, 2005), p. 155 *et seq.* including comprehensive evidence.

this may be considered to restrain rivals and can impair competition on the downstream market. On the other hand, such a refusal to deal may be justified if the facility has been developed by way of a genuine commercial effort to compete on the merits on the part of the undertaking in order to acquire an advantage on the downstream market. In such a case, the obligation to deal would negate the incentive to gain an advantage on the downstream market. Here, the protection of rivals must step back in favour of safeguarding the competitive process.[101]

V. DIRECT AIDS FOR PRODUCING AND BROADCASTING CONTENT

As was previously described in the introduction, competition rules have a neutral effect with regard to individual sectors or products. In particular, they are designed to safeguard the prerequisites for the economic success of competitive products and services. In the following part of the text, various exemptions from the applicability of general rules will be presented that may be beneficial in the specific context of producing and broadcasting content.

A. Article 81(3) EC – Exemptions General Ban on Cartels

As mentioned above, Article 81 EC deals with collusion among undertakings. The prohibition of agreements in restriction of free trade in Article 81(1) EC thus indirectly promotes the production of content by ensuring that undertakings do not replace competition, which bears many risks, with collusion. The competitive structure described above shall be preserved as an institution of the internal market based on the assumption that players on the market act autonomously. The purpose of the conditions presented for an exemption from the prohibition of agreements in restriction of free trade in Article 81(3) leg cit EC shall enable a case-by-case comparison of the restrictive effects of an agreement with its pro-competitive effects. Agreements, decisions of associations of undertakings or concerted practices are not subject to the cartel prohibition provided that they contribute to improving the production or distribution of goods or promote technical or economic progress and allow the consumers a fair share of the resulting benefits. Restrictions must not be imposed on the undertakings concerned that are indispensable to the attainment of these objectives or that afford such undertaking the possibility of eliminating competition in respect of a substantial part of the product in question. The effect of these exemption clauses can definitively be to 'directly' promote content in the sense of the typology of content-specific norms applied in this study.

101. *See* P. Thyri, [2005] *Wirtschaft und Wettbewerb*, 397 *et seq.*

The *UEFA Champions* League[102] case is a recent example. In this case the Commission exempted an agreement on joint selling arrangements of commercial rights to a league competition that normally would be included in the scope of the ban on cartels according to Article 81(3), as it provided a service that otherwise would not have been available to consumers. With regard to the restriction of competition (market foreclosure) that the Commission identified as relevant to distribution, however, the Commission set extensive requirements for the exemption. Thus, for example, the extended periods of the relevant agreements had to be reduced to a maximum of three years,[103] a more objective public procurement procedure had to be designed to give all suitable broadcaster the chance to put in informed bids for broadcasting rights on equal footing,[104] and television rights awarded to various companies had to be split into several smaller packages.[105]

B. Objective Justification According to Article 82 EC

Although Article 82 EC does not expressly provide for justification in the case of abuse of a dominant position on the market, the jurisprudence of the Community Courts acknowledges that unilateral action is excluded from the prohibition of abuse if it is objectively justified and proportional.[106] These decisions do not aim at an exemption of actions that would otherwise be deemed abusive behaviour, but strive for a suitable compromise between anti-competitive effects and objective justification.

VI. SAFEGUARDING UNDISTORTED COMPETITION FROM INTERVENTION BY THE MEMBER STATES

A. Resale Price Maintenance for Books

Resale price maintenance for books has been dealt before in this book and shall be only briefly mentioned here for the sake of completeness.[107] Limiting a retailer's freedom to set his price is 'black listed' in the vertical Block Exemption Regulation[108] (exception: maximum price and price recommendations) and

102. *UEFA Champions League*, Commission Decision 2003/778/EC, OJ 2003 L 291/25.
103. *UEFA Champions League*, Commission Decision 2003/778/EC, OJ 2003 L 291/25, para. 25.
104. *UEFA Champions League*, Commission Decision 2003/778/EC, OJ 2003 L 291/25, para. 27.
105. For further conditions for exemptions with which the Commission combated the market foreclosure effects of agreements *see* D. Geradin, (2005) 30 *European Law Review*, 75 *et seq*.
106. *Centre Belge d'Etudes de Marché Télémarketing v. SA Compagnie luxembourgeoise de télédiffusion*, Case No. 311/84 [1985] ECR 3261; *Hilti v. Commission*, Case No. T-30/89 [1991] ECR II-1439; *see Whish* [2003] 208 with further reference.
107. *See* Chapter 1, Section II.A.1 *above*.
108. Cf. No. 2790/1999, ABl 1999 L 336/21.

definitely renders a group exemption inapplicable. Also an exemption according to Article 81(3) EC seems hardly possible for such an agreement. However, Article 81(1) EC is not applicable to a legal requirement unilaterally setting the retail sale price. If governmental measures negate any scope for autonomous competitive activity or stipulate agreements in restraint of free trade, undertakings are dispensed of their responsibility under Article 81(1) EC. Under these circumstances such agreements do not result in any noticeable restriction of competition.[109] The ECJ made it clear that it is not an issue whether the governmental measure itself is in keeping with Community law.[110] If anti-competitive agreements are ordered, caused, facilitated or strengthened in their effect by a Member State, the Member State concerned is violating Community law, more specifically the principle of allegiance to the Community laid down in Article 10 EC with regard to the competition rules stipulated in Article 3(g) and 81 EC.[111]

B. Article 87 EC – Framework for State Aid in the Content Industry

Article 87(3)(d) EC holds that 'aid to promote culture and heritage conservation where such aid does not affect trading conditions and competition in the community to an extent that is contrary to the common interest is compatible with the Common Market'.[112] This exemption was introduced in the Treaty of Maastricht and has so far been applied mainly in the field of film aid.[113] In a Communication, the Commission has summarized the principles it applies in awarding aid to cinema films and TV productions according to Article 87(3)(d) EC since its decision on the French programme for a cinema production aid scheme.[114] The Communication emphasizes that such aids are to be assessed with a view to the fact that audio-visual works are created mainly to conserve the cultural heritage of a country and not to develop a particular economic sector. Other than fostering the content products themselves, and the cultural goals envisaged by them, these aids also have the indirect side effect of stimulating the film-production sector. In order to minimize their potential of distorting competition the Commission has listed a series of criteria in the above-mentioned Communication that must be met for such an aid to be regarded as compatible

109. Basic ECJ case, *Suiker Unie et al. v. Commission*, Case No. 40–48, 50, 54–56, 111, 113 and 114/73 [1975] 1663, paras 71 *et seq*.
110. *Commission and French Republic v. Ladbroke Racing*, Case No. C-359/95 P and C-379/95 P [1997] ECR I-6265, para. 33.
111. *Ministère public v. Asjes*, Case No. 209/84 – 213/84 [1986] ECR 1425, para. 72.
112. *See also* Chapter 1, Section II.C *above*.
113. Cf. M. Heidenhain, *Handbuch des Europäischen Beihilfenrechts* (Munich, Beck, 2003), Section 19 with additional supporting references.
114. Communication cinematographic and other audiovisual works, COM(2001) 534, OJ 2002 C 43/6.

with the Common Market.[115] In a second Communication the validity of these compatibility criteria was extended from 16 March 2004 to 31 June 2007.[116] As far as conceivable, the Commission applied these criteria most recently in a decision on the extension of aid schemes to support film and TV productions in the German Länder.[117] Previously, several national aid schemes to promote film and TV productions had been approved.[118]

In the print sector, the Commission recently approved a Danish state aid scheme that finances mailing costs through direct funding for certain non-profit magazines and journals. It is the goal of this scheme to promote a democratic exchange of ideas, the dissemination of cultural and social information and also the activities of certain associations.[119]

The Commission also focuses on public service broadcasters. A Communication[120] on this matter was published as early as 2001 followed by a FAQ memo in March 2005 summarizing present practice, especially in light of the most recent developments in case law of the ECJ on justification of state aid schemes.[121] Accordingly, the funding of public service broadcasters is basically subject to aid within the meaning of Article 87(1);[122] it can however be justified as a service of general economic interest according to Article 86(2).[123]

So far, the Commission has not recognized – according to the ECJ's *Altmark*-ruling generally possible – an exception from Article 87(1) for public service broadcasters. Following its approach in *Ferring*[124] the Court held in *Altmark* that a state measure does not come under Article 87 (1) EC, provided that it can be regarded as compensation for the services provided by the recipient undertakings in order to discharge public service obligations.[125]

---

115. For a detailed description of these compatibility criteria *see* Chapter 1, Section II.C.
116. Communication on the film industry, COM(2004) 171, OJ 2004 C 123/1.
117. Commission Decision N 411/2004 of 14 December 2004, <http://ec.europa.eu/comm/competition/state_aid/register/ii/#by_case_number>, 7 July 2006.
118. Cf. Commission Decision N 496/2004 of 3 November 2004; Commission Decision N 224/2004 of 30 June 2004; Commission Decision N 181/2004 of 16 June 2004; Commission Decision N 530/2003 of 16 December 2003; Commission Decision N 513/2003 of 16 December 2003; Commission Decision N 353/2003 of 10 December 2003; Commission Decision N 261/2003 of 15 October 2003; Commission Decision N 313/2004 of 6 December 2004; Commission Decision N 37/2003 of 1 October 2003 (all decisions available at <http://ec.europa.eu/comm/competition/state_aid/register/ii/#by_case_number>, 7 July 2006).
119. Press release IP/04/761 of 16 June 2004.
120. Communication public service broadcasting and state aid, OJ 2001 C 320/4.
121. 'Public service broadcasting and state aid – frequently asked questions', MEMO/05/73 of 3 March 2005.
122. Communication public service broadcasting and state aid, OJ 2001 C 320/4.
123. Communication public service broadcasting and state aid, OJ 2001 C 320/4.
124. *Ferring v. ACOSS*, Case No. C-53/00 [2001] ECR I-9067.
125. *Altmark Trans v. Nahverkehrsgesellschaft Altmark*, Case No. C-280/00 [2003] ECR I-7747, paras 87 *et seq*.; cf. P. Thyri, 'Gemeinwirtschaftliche Dienstleistungsaufträge zwischen Beihilfenanmeldung und Vergabeverfahren', [2003] *Österreichische Zeitschrift für Wirtschaftsrecht*, 126.

Beyond this compensation, the Court of Justice extends the test to be applied by four further criteria all of which must be fulfilled in order for the exemption of the prohibition of state aid to apply. (i) First, the recipient undertaking must actually have public service obligations to discharge, and the obligations must be clearly defined; (ii) Second the parameters on the basis of which the compensation is calculated must be established in advance in a transparent and objective manner; (iii) Third the compensation cannot exceed what is necessary to cover all or part of the costs incurred in the discharge of public service obligations, taking into account the relevant receipts and a reasonable profit (prohibition of excess costs); (iv) Fourth where the undertaking which is to discharge public service obligations, in a specific case, is not chosen pursuant to a public procurement procedure, the level of compensation needed must be determined on the basis of an analysis of the costs which a typical well run undertaking would have incurred in discharging those obligations, taking into account the relevant receipts and a reasonable profit for discharging the obligations.[126]

The ECJ thus does not treat these compensation payments as aid justified by Article 86(2) EC, but regards mere compensation payments as neutral from a competition point of view and thus not subject to the state aid rules. The practical consequences of the differing approaches are obvious: while in the first case the Commission is competent to undertake such an exclusive *ex-ante* examination of compensation aid, no such examination will take place if a case, according to the criteria of the ECJ, is not considered state aid as not covered by Article 87 in the first place.[127]

In the cases of public-service broadcasting examined so far, an exception according to *Altmark* cannot regularly be upheld due to the lack of *ex-ante* defined, objective and transparent parameters of compensation or due to the lack of a public procurement procedure or alternatively a calculation of the compensation on the basis of a cost analysis that a typically well run undertaking would have incurred in discharging the obligations in question.[128] Thus it is to be pointed to the general practise of the Commission as the supervisory authority for aids, differentiating between existing and new aids.[129] Article 88(1) EC sets out that the Commission continuously supervises existing national aid schemes in cooperation with the Member States. In addition, Article 88(1) EC provides that the Commission should propose appropriate measures to the Member States fostering the progressive development and functioning of the

126. *Altmark Trans v. Nahverkehrsgesellschaft Altmark*, Case No. C-280/00 [2003] ECR I-7747, paras 89–93.
127. Cf. A. Bartosch, 'The Relationship between Public Procurement and State Aid Surveillance – The Toughest Standard Applies?', (2002) 39 *Common Market Law Review*, 551, 562 *et seq*.
128. 'Public service broadcasting and state aid – frequently asked questions', MEMO/05/73 of 3 March 2005.
129. Cf. Communication public service broadcasting and state aid, OJ 2001 C 320/4, paras 20 *et seq*.

Common Market. Hence a constant review of existing aid schemes on the part of the Commission is provided for. Existing state aid has no further immediate legal consequences while in contrast, new aids are basically subject to the notification procedure and prohibition on bringing proposed measures into effect pursuant to Article 88(3) EC as long as they have not been approved by the Commission. Existing aids basically are those that have been notified and approved by the Commission. The concept used in Article 88(1) EC is defined more closely in Article 1(b) Procedural Regulation, which lists five specific categories.[130] In this context, Article 1(b) Procedural Regulation is essential and defines those aid schemes and individual aids as existing that were introduced prior to the entry into force of the Treaty in the respective Member States and are still applicable after the EC Treaty took effect. In contrast, Article 1(c) Procedural Regulation defines new aids from a negative point of view as 'all aids, i.e. aid schemes and new aids that are not existing aid, including changes in existing aids'.

According to these criteria, the Commission considers new systems of funding for public service broadcasting principally as subject to notification according to Article 88(3) EC. For existing aids in the field of public service broadcasting, the Commission proposes measures of continuous assessment and control according to Article 88(1) EC.[131]

As appears from the Commission Communication on public service broadcasting, from a content point of view, the Commission monitors (i) the definition of the public service obligation (ii) the conferring of the public service obligation and its supervision as well as (iii) the funding of the public service obligation and the principle of proportionality.

The public service obligation should be defined as precisely as possible in order to enable effective control. The Commission, however, limits itself with regards to the definition of the task for public service broadcasting to assessing the most obvious infringements.[132] With regard to conferral and supervision, the Commission emphasizes the role of an independent supervisory authority.[133] In essence, transparency of the financial relations concerned is the fundamental criteria for the proportionality analysis of a funding system. Thus the Commission holds the opinion that public service broadcasters are to disclose the source and the amount of all revenues from activities that are not public service activities.[134] Expenses not related to the public service activities should be clearly identified as expenses.[135] With regard to the principle of

130. Council Regulation 659/1999 laying down detailed rules for the application of Article 93 (now Article 88) of the EC Treaty, OJ 1999 L 83/1.
131. Communication public service broadcasting and state aid, OJ 2001 C 320/4, paras 20 *et seq*. 'Public service broadcasting and state aid – frequently asked questions', MEMO/05/73 of 3 March 2005.
132. OJ 2001 C 320/4, para. 36.
133. Communication public broadcasting and state aid, OJ 2001 C 320/4, paras 41 *et seq.*
134. Communication public broadcasting and state aid, OJ 2001 C 320/4, para. 54.
135. Communication public broadcasting and state aid, OJ 2001 C 320/4, para. 55.

proportionality, the Commission assumes that state aids may not exceed the net costs of a public service obligation.[136] As has been demonstrated by the example of the Danish public broadcasting company TV2 and the Dutch public service broadcaster NOS, the Commission takes a strict stance in enforcing this net cost principle. In the Danish case, the Commission ordered the reimbursement of EUR 84,400,000 plus interest due to overcompensation of the actual costs of providing a service in the general economic interest.[137] Recently, it also ordered the Dutch public service broadcaster to pay back EUR 76,300,000 in excess ad hoc funding.[138]

VII. SUMMARY AND CONCLUSION

It has been the goal of this chapter to point out the various ways the competition provisions of the EC Treaty affect and regulate the content industry by way of providing for competitive market structures. Without fostering the success of any given product or technology, the cartel prohibition in Article 81 EC, the prohibition to abuse a dominant position in Article 82 EC, the merger regulation, as well as the special rules for public undertakings in Article 86 EC and the state aid provisions in Articles 87 *et seq.* are thus designed to establish the precondition for economic success in a system of free markets.

Despite the fact that the competition rules are applicable across the board, their application, for the purpose of this chapter, has been categorized into rules governing the production level (upstream) and rules working at the distribution level (downstream). Horizontal cooperation for the production of content is an almost indispensable phenomenon. Such cooperation agreements must not necessarily pose a competitive threat. Notwithstanding, joint purchase or sale of content often come under Article 81 EC and are rigorously scrutinized, usually in the context of exclusivity. Here, duration and scope of the agreement are essential. It has also been found, that the practice of cross-platform bundling is particularly harmful as it can lead to market foreclosure.

The challenge of applying Article 82 EC in the content industry – as well as in technology driven markets in general – lies in correctly weighing incentives for entrepreneurial efficiency and innovation, aiming at market dominance against the potential for abuse once this position has been acquired. The rules developed for refusals-to-deal are of particular interest in the content markets.

While Article 82 EC is a tool for *ex-post* control of market power, merger review provides *ex-ante* control against the establishment of dominant firms through concentrations in the market. The Commission recurrently uses this tool to safeguard the competitive structure in the content markets.

---

136. Communication public broadcasting and state aid, OJ 2001 C 320/4, paras 57 *et seq.*
137. *See* press release IP/04/666 of 19 May 2004.
138. *See* press release IP/06/822 of 22 June 2006.

The distribution of content gives rise to many competition issues as well. Horizontal cooperation for the purpose of distribution (joint selling) is as widely practiced as vertical cooperation between companies operating at the production level and downstream companies. Joint selling is often exempted under Article 81 (3) EC as the cases of sports associations for sports content and collecting societies for music show. Much more problematic are exclusive distribution agreements with dominant buyers as they suck dry the content pipeline and thus lead to market foreclosure, denying entrants access to supply. In a vertical view, exploitative practices such as excessively high broadcasting charges have been identified as well. The Commission actively reviews these practices also in the field of merger control.

A slightly unorthodox view has been taken in this study in asking whether and how competition law may protect third parties and safeguard general interests. The answer must be that it is predominantly the final consumer who is protected if a functioning market structure renders competitive (non-exploitative) prices and high-quality products. While competition law never serves the direct protection of competitors, they can however directly benefit from the rules safeguarding a competitive market structure. In addition, Article 82(2)(a-d) EC shows that trading partners can be protected *vis-à-vis* dominant undertakings.

Without doubt, the competition law of the EC Treaty has been designed to serve the protection of the common market in that it prohibits agreements that share markets and, more specific, provides for a careful review of state aid linked to territorial usage clauses.

Asked if and how the competition rules of the EC can directly aid the production and broadcasting of content, Article 81(3) EC comes to mind. The conditions for exemption from the cartel prohibition give guidance as to how to design agreements in order to benefit from the exemption rule. By the same token, the concept of objective justification serves a similar purpose for Article 82 EC. Ultimately, adherence to the state aid provisions of Article 87 *et seq* EC can obviously directly promote the content industry as illegal aid from the Member States is threatened by nullity and an order to pay-back excessive aid might be rendered. In particular, the Commission is very active in reviewing aid relating to the movie industry as well as to the financing of public service broadcasting. In many cases however, such aid can be justified as a service of general economic interest according to Article 86(2) EC.

Overall, it can be concluded that a rigorous application of the competition rules is essential to the functioning of markets in the content industry. In the media and entertainment markets affected, dealing with market dominance is a particular challenge. It will be a continuing effort for competition enforcement to safeguard the pro-competitive potential lying in ongoing technological innovation and ever changing customer preferences in the future.

Chapter 3
Sector-specific Regulation at Infrastructure Level

Dragana Damjanovic

I. PRELIMINARY REMARKS: SECTOR-SPECIFIC REGULATION AT INFRASTRUCTURE AND CONTENT LEVEL

Sector-specific regulation of the content industry at European level exists on the one hand for the electronic communication infrastructures necessary to deliver eContent and on the other hand for the eContent itself. This chapter focuses on the infrastructure related sector-specific rules which are covered by the 2002 regulatory package for the electronic communication markets.[1] Although the subject matter of these rules is not the content industry itself, but their upstream markets, this is the electronic communications markets, they play – as will be displayed in the following in more detail – a vital role for the provision and development of content as well. The content related sector-specific regulations, at the European level mainly incorporated in the TWF Directive[2] and the E-Commerce Directive,[3] will be dealt with in the chapter on 'Sector-specific regulation at content level'.[4]

1. The measures are for download available: <http://europa.eu.int/information_society/policy/ecomm/index_en.htm>, 23 June 2006. For an overview of these measures, *see also* D. Damjanovic and M. Holoubek and H.P. Lehofer and K. Kassai and W. Urbantschitsch, *Handbuch des Telekommunikationsrechts* (Vienna, Springer, 2006) p. 18 *et seq.*
2. Directive 97/36/EC, OJ 1997 L 202/60.
3. Directive 2000/31/EC, OJ 2000 L 178/1.
4. *See* Chapter 4 *below*.

M. Holoubek, D. Damjanovic and M. Traimer (eds), *Regulating Content – European Regulatory Framework for the Media and Related Creative Sectors*, pp. 91–118

II. MARKET ENTRY AND ACCESS REGULATION IN THE ELECTRONIC COMMUNICATION MARKETS – ENSURING FUNCTIONING MARKET STRUCTURES IN THE CONTENT INDUSTRY

A. Infrastructure Regulation as Market Regulation

The main objective of the infrastructural sector-specific rules relevant for the content industry is to ensure functioning market structures. This is in general the case with specific regulatory models developed for network industries[5] that due to their distinct economic characteristics,[6] do not function on the basis of free competition and market rules as many other markets. The main aim of the specific regulations of these industries is thus to prevent market failure. The most important instruments used in the pursuit of this objective are market entry regulation and access regulation.

B. Regulation of Market Entry in the Electronic Communications Markets

1. Relevance for the Content Industry

The sector-specific market entry provisions of the regulatory framework for the communications markets[7] refer only to the electronic communications infrastructures and services,[8] not to the content itself. But they concern the commercial activity of providing content indirectly, insofar as the infrastructures they regulate are an indispensable precondition for the provision of certain content, namely the electronic content (eContent). With regard to the mere provision of content, Community law does not provide for any special market entry regulation. Rather, the mere provision of content within the European Union is, on the basis of the fundamental freedom to provide services according to Article 49 EC,[9] governed by the principle of freedom of access and of

5. To the main features of these specific regulatory models, *see* R.J. Pierce, Jr. and E. Gellhorn, *Regulated Industries in a nutshell* (4th edn, St. Paul, Minn, West Group, 1999); C. Henry and M. Matheu, 'New regulations for public services in competition' in *Regulation of Network Utilities. The European Experience*, C. Henry, M. Matheu, A. Jeunemaître (eds) (Oxford, Oxford University Press, 2001), p. 1.
6. *See* O. Shy, *The economics of network industries* (Cambridge, Cambridge University Press, 2001).
7. Cf. fn. 1.
8. For a definition of these terms *see* Articles 2(a) und (c) of the Framework Directive 2002/21/EC, OJ 2002 L 108/33.
9. On the application of this fundamental freedom of the EC treaty to the content industry *see also* Chapter 1, Section I.A. *above*.

free flow of information. This is expressly stated in the TWF Directive[10] for television broadcast services – which will be extended in the future to all audiovisual media services[11] – and in the E-Commerce Directive[12] for the so called 'information society services'.[13]

The relevant provisions for the communications infrastructures are primarily contained in the Authorization Directive,[14] which is one of the six directives within the 2002 regulatory package for the European communications markets.[15] Taking into account the concept of technological neutrality, which is a basic principle of the whole new legal framework for the electronic communications markets, the directive covers also communications infrastructures that are deployed for the transmission of content, such as, e.g., the digital TV platform as well as all the analogue TV and radio distribution systems over cable, satellite and terrestrial networks.

In addition, the Conditional Access Directive[16] is of relevance for the content industry. It governs the market entry of conditional access systems as a specific component of communications infrastructures.[17] They are defined as 'technical measures and/or arrangements whereby access to a protected radio or television broadcasting service in intelligible form is made conditional upon subscription or other form of prior individual authorization'[18] According to Article 3(2)(b) of the Conditional Access Directive, these systems shall be governed by the principle of freedom of access. Under this principle, the Member States may restrict the free movement of conditional access devices exclusively in order to outlaw the following infringements:

- the manufacture, import, distribution, sale, rental or possession for commercial purposes of illicit devices;

---

10. Article 2(a)(1) of the TWF Directive 97/36/EC, OJ 1997 L 202/60, provides for the content 'television broadcasts' that the access procedure shall not restrict market entry for reasons which fall within the fields coordinated by the directive. In detail, *see* H. Gersdorf, *Grundzüge des Rundfunkrechts* (München, Beck, 2003), p. 256.
11. For the extension of the scope of application of Community law provisions in the audiovisual media field *see* Chapter 4, Section I.B. *below*.
12. Article 4 Directive 2000/31/EC, OJ 2000 L 178/1, lays down the principle of freedom of access. According to this principle, the Member States shall ensure that the activity of an 'information society service' provider may not be made subject to prior authorization or any other requirement having equivalent effect (without prejudice to authorization schemes which are not specifically and exclusively targeted at information society services).
13. For a definition of such services *see* Part One, Chapter 3, Section III.
14. Directive 2002/20/EC, OJ 2002 L 108/21.
15. Cf. fn. 1.
16. Directive 98/84/EC, OJ 1998 L 320/54.
17. According to the scope of application of the regulatory package for the communications markets laid down in Article 1(1) Framework Directive 2002/21/EC, OJ 2002 L 108/33, they would, in general, also be covered by the Authorization Directive 2002/20/EC, OJ 2002 L 108/21. However, Recital 6 of the Authorization Directive expressly provides that the authorization of such systems is exclusively governed by the Conditional Access Directive 98/84/EC, OJ 1998 L 320/54.
18. Article 2(f) Framework Directive 2002/21/EC, OJ 2002 L 108/33.

- the installation, maintenance or replacement for commercial purposes of an illicit device;
- the use of commercial communications to promote illicit devices.

The primary goal of these provisions is to ensure an efficient and structured administration and with this an optimal use of the resources required for the installation of communication infrastructures. These resources include frequencies, rights of way and addressing elements (e.g. IP addresses). The optimal use of the frequencies is furthermore guaranteed by spectrum management at Community level, which precedes the market entry regulation process, this is the authorization and allocation procedures.[19]

2. General Versus Individual Authorization – Media and Culture Related Selection Criteria

The Authorization Directive is based on the principle of general authorization. The general rule according to this principle is that the Member States may only require the submission of a notification with regard to the economic activity of providing a communication infrastructure. This general principle applies to all infrastructures regardless of whether they are used for the transmission of data, voice or content.[20]

An individual authorization, which requires an individual administrative act by a regulatory authority before exercising the rights stemming from the authorization, shall only be admissible if such authorization is in fact required in order to guarantee the efficient administration and optimal use of certain resources – radio frequencies, numbers and rights of way. Such necessity shall, in particular, be assumed if a scarcity of resources already exists or is imminent without coordinated allocation.[21]

For an efficient allocation of the rights of use regarding these resources by the Member States or, more precisely, by the national regulatory authorities, the Authorization Directive provides for open, transparent and non-discriminatory procedures. Any restriction on the granting of rights of use for radio frequencies that infringes the fundamental freedoms of the market participants guaranteed pursuant to Articles 49 *et seq* of the EC Treaty must follow the general principle of proportionality that applies to Community law. According to this principle, the restrictions should be objectively justified and should not exceed what is necessary to achieve general interest objectives as defined by the Member States in conformity with Community law.[22] As a result, these provisions thus provide for an allocation of the resources according to economic efficiency criteria.

19. *See in particular* the Communication on Spectrum Management, COM(2005) 400 final.
20. Article 3 Authorization Directive 2002/20/EC, OJ 2002 L 108/21.
21. Article 5(1) Authorization Directive 2002/20/EC, OJ 2002 L 108/21.
22. Article 5(2) Authorization Directive 2002/20/EC, OJ 2002 L 108/21.

At the same time – again within the framework of the general principle of proportionality – they also allow for other specific criteria to be taken into consideration when it comes to allocating the radio frequencies used for the provision of content.[23] This is particularly true for media pluralism or cultural diversity aspects that traditionally play a crucial role in the allocation process of frequencies for the transmission of broadcasting content services in the Member States.[24] The purpose of this exception clause is to enable the Member States to pursue by the instrument of market entry regulation in the content industry not only functioning market structures but also a functioning media landscape. However, infrastructure related sector-specific regulation at Community level does not contain a more detailed determination of such selection criteria that take into consideration aspects of cultural and media policy.

C. Regulation of Access to Communications Networks and Services

1. Relevance for the Content Industry

Sector-specific access regulation is a concept[25] that was initially developed for the telecommunications sector after the abolition of the state monopolies in this industry, at a time when there was just one infrastructure operator on the telecommunications markets. The purpose was to create the requirements facilitating the development of competition on the telecommunications markets, in a first step on the service level only, by imposing on these infrastructure operators[26] the obligation to open up their networks to other market participants. Competition on the service level should then lead to competition at an infrastructural level. The initial aim of access regulation is thus to create and ensure functioning market structures.

In the meantime – more than a decade after the opening of the markets – competitive structures have developed in the telecommunications sector, not

23. Article 5(2) Authorization Directive 2002/20/EC, OJ 2002 L 108/21.
24. A regular selection criterion is, e.g., in how far the programme that is to be broadcast via the frequencies to be allocated may contribute to media diversity. Cf., e.g., Section 7 of the Austrian Act on Private Television ('PrTV-G') (Federal Law Gazette 'BGBl' 84/2001 as amended 169/2004): [. . .] the regulatory authority shall give priority to the applicant who [. . .] in general offers a better guarantee for a wider media diversity and from whom an individual programme offer that takes into consideration the interests of the area of supply is to be expected [. . .]'.
25. As to this concept *see in particular* J. Kühling, *Sektorspezifische Regulierung in den Netzwirtschaften* (München, Beck, 2004) p. 164 *et seq.*
26. In Austria this was what is today known as Telekom Austria AG. As to the beginnings of the liberalization process in the telecommunications sector in Europe, *see* P. Larouche, *Competition Law and Regulation in European Telecommunication* (Oregon, Hart Publishing, 2000).

least on the basis of this concept of network access regulation.[27] However, the communications sector is due to its specific technical and economic characteristics as a network industry[28] still confronted with the problem of the so-called digital gatekeepers – a term which refers to vertically integrated enterprises that control infrastructural facilities that might constitute bottlenecks, or at least potential bottlenecks, for their competitors. This competition problem in the communication markets[29] is hard to control, at least at the moment, with the tools of general competition law.[30]

Sector-specific access regulation was therefore maintained in the telecommunications sector, even if competitive structures have developed to a certain extent. But the rules had to be adapted to the evolving competitive environment. Furthermore their scope had to be expanded to include all communications infrastructures, because the problem of the digital gatekeepers not only concerns telecommunications networks (in a narrow meaning) but rather all communications infrastructures including, without limitation, also the platforms used for the transmission of content.[31] This adaptation was implemented in the course of the amendment of the legal framework for telecommunications and the development of a new regulatory framework for the entire electronic communication markets in the year 2002.[32]

In particular with regard to the platforms developed for the transmission of digital television,[33] a series of new commercialization activities and transport

27. *See* the Communication Report 2005, COM(2006) 68.
28. Cf. fn. 6.
29. Regarding the problems of digital gatekeepers in communication markets *see* Damjanovic, *Regulierung der Kommunikationsmärkte unter Konvergenzbedingungen* (Wien, Springer WienNewYork, 2002), p. 101 *et seq.*
30. For the application of general competition rules in the communications markets, in particular with regard to the digital gatekeeper problem, *see* P. Larouche [2000] p. 165 *et seq.*
31. At the moment these are primarily the analogue and digital broadcasting distribution systems. The PC broadband networks and the mobile platforms of the third mobile generation only slowly start to develop into platforms that are actually suitable for the distribution of content that requires high transmission rates. For more detail *see* the EITO, *European Information Technology Observatory 2005* (Mainz, Eggebrecht-Presse KG, 2005).
32. For more information on this process, *see* <http://europa.eu.int/information_society/policy/ecomm/history/index_en.htm.>, 23 June 2006.
33. These are designed as multi-platforms, which are not only suitable for the transmission of traditional 'televisions broadcasts' (the linear audiovisual media services) but also of various other content and communications services. Cf. *Impact Study of Measures (Community and National) Concerning the Promotion of Distribution and Production of TV Programmes Provided for Under Article 25(a) of the TV Without Frontiers Directive – Final Report,* prepared by David Graham and Associated Limited for the Audiovisual, Media and Internet Unit Directorate-General Information Society and Media European Commission (24 May 2005).

services have led – in spite of the multiplication of transmission capacities entailed by digitalization – to the emergence of new digital gatekeepers and thus barriers to entry in the content industry.[34] These barriers include:

- programme bundling as a sales and distribution platform;[35]
- the conditional access system,[36] a technology that aims at reserving the right to receive paid-for content to authorized viewers;
- the interfaces for programme applications[37] where the parameters of the interface are not known and freely available, which is the case with so-called proprietary API technologies;[38]
- the programme navigators (electronic programme guides and similar display and orientation guides), which are electronic user guidance systems that provide the viewer with an overview of all available programmes and services, and
- multiplexing where the various services to be transmitted via a multiplex platform are bundled into one transport data stream.

Sector-specific access regulation on the basis of the Access Directive[39] ensures access to electronic communications platforms (including all technical infrastructure facilities and services necessary to transmit content)[40] beyond the provisions of general competition law.[41] Its primary aim is to create and

34. For an overview *see* W. Schulz and W. Seufert and B. Holznagel, *Digitales Fernsehen. Regulierungskonzepte und – perspektiven* (Leske&Budrich, 1999) p. 52 *et seq*; N. Helberger, *Controlling Access to Content. Regulating Conditional Access in Digital Broadcasting* (The Hague, Kluwer Law International, 2005), p. 10 *et seq.*
35. Which, in contrast to the other items listed here, does not form part of the infrastructure but is a content service. Cf fn. 58.
36. For a definition *see* Article 2(f) Framework Directive 2002/21/EC, OJ 2002 L 108/33 and cf. in this Section further *above*.
37. Article 2(p) Framework Directive 2002/21/EC, OJ 2002 L 108/33: 'the software interfaces between applications, made available by broadcasters or service providers, and the resources in the enhanced digital television equipment for digital television and radio services.'
38. In the meantime the companies involved in the Digital Video Broadcasting Project (DVB) have developed a specification for an open European API for digital television – the Multimedia Home Platform (MHP) – that has been approved as a technical specification by ETSI (European Telecommunications Standards Institute) and consequently been included in the list of standards and specifications for electronic communications networks and services (OJ 2002 C 331/4) by the European Commission pursuant to Article 17 of the Framework Directive 2002/21/EC. The purpose is to encourage, but not oblige, the industry to use the MHP standard. For details *see* <www.mhp.org>, 23 June 2006 and Section IV.B *below*.
39. Directive 2002/19/EC, OJ 2002 L 108/7.
40. For a definition of the terms communications infrastructures and services and thus for the scope of application of the Access Directive, *see* Part One, Chapter 3, Section III.
41. For the application of general competition rules in the communications sector cf. fn. 30, and in particular with regard to conditional access systems cf. N. Helberger [2005] p. 119 *et seq.*

ensure sustainable competition and functioning market structures in the electronic communications markets. Beyond this, the Access Directive indirectly also contributes, as it provides a right of access to content services as well,[42] to the free flow of information on the European electronic communications markets and with this to the functioning of a market place for opinions. At least, these provisions ensure that there is diversity of content providers on the electronic communications markets. It is, however, to be doubted whether this fact alone, i.e. the mere increase in the number of market participants, will necessarily result in a diversity of opinions.[43] But at least it creates an environment which increases the likelihood of receiving a greater diversity of content.[44] By doing so, the sector-specific access regulation, which relates primarily to the infrastructure level, is also of material importance to the content industry for the scope of electronically transmitted content.

2. The General Access Regulation Regime for the Communications Markets

The access regulation regime for the communications markets laid down in the Access Directive[45] is primarily based – following the model of free market economy – on the autonomy of the contracting parties. According to this principle, agreements regulating access to the communications infrastructures have to be primarily negotiated among the market participants themselves. Only on markets without efficient competition, where the negotiating positions of individual market participants are stronger and, therefore, dependencies among the market participants exist, regulation measures, i.e. the imposition of specific access rules shall be possible.

The Access Directive delegates the analysis, which markets lack efficient competition, which competition problem this entails and whether such problems justify the imposition of specific access obligations, largely to the national regulatory authorities. They have to decide on a case by case basis. The Directive only governs the procedure according to which the national regulatory authorities have to carry out their analyses and defines the fundamental principles that shall guide their decision-making. Accordingly, the national regulatory

42. On the basis of its technology-neutral approach, the Access Directive applies to all platforms, irrespective of the services transmitted.
43. A multitude of content providers does not necessarily lead to diversity of content. In particular, the pressure of competition, the economic concentration of the production capacities and the target group maxim are factors that reduce diversity.
44. Cf. W. Schulz and W. Seufert and B. Holznagel [1999] p. 94.
45. Directive 2002/19/EC, OJ 2002 L 108/7.

authorities have to apply the following three-staged process when making their decisions:

- As a first step, they have to define the relevant partial markets, meaning the product and services markets in the electronic communications sector which are eligible for ex ante regulation,
- as a second step they have to identify the companies on these markets that have considerable market power, and
- finally, as a third step, they have to determine which problems of competition (if any) this considerable market power entails on the relevant market, and which regulatory measure is best suited to prevent this competition problem. The obligation to grant access is only one of many possible regulatory options mentioned in the Access Directive.[46]

The fundamental principles to be applied by the national regulatory authorities in this three staged decision-making process include the principle of market economy – the market analysis shall be based on economic criteria and carried out according to competition law methodology[47] – and the principle of proportionality. According to the principle of proportionality the obligation in question must be proportionate to the nature of the problem identified.[48] Furthermore, the criteria under which access has to be granted must be objective, transparent, proportional and non-discriminatory.

The Directive itself does not determine the market analysis process and its underlying basic principle of market economy in more detail; but it leaves to the European Commission the competence to specify, by means of a recommendation on the relevant product and services markets[49] and by means of guidelines for the determination of the significant market power,[50] how this principle of market economy has to be applied in the market analysis process. At a first glance, these specifications by the European Commission in the form of recommendations and guidelines might appear to be no more than soft law provisions. In fact, however, they constitute binding criteria as pursuant to

46. In detail, D. Damjanovic et al [2006] p. 144 *et seq.*
47. Cf. in particular Recital 13 of the Access Directive, OJ 2002 L 108/7. Article 5 of the Access Directive also expressly provides that national regulatory authorities shall exercise their responsibility in a way that promotes efficiency, sustainable competition, and gives the maximum benefit to end-users.
48. Cf. Recital 15 of the Access Directive 2002/19/EC, OJ 2002 L 108/7. Guidelines as to which regulatory instruments are to be seen as suitable remedies in a specific case can be found in a document prepared by the European Regulators Group (ERG). In this document the ERG identifies four major market constellations and 27 standard competition problems and assigns to each standard competition problem the suitable regulatory instruments Cf. ERG Common Position on the approach to appropriate remedies in the new regulatory framework, ERG(03)30rev1 <http://www.erg.eu.int/doc/whatsnew/erg_0330rev1_remedies_common_position.pdf.>, 23 June 2006.
49. Recommendation on Markets, OJ 2003 L 190/13.
50. SMP Guidelines, OJ 2002 C 165/6.

Article 7(4) of the Framework Directive[51] they can ultimately be imposed on the Member States.[52]

3. The Specific Access Regulation Regime for the Field of Digital Television

Beyond this general access regulation framework, Article 6 of the Access Directive contains specific provisions for the field of digital television, or more precisely for conditional access systems[53] used for the transmission of digital (pay) television.[54] This regime differs from the general access regulation regime insofar as, on the one hand, the conditions under which access to the system must be granted are defined in the directive in greater detail.[55] On the other hand, it allows the Member States to impose the obligation of granting access not only to infrastructure operators with considerable market power but to all operators of conditional access systems, irrespective of their market shares and thus to deviate slightly from the principle of market economy. But the Member States can only make use of this specific provision if its application is necessary in a democratic society, to enable the widest possible group of end users access to the new digital radio and television services. If an adequate supply of the population can be guaranteed by the general access regulation regime, this is by a mere market orientated regulatory approach,[56] Article 6 does not allow for an extension of the obligation to grant access to all operators. Whether the general access regulation regime can already provide for an adequate supply or not must be assessed by the Member States at regular intervals.

If necessary, the Member States can expand the scope of this specific access regulation regime to other technical infrastructural facilities and/or services of digital television, namely the application programme interfaces (APIs) and the electronic programme guides (EPGs),[57] but not to programme bundling as this service is qualified as a content service.[58]

---

51. Directive 2002/19/EC, OJ 2002 L 108/33.
52. In the course of this so-called consultation procedure the national regulatory authorities must submit draft decisions to the Commission requesting its opinion; in certain cases the Commission may request the national regulatory authority to '... withdraw the draft measure'.
53. Cf. fn. 36.
54. Such a special regulatory regime for conditional access systems did already exist, before the new package of measures for the communications markets was issued in 2002. They were stipulated in the Directive 95/47/EG (repealed), which contents, more or less unchanged, have been integrated into the Access Directive 2002/19/EC, OJ 2002 L 108/7.
55. *See* Annex I of the Access Directive 2002/19/EC, OJ 2002 L 108/7.
56. Cf. Article 6(3) Access Directive 2002/19/EC, OJ 2002 L 108/7.
57. Article 5(1)(b) of the Access Directive 2002/19/EC, OJ 2002 L 108/7.
58. The offer to sell a package of radio or television content is to be qualified as a content service (and not as a communications infrastructure or communication service). Programme bundling is not, therefore, subject to the obligations for electronic communications

D. Capability of the Market Entry and Access Regulation Regime to Ensure Cultural and Democratic Policy Objectives – Problem Analysis

The Community law framework grants the Member States the freedom to use the primarily market-oriented instrument of market entry regulation to pursue cultural aims in the content industry as well, this is to preserve media pluralism and cultural diversity and, with this, the promotion of qualitative content. But in view of the technical developments and related structural changes in the communications and content industry, in particular the successive elimination of scarce resources for the transmission of content, it has to be questioned whether the instrument of market entry regulation will be capable to preserve media pluralism, diversity of opinion and the promotion of qualitative content still in the future.[59] It's to assume that in the future rather access regulation will be of importance as an instrument for guaranteeing diversity of opinion.[60] But access regulation (at least at European level) is designed, basically, on a pure market orientated regulatory approach. It's only applied where there is an absence of effective competition which has to be assessed according to purely economic criteria. Pluralism and cultural diversity are principally not of relevance in this context. This is, within the context of the new regulatory framework for the electronic communications markets, expressly affirmed by the so called concept of separated regulation of content and infrastructure.[61]

On the other hand, though, to some extent also the merely market orientated access regulation regime encourages media pluralism by taking into account that content is not only an economic but primarily also a cultural good. It ensures, at least indirectly, by providing open platforms, a diversity of content providers. That does not necessarily have to result in diversity of opinion per se, but after all more content is given a chance of being received. In addition, the special access regulation regime for the platforms of digital television on basis of Article 6 Framework Directive, shows that by a deviation from purely economic criteria, media and cultural policy aspects may also be achieved directly through the regulatory instrument of access regulation.[62]

---

infrastructures and services laid down in the Access Directive. *See* Recital 2 of the Access Directive 2002/19/EC, OJ 2002 L 108/7.

59. *See*, e.g., K.H. Ladeur, 'Rundfunkaufsicht im Multimediazeitalter' [2000] *Kommunikation&Recht*, 176 *et seq.*
60. *See* W. Hoffmann-Riem, *Regulierung der dualen Rundfunkordnung* (Baden-Baden, Nomos, 2000) p. 136 *et seq.*
61. Cf. Recital 5 of the Framework Directive 2002/21/EC, OJ 2002 L 108/33: 'This framework does not therefore cover the content of services; and is therefore without prejudice to measures taken at Community or national level in respect of such services, in compliance with Community law, in order to promote cultural and linguistic diversity and to ensure the defence of media pluralism [. . .]'.
62. This is in line with the principle of separate regulation of infrastructure and content because this principle allows taking into consideration the connections between the regulation of

E. SUMMARY

Sector-specific regulation in the content industry at the infrastructural level – seen as a regulatory model developed for network industries because of their special economic characteristics – aims at ensuring functioning market structures. The most important instruments used in the pursuit of this objective are market entry regulation and access regulation.

Market entry regulation – laid down in the Authorization Directive and the Conditional Access Directive – refers only to the communications infrastructures and services, not to the content itself. Insofar it plays only an indirect role for the content industry, to be accurate the electronically transmitted content. The mere provision of content within the European Union is, on the basis of the fundamental freedom to provide services according to Article 49 EC, governed by the principle of freedom of access and of free flow of information.

Its primary aim is to guarantee the optimal use of the resources required for the establishment of communications infrastructures and thus *inter alia* also for the provision of content. This is to be achieved primarily by the imposition of a general authorization system. Only in exceptional cases – in the case of scarcity of resources – an individual authorization system may be provided for, meaning that the resources will be allocated by means of an individual administrative act on the basis of economic efficiency criteria. In the case of resources that are used for the distribution of television and radio broadcasts, the Authorization Directive allows for a deviation from these economic efficiency criteria, and for the consideration of aspects of media and cultural policy. This makes it possible for the Member States to use the control instrument of market entry regulation in pursuit of objectives like media pluralism and cultural diversity. In view of technical developments and related structural changes in the communications and content markets, it's to assume that, in the future, these objectives can – only to a limited extent – be achieved by means of market entry regulation. At the infrastructural level, network access regulation will instead become of crucial importance as an instrument for guaranteeing cultural and democratic policy objectives.

Access regulation, which guarantees access to communications platforms beyond what is assured by general competition law, is of relevance for all content providers that need electronic platforms in order to reach their customers. They may demand access from any infrastructure operator that is obliged to grant access according to the access regulatory regime for the communications markets laid down in the Access Directive. In general this is the case if the infrastructure operator has a considerable market power and is furthermore involved in different stages of the production process, so that he exercises

---

transmission and the regulation of content. *See* Recital 5 of the Framework Directive 2002/21/EC, OJ 2002 L 108/33. Such connection exists in the case of network access regulation because of its crucial importance for enabling the access of the public to a wide range of media content.

control over the infrastructural facilities which might result in bottlenecks for their competitors. In addition, Community law provides for specific provisions in the field of digital television based on the special importance of the broadcasting market for a democratic society. The infrastructure operators for digital television, in particular the conditional access system providers may, therefore, be subject to the obligation to grant access, even if they do not have a dominant position in the market.

III. ENSURING A BASIC SUPPLY OF THE POPULATION WITH CONTENT – PROTECTION OF THIRD PARTY AND FURTHER GENERAL INTERESTS

A. THE PUBLIC INTEREST IN THE CONTENT MARKETS

Network industries usually supply services which are of public interest. Therefore, as a rule, the aim of sector-specific regulatory regimes for network industries is not only to ensure functioning market structures but usually also to safeguard certain public interests.[63] On the content markets, this public interest consists in ensuring a basic supply of the population with content, and in particular with regard to the online content markets which form a central part of the future information society, to prevent the emergence of a 'digital divide', this is of a two-class society between people who have access to modern electronic communications services and those who do not.[64]

At the level of sector-specific infrastructure market regulation this objective is guaranteed by the concept of open access for everyone to electronic communications infrastructures and thus also to the content that is transmitted through them.[65] It is implemented at the European level by various provisions: firstly by the universal service regime and the must-carry provisions according to the Universal Service Directive,[66] secondly by the provisions on the broadcasting of major events according to the TWF Directive[67] and finally by the provisions

63. For an overview of the sector-specific regulatory regimes for network industries at the European level, in particular with respect to the public interest of these industries, *see* the Green Paper Services of General Interest, COM(2003) 270.
64. For this central policy concern with regard to the future information society *see* the numerous studies and reports on this issue at the eEurope 2005 website <http://europa.eu.int/information_society/eeurope/2005/index_en.htm>, 23 June 2006, and most recently the eInclusion and the Digital Divide Forum Report (both July 2005 and both available for download at the eEurope 2005 website).
65. Ensuring accessibility to infrastructures and content is also a focal point of the i2010 Initiative. The achievement of this social and democratic policy objective is to contribute to the development of an information society in Europe which includes all people, offers high-quality public services and contributes to the improvement of the quality of life. Cf. Communication i2010, COM(2005) 229. For this initiative *see* Chapter 1, Section III, *above*.
66. Directive 2002/22/EC, OJ 2002 L 108/51.
67. Directive 97/36/EC, OJ 1997 L 202/60.

on the special role and importance of the public service broadcasters, laid down in the EC treaty.

B. Universal Service Regime

The sector-specific provisions for the protection of third parties and further general interests at the level of infrastructural regulation are contained in the so-called Universal Service Directive,[68] which aims at guaranteeing access by the public to certain electronic communications infrastructures and services, which are collectively referred to as universal services.[69] As the universal service regime is designed only to offer a basic, not an optimal supply of the population, the term universal service presently covers only the following services:

- connection to the public telephone network at a fixed location and
- access to publicly available telephone services.

Within this scope, the universal service regime is only of limited relevance for the content industry as it only guarantees voice-related services and a simple Internet access using the traditional public telephone network which – particularly when compared to broadband technologies[70] – is hardly suitable for the transmission of content.[71]

The inclusion of broadband services, which would also ensure access to a broad range of digital content, into the scope of the universal service has been discussed at the European level in the course of the review and evaluation of the Universal Service Directive;[72] eventually, such an inclusion was rejected, as a broadband connection is not yet required for normal participation in Europe's society and thus the absence of access to such a connection does not (yet) result in social marginalization.[73]

---

68. Directive 2002/22/EC, OJ 2002 L 108/51.
69. Articles 3 to 7 of the Universal Service Directive 2002/22/EC, OJ 2002 L 108/51, describe the services forming part of the universal service.
70. DSL, cable, mobile and wireless technologies offer fast Internet access which is in particular suitable for the transmission of digital content.
71. Internet access at a transmission rate of 56 kbit/s basically facilitates only the transmission of publishing content (electronic print media) and to a limited extent also of audio content (MP3), but not of audiovisual content (webcasting, streaming, ...). For the transmission of such content, considerably higher transmission rates are required. *See also* EITO [2005] p. 89 *et seq.*
72. Article 15 of the Universal Service Directive 2002/22/EC, OJ 2002 L 108/51, provides for a periodic review of the scope of the universal service and for the possibility of redefinition of the scope in order to adapt it to the technological and economic developments on the communications markets and the related demands of the population. Cf. the Commission Communication on the review of the scope of the universal service, COM(2005) 203.
73. According to Article 15 Universal Service Directive 2002/22/EC, OJ 2002 L 108/51, the criterion 'used by the majority of subscribers' would be a requirement for the inclusion of

Apart from sector-specific market regulation, a number of soft law measures[74] pursue the expansion of broadband in the Member States, particularly to remote and rural areas where the population is dispersed and the efficacy of the market is weak. These soft law measures include, for instance, funding programmes, such as the use of Structural Funds to enable less favoured areas to come to the forefront of the development of the information society.[75]

C. MUST-CARRY PROVISIONS

Apart from the above described universal service regime, which obliges the market players to provide the public with certain electronic communications infrastructures and thus only indirectly with content, the Universal Service Directive also contains a provision that directly relates to the content itself. Article 31 of the Universal Service Directive provides for transmission obligations for certain infrastructure operators[76] with regard to the distribution of radio and television broadcasts. But the provision is worded as an optional provision only, meaning that it does not impose the obligation to the infrastructure operators itself. It only determines the conditions under which the Member States are allowed to provide for such transmission obligations. Therewith it intends to ensure that the imposition of such obligations to certain infrastructure operators does not exceed a reasonable extent,[77] as this might result in adverse effects for the internal market with regard to the content industry. Its primary purpose, thus, is not to promote such transmission obligations and with it the supply of the population with content, but rather to concretize the conditions under which the Member States can pursue such social and cultural policy objectives in a generally free market environment. In other words, Article 31 of the Universal Service Directive substantiates the principle of proportionality,[78] which – in the context of the provision of services of general

---

a communication service to the universal service regime. The next revision of the Universal Service Directive has been scheduled for 2006 (cf. Communication i2010, COM [2005]229).

74. Cf. the Communication: National Broadband Strategies, COM(2004) 369.
75. The Commission issued guidelines on the criteria and modalities for the use of Structural Funds for electronic communications. *See* Guidelines on Structural Funds, SEC(2003) 895.
76. According to Recital 44 of the Universal Service Directive 2002/22/EC, OJ 2002 L 108/51, these include the operators of cable, satellite and terrestrial broadcasting networks. Providers of sales and distribution platforms for broadcasts (cf. fn. 58) are not referred to as infrastructure operators but as providers of content services; they are therefore not subject to the must-carry obligation according to Article 31 of the Universal Service Directive. The Member States are free to provide for special obligations (such as, for instance, diversity and transparency obligations) for such operators, provided that they are compatible with Community law, in particular the general competition law (cf. Recital 45 of the Universal Service Directive 2002/22/EC, OJ 2002 L 108/51).
77. *See*, to this effect, the Working Document of the Open Network Provision Committees, 10 (14 June 2002).
78. For a detailed analysis of the principle of proportionality *see* H. Schweitzer, *Daseinsvorsorge, 'service public', Universaldienst* (Baden-Baden, Nomos, 2002) p. 171 *et seq.*

interest – is laid down in Article 86(2) of the EC Treaty. So it provides that must-carry obligations may only be imposed on networks which constitute for the end users principal means to receive radio or television broadcast services. Furthermore the obligations must be necessary to meet clearly defined general interest objectives[79] and they have to be proportionate and transparent. Finally, it has to be reviewed periodically, whether all these preconditions for the imposition of must-carry obligations are fulfilled.

D. Broadcasting of Major Events

Access for everyone to 'major events' on television broadcast[80] – including, e.g., important cultural events such as the New Year's Concert or major sporting events such as the World Cup – are of crucial importance in the context of guaranteeing a basic supply of the public with content as well as the fundamental right to information,[81] as determined by Article 10 ECHR.[82]

Community law does not itself guarantee the access for everyone to 'major events' but it enables the Member States to ensure, pursuant to Article 3a of the TWF Directive,[83] that such events are not broadcast on an exclusive basis so that a substantial part of the public is deprived from the access to such content and thus from its fundamental right to information. To put it simply: the provision enables the Member States to guarantee the access of the public to major events on free-to-air-television.

The Member States may freely decide whether or not to take such measures. In particular, it is left to them to define the events of major importance for society within the meaning of said provision.[84] Article 3a(2) provides that the Member States shall notify the European Commission of any such measures taken and that the Commission shall verify that such measures are compatible

79. They may also include the transmission of services specifically designed to enable appropriate access by disabled users. Cf. Recital 43 of the Universal Service Directive 2002/22/EC, OJ 2002 L 108/51.
80. For the economic and cultural significance of major events *see* M. Schoenthal, 'Major Events and Reporting Rights' (2006) 04, Iris Plus, Legal Observations of the European Audiovisual Observatory, 1 *et seq.*
81. *See also* N. Helberger [2005] p. 67 *et seq.*
82. Article 10 of the ECHR protects the 'free flow of information to the public in general'. Cf. ECHR *Geillustreerde Pers N.V. v. the Netherlands* Case No. 51786 [1976] paragraph 85.
83. Directive 97/36/EC, OJ 1997 L 202/60. Or under international law, Article 9a of the Council of Europe's Convention on Transfrontier Television.
84. Recital 21 of the TWF Directive 97/36/EC, OJ 1997 L 202/60, states that these should be outstanding events which are of interest to the general public. In Recital 14 the Olympic Games and football events are mentioned by way of example. For Austria, the relevant provision – Ordinance on events of major importance for society, Federal Law Gazette 'BGBl' II 305/21 – lists, e.g., the New Year's Concert or the Vienna Opera Ball as such events of major importance for society.

with Community law.[85] Such a Commission decision has binding legal effects and is therefore open to challenge.[86]

E. The Special Importance and Role of Public Broadcasting Within the EU

The central role of audiovisual media for the functioning of today's democratic societies and in particular for the development and communication of social values and the consequential need for a special public interest regulation of this sector is generally recognized by Community legislation.[87] The special contribution of the public service broadcasters in this respect[88] is specifically taken into account by giving the Member States the possibility of supporting public broadcasting and, thereby, actively promoting media diversity. This has been fundamentally laid down in the Amsterdam Protocol according to which 'the provisions of the Treaty establishing the European Community shall be without prejudice to the competence of the Member States to provide for the funding of public service broadcasting [. . .]'. The competence of the Member States for determining the remit and the financing of public service broadcasting, with reference to the outstanding role it plays for the social, democratic and cultural life in the European Union, has been reaffirmed in a Council resolution,[89] a Communication from the Commission on the application of state aid rules

85. According to M. Traimer, 'Neufassung der EU-Richtlinie Fernsehen ohne Grenzen verabschiedet' [1997] *Medien und Recht,* 128, this notification obligation can be traced back to the fact that this regulatory interference in the content markets might affect sensitive fundamental rights and rights granted by EC law. In detail on the compatibility of this provision with Community law *see* Altes in *Beck'scher Kommentar zum Rundfunkrecht*, Hahn/Vesting (eds) (München, CH Beck, 2003) para. 69 *et seq.*
86. Cf. *Infront WM AG v. Commission of the European Communities,* Case No. T/33/01 [2005] ECR 0. The case followed an action brought by Infront WM AG (previously the Kirch Group) against the list drawn up by the UK. Since the action was upheld on the grounds of procedural infringements, the judgment does not comment on the material legitimacy of measures taken by the Commission under Article 3a or of list regulations adopted by Member States.
87. In general *see, e.g.*, the Communication: Services of general interest, COM(2000) 580.
88. Regarding the function of public service broadcasting *see* in detail '*The digital age: European audiovisual policy. Report from the high-level group on audiovisual policy* (Brussels-Luxembourg, 1998). Available: <http://ec.europa.eu/comm/avpolicy/docs/library/studies/finalised/hlg/hlg_en.pdf>, 23 June 2006. According to this Report public service broadcasting 'has an important role to play in promoting cultural diversity in each country, in providing educational programming, in objectively informing public opinion, in guaranteeing pluralism and in supplying democratically and free-of-charge, quality entertainment'. Furthermore, broadcasting is generally perceived as a very reliable source of information and represents, for a not inconsiderable proportion of the population, the main source of information. It thus enriches public debate and ultimately ensures that all citizens participate to a fair degree in public life.
89. Resolution 1999/C 30/01, OJ 1999 C 30/01.

to public service broadcasting[90] and finally in the Green Paper on services of general interest.[91]

The freedom of the Member States laid down in these documents to freely decide on the tasks and the extent of financial support of their public service broadcasting companies is, however, significantly limited by the application of the EC fundamental freedoms and the EC competition rules and the, from these rules resulting principle of proportionality,[92] laid down in Article 86(2) of the EC Treaty. According to this principle the Member States' regulations on the remit and financing of their public service broadcasters have to be proportionate, meaning that they have to comply with the EC treaty and in particular the aforementioned fundamental freedoms and competition rules, unless their application would prevent the public service remit from being fulfilled. In detail, the Amsterdam Protocol reads: 'insofar as such funding is granted to broadcasting organizations for the fulfilment of the public service remit as conferred, defined and organized by each Member State, and insofar as such funding does not affect trading conditions and competition in the Community to an extent which would be contrary to the common interest, while the realization of the remit of that public service shall be taken into account'. This is further specified in the Resolution on public service broadcasting[93] and in the Resolution on state aid for broadcasting,[94] according to which a broad definition of the public service remit is deemed acceptable, in particular in order to facilitate the further development and diversification of public service broadcasting activities in the digital age. After all, 'public service broadcasting must be able to continue to provide a wide range of programming in accordance with its remit as defined by the Member States in order to address society as a whole. In this context it is legitimate for public service broadcasting to seek to reach wide audiences', as in practice wide audiences are an indispensable requirement for the broadcasters to be able to fulfil their public remit.

F. Analysis of the Public Interest Regulation at Infrastructure Level – Problematic Aspects

1. Transition from Analogue to Digital Technologies

The planned transition from analogue to digital technologies within the European Community is a challenge to the task of ensuring basic supply of the population with certain content. The European Commission recently issued a Communication on accelerating the transition from analogue

90. OJ 2001 C 320/4.
91. COM(2003) 270.
92. Cf. fn. 78.
93. OJ 1999 C 30/1.
94. OJ 2001 C 32/4.

to digital broadcasting[95] in which it proposes early 2012 as the latest analogue switch-off date, taking into consideration the switchover plans prepared by the Member States under the 'eEurope' Action Plan and an Opinion recently submitted by the Radio Spectrum Policy Group.[96] However, in this paper the Commission fails to discuss the central question of how the basic supply of all citizens with television and radio services is to be guaranteed in the course of this transition process.

2. Access to Broadcasting and Programme Rights on a Sector-Specific Basis

Apart from enabling the Member States to guarantee access of the public to important events, as described above, Community law does not yet contain any sector-specific provisions on ensuring access to broadcasting and programme rights.[97] Such access is not covered by the Access Directive[98] as broadcasting and programme rights are content services and the Access Directive contains exclusively regulations regarding the access to infrastructure. The TWF Directive,[99] which contains the sector-specific regulations relating primarily to content, does not (yet) provide for such access regulation either.[100]

This lack of regulation on a sector-specific basis in this context has often been criticized because it may jeopardize media pluralism and the fundamental right to freedom of information.[101] It has been argued that, with the provisions of general competition law alone,[102] it is impossible to keep access to programme resources and programme rights sufficiently open. This may result in adverse effects for the content markets as to the range of content services offered which in turn might hamper the development of media pluralism and cultural diversity.

---

95. COM (2005) 204 final.
96. Available for download at <http://rspg.groups.eu.int/doc/documents/meeting/rspg5/rspg04_55_opinion_digit_switchover.pdf>, 23 June 2006.
97. The European Convention on Transfrontier Television (ECTT) contains a right to short reporting. For this provision in more detail N. Helberger, *The 'Right to Information' and Digital Broadcasting: About Monsters, Invisible Men and the Future of European Broadcasting Regulation* (2006) 2 Entertainment Law Review, 70 *et seq*. On the EC level, of course, the general competition rules are applicable to the issue of access to broadcasting and programme rights. Cf. Chapter 2, Section I.C.2. *above*.
98. Directive 2002/19/EC, OJ 2002 L 108/7.
99. Directive 97/36/EC, OJ 1997 L 202/60.
100. The Information Society Directive 2001/29/EC, OJ 2001 L 167/10, only allows the MS to provide for limitations for exclusive marketing.
101. *See, e.g.*, B. Holznagel, 'Der Zugang zu Premium-Inhalten: Grenzen einer Exklusivvermarktung nach Europäischen Recht' [2005] *Kommunikation & Recht*, 385 *et seq*; For reform proposals *see* N. Helberger [2006] p. 70.
102. Cf. fn. 97.

For this reason, it is being discussed, in the course of the revision of the TWF Directive,[103] to introduce a coordinated regulation system for such access on a Community level, at least for programme extracts – referred to as the 'right to short reporting'. In the present draft of the future directive it is specified that the trans/frontier access to short reports for use in information programmes should be non-discriminatory. Member States which already have conventional rules or agreements on the retransmission of audiovisual extracts have to introduce a provision requesting other Member States to ensure that broadcasters within their jurisdiction give other Member States' broadcasters non-discriminatory access to programme extracts for use in information programmes.[104]

3. Political Consensus Regarding the Role of the Public Service Broadcasting Organizations within the Community?

Although the special role of public service broadcasting has, in principle, been laid down in Community law, there is increasing concern about possible distortions of competition resulting from this special position of the public service broadcasters,[105] in particular due to a too broadly defined public remit and the consequentially excessive funding of the public service broadcasters by the Member States. For this reason, aspects of competition law in context with public service broadcasting have recently been discussed at the Community level more intensely.[106]

The question, to what extent public financing of public service broadcasting is proportionate in the meaning of Article 86(2) EC treaty and thus compliable with the general competition rules,[107] leaves a lot of appreciation margin, as the numerous state aid decisions, the European Commission has meanwhile issued on the compatibility of various state financing regulation for public service broadcasters quite clearly show.[108] In the light of these developments,

103. For more information on this revision process, *see* Liverpool Audiovisual Conference (Liverpool, 20–22 September 2005) <http://ec.europa.eu/comm/avpolicy/reg/tvwf/modernization/liverpool_2005/index_en.htm>, 23 June 2006.
104. Cf. Recital 27 and Article 3b of the Proposal for a directive amending the TWF Directive 89/552/EEC, COM (2005) 646 final.
105. Regarding the market structures and the development of the broadcasting industry, *see* the Impact study (cf. fn. 33).
106. The discussion was started by a series of state aid related concerns filed with the European Commission by private media companies against various activities of public service broadcasters in Europe and their funding. For an overview to these decisions *see* Depypere/Tigchelaar, '*Competition Policy Newsletter*' [2004] p. 19 *et seq.* Beck D. *et al, Service Public unter Druck? Die Auswirkungen der EU-Transparenzrichtlinie auf den öffentlichen Rundfunk* (Zürich, Rüegger, 2004).
107. *See* Commission communication public service broadcasting and state aid, OJ 2001 320/4.
108. *See* in this context the preliminary views of the European Commission on state financing of the public service broadcasters in Germany, D/51650 (Brussels, 3.3.2005) and of RTÉ and TnaG (TG4), Ireland, D/51652 (Brussels, 3 March 2005).

political consensus regarding the role of public service broadcasting within the European Union is on very shaky ground. Many doubt whether such consensus still exists at all, in particular regarding its role in the digital age and especially when it comes to online services. For these reasons, a revision of the European broadcasting law is required in order to be able to continue to ensure the key role of public service broadcasting alongside private broadcasting, while at the same time safeguarding competition structures on these markets. On the one hand, the conditions under which the Member States can support their public service broadcasters have to be elaborated in more detail at the EC level; on the other hand, EU broadcasting law has to be adjusted to the new technological and economic environment of this sector, characterized by digitalization, convergence and the emergence of various new audiovisual media services.[109]

G. SUMMARY

On the content markets, guaranteeing the basic supply of everyone or, in other words, open access for all to the electronic communication infrastructure and the content[110] that is transmitted by them, is a specific public interest and social objective. It is implemented, *inter alia*, by means of sector-specific market regulations on an infrastructural level.

The individual provisions can be found in

- the Universal Service Directive,[111] which guarantees the transmission of content via a simple internet connection on the one hand, and provides for the imposition of 'must-carry' obligations on certain network operators with regard to certain radio and television programmes by the Member States, on the other;
- the TWF Directive[112] which in Article 3a provides a legal basis that enables the Member States to guarantee basic supply of so-called 'major events' on television broadcast;
- and in the EC Treaty (the Amsterdam Protocol) which lays down the special role and importance of public service broadcasting for guaranteeing such a basic supply with content, and therefore permits the installation

---

109. *See* the issues paper 'Media Pluralism – What should be the European Union's role?' (available for download at <http://europa.eu.int/comm/avpolicy/revision-tvwf2005/consult_en.htm>, 23 June 2006). *See also* the opening speech by Ruth Hieronymi, 'The key role of public service broadcasting in European society in the 21st century' (2005) 1 *European Broadcasting Union, Diffusion* <http://www.ebu.ch/en/union/publications/diffusion/index.php>, 23 June 2006.
110. In particular the content that is of major importance for society in the meaning of being essential for everyone in order to be able to participate fully in the European society.
111. Directive 2002/22/EC, OJ 2002 L 108/51.
112. Directive 97/36/EC, OJ 1997 L 202/60.

of a dual radio broadcasting system, meaning the parallel provision of services on the broadcasting markets as well as by private entities and the State.

Proceeding on the assumption that the optimal allocation of resources in the interest of society as a whole is normally best guaranteed by an open market economy with free competition, the above analysed public interest provisions within the framework of sector-specific market regulation are designed as subsidiary provisions at EC level, meaning that they only allow for special socio-politically and culturally motivated interventions in the content industry if the public interest cannot be safeguarded by functioning market structures.

Apart from this, it's to bear in mind that the primary purpose of these provisions at EC level is not to directly promote basic supply of content by determining the here fore necessary regulatory instruments,[113] but only to set up a harmonizing framework within which the Member States may become active in order to realize these socio-political and cultural aims on the content markets. The central intent of Community law in the given context is thus to define principles according to which the realization of public interests on the content markets may also be guaranteed in a primarily market economy oriented environment. Striking the right balance is not an easy task as can be seen from the discussion on the implementation of special access regulation for broadcasting and programme rights into Community law, or on the financing of public service broadcasters.

IV. STANDARDIZATION ACTIVITIES IN THE CONTENT INDUSTRY – PRESERVATION OF THE SINGLE MARKET

A. Standardization in the Online Content Market – A Primarily Market Led Process

The realization of the single market in high-technology areas, as, for instance, the online content market depends crucially on commonly developed standards in these industries. The existence of standards is a requirement for the functioning of interoperability in the electronic communications markets, which in turn makes it possible for the content providers to offer their services on any (technologically) suitable platform and, in particular, also on a trans-national level. The end-users, on the other hand, can receive through their devices various services via diverse platforms.[114] Interoperability thus also plays a central role

113. The universal service regime (*see* Section B *above*) is an exception in this context.

114. For the network operator interoperability means the ability to cooperate with other network operators. Regarding the various aspects and the concept of interoperability cf. Commission Staff Working Document on Barriers to widespread access to new services

for ensuring a large selection of content and a broad access of the population to this content and with it freedom of information and media pluralism.

Standardization on the electronic communications markets which is set to facilitate such interoperability is, following the general new concept of European standardization, designed primarily as a market-oriented process, i.e. a process that is predominantly led by the industry itself.[115] According to Article 17 of the Framework Directive[116] the Commission's task in this process is, first of all, to publish a list of standards and/or specifications to serve as the basis for encouraging the harmonized provision of electronic communications networks and services and where necessary request that standards be drawn up by the European standards organizations. Only if these measures do not suffice to ensure the interoperability of services, the implementation of common standards may be made compulsory on a Community level to the minimum extent strictly necessary.[117]

B. Specific Standardization Measures for Digital Interactive Television

Apart from Article 17 of the Framework Directive[118] which follows the general concept of standardization, further specific rules have been issued in the course of the 2002 regulatory package for the electronic communications markets, which shall ensure standardization in the field of digital interactive television. These provisions have to be seen in the light of the very moderate progress in the development of uniform standards, and the resulting remaining barriers for open platforms in the field of digital television.[119]

Article 4(2) of the Access Directive[120] provides, for instance, that public electronic communications networks established for the distribution of digital television services shall be capable of distributing wide-screen television services[121] and programmes. Network operators that receive and redistribute

---

and applications of the information society through open platforms in digital television and third generation mobile communications (in the following Commission Staff Working Document on barriers to widespread access) <http://pm2.activenavigation.com/facade/europa.eu.int/information_society/activities/consultations/docs/open_platforms-en.pdf>, 23 June 2006.

115. More on this 'industry led approach' of European standardization Holoubek 'Normung' in *Handbuch des öffentlichen Wirtschaftrechts II,* Holoubek/Potacs (eds) (Wien, Springer, 2002) p. 23 *et seq.*
116. Directive 2002/21/EC, OJ 2002 L 108/33.
117. Cf. Article 17(3) Framework Directive 2002/21/EC, OJ 2002 L 108/33.
118. Directive 2002/21/EC, OJ 2002 L 108/33.
119. Cf. the Commission Staff Working Document on barriers to widespread access, p. 12 *et seq.*
120. Directive 2002/19/EC, OJ 2002 L 108/7.
121. According to Article 2d of the Access Directive 2002/19/EC, OJ 2002 L 108/7, this means a television service that consists wholly or partially of programmes produced and edited to

wide-screen television services or programmes shall maintain that wide-screen format. It is assumed that making the wide-screen format 16:9 compulsory will contribute to the market penetration of digital television.[122]

For the same reason, but especially in order to encourage the switchover from analogue to digital technologies, Article 24 of the Universal Service Directive[123] obliges the Member States to ensure the interoperability of the consumer digital television equipment. According to this provision, the manufacturers of consumer equipment, intended for the reception of digital television signals, must use the common European scrambling algorithm and/or provide free-to-air reception. Manufacturers of analogue television must ensure that television sets with a screen diagonal of more than 42cm, are fitted with one connection to digital receivers.[124]

Finally, Article 18 of the Framework Directive instructs the Member States to encourage, on their markets, the use of open application programming interfaces (APIs)[125] or to otherwise guarantee that providers of digital television services receive all the information regarding the API used on fair, reasonable and non-discriminatory terms as is necessary to provide all services supported by the API in a fully functional form. However, this provision is a 'soft law' measure only encouraging the development of such an open standard without requiring it in a binding manner.

In fact, most APIs on the European market are still proprietary and are not interoperable at the end-user devices level, so that most of these APIs are not capable of transmitting data formatted for other APIs. This has an adverse effect on the user's freedom of choice and thus, in general, on the free flow of information, media pluralism and cultural diversity in Europe. With the 'Multimedia Home Platform' (MHP) a common open API standard has been developed by the industry and approved as a technical specification by the competent European standards organization ETSI. Whether, and to what extent, these standards will be accepted on the market on a voluntary basis remains open to doubt.[126] For the time being, it is still hoped that market forces will cause a gradual transition from the proprietary to the open systems by the voluntary use of such standards. Should this not happen within a reasonable period of time – and progress in this regard has to be reviewed by the Commission on

---

be displayed in a full height wide-screen format. The 16:9 format is the reference format for wide-screen television services.

122. Cf. the Commission Staff Working Document on the contribution of wide-screen television, SEC(2004) 46.
123. Directive 2002/22/EC, OJ 2002 L 108/51.
124. As to the individual equipment *see* the specifications according to Annex VI of the Universal Service Directive 2002/22/EC, OJ 2002 L 108/51.
125. For a definition, *see* the Commission Staff Working Document on barriers to widespread access, p. 11, and in greater detail as to what this term includes: Commissions Staff Working Document on interoperability, SEC(2004) 346, p. 2.
126. Cf. the Commission Staff Working Document on barriers to widespread access, p. 14.

an annual basis[127] – there is also the possibility of a binding stipulation of such standards by the Commission according to Article 18(3) of the Framework Directive.

C. Other Standardization Activities in the Content Industry

The Commission has instructed the CEN[128] to develop a European standard for the cataloguing and indexing procedures for cinematographic productions and for the interoperability of film databases.[129] This is to guarantee cooperation of the Member States in the restoration and conservation of film heritage (including digitalization) and to encourage networking of European archival data. The standardization is to contribute to a better use of the European film heritage and thus to the preservation of the single market in the audiovisual area.[130]

D. Problematic Aspects with Regard to the Standardization Processes on the Content Markets

The development of unified open standards in the area of digital television is progressing more slowly than hoped for, which is having an adverse impact on the development of the market for digital television. This fact has recently caused increased debate at the Community level as to whether the formulation of one or more binding standards in this area would not be a better solution than the presently pursued approach of keeping regulatory interference as little as possible in this area.[131]

One of the main disadvantages of the latter approach is that it does not provide clarity as to which technology will prevail in the field of digital television and, therefore, it fails to provide the market players – the content providers, developers of other applications for these platforms as well as the manufacturers of the devices – with a secure environment for making their market decisions. For the content providers that primarily means that they have to design their content in such a manner that it can be transmitted via various APIs which of course involves additional costs. In addition, this approach offers hardly any

---

127. Most recently reviewed by the Commission Staff Working Paper on interoperability, SEC(2004) 1028.
128. CEN stands for Comité Européen de Normalization (European Committee for Standardization). For more information *see* <http://www.cenorm.be/cenorm/index.htm>, 23 June 2006.
129. Cf. GD INFSO A/01 v. 14 March 2005.
130. *See also* the Proposal for a recommendation on film heritage, COM(2004) 171 final.
131. Regarding the related problems and possible solution approaches *see* the Communication on interoperability, COM(2004) 541 final.

protection to the consumers as it cannot be guaranteed that they will be able to use all services offered in the field of digital television with a single end-user device.

Basically, all of these problems could be resolved by means of further regulatory intervention within the meaning of further standardization activities. What, however, speaks against it is that a binding specification of a standard may turn out to be a barrier to future infrastructure investment. Given the high share of end-user devices with non-standardized APIs, the subsequent introduction of a uniform standard would either involve high costs for the exchange of the devices, or would force the end-users to accept a limited scope of functions of their devices.

Taking these arguments into account and given the fact that the digital television sector is still an immature market, the European Commission advocates the preservation of the status quo. The finding of solutions to guarantee interoperability is to remain, primarily, the responsibility of the market. The tasks of the Member States is to be limited to supporting this market process by means of incentive mechanisms. The possible promotional actions suggested by the European Commission include:[132]

- the creation of MHP Groups in every Member State;
- the granting of national subsidies for the development of end-user devices that are compatible with the common standard;
- the publication of further standards by the Commission;
- ensuring access to proprietary systems for third parties beyond the provisions of general competition law by means of sector-specific 'access regulation'.[133]

E. Summary

Interoperability plays a central role for ensuring a large selection of content and thus in general for securing freedom of information and pluralism on the content markets. On the communication markets, standardization processes that are to guarantee interoperability are primarily led by the market itself. Only in the field of digital television, Community law provides for special regulations by means of standardization. However, these provisions are merely 'soft law' clauses with the objective of encouraging the development of common standards by the industry without demanding them in a legally binding manner.

---

132. *See* the Commission Staff Working Document on interoperability, SEC(2004) 346.
133. For details *see* Section II.C. *above*.

V. DIRECT PROMOTION OF THE PRODUCTION AND DISTRIBUTION OF CONTENT

Within the framework of sector-specific regulation of the communications and content markets at the infrastructural level, Community law does not provide for provisions that directly aim at promoting the production and distribution of content, respectively at ensuring pluralism and cultural diversity. But of course, all of the above analysed sector-specific provisions for ensuring functioning market structures, for preserving the single market and for protecting third parties and other general interests, at least indirectly also boost the production and distribution of content and thus diversity of opinion.

VI. SUMMARIZING EVALUATION – RECIPROCITY AND INTERCONNECTIONS BETWEEN THE VARIOUS REGULATORY INSTRUMENTS IN SECTOR-SPECIFIC REGULATION AT INFRASTRUCTURE LEVEL

The substantial function of the above described sector-specific regulations, is to ensure functioning market structures on the electronic communications infrastructure markets. As these form an upstream market of the online content industry, the here discussed sector-specific provisions – even though they only regulate the infrastructure level – are of crucial importance for the functioning and development of the online content industry as well. Therefore, in this survey, it also refers to these rules as sector-specific market regulations of the content industry.

Access regulation to networks or the promotion of the development of uniform standards with regard to the infrastructure facilities, for instance, ensure open communications platforms and thus also open access to the communications infrastructure for content providers. And this not only guarantees functioning market structures on the online content markets, but also, the free flow of information within the EU, which, in turn, also promotes other central values than market efficiency within the content industry, as freedom of opinion, media pluralism and cultural diversity.

Provisions within this sector-specific market regulations framework, which pursue other objectives than securing functioning market structures – primarily to provide a basic supply of infrastructure and content for the population and with it the right to information for everyone – have been designed as exceptional clauses and subsidiary provisions only, meaning that according to the principle of proportionality under Community law they shall only apply if the social, cultural and democratic policy objectives within the content industry cannot be accomplished by the market itself, this is without other interventions into these markets than those ensuring functioning market structures, as such 'public interest' interventions, if too excessive, may create unnecessary barriers to free economic activity, destroy market incentives, impair the economic results and thus have an overall subsequent adverse effect on the functioning of these markets.[134]

Whether functioning market structures and competition already exist to an extent which is sufficient to ensure these central values of the content industry – a basic supply of the population with content, freedom of information and diversity of opinion – respectively whether the market under the conditions of competition alone at all is capable to achieve these values, is a complex question, which requires a broad political debate firstly, on the social and cultural objectives that are to be pursued on these markets by 'public interest' regulation and secondly, on the extent to which these objectives are to be pursued at EC level. And this debate needs to go hand-on-hand with an in-depth economic analysis of the structures of the content markets as to find out to what extent the market alone is capable to fulfil these objectives. Especially in the quickly changing sector of the electronic content industry this debate and analysis have to be subjected to a continuous re-evaluation as well.

134. For an economic analysis on market regulation *see* Phillips C.F., *The Regulation of Public Utilities. Theory and Practice* (Virginia, Public Utilities Reports, Inc, 1985) p. 35 *et seq.*

Chapter 4
Sector-specific Regulation at Content Level

Christoph Bezemek/Gregor Ribarov

I. PRELIMINARY REMARKS

A. Objects and Systemization of Sector-specific Regulation at Content Level

Sector-specific regulation at content level deals with legal provisions that directly regulate the service content itself, in other words the act of producing and distributing content. This includes all sector-specific provisions that, unlike the regulations described in the preceding chapter,[1] do not address the market structures of the content industry, but rather directly concern the goods produced for this market by regulating either the content itself or the means used to distribute it. Such regulations for content broadcast via television are contained in the Television without Frontiers Directive,[2] as regulations for so-called information society services[3] are enclosed in the E-Commerce Directive.[4] In addition, Community Law also features a few individual product-related regulations, which, due to the specific properties of the product in question or the impact it may have, also standardize corresponding advertisement. As they contain subject-matter regulations governing the performance of content – *see*

1. *See* D. Damjanovic in Chapter 3 *above*.
2. Television without Frontiers Directive 97/36/EC, OJ 1997 L 202/60. In reference to the amendments as compared to the original version, cf. in particular M. Traimer, 'Neufassung der EU-Richtlinie 'Fernsehen ohne Grenzen' verabschiedet' (1997) 3 *Medien und Recht*, 127 *et seq*. *See also* the Proposal for a directive amending the Television without Frontiers Directive 89/552/EEC, COM (2005) 646 final.
3. For a definition of information society services *see* Section I.C.
4. Directive 2000/31/EC, OJ 2000 L 178/01.

M. Holoubek, D. Damjanovic and M. Traimer (eds), *Regulating Content – European Regulatory Framework for the Media and Related Creative Sectors*, pp. 119–149

for example the Tobacco Directive[5] – they are to be considered in the given framework as well.

Differentiations between the regulations addressed in this Section can be made according to whether they are sector-specific, or 'vertical' (i.e. they are addressed toward a specific medium or a specific content category) or 'horizontal' (i.e. they cut across the boundaries of specific media) (*see* Fig. 1).

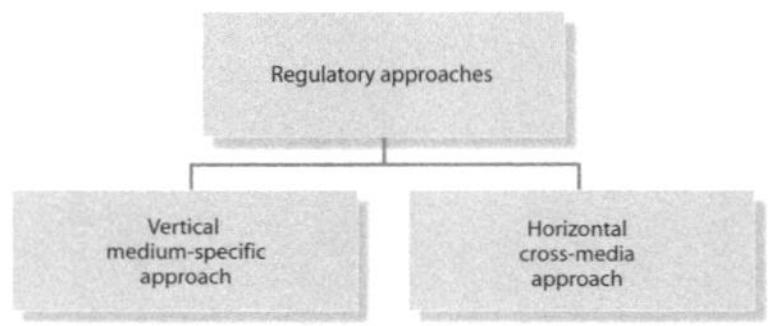

Figure 1: Regulatory Approaches

Furthermore, depending on whether subject-matter provisions regarding content or merely the distribution method (limiting the hours in which it may be broadcast, etc.) are stipulated, regulations can also be broken down into qualitative and quantitative regulatory measures (*see* Fig. 2).

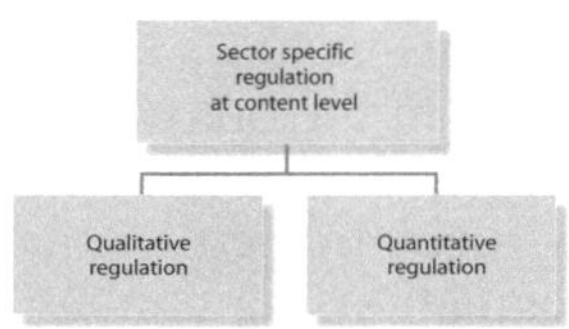

Figure 2: Sector-specific regulation at content level

Taking this contrast one step further, the qualitative content regulation that is subject-matter-related can be differentiated into commercial content or other kinds of content, and, within the latter, into content for informative purposes or content for entertainment purposes. Commercial content is generally defined as content that serves to promote a product, a service or a brand. This definition covers all forms of advertising and sponsoring for which financial consideration is made (*see* Fig. 3).[6]

5. Directive 2003/33/EG, OJ 2003 L 152/16.
6. *See* R. Hieronymi, 'Rules applicable to audio-visual content services' Report given at the Liverpool Audiovisual Conference (Liverpool, 20–22 September 2005) <http://ec.europa.eu/comm/avpolicy/reg/tvwf/modernisation/liverpool_2005/index_en.htm>,23 June 2006.

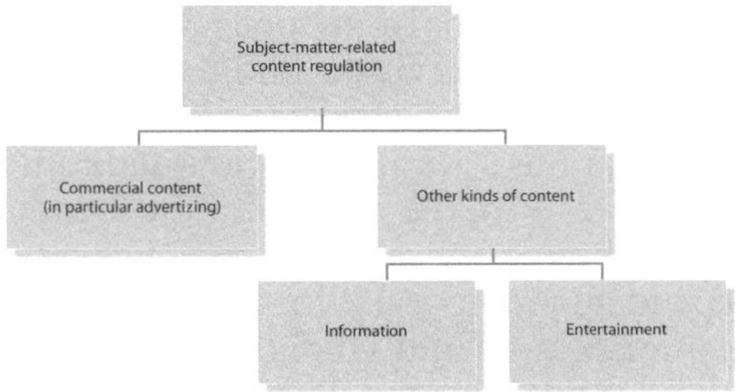

Figure 3: Subject-matter-related Content Regulation

B. Development of Sector-Specific Regulation at Content Level

The evolution of technology, including the concomitant media trends towards uniformity (the keyword being 'multi-media'), has forced content regulation to rethink out-dated differentiations focusing on a particular medium, and instead aim at global solution models.[7] This has already taken place on the infrastructural level with the creation of a uniform space for all communication networks and services.[8] This step has yet to be taken with respect to the legal framework governing content itself. The reworking of the Television Directive[9] is focussing on doing just that – as its current scope of application,[10] limited only to television broadcasts, certainly is too narrow. Although the services outside of the directive's scope are not left unregulated, they are not subject to its special regulatory regime pursuing cultural, socio-political and democratic objectives. Instead the E-Commerce and Universal Service Directive, with their solely economic oriented approach concentrating on commercial communication will apply. This shows that regarding the future audiovisual media service directive the question of its scope of application is important, because that is how the principle direction of European regulation for audiovisual media services will be determined.

The consultations concerning the future of the Television Directive entered their final phase at the Liverpool Conference held in October 2005.[11] The regulations contained in the Directive have been analysed and reviewed at many stages. In its Communication on the future of European regulatory audiovisual

7. As stated by M. Traimer, 'Europäische Rahmenbedingungen staatlicher Medienregulierung im Lichte der Konvergenz' [2000] *Journal für Rechtspolitik*, 137.
8. For an overview on the regulation at infrastructural level *see* D. Damjanovic in Chapter 3 *above*.
9. Television without Frontiers Directive 97/36/EC, OJ 1997 L 202/60.
10. For a definition of television broadcast *see* Article 1(a) of the Television without Frontiers Directive, OJ 1997 L 202/60 and also in Part One, Chapter 3, Section III.
11. Liverpool Audiovisual Conference (Liverpool, 20–22 September 2005) <http:// ec.europa.eu/comm/avpolicy/reg/tvwf/modernisation/liverpool_2005/index_en.htm>, 23 June 2006.

policy,[12] which draws its conclusions from public consultation, the Commission took the position that a thorough revision would be necessary. Furthermore, it initiated the work of focus groups which were to investigate the need for specific modifications of the regulations governing audiovisual content over the last two years. So-called Issue Papers were the product of the focus groups: Rules applicable to Audiovisual Content Services, Cultural Diversity and Promotion of European and Independent Audiovisual Production, Commercial Communication and Protection of Minors and Human Dignity, Right of Reply, which formed the foundation for adapting the Television Directive.

Recently the Commission has submitted a corresponding draft amendment.[13] The purpose of the new Directive (the so-called Audiovisual Media Services Directive), as stated by the Commission in its Communication 'i-2010',[14] is to build towards an integrated approach to information society and audiovisual media policies in the EU. It will therefore focus on regulating audiovisual media content in general instead of merely television, thereby also applying to services aside from classic television programmes.

Audiovisual media services are defined as services,[15] which have the principal purpose[16] of providing moving images with or without sound, in order to inform, entertain or educate, to the general public by electronic communications networks.[17] This definition now provides for a basic stock of norms applicable to every audiovisual media service. Such cross-media regulation, however, does not preclude graduated and more specific rules where they are needed. According to different types of distribution, the audiovisual media services are to be broken down into linear and non-linear services. Regardless of the broadcast platform used, all on-demand services will probably be included among non-linear content (such as video-on-demand). This way the commission wants to bypass the demarcation problems with the already mentioned e-Commerce Directive and its definition of information society services.[18]

The difference between those 'non-linear' media services and the 'linear' services is the fact that the former offer viewers the option of deciding for

12. Communication of the future European regulatory audiovisual policy, COM(2003) 784.
13. *See* the Proposal for a directive amending the Television without Frontiers Directive 89/552/EEC, COM (2005) 646 final.
14. Communication i2010, COM (2005) 229.
15. Meaning services as laid out in the Articles 49 and 50 of the EC Treaty.
16. This formulation has already met criticisms as being too vague not determining when the criteria of 'principal purpose' are met. Recital number 14 of the Proposal for the directive however indicates that all those services are to be excluded, where any audiovisual content is merely incidental to the service and not its principal purpose. An example stated in the same recital is a website containing audiovisual elements only in an ancillary manner, like e.g. elements with graphic animation, short advertising spots, etc...
17. Article 1(a) as amended by the Proposal for a directive amending the Television without Frontiers Directive 89/552/EEC, COM (2005) 646 final.
18. T. Kleist/A. Scheuer, 'Audiovisuelle Mediendienste ohne Grenzen' (2006) 3 *MultiMedia und Recht*, 128.

themselves what they want to see and when they want to see it.[19] This shows the necessity to also differentiate in regulation: whereas for the non-linear services a basic framework of general rules may suffice, for linear ones – those for which the responsible organizers compile a fixed programming schedule for the day (e.g. traditional television programming or the so-called near video-on-demand formats) – additional rules of regulation will apply.

II. THE PROTECTION OF THIRD PARTIES AND FURTHER PUBLIC INTERESTS

A. Review of Status Quo

1. Regulation of content for the protection of human dignity,[20] as well as the protection of other fundamental values of a democratic society[21]

The specifications for the protection of human dignity and fundamental values are all of a qualitative nature, in other words regulating content with subject-matter specifications. Regarding commercial content broadcast during television programmes, Article 12(a) of the Television Directive[22] stipulates that television advertising and teleshopping are not to prejudice respect for human dignity. Furthermore, according to Article 12(b) of the Directive, television advertising and teleshopping may not include any discrimination on grounds of race, sex or nationality. The article also prohibits television advertising and teleshopping from being offensive to religious or political beliefs (c), encouraging behaviour prejudicial to health or to safety (d) or to the environment (e).

As concerns other types of content – like broadcasts – Article 22a of the Television Directive instructs the Member States to also ensure that those do not contain any incitement to hatred on grounds of race, sex, religion or nationality.

For television advertisement, Article 12a of the Television Directive provides for absolute protection of human dignity; however, it does not with regards to other kinds of content. In matters of religion and nationality, there is a clear gap between commercial and other kinds of content as well. While commercial content must refrain from being discriminating or prejudicial, restrictions on other content are made only on a more invasive degree of incitement

---

19. Cf. the definition in Article 1(1) (e) as amended by the Proposal for a directive amending the Television without Frontiers Directive 89/552/EEC, COM (2005) 646 final.
20. For existing 'soft law' cf. in particular the Recommendation on the Protection of Minors and Human Dignity, OJ 1998 L 270/48. For the implementation, *see* the Decision on Combating Illegal and Harmful Content on Global Networks, OJ 2003 L 162/1.
21. The term used in the given context of fundamental values of a democratic society follows the guarantees and objectives of the Charter of Fundamental Rights – Article II 61 *et seq.* in Part II of the treaty establishing a Constitution for Europe.
22. Television without Frontiers Directive 97/36/EC, OJ 1997 L 202/60.

to hatred. The problem areas health, safety and protection of the environment are completely left by the wayside in terms of other content. This supposed contradiction in values can be explained by the different level of protection that commercial and other content enjoy in the context of Article 10 of the European Convention on Human Rights.[23]

2. Regulation of Content for the Protection of Minors[24]

As already indicated by the Commission in its 1996 'Green Paper on the Legal Protection of Minors and Human Dignity in Audiovisual and Information Services'[25] the advent of new audiovisual and information services requires the adaptation of current regulations for the protection of minors.

In several Member States general statues cover the principle of the protection of minors regardless of media, prohibiting minors the access to materials detrimental to their development but whose use by adults is not subject to sanctions. Then again other Member States have media-specific statues. However, the problem remains the same in every case: implementing measures for the protection of minors in such a way, so as to prevent them from obtaining materials posing a danger to them without completely impeding access to these materials for adults.[26] Although special software that filters out undesirable content is already available and various initiatives try to classify content in the Internet,[27] this goal still is hard to achieve. Specific regulations governing all audiovisual content and information services on the European level are lacking, as to date regulations for protecting the physical, mental and moral development of minors are only provided for with regard to the medium television.[28] There is no clear regulatory mandate, however, from the Community applicable to other media and information services concerning the protection

23. Cf. C. Graberwarter, *Europäische Menschenrechtskonvention* [2005] pp. 245 *et seq.*
24. With regard to existing 'soft law' cf. fn. 19.
25. Green Paper on the Legal Protection of Minors and Human Dignity in Audiovisual and Information Services, COM (96) 483.
26. In this context Spoerr/Sellmann speak of a 'system that takes interests into account' which should guarantee the protection of minors that is as comprehensive as possible, but may also note allowed to restrict too severely the interests of the users and provider with regard to freedom of information. W. Spoerr and C. Sellmann, 'Informations- und Kommunikationsfreiheit im Internet' [2004] *Kommunikation & Recht*, 372. Cf. also Recital 32 in the Proposal for a directive amending the Television without Frontiers Directive 89/552/EEC, COM(2005) 646 final.
27. M. Bock and J. Wöbke, [1997] *Betriebs-Berater*, 16. For instance, databases of websites that contain objectionable content can be set up; the PICS (Platform for Internet Content Selection Initiative) is relatively far along in the classification based on voluntary self-regulation. *See* <http://www.w3.org/PICS/>, 23 June 2006.
28. The general necessity of such rules is expressly stated in the 32nd Recital of the Television without Frontiers Directive 97/36/EC, OJ 1997 L 202/60.

of minors.[29] The foundation for the measures ensuring the protection of minors regarding audiovisual and information services was laid in a Council Recommendation[30] in 1998, however, these first steps have not yet evolved into specific regulations. The currently applicable E-Commerce Directive merely mentions the issue in Article 16 (1) which only includes a call for the Commission and Member States to encourage the drawing up of codes of conduct regarding the protection of minors and human dignity. As efforts are being made to extend the scope of the Television Directive's[31] basic regulatory framework to audiovisual media services,[32] this would also mean to apply the requirements for protecting minors to non-linear services, right now only being subject to the rules in the E-Commerce Directive.

The requirements for protecting minors currently mandated by the Television Directive are primarily of a qualitative or substantive nature.[33] By this token, television advertisement and teleshopping may not, according to Article 15(1) of the Television Directive, be specifically aimed at minors, and in particular depict minors consuming alcoholic beverages. Article 16(1) of the Directive stipulates that television advertising may not directly exhort minors to buy a product or a service by exploiting their inexperience or credulity (a), nor directly encourage minors to persuade their parents or others to purchase the goods or services being advertised (b), nor exploit the special trust minors place in parents, teachers or other persons (c), nor unreasonably show minors in dangerous situations (d). Paragraph 2 of this article applies the requirements enumerated in paragraph 1 to teleshopping, with the additional stipulation that teleshopping may not exhort minors to contract for the sale or rental of goods and services.[34]

With regard to other content, Article 22(1) of the Television Directive obligates the Member States to take appropriate measures to ensure that television broadcasts by broadcasters under their jurisdiction do not include any programmes which might seriously impair the physical, mental or moral development of minors, in particular programmes that involve pornography

29. W. Berka, 'Conent-Regulation im Lichte der Konvergenz' [2000] Journal für Rechtspolitik, 197. For Berka ensuring a certain fundamental standard in the protection of minors for fields that do not come under the scope of the Television without Frontiers Directive on constitutional law grounds (considerations under equality law or in any case with regard to fundamental legal obligations to protect) is necessary.
30. Recommendation on the Protection of Minors and Human Dignity, OJ 1998 L 270/48.
31. General information can be found at <http://ec.europa.eu/comm/avpolicy/reg/tvwf/modernisation/index_en.htm>, 23 June 2006.
32. Cf. in particular Article 3d as amended by the Proposal for a directive amending the Television without Frontiers Directive 89/552/EEC, COM (2005) 646 final.
33. Cf. T. Kleist/A.Scheuer, 'Neue Regelungen für audiovisuelle Mediendienste' [2006] *MultiMedia und Recht*, 206 *et seq.*
34. Based on the country of transmission principle (*see* Section IV.A in this Chapter), in this context receiving states are forbidden to subject television advertising from other Member States under their jurisdiction as this would amount to a double regulation. *De Agostini ua*, Cases No. C-34/95, C-35/95, C-36/95, [1997] ECR I-03843.

or gratuitous violence. The measures provided for in paragraph 1 are also applicable to other programmes which are likely to impair the physical, mental or moral development of minors, except where it is ensured, by selecting the time of the broadcast or by any other technical measure, that minors in the transmission area will not normally hear or see such broadcasts. When such programmes are broadcast in uncoded form, Article 22(3) obligates the Member States to ensure that they are preceded by an acoustic warning or are identified by the presence of a visual symbol throughout their duration. The measures the Member States take against broadcasts likely to cause development impairment are differentiated by considering the gravity of the potential impairment, a necessarily vague term. Pornography and gratuitous violence are explicitly mentioned in the demonstrative framework of Article 22(1) of the Television Directive as indicated above. The challenge of achieving an adequate differentiation is made abundantly clear against the backdrop of these two terms alone. In any case, the provisions contained in paragraph 1 cover so-called splatter[35] or hardcore[36] formats. Considering the stringency of the intervening measures with regard to such broadcasts, merely potentially (i.e. not seriously) impairing depictions, such as usual erotic or action films, are subject to the provisions contained in paragraph 2. Regarding these programmes it is adequate to block them either by using technical means or by selecting the time of broadcast. By systematically, and especially teleologically interpreting these provisions, it can be inferred that Article 22(3) of the Directive only applies – in this sense – to programmes that do not cause serious impairment.

From a quantitative point of view, Article 11(5) of the Television Directive stipulates that the broadcast of children's programmes with a scheduled duration of less then 30 minutes is not to be interrupted by advertising or teleshopping. For the future, this duration will likely be extended slightly due to the harmonization of relative time spans.[37]

3. Regulation of Content for the Protection of Health

Although regulatory provisions for protecting health are, according to their very nature, to be included under the heading of consumer protection norms, their objectives are clearly distinct. These provisions therefore shall be dealt with separately.

Unlike any other group of regulations, those governing the protection of health are characterized by media-related as well as cross-media regulatory provisions. The media-related or sector-specific provisions are laid down in the Television Directive.[38] Cross-media provisions, or those which apply to

35. Horror films which focus on the depiction of explicit violence and bloodthirstiness.
36. The explicit depiction of sexual activities displaying the sexual organs during the act.
37. Cf. Article 11(2) as amended by the Draft for a Proposal for a directive amending the Television without Frontiers directive 89/552/EEC, COM (2005) 646 final.
38. Television without Frontiers Directive 97/36/EC, OJ 1997 L 202/60.

all content, can be found in the Directive on Tobacco Advertising[39] and the Medicinal Products Directive.[40]

As for content regarding 'television advertisement and teleshopping[41] for alcoholic beverages', Article 15 of the Television Directive contains subject-matter provisions governing the protection of health. In particular, they may not link the consumption of alcohol to enhanced performance or to driving, nor may they create the impression that the consumption of alcohol contributes to social or sexual success, and in general, moderation in alcohol consumption may not be presented in a negative light.

Furthermore, the Medicinal Products Directive contains qualitative restrictions on the advertisement of medicinal products relevant not only for television advertisement, but also for commercial advertising in general, irrespective of its media platform. Accordingly advertisements for medicinal products must present the properties of the medicinal product objectively and without exaggeration and may not be misleading (Article 87(3)). Advertising medicinal products that are available on medical prescription only is prohibited (Article 88 1st bullet point). Certain elements, such as those that apply either exclusively or mainly to children, are prohibited per se in the advertisement of medical products (cf. the catalogue under Article 90).

Quantitatively speaking, Article 13 of the Television Directive generally prohibits any kind of television advertising and teleshopping for cigarettes and other tobacco products. Television advertising for medicinal products and medical treatments that are only available on medical prescription are barred pursuant to Article 14(1) of the Television Directive. The same applies with regard to teleshopping for certain medicinal products,[42] as well as for medical treatments. Article 17(2) of the Television Directive also forbids the sponsoring of television programmes by companies whose main activities are manufacturing cigarettes and other tobacco products. Within the meaning of Article 14(1) of the Television Directive, sponsoring is also prohibited for certain medicinal products and medical treatments.[43]

Administrative provisions in the individual Member States are to be approximated pursuant to Article 1(1) of the Tobacco Directive in terms of the press, other printed publications, radio broadcasting and the information

39. Tobacco Directive, OJ 2003 L 152/16.
40. Directive 2001/83/EC, OJ 2001 L 311/67.
41. In the future the scope of these provisions will be extended in general to audiovisual commercial communication. Cf. Article 1(f) in conjunction with Article 3g (e) as amended by the Proposal for a directive amending the Television without Frontiers directive 89/552/EEC, COM (2005) 646 final.
42. Those that require approval for being brought out onto the market within the meaning of the Medicinal Products Directive, OJ 1965 L 22/369 (recently amended by Directive 93/39/EEC, OJ 1993 L 214/22).
43. In the future this rule will be applicable to all audiovisual media services. Cf. Article 3h (2 and 3) as amended by the Proposal for a directive amending the Television without Frontiers directive 89/552/EEC, COM (2005) 646 final.

society services. The permissibility of advertising for tobacco products is clearly restricted[44] pursuant to Article 3(1) of the Tobacco Directive[45] with regard to printed publications. This kind of advertising is also not permitted in information society services[46] (Article 3(2) of the Tobacco Directive). Prohibitive regulations are also in place for advertising or sponsoring in radio broadcasting[47] (Article 4 of the Tobacco Directive).

4. Regulation of Content for the Protection of Consumers

It is certainly no surprise that in consumer protection detailed regulations are in place. Aside from special issues (such as tobacco advertising), in which qualitative intervention can be adapted to the specific regulatory subject-matter, the objective in the abstract area of consumer protection, aside from the possible deception of consumers, is to prevent them from being permanently bombarded by advertising messages of whatever kind.[48] Qualitative intervention means, in essence, mandatory identification and prohibitions on execution, while quantitative provisions restrict broadcasting times.

The regulations relevant to television advertising and teleshopping content can be found in the Television Directive; pursuant to Article 10 of this Directive, television advertising and teleshopping must be readily recognizable as such and kept quite separate from other parts of the programme by optical and/or acoustic means (paragraph 1); Isolated advertising spots are to remain the exception; (paragraph 2); advertising is not to use subliminal techniques (paragraph 3); and surreptitious advertising is prohibited (paragraph 4). Pursuant to Article 17(a) of the Television Directive, the content and scheduling of sponsored programmes may in no circumstances be influenced by the sponsor in such a way as to affect the responsibility and editorial independence of the broadcaster in respect of programmes. Article 17(b) of the Television Directive states that sponsored programmes must be clearly identified as such by the name and/or logo of the sponsor at the beginning and/or the end of the programmes. This regulation, however, is to be interpreted so as to ensure that this information as regards the sponsor is not prohibited in other places.[49] In accordance with Article(c) of the Television Directive, sponsored programmes must not encourage the purchase or rental of the products or services of the sponsor or a third party. Article 17(3) states that news and current affairs programmes may not be sponsored. In the future the mandatory identification of sponsored

44. Specifically to those exclusively intended for persons active in tobacco commerce and to publications that are printed and published in third countries, provided that these are not primarily intended for the Common Market.
45. Tobacco Directive, OJ 2003 L 152/16.
46. For a definition of information society services *see* Section I.C.
47. Therefore they are not only limited to television, but also include radio broadcasting services.
48. *EC Commission v. Netherlands*, Case No. C-353/89 [1991] ECR I-4069.
49. *RTI*, Cases No. C-320–94, C-328–94, C-329–94, V-337/94 [1996] ECR I-06471.

programmes may be extended to the full duration of their broadcast. 'Product placement' until now not having been subject to the directive's regulation, will most likely have its place in the new Audiovisual Media Services Directive, as the proposal already includes provisions requiring mandatory identification.[50] The differentiation between product placement, surreptitious advertising and sponsoring however is still being heavily discussed[51] and might lead to a differing wording in the final text.

Furthermore, Article 11(1) of the Television Directive states that advertisements and teleshopping spots are to be inserted between programmes. Provided the conditions contained in paragraphs 2 to 5 of this Article are fulfilled, advertisements may also be inserted during programmes in such a way that the integrity and value of the programme, taking into account natural breaks, the duration and nature of the programme, and the rights of rights-holders are not prejudiced. In programmes consisting of autonomous parts, or in sports programmes and similarly structured events and performances containing intervals, advertising and teleshopping spots are only to be inserted between the parts or in the intervals (paragraph 2). The transmission of audiovisual works, such as feature films and films made for television,[52] provided their scheduled duration is more than 45 minutes, may be interrupted once for each period of 45 minutes.[53] A further interruption is allowed if their scheduled duration is at least 20 minutes longer than two or more complete periods of 45 minutes. Where programmes, other than those covered by paragraph 2, are interrupted by advertising or teleshopping spots, a period of at least 20 minutes should elapse between each successive advertising break within the programme (paragraph 4). Advertising and teleshopping is not to be inserted in any broadcast of a religious service. News and current affairs programmes, documentaries and religious programmes, when their scheduled duration is less than 30 minutes, are not to be interrupted by advertising or by teleshopping (paragraph 5).[54] As in other citations, the approach in this regulation is the content-dependent preclusion of commercial content. Religious programming in particular, as with

50. Cf. 3h as amended by the Proposal for a directive amending the Television without Frontiers directive 89/552/EEC, COM (2005) 646 final. What has been subject to discussion here is mainly the difficulty of differentiating between product placement, surreptitious advertising and sponsoring.
51. *See* the *Progress Report of the Council on the Proposal*, 9134/06 (10 May 2006).
52. With the exception of serials, series, light entertainment programmes and documentary films. Made-for-television films which were designed to include breaks for inserting advertising spots come under the term 'films made for television' in the text. With regard to the frequency of the interruptions, these therefore are entitled to increased protection. *RTL*, Case No. C-245/01 [2003] ECR I-12489.
53. This duration also includes the time allotted to advertising, the so-called 'gross principle'. Cf. *ARD/Pro Sieben*, Case No. C-6/98 [1999] ECR I-07599. Pursuant to Article 3 the opinion of the ECJ authorizes the Member States to take stricter measures and introduce the net principle (without calculating the time allotted to advertising).
54. The provisions contained in the above-mentioned paragraphs apply to a programmed broadcasting time of at least 30 minutes.

those which claim to present information objectively, must not be exploited for commercial purposes.[55] In all likelihood, future regulations will be based on comparative provisions (minimal changes to the time intervals as they pertain to interruptions may be possible), however, simplifications are on the horizon with the proposal for a new directive.[56]

Regarding the upper limit of the amount of broadcast time allotted to advertising[57] and teleshopping spots,[58] Article 18(1) of the Television Directive sets a total limit of 20 per cent of the daily transmission time. Transmission time for advertising alone may not exceed 15 per cent of the daily transmission time. The amount of spot advertising within a given one-hour period is not to exceed 20 per cent (paragraph 2). In future this rather complex regulation will most likely make way for a unified limit applicable regardless of the advertising format.[59]

Furthermore, in view of the current legal situation, one peculiarity should be pointed out, namely that teleshopping windows dedicated to teleshopping broadcast by a channel not exclusively devoted to teleshopping are to be of a minimum uninterrupted duration of 15 minutes. (Article 18a(1) of the Television Directive). The maximum number of windows per day is eight. Their overall duration may not exceed three hours per day. They must be clearly identified as teleshopping windows by optical and acoustic means (paragraph 2). In the context of this regulation, the setting of a minimum duration pursues a quasi 'reverse regulatory approach'. With additional mandatory identification, qualitative and quantitative elements are present. It remains to be seen whether this approach will be included in the framework of the new regulations or whether it will fall victim to the trend toward simplification.[60]

Apart from television other audiovisual media content is not left unregulated but may fall under the definition of information society services becoming subject to the E-Commerce Directive's regulatory regime. In the same directive Article 6 *et seq* regulates information and other legal requirements with regard to commercial communication.[61] It must be clearly identifiable as such

55. Cf. *EC Commission v. Netherlands*, Case No. C-353/89 [1991] ECR I-4069, para. 45.
56. Cf. Article 11(2) as amended by the Draft for an Audiovisual Media Services Directive.
57. Pursuant to Article 18(3) of the Television without Frontiers Directive 97/36/EC, OJ 1997 L 202/60, announcements made by the television broadcaster in connection to its own programmes and ancillary products directly derived from these programmes, as well as public service announcements and charity appeals are not considered advertising within the meaning of Article 18 of the Television without Frontiers Directive.
58. With the exception of those under Article 18a of the Television without Frontiers Directive, OJ 1997 L 202/60.
59. Cf. Article 18 as amended by the Proposal for a directive amending the Television without Frontiers directive 89/552/EEC, COM (2005) 646 final.
60. Ibid. the Proposal deletes Article 18a of the old version.
61. Article 2(f) defines commercial communication as any form of communication designed to promote, directly or indirectly, the goods, services or image of a company, organization or person pursuing a commercial, industrial or craft activity or exercising a regulated profession. Pursuant to Article 2(f) bullet points 1 and 2, the mere fact of having a domain

(Article 6(a)), the natural or legal person on whose behalf the commercial communication is made must be clearly identifiable (Article 6(b)), promotional offers, (discounts, premiums, etc.) if permitted in the Member State where the service provider is established, must be clearly identifiable as such, and the conditions which are to be met to qualify for them are to be easily accessible and be presented clearly and unambiguously (Article 6(c)), and the same applies analogously to promotional competitions or games, (Article 6(d)).

As far as an unsolicited commercial communication is concerned (so-called spamming), Article 7 of the E-commerce Directive – presuming its permissibility in the respective Member State[62] – contains comparative requirements. Such commercial communication is to be identifiable clearly and unambiguously as such as soon as it is received by the recipient (paragraph 1). Furthermore, the Member States are obligated to ensure that service providers undertaking unsolicited commercial communication by electronic mail regularly consult and respect the opt-out registers in which natural persons not wishing to receive such commercial communications can register themselves (so-called Robinson lists)[63] (paragraph 2). Member States are also to ensure that the use of commercial communications which are part of, or constitute, an information society service provided by a member of a regulated profession[64] (e.g. doctors) is permitted subject to compliance with the professional rules regarding, in particular, the independence, dignity and honour of the profession, professional secrecy and fairness towards clients and other members of the profession (Article 8(1) of the E-Commerce Directive).

Provisions for combating misleading advertisement[65] are used to conduct consumer protection objectives. Pursuant to Article 4(1) of Directive 84/450/EEC[66] as amended by Directive 97/55/EC[67] mandated in the interest of the consumer, competitor and the general public to create suitable and effective tools for combating misleading advertising.[68] According to Article 2(2) misleading advertising is defined as 'any advertising which in any way, including its presentation, deceives or is likely to deceive the persons to whom it is addressed or whom it reaches and which, by reason of its deceptive nature, is likely to affect their economic behaviour or which, for those reasons, injures or is likely to

---

name or communicating information that is not advertising, such as 'independent product promotion' do not in themselves constitute commercial communications. Cf. R. Kilches, 'Electronic Commerce Richtlinie' [1999] *Medien & Recht*, 3 *et seq.* with further citations.

62. Cf. D. Damjanovic, 'Öffentlich-rechtliche Aspekte des E-Commerce' in *Handbuch Öffentliches Wirtschaftsrecht*, M. Holoubek and M. Potacs (eds.) (Springer, 2002) p. 1143.
63. Register of those persons who desire no access to commercial communication.
64. Pursuant to Article 2(g) of the E-Commerce Directive all profession within the meaning of Article 1(d) of the Directive 89/48/EEC, OJ 1989 L 19/16, or Directive 92/51/EEC, OJ 1992 L 209/25 as amended by Directive 97/38/EC, OJ 1997 L 184/31.
65. These regulations definitely pertain to further interests, such as those of competitors.
66. OJ 1984 L 250/17.
67. OJ 1997 L 290/18. Directive 97/55/EC, OJ 1997 L 290/18.
68. With regard to unfair business practices in general cf. Directive 2005/29/EC, OJ 2005 L 149/22.

injure a competitor.' In determining whether advertising is misleading, Article 3 demands that account be taken of all its features, and in particular of any information it contains concerning the characteristics of goods or services, the price and the like. For comparative advertising – in other words advertising that directly or indirectly identifies a competitor or the products or services offered by a competitor (Article 2 – 2a) – the regulation contained in Article 3a (as far as comparison is concerned) applies under certain circumstances. Among other things, it may not be misleading, nor run the risk of failing to differentiate between the advertiser and the competitor, nor unfairly exploit the reputation of a brand.

5. Regulation of Content for the Protection of Personal Rights

Regarding content broadcast via television, Article 23 of the Television Directive regulates a right of reply for every natural or legal person whose legitimate interests have been damaged by an assertion of incorrect facts in a television programme. The reply must take place within a reasonable time period after the receipt of a legitimate application for the exercise of the right of reply in a timely, objective and adequate manner in relation to the programme for which the application applies. The Directive on Privacy and Electronic Communications[69] also serves to protect fundamental rights and freedoms, in particular the right to privacy, with respect to the processing of personal data in the electronic communication sector (Article 1(1)). The right to privacy and personal communication is protected from unsolicited communications ('spamming') cited in Article 13 – these include communications in which automated calling systems, facsimile machines or electronic mail for the purposes of direct marketing are used. Article 13 stipulates that these methods may only be used if prior consent has been given. In any event, the practice of sending electronic mail for purposes of direct marketing disguising or concealing the identity of the sender on whose behalf the communication is made, or without a valid address to which the recipient may send a request that such communications cease, is prohibited. Regarding the processing of personal data, Article 5 requires Member States to prohibit listening, tapping, storage or other kinds of interception or surveillance of communications and the related traffic data. This represents an attempt to guarantee the right to the protection of personal data as enshrined in the Charter of Fundamental Rights.

Article 7 of the Charter of Fundamental Rights[70] (Article II-67 of the European Constitution) and Article 8 of the European Convention on Human

69. Directive 2002/58/EC, OJ 2002 L 201/37.
70. With regard to the general recognition of the fundamental right to the protection of privacy, regardless of the function of the Charter of Fundamental Rights as a source of recognition of rights, cf. recent precedents, e.g. *KPN Telekom*, Case No. C-109/03, [2004], ECR I-11273, as well as *Commission v. Netherlands*, Case No. C-350/02, [2004], ECR I-6213.

Rights provide the foundation for regulating fundamental rights in this context. Relying on the prevailing interpretation,[71] at least for the Charter of Fundamental Rights, that precedents of the European Court of Human Rights represent an imminent component of the European Community's code of fundamental rights, far-reaching possibilities for restricting the freedom of the press can be assumed with regard to respect for personal privacy and family life based on recent developments. The ECHR also assumed a restrictive interpretation of the term 'public figure' in the ruling it handed down in Hannover/Germany 2004.[72] The weighing of the fundamental rights of freedom of speech on one hand and the protection of privacy on the other must, according to the court, take into account the question of whether the publication of articles of photographs contributes to a debate of general public interest. Reporting about the purely private activities of a merely 'relative person of contemporary history' does not meet this requirement. Primarily the above-mentioned narrow term of 'absolute person of contemporary history' seems to be problematic in this context. Should the restrictive track taken by the ECHR in actuality lead to subsuming only political functionaries under this term, this would constitute an attack on the media's perception of its core responsibility, namely as 'public watchdog'.[73]

B. Analysis of the Problem

The objective of the new Audiovisual Media Services Directive is to cover the classic linear television programme, as well as the non-linear media services, in other words services where users decide for themselves which programme they want to see. This way the demarcation problems with information society services regulated by the E-Commerce Directive could be solved[74] in favour of a more comprehensive regulation, which makes the most sense. If no guarantees for certain minimum standards are in place for all content services, users could undermine protections of the rights of third parties simply by switching to a different medium and that should not be the case. In expanding the regulatory scope, naturally the question of possible regulatory options arises. In principle, there are two antithetical positions. The first represents comprehensive control by the state, while the other represents self-regulation by society. According to *Schmidt-Preuß*, self-regulation by society represents the 'individual or collective pursuit of private interests in the enjoyment of fundamental freedoms

71. Cf. S. Griller, 'Der Anwendungsbereich der Grundrechtscharta' in *Gundrechte für Europa – Die Europäische Union nach Nizza*, S. Griller and A. Duschanek (eds) [2002] p. 158.
72. ECHR, *Von Hannover*, Case No. 59320/00 [2004].
73. Cf. D. Ennöckl / M. Windhager, '"Paparazzi-Fotos" von Prominenten' [2004] *Medien & Recht*, 246.
74. T. Kleist / A. Scheuer, 'Audiovisuelle Mediendienste ohne Grenzen' (2006) 3 *MultiMedia und Recht*, 128.

for one's own legitimate benefit.'[75] Regulation by the state, however, shapes the framework in which we live, in the broader sense, by exercising public powers. The situation naturally becomes interesting when trying to establish a position between these two extremes. That's where we find the model that strikes the best balance between the 'state and the private sphere', namely the model of regulated self-regulation or also co-regulation. The state, or in our case the European Union, regulating more and more through 'soft law' and promotional instruments has encouraged voluntary, private initiatives as a contribution toward meeting public responsibilities.

While the usual regulatory measures can be seen as sufficient for 'classic' television formats, its applicability for other audiovisual media is widely questioned. At first glance it can be seen as an alternative to require providers to label content and filter it through positive and negative lists. However, positive lists have the potential to strongly limit the access to information, perhaps too strongly. On the other hand recording all illegal content on negative lists is currently technically impossible and will most likely remain so in the near future as well. This is because content cannot be blocked precisely from a central location. Filters can be circumvented by users and drawing up negative lists is also very expensive, a factor that should not be underestimated.[76] Furthermore, classic regulation cannot keep up with arduous decision-making processes as a rule, given the fast pace of development in the multimedia sector. In other words, the limits of detailed regulation have been reached.[77] Regarding the regulation of non-linear services, the possibilities are therefore limited to co-regulation and thereby to provisions that have the character of a recommendation and to incentives for private initiatives, as is already visible in current Community regulations.[78] As for the Community, there is a trend to let these models play a greater role.[79]

Another problem is compliance with regulations under constitutional law, based on which care must be taken that other fundamental rights, in particular the freedom of speech, the press and information, are not left by the wayside in favour of protecting the rights of third parties. Regulating certain content too narrowly for the protection of persons, for example minors, entails the danger

---

75. M. Schmidt-Preuß, 'Verwaltung und Verwaltungsrecht zwischen gesellschaftlicher Selbstregulierung und staatlicher Steuerung' in *Veröffentlichungen der Vereinigung der deutschen Staatsrechtslehrer*, Vol. 56 (De Gruyter, 1997) pp. 162 *et seq.*
76. K. Köhntopp / M. Köhntopp / M. Seeger, 'Sperrungen im Internet' [1998] *Kommunikation & Recht*, 25.
77. *T. Kleist* / *C. Palzer*, 'Medien Jugendschutz und Demokratie' <http://www.emr-sb.de/EMR/HSFKFSF.pdf>, 23 June 2006.
78. Cf. the Recommendation on the Protection of Minors and Human Dignity, OJ 1998 L 270/48. Unlike Directives, Recommendations are not legally binding and serve merely to urge the Member States to adopt a particular behaviour (*see* Article 249(5) of the EC Treaty).
79. Cf. Recital 25 in the Proposal for a directive amending the Television without Frontiers directive 89/552/EEC, COM (2005) 646 final.

of having an unintentional impact, in this case on adults.[80] As far as the user is concerned, this thus results in a kind of 'information blocking'[81] and may make it unduly difficult for providers to disseminate content. The reason for this problem is seen, among others, in the flood of technology and in the resulting overburdening of state structures. Co-regulation could possibly minimize the dangers of 'overregulation', as those involved have to be in agreement with each other on the scope and the government's implementation and can apply the experiences they have gained from day-to-day practice.

As experience with the co-regulation model is lacking, it is as yet somewhat unclear how this approach would develop in detail. It is therefore difficult to say to what extent co-regulation should actually be implemented in the interplay between state-control versus private initiative without further analysis.

C. SUMMARY

In the related secondary legal framework, numerous regulations already exist that directly limit content in both a qualitative and quantitative manner for the protection of third parties. Content is regulated in varying degrees depending on its nature for the protection of human dignity. The Television Directive differentiates between advertising and other kinds of content, thereby definitively prohibiting only the commercialized depiction of violations of human dignity. Qualitative regulations can be found in the protection of minors, for example as indicated in Article 22 of the Television Directive which ties into the endangerment of physical, mental and moral development; there are also quantitative regulations which prohibit advertising interruption during children's programmes up to a certain duration. Protection of the consumer and health also number among the factors worthy of protection for which content is regulated. The Television Directive furthermore wholly prohibits, for instance, advertising for specific goods that are dangerous to human health, such as tobacco products in Article 13, and Article 10 demands that advertising and teleshopping be clearly indicated as such. Regarding personal rights, Article 23 of the Directive stipulates a right of reply that any person is entitled to whose legitimate interests have been prejudiced by assertions of false information in a television programme. The above-mentioned Television Directive regulates content according to specific sectors; its regulations are limited to television programme and television advertising.

The protection of fundamental and personal rights, in particular the rights of minors, furthermore the protection of health, consumer interests and the

80. For this reason Recital 32 in the Proposal for a directive amending the Television without Frontiers directive 89/552/EEC, COM (2005) 646 final, also states that all measures taken to protect minors and human dignity must be carefully balanced with the fundamental right to freedom of expression.
81. W. Spoerr and C. Sellmann, 'Informations- und Kommunikationsfreiheit im Internet' [2004] *Kommunikation & Recht*, 367.

interest of rights-holders are all relevant outside of the medium of television as well. For this reason, provisions inspired by these regulations contained in the Television Directive can also be found in other directives. Relevant in this context are the E-Commerce and Data Protection Directives. The latter protects privacy and personal communication from unsolicited communications ('spamming') in Article 13. The E-Commerce Directive stipulates in principle standards for individually accessible electronic commercial communication. The Tobacco and Medicinal Products Directives contain provisions for protecting the rights of third parties as well. These regulations pursue their objective in protecting health in a cross-media approach, unlike the Television Directive.

The future Audiovisual Media Services Directive is intended to pursue a comprehensive concept that at least cuts across audiovisual media in order to include the non-linear services that are not addressed by many regulations. The expansion of these regulatory efforts cannot take place on the basis of a classic, state-controlled approach for several reasons,[82] but should rather take place with the help of private initiatives. The extent, to which the relatively new approach of so-called co-regulation can really be used to pursue these objectives in cooperation with various interest groups and with the goodwill of the content industry, is difficult to judge at the moment due to a lack of experience with these kinds of models. Unlike state control, co-regulation can potentially minimize the danger of overregulation. Overregulation indeed poses a threat to certain fundamental rights and freedoms, as the overzealous restriction of content for the protection of third parties may impact the rights of those who were not the target of the regulation. It is not easy to identify the reasons for this. Among other things, the flood of technology and the resulting overburdening of state structures have been cited in the discussion. Co-regulation may help to avoid this kind of situation, as those involved have to agree on the scope and the implementation of the government, and can apply the experiences they have gained from day-to-day practice.

III. PROMOTING PRODUCTION AND DISSEMINATION OF CONTENT

A. REVIEW OF STATUS QUO

1. Direct Promotion of Content

In addition to various European action and funding programmes – principally the MEDIA-Plus and MEDIA-Training, the EU's cultural programme, as well as the funding programmes[83] in the framework of Initiative i2010 –

82. Cf. Section II.B in this Chapter.
83. For general information on the funding programmes cf. M. Seifert, in Chapter 1, Section III.B *above*.

the Television Directive also directly promotes the production and the dissemination of content, in particular by prescribing quotas. Article 4 of the Television Directive requires Member States to ensure, where practicable and by appropriate means, that broadcasters reserve a majority proportion of their transmission time for European works, excluding the time appointed to news, sports events, games, advertising and teletext services.[84] Article 5 of the Television Directive demands that Member States ensure, where practicable and by appropriate means, that broadcasters reserve at least 10 per cent of their transmission time, excluding the time appointed to broadcasts within the meaning of Article 4 (supra) or alternately at least 10 per cent of their programming budget, for European works created by producers who are independent of broadcasters. This percentage is to be achieved gradually – newer works are to receive an appropriate percentage, including those which are broadcast within five years after being produced.

These regulations refer primarily to television programmes only. Indirectly, however, they naturally have a positive impact on the production of European audiovisual works, in particular on feature films, as well, as the latter are regularly also broadcast within the context of television programmes.

2. Indirect Promotion of Content

a. Promotion through tax breaks for film and television

This kind of promotion primarily takes a two-pronged approach. On one hand, using the classic means of depreciation and amortisation where procurement and production can be written off over a short time period. The other approach entails using a system of tax credits that originated in Canada. Here, a producer receives a state grant depending on the sum of the taxes that the employees of the production company are required to pay, amounting to, for example, up to 20 per cent of sum total of taxes to be paid by the employees.[85]

b. Promotion by limiting regulatory possibilities

A fundamental norm that places restrictions on the regulation of content both quantitatively and qualitatively is Article 10 of the European Convention of Human Rights. This regulation guarantees the fundamental right of freedom of expression. By its wording this article also applies in addition to the freedom

84. For the term 'European works' cf. Article 6 of the Television Directive, OJ 1997 L 202/60. Roughly speaking, these include works from Member States, but also works from European third countries if these countries are signatories to the Council of Europe's Convention on Transfrontier Television or are closely involved either contractually or de facto with the production via Member States – this must in any case be proportional.
85. Cf. O. Castendyk, 'Förderung der audiovisuellen Produktion in Europa' in *Die Zukunft der Fernsehrichtlinie*, EMR (eds.) (Nomos, 2005), p. 99; on the indirect promotion of content through tax breaks cf. M. Hofstätter, in Chapter 6 *below*.

to receive and impart information and ideas without interference by public authority and regardless of frontiers. These freedoms can be subject to restriction under the conditions listed under Article 10(2) of the European Convention of Human Rights.

The possibility of restrictions varies according to degree depending on the area in question. Also the European Court of Human Rights gives the Member States – for example as regards freedom of the press, since, as the ECHR described it, the press plays a special role within a democracy as 'public watchdog'[86] – only limited leeway in their judgement whether the criteria as contained in paragraph 2 are given. Restrictions on disseminating content in the form of commercial communication are subject to less strict control by the ECHR.[87] For this reason, the advertisement is given even more leeway in assessment, as it does not have the same essential significance for a democratic society as non-commercial communication does. Thus the ECHR has restricted itself when interfering with the freedom to advertise to efforts verifying whether the interference is fundamentally justified and proportionate. According to the criterion of contributing to a democratic society, a differentiation between commercial and non-commercial communication is made. The logical conclusion of this is that advertising fundamentally enjoys less protection under Article 10 of the European Convention of Human Rights; in other words more profound state intervention is permissible in commercial communication as compared to other kinds of content. However, this line cannot be drawn very clearly every time, and it is not expressly regulated. Rather, it has developed over a longer period of time based on case law of fundamental rights. It becomes even more delicate when making a further distinction among non-commercial communication between information and entertainment. Here as well, a varying significance for the state of a democratic society must fundamentally be presupposed; however, in individual cases it quickly becomes questionable whether a piece of information is significant for the public or serves purely to entertain, as for example the Hannover/Germany case[88] has shown recently.

Radio broadcasting has a special status with regard to content. In the cases GROPPERA,[89] LENTIA[90] und TELE 1,[91] the ECHR found that any restriction on the freedom of broadcasting constituted an infringement of Article 10 of the European Convention on Human Rights. However, for a long time it was unclear whether and how such infringements could be justified. Article 10 of the European Convention on Human Rights presupposes a certain special status for broadcasting as compared to other mass media outlets, inasmuch as

86. ECHR *Lingens*, Series A Case No. 103, para. 42. Cf. ECHR *Sunday Times*, Series A Case No. 30 in which the ECHR stressed the significance of the press for the freedom of expression.
87. ECHR *Barthold*, Series A Case No. 90 and *Markt Intern*, Series A Case No. 165.
88. ECHR *Von Hannover*, Case No. 59320/00 [2004].
89. ECHR *Groppera Radio AG* et al, Series A Case No. 173.
90. ECHR *Informationsverein Lentia*, Series A Case No. 276.
91. ECHR *Tele 1* PrivatfernsehgesellschaftmbH, Case No. 32240/96 [2000].

Article 10(1)(3) of the European Convention on Human Rights states that the signatory states of the European Convention on Human Rights may 'require the licensing of broadcasting, television or cinema enterprises.' This express right to issue licences laid out in Article 10(1)(3) of the European Convention on Human Rights firstly makes it clear that the legislator may subject broadcasters – unlike press undertakings – to a preventative state-controlled licensing process. This licensing right contained in Article 10(1)(3) of the European Convention on Human Rights gives the possibility to the legislator of pursuing certain objectives in broadcasting regulation that go beyond the legitimate aims of intervention in Article 10(2) of the European Convention on Human Rights.

In addition to technical grounds such as scarcity of frequencies, which will not allow a completely free market, a content wise aspect provided the key for the possibility of preventative control. What is meant primarily is the great influence audiovisual media have on the population, which supports the idea of regulating broadcasting more narrowly than other kinds of mass media where plurality and balance of programming should be guaranteed. However, this does not mean that Article 10(1)(3) of the European Convention on Human Rights could be used to regulate content directly, as the question of permissibility of providing communication infrastructure, even when taking into consideration contentwise and cultural aspects, remains. In light of new broadcast technologies, such as DVB-T[92] or the Internet the problem of frequency capacity is slowly but surely losing significance. The impact of the programming aspect of the notion of broadcasting according to the European Convention on Human Rights might be interesting. The point of departure, of course, had been that broadcasting as a rule represents passive entertainment for listeners and/or viewers. Viewers do not seek out what they want to see intentionally, but are rather confronted with a programme put together by someone else (broadcaster). As a result, the element of programming content takes on a central significance for understanding the notion of broadcasting. New possibilities offered by technology are increasingly changing the role of the consumer, which is also illustrated in day-to-day nomenclature. Viewers are no longer passive recipients, but rather actively shape what they see – they become users who, for instance with *video on demand*, put together their own programming. But since this way, the conditions for the definition of broadcasting under Article 10(1)(3) are not fulfilled, the right reserved to the state for issuing licences could become irrelevant for these cases.

In summary it must be stated that securing diversity in the media forms a central argument for regulating content. The objective of pluralism in the

92. Digital video broadcasting is the transmission standard for digital television in Europe which has prevailed. The addition '-T' stands for 'terrestrial', whereby the variants '-S' for 'satellite' or '-C' for 'cable' are also possible. For an introduction to the issue cf. S. Himberger, 'Digitales terrestrisches Fernsehen in Österreich' [2005] *Medien & Recht*, 159 *et seq.*

media is directly linked to the fundamental definition of freedom of expression for the democratic society.[93] Mass media have a special significance for guaranteeing the public communication process, which, in turn, is essential in a democracy. Ensuring pluralism is, however, not an objective that can justify any restriction whatsoever, as a democratic society has also to guarantee additional fundamental and personal rights that must be weighed against the freedom of expression and pluralism in the media.

B. Analysis of the Problem

The quota regulation contained in the Television Directive points to numerous problematic aspects. Even the legal foundation of this regulation is questionable as the quota regulation can be seen as a culture policy measure over which the Community has no competence.[94] The fact that the European Union primarily regulates the subject-matter of programmes, an economic matter presupposed for regulatory competence, is not at stake, and the quota regulation can therefore not be based on Article 47(2) in conjunction with Article 66 of the EC Treaty. This is, however, mistaken, inasmuch as the quota regulation at least indirectly improves the use of European production and therefore competitiveness of the European programming industry. This qualifies the regulation apart from the cultural policy aspect as an economic policy measure as well and justifies the use of Article 47(2) of the EC Treaty as a foundation.[95] Article 47(2) in conjunction with Article 66 of the EC Treaty is also aimed at easing the free movement of services. It remains to be seen whether this freedom will rather be restricted by the subject-mater provisions of the quota regulation. This hypothesis has found at least partial support.[96] On the other hand television broadcasters are favoured inasmuch as the cited European works are often produced by the broadcasters themselves.[97]

A further objection refers to the criterion of proportionality: The quota regulation's aim is to eliminate national restrictions that favour national cultural

93. Article 10 protects not just the opinion of the majority, but also that of the minority, be it worrisome or injurious. '..*Such are the demands of that pluralism, tolerance and broadmindedness without which there is no 'democratic society'* ECHR *HANDYSIDE*, Series A Case No. 24.
94. F. Ossenbühl, *Rundfunk zwischen nationalem Verfassungsrecht und europäischem Gemeinschaftsrecht* (Frankfurt, Alfred Metzner Verlag, 1986), p. 15. Measures Concerning broadcasting activities can only be justified on special economic-political competence grounds. For more reprimands *see* R. Weber et al (eds), *Kulturquoten im Rundfunk* (Baden-Baden, Nomos, 2006), p. 193.
95. O. Castendyk, 'Förderung der audiovisuellen Produktion in Europa' in *Die Zukunft der Fernsehrichtlinie*, EMR (eds) (Baden-Baden, Nomos, 2005), 101.
96. A. von Bogdandy, 'Europäischer Protektionismus im Medienbereich' (1992) 1 *Europäische Zeitschrift für Wirtschaftsrecht*, 14 *et seq.*
97. O. Castendyk, 'Förderung der audiovisuellen Produktion in Europa' in *Die Zukunft der Fernsehrichtlinie*, EMR (eds.) (Nomos, 2005), 101.

identity and work to the detriment of the free movement of services. But such restrictions can only be in place where a priori a criterion for the permissibility of such restrictions is met. This criterion is an interest of the general public, primarily to protect one's own cultural identity. The problem now is that cultural identity is not only affected by the broadcasting of programming from within but at least to the same extent from outside of Europe, which is why national restrictions still remain justified due to the rising market share of programming mainly from the USA.[98]

A further interest of the general public could also be seen in upholding certain quality standards in programming. Here, on the other hand, the quota regulation does not act directly, as the quota addresses quantitative, rather than qualitative characteristics. In light of this consideration, the question of proportionality of the quota regulation arises,[99] because it seems rather inefficient in its impact compared to its strong regulatory interventions.

Indeed, attention must be given to the fact that the Council has significant leeway for evaluation in examining the suitability and necessity of a legal act of the EC. The ECJ has again and again allowed the Council this leeway,[100] which is why it would appear improbable that the ECJ would cast doubt on the quota regulation according to the criterion of proportionality.[101]

Additional unanswered questions also concern the obligated parties according to the quota regulation (Are these the broadcasters all together or is it each broadcasting corporation individually?), the definition of a 'European work', or even and 'independent producer'.

Little is likely to change with regard to the promotion of European and independent audiovisual production in the future, as the majority of the Member States have supported maintaining the status quo. According to the Issue Paper,[102] producers, scriptwriters and unions proposed raising the minimum quota for European works; however, several Member States and private broadcasters opposed the quota and disproportionate interference in programming freedom.

According to the data in the study on the impact of measures for promoting the dissemination and production of television programmes pursuant to

---

98. *See* fn. 95.
99. K. Hailbronner / C. Weber, 'Möglichkeiten zur Förderung der europäischen Kultur in Rundfunk und Fernsehen anhand der Fernsehrichtlinie der EG' (1997) 14 *Die Öffentliche Verwaltung*, 565.
100. *Schröder*, Case No. 40/72 [1973] ECR 142.
101. O. Castendyk, 'Förderung der audiovisuellen Produktion in Europa' in *Die Zukunft der Fernsehrichtlinie*, EMR (eds.) (Nomos, 2005), 102.
102. H. Weber, 'Cultural Diversity and promotion of European and independent audiovisual production', Report given at the Liverpool Audiovisual Conference (Liverpool, 20–22 September 2005) <http://ec.europa.eu/comm/avpolicy/reg/tvwf/modernisation/liverpool_2005/index_en.htm>, 23 June 2006.

Article 25a of the 'Television without Frontiers'[103] Directives, the broadcast timeshare of European works has increased significantly. The authors of the above-mentioned issue paper presumed that these regulations have strengthened the European audiovisual industry as a whole, which is why the broadcast timeshare was described in the paper as thoroughly appropriate. Still it remains unanswered by whom the gain of European works in market shares is borne by. If it were mostly national programmes that are affected, the shares of e.g. US American programmes could have risen as well, which would indicate that the success proclaimed by the paper is only a relative one. In this context it is clear that the role of non-linear services, which have great potential regarding market share and profits, is growing. For several medium-sized television broadcasters this may mean stiffer competition with online services and telecommunication service providers who also wish to transmit e-content. These facts actually speak in favour of approximating the conditions for all distribution platforms and expanding the quota regulation in order to keep from distorting competition in favour of the new 'non-linear' services. It would be incomprehensible why despite their potential for making a large contribution toward promoting European works in the new media, should be exempted. For this reason Recital 35 of the proposal for an Audiovisual Media Services Directive states that non-linear audiovisual services should also advance the production and distribution of European works. Article 4, which contains the quota regulation, remains unchanged.

This also indicates the need for regulation in a new Audiovisual Media Services Directive, whereby there has been a lively discussion on how to do it. Several stakeholders wanted to impose a binding contribution for non-linear services to promote European productions, while others thought it premature, that there would be the risk of impeding the development of new programming. The aforementioned Issue Paper vacillated between advocating a review clause and a middle-of-the-road option in the form of a non-binding instrument which would send a positive signal to European producers of content, while at the same time would achieve an approximation of the competitive conditions between the various platforms.[104] In the proposal for the new directive Article 3f is referring to media service providers urging the Member States to ensure that such providers promote production of and access to European works.[105] Article 4 however is not amended leaving non-linear services outside the scope of the quota regulation.

103. Impact Study concerning the Distribution and Production of TV Programmes 2005 <http://ec.europa.eu/comm/avpolicy/info_centre/library/studies/index_en.htm>, 23 June 2006.

104. Cf. fn. 98.

105. Also the recitals in the Proposal for a directive amending the Television without Frontiers Directive 89/552/EEC, COM (2005) 646 final, mention the issue. Recital 35 says: '*Non-linear services have the potential to partially replace linear services. Accordingly they should where practicable promote the production and distribution of European works and thus actively contribute to the promotion of cultural diversity. It will be important to regularly re-examine*

C. Summary

In principle, it is possible to promote content directly with regulatory measures, such as the quota regulation contained in the Television Directive or via political programmes, or indirectly with tax breaks for content. Indirect regulations that place certain limitations on content regulation to minimize the danger of overregulation as explained in VI.B.2 also have served to promote content. It is achieved primarily by regulating the fundamental right to freedom of expression and the freedoms of the press and information as described in Article 10 of the European Convention on Human Rights. This means that limits are placed on content regulation in the media for the protection of fundamental and personal rights of third parties. Article 10 of the European Convention on Human Rights guarantees a minimum of protection from infringements in order to also ensure the dissemination of content in terms of freedom of information, as is vital in a democratic society.

After this overview the potential of these various promotional approaches to have an impact seems to be quite diverse and difficult to put a value on. The direct promotion of content using the quota regulation is certainly the most controversial from a law policy perspective. It is easy to cast doubt on the criterion of proportionality, although, considering the above-mentioned significant leeway allowed to the Council in determining necessity, it has prevailed against all objections to date. It remains questionable what the reaction to the shift on the dissemination of content from linear to increasingly non-linear services will be. Will we see demands for quotas for providers of these new services and for the approximation of the various transmission channels, analogous to the regulations for the protection of the rights of third parties? This is a question that has not yet been decided, as is obvious in light of the discussions in the focus groups and beyond.

IV. MAINTAINING THE SINGLE MARKET

A. Review of the Status Quo

Naturally, what all of the above-mentioned regulations have in common is that they contribute to maintaining the single market by legal approximation. The following remarks deal in particular with the provisions of sector-specific regulation at content level whose objective is to directly and constitutively harmonize the market. These include in particular the various principles developed for the harmonization of legal norms; the affected market principle and the country of transmission principle (country of origin principle).

---

the appplication of the provisions relating to the promotion of European works by audiovisual media services.'

In terms of the collision of laws, the application of the market rule, at least in international private law, can be presumed based on the majority of regulations of the individual Member States.[106] An application of this kind also corresponds to the supposition contained in Article 5 of the draft for the Rome II Regulation[107] that in the case of unfair competition the closest connection exists to the State in which the damaging action has an impact.[108] In so-called multi-state competition[109] applying the affected market rule is, however, of little practicability. The larger the number of competent legal systems, the more difficult it becomes to assess the lawfulness of competitive acts for each market according to its market laws.[110] Within the scope of application of the Television Directive – meaning content broadcast during television programmes – the country of origin principle ('country of transmission principle') applies pursuant to Article 2 for this reason. Television broadcasters are therefore primarily subject to the jurisdiction of the Member State in which they are deemed established. The criteria for determining which country that is are the location of the head office, the place of employment of the majority of the staff and in which Member State the key decisions are made with regard to programming (paragraph 3). If the above-listed criteria are insufficient to determine the Member State of the head office, the following additional criteria come into play: they use a frequency granted by that Member State, they use satellite capacity appertaining to that Member State, they do use a satellite up-link situated in that Member State. If it is still not possible to determine which Member State has jurisdiction, jurisdiction is to be exercised by the Member State in which the broadcaster is established pursuant to Article 52 *et seq* of the EC Treaty.

Within the scope of the E-Commerce Directive, i.e. for information society services, Article 3 of the Directive regulates the country of origin principle as a fundamental principle.[111] Member States may not, for reasons falling within

106. Cf. for the field of competition law, for example Section 48 para. 2 of the Austrian Act on International Private Law (ÖIPRG) (Federal Legal Gazette 304/1978), Article 136 of the Swiss Act on International Private Law (schwIPRG) (AS 1998 1776), Article 40 para. 1 Introductory Statue to the German Civil Code (EGBGB) (German Federal Law Gazette I, 2494).
107. Draft for a Regulation of the European Parliament and the Council on the Law Applicable to Non-Contractual Obligations, COM (2003) 427 final.
108. N. Dethloff, 'Europäisches Kollissionsrecht des unlauteren Wettbewerbs' (2000) 4 *Juristenzeitung*, 181.
109. Competition action impacts on several markets, which is inherent to the nature of cross-border television and the Internet.
110. N. Dethloff, 'Europäisches Kollissionsrecht des unlauteren Wettbewerbs' (2000) 4 *Juristenzeitung*, 181.
111. Cf. in general for this development A. Scheuer / P. Strothmann, (2001) 9 *MultiMedia & Recht*, 577, as well as with regard to the E-Commerce Directive G. Spindler / M. Fallenböck, 'Das Herkunftslandprinzip der E-Commerce-Richtlinie' [2002] *Zeitschrift für Rechtsvergleichung, internationales Privatrecht und Europarecht*, 214.

the coordinated field,[112] restrict the freedom to provide information society services from another Member State (paragraph 2). Deviating measures may be taken with regard to a particular information society service on grounds such as public security, health, and safety or consumer protection. A service provider is deemed established if it effectively pursues an economic activity using a fixed establishment for an indefinite period. The presence and use of the technical means and technologies required to provide the service do not, in themselves, constitute an establishment of the provider (Article 2(c)). The regulations enacted within the meaning of the country of origin principle within the meaning of paragraph 2 are not applicable to certain fields listed in the Annex of the Directive (paragraph 3). Worth highlighting are in particular are copyright, neighbouring rights, the freedom of the parties to choose the law applicable to their contract, contractual obligations concerning consumer contacts and the permissibility of unsolicited commercial communications by electronic mail.

B. Analysis of the Problem

In this specific context the different treatment of content that is transmitted electronically and of content that is not when applying the principles of harmonization may be problematic.[113] As regulations of other kinds of content are taken horizontally (such as in the Medicinal Products Directive and the Tobacco Directive) in contrast to information society services or television and are therefore oriented toward the affected market principle, in this field, differing regulatory regimes could end up being applied to the same content, only because its distribution via different media. Advertisement on the Internet would therefore be subject to other standards based on the jurisdictional basis of the country of origin principle than the same advertisement disseminated in a cross-border printed medium. This has evoked fears of an 'online-offline chaos'[114] which has not entirely been dispelled as yet. Perhaps printed media, aimed at being distributed in several countries having separate national editing desks in most cases can be reasonably required to adhere to respective intrastate laws; however, it seems questionable whether it can be seen as appropriate if

112. Pursuant to Article 2(h) of the E-Commerce Directive 'requirements laid down in Member States' legal systems applicable to information society service providers or information society services, regardless of whether they are of a general nature or specifically designed for them.' The coordinated field concerns requirements with which the service provider has to comply in respect of the taking up of the activity of an information society service or the pursuit of the activity of an information society service.
113. Cf. K. Ladeur, *Das Werberecht der elektronischen Medien* (Verlag Recht und Wirtschaft, 2004), p. 54 *et seq.*
114. J. Apel / T. Grapperhaus, 'Das Offline-Online-Chaos oder wie die Europäische Kommission den grenzüberschreitenden Werbemarkt zu harmonisieren droht' [1999] *Wettbewerb in Recht und Praxis*, 1253.

the Internet site of a printed medium containing the same content should be subject to regulations that are different than those imposed on the printed medium itself.[115] It is possible that new ground must be broken with regard to cross-media congruency of content in order to contribute adequately to the realization of a Single Market.

In any case the establishment criterion seems to be a suitable instrument for television and information society services. This is evident as the discussions of experts which formed the basis for the issue papers present issued a clear appeal for adherence to the country of transmission principle to form the core of the Television Directive and the future Audiovisual Media Services Directive.[116] Expanding the regulations in the Television Directive relevant to this specific context to include 'audiovisual media services' or institutionalizing the 'media services provider' seems probable with the further development of the prevailing regulations. However, problems could arise in applying this principle, namely in constellations where the respective broadcaster is not established in any Member State. Furthermore the question of the jurisdiction of individual Member States, if non-linear audiovisual services are included in the Draft Audiovisual Media Services Directive also arises. It was also those issues in particular that were touched on in the issue paper,[117] whereby the following perspectives can be summarized as follows.

In the case of linear audiovisual services the country of origin principle is to be maintained as an essential principle. In light of experiences with broadcasts containing incitement to hatred a reversal of the order of the accountability criteria could be possible in favour of the use of broadcasting facilities. The ability to apply this to so-called multiplex operators[118] still seems questionable.

With regard to non-linear services, the location at which the editorial decisions concerning the non-linear services are made, as well as the location of establishment of the non-linear services provider (analogously applying the establishment criterion under the E-Commerce Directive) could be used for the purpose of determining legal jurisdiction. All in all, it seems likely that the criteria contained in the Television Directive will be adapted comprehensively, and therefore based primarily on the accumulation of the above-mentioned elements.[119] Concerning providers who are not established in any EU Member State, in particular the setting up of a registration procedure, similar to the

115. Cf. also specifically the 15th Recital of the Proposal for a directive amending the Television without Frontiers Directive 89/552/EEC, COM (2005) 646 final.
116. *See* R. Hieronymi, 'Rules applicable to audio-visual content services' Report given at the Liverpool Audiovisual Conference (Liverpool, 20–22 September 2005) <http://ec. europa. eu/comm/avpolicy/reg/tvwf/modernisation/liverpool_2005/index_en.htm>, 23 June 2006.
117. Ibid.
118. The method bundles signals from various sources for satellite transmission.
119. Cf. Article 2(3) as amended by the Proposal for a directive amending the Television without Frontiers Directive 89/552/EEC, COM (2005) 646 final.

one in the VAT Directive,[120] has been mentioned. These providers could register accordingly in a Member State and would then be subject to the relevant laws of that country. In the case of providers that do not register, any country in which the respective service is available would have the authority to take action; the provider would then be subject to multiple regulations.

A partial deviation from the principle of establishment could also be introduced to the future Audiovisual Media Services Directive as a new regulatory aspect. The idea is to subject media services providers who pursue the majority of their activities in a Member State other than the Member States where they are deemed established, with the intent to circumvent national laws within the regulatory framework of the directive, to the legal sovereignty of the respective Member State. So as to avoid undermining the objectives of the Directive, such an action taken by a Member State should be tied to additional criteria, such as a primary application to the state of establishment, notifying the Commission, etc.[121]

C. SUMMARY

The country of origin principle (country of transmission principle) applies to the scope of application of the Television Directive and the E-Commerce Directive. Accordingly, the laws of the Member State in which the service provider or the television broadcaster is established are to be applied. For media not distributed electronically, the affected market principle will still prevail, meaning that the laws of the Member State will apply whose market is affected by the respective action. As a result of this incongruence, the same content can also be subject to other laws that apply to specific media. Overall, the practical problems can be eliminated from the resulting constellations perhaps. In any case, there does seem to be a need for action for maintaining legal stringency.

V. CONCLUSIONS

Sector-specific regulation at content level encompasses legal provisions that directly regulate the performance of content, i.e. the activities of producing and disseminating content.

These regulations place qualitative (pertaining to the subject matter) and quantitative (pertaining to the method used in dissemination) restrictions on content primarily for the protection of third parties. Corresponding legal provisions also exist, however, to promote production and distribute content (directly

120. Directive 2002/38/EC, OJ 2002 L 128/41.
121. Cf. Article 2(7) *et seq.* as amended by the Proposal for a directive amending the Television without Frontiers Directive 89/552/EEC, COM (2005) 646 final.

and indirectly) as well. By deliberately determining the country of origin principle for particular content – mainly for e-content – content regulation in the narrower sense is used to maintain the Single Market. On the other hand, securing functioning market structures does not play a major role in sector-specific regulation at content level.

Regulations for the protection of third parties can be found primarily in the Television Directive and refer predominantly to content, that is transmitted during television broadcasts. Concerning other audiovisual media, sector-specific regulation for the protection of third parties for information society services can be found in the E-Commerce Directive. Since the latter follows a different, mainly economically focused regulatory approach, until now there is no so-called 'level-playing-field'. However the proposal for a directive amending the Television Directive is extending the scope of application generally to audiovisual content services. The Medicinal Products and the Tobacco Directives also contain provisions that regulate on a horizontal basis (meaning all content, in particular content not transmitted electronically) – these regulations primarily serve to protect consumer health. The data Protection Directive also has similar provisions aimed at protecting personal rights.

Directly regulating measures are used to regulate content for promoting the production and distribution of content; this includes the quota regulation contained in the Television Directive, as direct and indirect measures, such as tax breaks. Regulations that limit restrictions in content also serve to promote content regulation indirectly. Here, the focus of Article 10 of the European Convention on Human Rights restricts content regulation with the aim of protecting particular public interests. Although the quota regulation may have achieved the desired effects, it still poses a great deal of, as yet, unanswered questions. Above all, however, the lack (due to competence issues) of related qualitative regulations is also mentioned with regard to deficiencies in its construction. In particular, the regulation's lack of efficiency, cited as a result, has been criticized. Furthermore the legal foundation and the proportionality of the provision have additionally been the subject of much debate.

The country of origin principle was enshrined in the Television Directive and the E-Commerce Directive with the aim of preserving the Single Market, according to which, television broadcasters come under the jurisdiction of the Member State in which they are established. In the case of the linear audiovisual services within the scope of the Television Directive, the establishment criteria are based on the head office, the place of employment of the majority of the staff and on the question in which Member State the key programming decisions are made. Within the scope of the E-Commerce Directive a service provider is deemed established if it effectively pursues an economic activity using a fixed establishment for an indefinite period. As a result, the Member States are prohibited from restricting the distribution of the content referred to by the above-mentioned Directives on grounds that pertain to their field of regulation. The affected market principle applies to other kinds of content, i.e. content disseminated offline in particular, if no regulation to the opposite effect exists. The law to be applied is determined according to the Member State in which the content has a specific effect. The consequence is that the content transmitted via different media can be subject to differing legal treatment. It remains to be seen just how relevant this will turn out to be in practice. In order to avoid any contradiction in interpretation further legal approximation appears desirable.

Concerning sector-specific regulation at content level the main goal is to overcome the difficulties that arise in light of the broad coherence of content against the backdrop of existing albeit gradually diminishing differences between the media transmitting the content. In conclusion, with regard to future regulation, the question of how far-reaching it will have to be and which services it will cover, is going to be central. Subsequently, given the wide scope of application, the practical enforcement of the regulatory measures (in particular with regard to the protection of minors) will most certainly raise concomitant problems.

Chapter 5
Copyright and Related Rights

Margit Nemetz/Mathias Neubauer/Andreas Wiebe

I. LEGAL PROTECTION OF CONTENT – PROMOTION OF THE PRODUCTION AND DISTRIBUTION OF CONTENT

A. REVIEW OF THE STATUS QUO

Of the various protective systems under the law on intellectual property rights, it is mainly copyright and neighbouring rights which are of relevance for promotion of the production and distribution of content. For this reason, they will form the core of this section. Other industrial property rights such as, trademark rights, may also gain ancillary importance, but are not primarily aimed at the promotion and distribution of content. This section will not only treat regulations that directly serve the purpose of protecting the authors and holders of neighbouring rights but also provisions of those who offer and distribute third party content or 'improve' such content by offering value-added services.

1. Database Directive

The objective of the Database Directive 96/9/EC is to encourage the creation of databases as important elements of the information society. It establishes a dual system of protection for databases. The protection by copyright is aimed at promoting creativity regarding the selection and arrangement of the data. The newly introduced *sui generis* right serves the purpose of protecting investment in the creation of databases.[1]

1. Cf. Recitals 7 *et seq.* of the Directive 96/9/EC on the legal protection of databases, OJ 1996 L 77/20.

M. Holoubek, D. Damjanovic and M. Traimer (eds), *Regulating Content – European Regulatory Framework for the Media and Related Creative Sectors*, pp. 151–190

With the introduction of this *sui generis* right, the legislator pursued a broad approach to protection. After the court of first instance had initially supported this approach in most of its decisions, the ECJ, in its cases 'William Hill'[2] and 'Fixtures',[3] applied a restrictive interpretation which narrowly limited the protection to investments that have flowed into the actual creation of the database and that can be distinguished as having been made for that purpose.[4] Another decision with a restrictive effect was handed down by the Federal Court of Justice[5] in Germany in the 'Paperboy' case regarding the question of whether the *sui generis* right was infringed by the insertion of hyperlinks. The advantage of these decisions is, however, that they facilitate the provision of value-added services and access to information in general.

2. Information Society Directive

Directive 2001/29/EC ('Information Society Directive') serves the purpose of providing a high level of protection in the field of intellectual property in order to ensure the maintenance and development of creativity[6] and guarantee the necessary resources for the cultural creativity and productivity in Europe.[7] The focus is on harmonizing the powers and admissible limitations of copyright. The objective of such harmonization is an adaptation to digital media and a comprehensive protection of the rightholders.

a. Reproduction Right

The reproduction right laid down in Article 2 has been deliberately defined in a broad manner[8] and covers any direct and indirect, temporary and permanent reproduction. It is therefore being adapted to the new characteristics of information technology and includes a comprehensive approach to protection.

---

2. *British Horseracing Board Ltd and Others v. William Hill Organization Ltd*, Case No. C-203/02 [2004] ECR I-10415.
3. *Fixtures Marketing Ltd v. Organismos prognostikon agonon podosfairou AE*, Case No. C-338/02 [2004] ECR I-10549.
4. Cf. A. Wiebe, 'Europäischer Datenbankschutz nach 'William Hill' – Kehrtwende zur Informationsfreiheit?' [2005] *Computer und Recht*, 169.
5. Federal Court of Justice BGH, 17 July 2003, I ZR 259/00, [2003] *Computer und Recht*, 902 (*Nolte*) = [2003] *MultiMedia und Recht*, 719 (*Wiebe*) = [2003] *TeleKommunikations- und MedienRecht*, 438 (*Neubauer*).
6. Cf. Recital 9 of the Directive 2001/29/EC on the harmonization of certain aspects of copyright and related rights in the information society, OJ 2001 L 167/10.
7. Cf. Recital 11 of the Information Society Directive, OJ 2001 L 167/10.
8. Cf. Recital 21 of the Information Society Directive, OJ 2001 L 167/10; *see also* H. Wittmann, 'Die EU-Urheberrechts-Richtlinie – ein Überblick' [2001] *Medien und Recht*, 144.

b. Communication, Including Making Available, to the Public

The right of communication to the public, including the right of making available to the public, is harmonized in Article 3 of the Directive. This right is to be construed broadly and, in implementation of the WCT and the WPPT, clarifies that interactive transmissions over the Internet are also to be attributed to the rightholder.[9]

c. Limitations and Free Uses of Works

The copyright legislations of the Member States show a wide range of limitation provisions of differing scope. In most countries, the exemptions have been defined precisely. In British copyright law, however, regulations on fair dealing are used which, although exhaustive, nevertheless are reminiscent of general clauses which show parallels to the general clause of 'fair use' that is typical for U.S. law.

Article 5 of the Directive brings about a certain European-wide harmonization and thus also a certain degree of legal certainty for the holders and providers of content. The limitations with regard to the reproduction right and the right of communication to the public are listed exhaustively, so that no further restrictions of these rights are admissible. However, apart from Article 5(1) all limitations have optional character. The reason for that can be found in the different legal traditions of the Member States.[10] Especially in this area it is of great importance to take into account cultural distinctions.

According to the Information Society Directive, it will be possible to maintain the system of lump-sum remuneration schemes through collecting societies; the requirement of replacing such schemes by DRM systems could not be successfully established under the Information Society Directive.[11]

d. Legal Protection of Technological Protection Measures

Article 6 governs the protection against circumvention of any effective technological measures, including the protection against preparatory acts, and Article 7 protects information that is required for digital rights management systems. The circumvention of protection measures under the copyright limitations by means of self-help is prohibited, meaning that the limitations cannot be directly enforced within the meaning of a 'right to hack'.[12]

9. Cf. D. Kröger, 'Die Urheberrechtsrichtlinie für die Informationsgesellschaft – Bestandsaufnahme und kritische Bewertung' [2001] *Computer und Recht*, 318.
10. Cf. N. Flechsig, 'Grundlagen des Europäischen Urheberrechts' [2002] *Zeitschrift für Urheber- und Medienrecht*, 9.
11. Cf. G. Spindler, 'Europäisches Urheberrecht in der Informationsgesellschaft' [2002] *Gewerblicher Rechtsschutz und Urheberrecht*, 112.
12. Cf. M. Neubauer, 'Technische Schutzmaßnahmen und Recht' in *Internetrecht*, A. Wiebe (ed) (Wien, Springer, 2004), p. 119.

e. *Sanctions Under the Information Society Directive*

Article 8 of the Directive governs the obligation of the Member States to provide for suitable sanctions and remedies. In Austria, the right to receive information from intermediaries – which basically refers to access providers – has already been laid down in Section 87b Paragraph 3 of the Austrian Copyright Act ('UrhG') on the basis of Article 8(3) of the Directive. In other countries, such as Germany, no provisions to that effect have been introduced; it is likely that, together with other provisions regarding sanctions and remedies, they will be introduced on a Community level in the course of the implementation of the Enforcement Directive 2004/48/EC.[13]

3. Enforcement Directive

The Enforcement Directive 2004/48/EC[14] harmonizes and encourages the enforcement of intellectual property rights and serves the purpose of promoting and distributing content as it increases the incentive function of copyright. The Directive provides for a right to obtain information from infringing parties and third parties, including without limitation access providers, requirements regarding the preservation of evidence and claims for injunction and damages. It is planned to add some criminal measures.[15]

4. Country-of-origin and Country-of-transmission Principles and Exceptions

a. *Country-of-transmission Principle*

The Cable and Satellite Directive 93/83/EEC[16] governs the cross-border exploitation of programmes via satellites and the cable retransmission of programmes. It provides for a special rule with respect to the applicable law. According to the country-of-transmission theory, programmes broadcast via satellite shall be subject to the jurisdiction of the Member State from which the programme signal is being transmitted to the satellite. The act of communication to the public by satellite occurs solely in the Member State where, under the control and responsibility of the broadcasting organization, the programme-carrying signals are introduced into an uninterrupted chain of communication leading to the satellite and down towards the earth, meaning

13. Directive 2004/48/EC on the enforcement of intellectual property rights, OJ 2004 L 195/16.
14. OJ 2004 L 195/16.
15. Proposal for a directive on criminal measures aimed at ensuring the enforcement of intellectual property rights, COM(2005) 276 final.
16. OJ 1993 L 248/15.

in the State where the programme is introduced.[17] The contents and scope of the right to satellite broadcasting are therefore generally governed by the laws of the country of transmission. In contrast, the application of the country of reception would have meant that a broadcasting company would have had to guarantee legal protection in all countries of reception prior to broadcasting. Catch-all provisions prevent any circumvention of the country-of-transmission principle by transferring the broadcasting activities to a non-Community state.[18]

To make sure that the country-of-transmission principle does not have any undesired effects, all Member States have to provide for a minimum level of protection for authors and holders of neighbouring rights which was achieved by means of the Rental Directive[19] and the Cable and Satellite Directive.[20] The exclusive right of the author to the communication to the public by satellite should be recognized in all Member States. It shall be impossible to acquire this right without entering into a contract.[21] It is ensured that the unauthorized broadcasting of encrypted programme-carrying signals is deemed to be public communication.[22]

b. Country-of-origin Principle

The E-Commerce Directive 2000/31/EC lays down the application of the country-of-origin principle for the services of the information society.[23] This principle has been developed after the model of the country-of-transmission principle and ultimately results in an information society service in the coordinated field only having to meet the legal requirements of the Member State in which the service provider is domiciled. If the requirements of all Member States in which the provider's information society service was available had to be obtained, this would run counter to the realization of the internal market and the harmonization of the legal framework for the information society. However, the copyright, the neighbouring rights and the industrial property rights are expressly exempt from the country-of-origin principle because these

17. Article 1(2)(b) of the Directive 93/83/EEC on the coordination of certain rules concerning copyright and rights related to copyright applicable to satellite broadcasting and cable retransmission, OJ 1993 L 248/15; G. Kucsko, *Geistiges Eigentum* (Wien, MANZ, 2004), pp. 1092, 1190.
18. Article 1(2)(d) of the Cable and Satellite Directive, OJ 1993 L 248/15; T. Dreier in *Europäisches Urheberrecht*, M. Walter et al. (eds), (Wien, Springer, 2001), Article 1 Cable and Satellite Directive, margin No. 23 *et seq.*
19. OJ 1992 L 346/61.
20. T. Dreier in M. Walter et al. [2004] margin No. 13, 23, Article 4, margin No. 1.
21. G. Kucsko [2004] p. 1185; T. Dreier in M. Walter et al. (eds) (2001) margin No. 23.
22. Article 1(2)(c) of the Cable and Satellite Directive, OJ 1993 L 248/15; cf. T. Dreier in M. Walter et al. [2001], margin No. 20.
23. Article 3 of the Directive 2000/31/EC on certain legal aspects of information society services, in particular electronic commerce, in the Internal Market, OJ 2000 L 178/1.

areas are strongly regulated by international conventions and Community law and governed by the principle of territoriality.[24]

The country-of-origin principle has also been laid down in the Television without Frontiers Directive 97/36/EG.[25] This Directive does not contain any general exceptions but only provides for exceptions in individual cases, for instance for the purposes of the protection of minors. That means that the country-of-origin principle under the Television without Frontiers Directive applies to broadcasting-related programme and language requirements and the advertising right, in particular regarding the prohibition of advertising and teleshopping spots.[26]

5. Rights Management and Collecting Societies

European directives always refer to collecting societies[27] and also proceed on the assumption that collecting societies are active in all Member States.[28] Although no harmonization has yet been achieved in this area, the necessity of increased transparency and efficiency with regard to the activities performed by collecting societies has been recognized.[29] The national collecting societies only become active within the respective Member States which results in an ‘offline’ and ‘online’ market allocation along the national borders of the Member States.

6. Resale Rights Directive

In practice, artists usually still sell their works at modest prices while their value on the art market is later often enhanced enormously. Until now, it was impossible for the artists to benefit from the enormous prices fetched by their works once they had sold them. But the Directive 2001/84/EC on the resale right[30] for the benefit of the author of an original work of art, which must be implemented into national law by 1 January 2006, lays down the artist’s claim to a share in the selling price against the seller provided that the seller is a representative of the art market.

---

24. Explanatory remarks 817, Protocol No. 43 of the 21st Session of (Austrian) Parliament.
25. Directive 97/36/EC amending Council Directive 89/552/EEC on the coordination of certain provisions laid down by law, regulation or administrative action in Member States concerning the pursuit of television broadcasting activities, OJ 1997 L 202/60.
26. C. Brenn, *Das ECG – E-Commerce-Gesetz* (Wien, MANZ, 2002), p. 315.
27. Articles 1, 9 of the Cable and Satellite Directive, OJ 1993 L 248/15; Recital 26 of the Information Society Directive, OJ 2001 L 167/10.
28. Recitals 17 *et seq.* of the Information Society Directive, OJ 2001 L 167/10; Recital 28 and Article 6 of the Directive 2001/84/EC on the resale right for the benefit of the author of an original work of art, OJ 2001 L 272/32.
29. *See* Communication from the Commission: The Management of Copyright and Related Rights in the Internal Market, COM(2004) 261 final, 8; Recital 17 of the Information Society Directive, OJ 2001 L 167/10; Recital 28 of the Resale Right Directive, OJ 2001 L 272/32.
30. OJ 2001 L 272/32.

7. Harmonization of Copyright Contract Law

On a European level, harmonized provisions regarding copyright contract law can be found only sporadically. The Rental Directive, for instance, provides for a right of the author and the artist to receive equitable remuneration which must not be waived.[31] In addition, there are some single provisions contained in the Software Directive, the Cable and Satellite Directive and the Database Directive. For the time being, it is not planned to carry out a comprehensive harmonization of the copyright contract law.[32]

8. Consolidation of the European copyright laws

Since 2002, the Commission has been revising the *acquis communautaire* in the field of copyright law with the objective of ensuring the functioning and the coherence of the internal market. The copyright directives of the 'first generation'[33] are to be reviewed as to whether they are coherent with the new directives, including without limitation Directive 2001/29/EC, and in how far there are still deficits in legal protection.[34] A consultation to that effect was carried out in the year 2004. [35]

B. Problem Analysis

1. Scope of the Database Protection

The scope of the *sui generis* right for the protection of the investments into databases had been unclear for a long time as it had been introduced as a new type of right by the European legislator and there was only experience with more or less related national industrial property rights. Now the ECJ, in its decisions William Hill[36] and Fixtures,[37] has drawn up guidelines for the interpretation of the most important requirements for protection. In doing so,

---

31. Article 4 of the Directive 92/100/EEC on rental right and lending right and on certain rights related to copyright in the field of intellectual property, OJ 1992 L 346/61.
32. Cf. in more detail S. von Lewinski, 'Kapitel VIII. Urhebervertragsrecht' in *Europäisches Urheberrecht*, M. Walter et al. (eds) margin Nos. 77–90; *see* Communication on copyrights, COM(2004) 261, 13.
33. Directive 91/250/EEC on the legal protection of computer programs, OJ 1991 L 122/42; Rental Directive, OJ 1992 L 346/61; Cable and Satellite Directive, OJ 1993 L 248/15; Directive 93/98/EEC, OJ 1993 L 290/9; Database Directive, OJ 1996 L 77/20.
34. IP/04/955, Commission launches consultations on fine-tuning of legislation (press release 19 July 2004).
35. IP/04/955 Commission launches consultations on fine-tuning of legislation; Commission Staff Working Paper on the review of the EC legal framework in the field of copyright and related rights, SEC(2004) 995.
36. ECJ Case C-203/02, *William Hill*, [2004] ECR I-10415.
37. ECJ Case C-338/02 et al., *Fixtures Marketing*, [2004] ECR I-10549.

the ECJ sent a strong signal for a narrow definition of the rights of the makers of databases. This referred in particular to three criteria for legal protection. On the one hand, when giving the reasons for protection, the investments qualifying for protection were strongly limited by means of a restrictive separation from investments made into the generation of data. Eligible investments include exclusively expenses for the search, collection and review of existing data which can demonstrably be separated from the expenses for the generation of the data. This does not only result in definition problems but also in the lack of protection for spin-off databases where either the substantial investment flowed into the research of the data and/or where it is very difficult to separate the expenses for the data collection from those incurred for the data generation. This concerns for instance journalistic information and measuring data for the production of weather charts.[38]

Regarding the scope of protection which refers to the taking of substantial parts of a database, the eligible elements were limited to the amount of investments made into the part taken over, and qualitative elements such as a special updating of the information or its specific value for the users were disregarded. The transfer of insubstantial parts, which is also prohibited under certain conditions, was degraded to a misuse provision which put a halt to all attempts of an expansion of the scope of protection by means of this supplementary criterion. What remains unclear is the scope and the dogmatic foundation of the 'right of consultation' mentioned by the court according to which the mere query of a published database is not prohibited.

In a phase in which the practical significance of the right of the maker of the database is emerging but has not yet become fully recognizable, the ECJ has strongly limited the scope of this right by means of a narrow interpretation oriented towards the legislative objective and thus has created the antipode of the broad approach of the Database Directive. Achieving a reconciliation of interests in the diametrical relationship between incentive by means of protection on the one hand and access to information on the other hand is the basic issue of the law on intellectual property. For databases, as important components of the information society, the narrow interpretation of the ECJ is in conflict with the broad legal protection intended by the legislator. Although the case law in this respect does make the offering of value-added services easier, it might also, on the other hand, reduce the incentive for creating databases because it facilitates the cost-free realization of competing offers from third party databases.

Harmonization of the limitation for temporary reproductions after the model of Article 5(1) of the Information Society Directive is being discussed, both with regard to database law and software; an introduction of a limitation for the benefit of users with a disability is being considered.[39]

---

38. Cf. A. Wiebe, 'Europäischer Datenbankschutz nach 'William Hill' – Kehrtwende zur Informationsfreiheit?', 171.
39. Cf. SEC(2004) 995, 7, 12.

2. Information Society Directive

a. Lack of Clarity Regarding the Scope of the 'Making Available' Right

The right of communication to the public including the right of making available to the public has to be construed in a broad sense.[40] Despite the intended comprehensive regulation, gaps in the protection and problems of definition can be identified with regard to certain types of transmission. Near-on-demand services, webcasting, push services and pay TV are covered by the general right of communication to the public.[41] There are, however, problems of differentiation from the broadcasting right, which for instance does not exist for all of the neighbouring rights. It is, for instance, questionable whether delayed downloads via peer-to-peer networks (P2P), where the downloading users cannot determine the point in time of the transmission themselves, are still covered by the right of making available to the public.

A point that still needs clarification is the application of the right of communication to the public to the use of works in intranets and for the purposes of e-learning. According to the relevant definition, a limited group of users with personal affiliations is not considered to be public under the laws applicable in Austria and Germany.[42] Accordingly, school classes are not deemed to be public.[43] On the other hand, however, Section 52a of the German Copyright Act ('UrhG') provides for a limitation in favour of schools and universities and also covers the making available to the public for purposes of instruction in schools. At the same time, Section 52a of said act expressly restricts the use to an 'exactly defined group' which would not be necessary if the user group of a school class was considered to be non-public in any case and therefore also defined. As a result, the criterion of personal affiliation will therefore have to be taken into primary consideration and defined in such a narrow way that it does not apply to school classes or students attending university lectures. Thus, this constitutes a regular act of making available to the public according to Article 3 of the Information Society Directive which is in the interest of a comprehensive protection of the content providers.

---

40. Cf. Recital 23 of the Information Society Directive, OJ 2001 L 167/10.
41. Cf. M. Walter, 'Ministerialentwurf einer UrhGNov 2002 – Ausgewählte Aspekte' [2002] *Medien und Recht*, 218; M. Fallenböck, 'Urheberrecht in der digitalen Ökonomie: Die EG-Urheberrechtsrichtlinie und ihre Umsetzung' [2002] *ecolex*, 104; T. Dreier, 'Die Umsetzung der Urheberrechtsrichtlinie 2001/29/EG in deutsches Recht' [2002] *Zeitschrift für Urheber- und Medienrecht*, 30.
42. Cf. W. Dillenz, *Urheberrecht* (Wien, Springer, 2004), copyright Section 18 margin No. 9.
43. T. Dreier/G. Schulze, *Urheberrechtsgesetz* (München, C.H.Beck, 2004), Section 15, margin No. 45 with reference to J. von Ungern-Sternberg, in *Urheberrecht Kommentar*, G. Schricker and et al (eds), (2nd edn, München, C.H.Beck, 1999), Section 15, margin No. 72.

Article 3(2) fails to mention the database right.[44] Although database law also includes a right of exploitation of online transmissions, these provisions are not congruent, at least not according to their wording, so that differences cannot be ruled out.

b. Allocated Uses

The limitation provisions and/or the free uses of works serve the purpose of balancing the interests of the holders of the rights and the concerns of the general public and will therefore be analyzed in greater detail under item C below. The scope of these limitations is, however, of relevance with a view to the protection of the providers of value-added services. The protection of authors and other rightholders should leave sufficient latitude for the provision of informational value-added services because these services can also be provided by content providers. Here, it is necessary to strike a balance: in general, the author is also to benefit from new and expanded possibilities of use.[45] What needs to be clarified is, however, whether this is also to include more remote uses on secondary and downstream markets.[46]

Article 5(1) of the Information Society Directive provides for a limitation regarding browsing and caching as technological processes that cannot be used separately for economic purposes. But this obviously does not include the reproductions that are the result of the automated searching and indexing of websites by means of search engines. An 'implied licence' conferred by putting content on the Internet cannot be generally assumed. Apart from search engines that serve primarily informative purposes, specialized search engines may also be used to realize 'parasite' competitive products using hyperlink technology which might affect the economic interests of the content providers.[47]

The scope of the limitation regarding teaching purposes provided for in Article 5(3)(a) of the Information Society Directive is of relevance for the providers of e-learning systems with a view to the use of existing material. Where this limitation does not leave any latitude, license agreements must be entered into with the rightholders. The Information Society Directive does leave room for national regulations in this respect. For example, Section 42 Paragraph 6 of the Austrian Copyright Act ('UrhG') bans reproduction for use in schools from works that, according to their nature and designation, are designed for use in schools or for teaching purposes. In Germany, there is no such ban with regard to the reproduction right, but there is one for the right of

44. Cf. to this effect, *N. Flechsig*, 'Grundlagen des Europäischen Urheberrechts', 5 *et seq.*
45. Cf. M. Rehbinder, *Urheberrecht* (12 edn, München, C. H.Beck, 2002), Section 8, margin No. 82 *et seq.*
46. T. Dreier, 'Die Umsetzung der Urheberrechtsrichtlinie 2001/29/EG in deutsches Recht', 34.
47. Cf. to this effect A. Wiebe, 'Abwehr unerwünschter Links' in *Hyperlinks*, S. Ernst/I. Vassilaki/A. Wiebe (eds), (Köln, Verlag Otto Schmidt, 2002), Chapter B. margin nos. 73 *et seq.*; M. Neubauer in note to Federal Court of Justice BGH 17 July 2003, I ZR 259/00 – *Paperboy* – [2003] *TeleKommunikations- und MedienRecht*, 445.

making available to the public within the meaning of the Directive, Section 52 a Paragraph 2 of the German Copyright Act and Section 46 of the draft bill on copyright reform ('second basket' – 'zweiter Korb').[48] In contrast, the making available to the public has not been expressly ruled out in Austria, but its prohibition results from Section 42 Paragraph 5, 18a of the Austrian Copyright Act.[49]

With regard to the free use of works for electronic press reviews, the limitation provided for by Article 5(3)(c) is of relevance and again requires clarification.[50] In Austria, electronic press reviews in the form of an electronic research database without editorial treatment seem to be generally prohibited.[51] The result of the German jurisprudence of the Federal Court of Justice is similar; according to the Court's decisions, however, press reviews that are transmitted electronically but whose function and uses do not exceed that of traditional press reviews are admissible.[52] In literature, this is observed critically with a view to the Information Society Directive.[53] Since the digital use might potentially impair the interests of the authors, the courts and the legislator are very restrictive when it comes to expanding the limitations to include electronic press reviews. Nevertheless, the free use of works for one's own use according to Section 42 Paragraph 1 of the Austrian Copyright Act was extended from 'paper and similar carriers' to include 'analogue use(s)'. According to the legislative materials, these analogue uses also include scanning, as only a copy of the template can be reproduced, which shows a rather broad interpretation. If, however, it is taken into consideration that the file produced in the course of a scanning process can both be distributed via digital networks and edited by means of conversion into a suitable format, it becomes evident that this regulation can no longer invoke the exception provided for in Article 5(3)(o) of the Information Society Directive which applies exclusively to analogue uses.[54] This has been clarified in the adopted version by means of reference to analogue forms of use. The preparation of electronic press reviews is therefore not covered by the exemption.[55] The preparation by third parties within the scope

48. German Federal Ministry of Justice, 'Draft Bill for a second law on the regulation of copyright in the information society' <www.urheberrecht.org/topic/Korb-2/bmj/760.pdf>, 27 September 2004.
49. Cf. M. Neubauer, 'Urheberrecht und digitale Netze' in *Internetrecht*, A. Wiebe (ed), (Wien, Springer, 2004), 74.
50. Cf. dazu auch H. Wittmann [2001] 145; G. Spindler [2002] 114.
51. Cf. M. Neubauer in Wiebe [2004] p.75.
52. Federal Court of Justice 11 July 2002, I ZR 255/00, [2002] *Computer und Recht*, 827.
53. Cf. C. Berger, 'Elektronische Pressespiegel und Informationsrichtlinie' [2004] *Computer und Recht*, 360.
54. Cf. A. Wiebe, 'Das neue "digitale" Urheberrecht – Eine erste Bewertung' [2003] *Medien und Recht*, 311; M. Fallenböck/S. Nitzl, 'Urheberrechtliche Rahmenbedingungen für elektronische Pressespiegel' [2003] *Medien und Recht*, 102. Regarding conformity with the directive cf. also M. Walter, 'Ministerialentwurf einer UrhGNov 2002 – Ausgewählte Aspekte', 223.
55. Section 44 Paragraph 1 of the Austrian Copyright Act ('öUrhG') is not applicable to electronic press reviews, cf. Austrian Supreme Court OGH 12 June 2001, 4 Ob 140/01v, [2001]

described whose possibilities do not exceed that of analogue use is conceivable, at least in Austria and Germany, (cf. Section 42a Sub-paragraph (3) of the Austrian Copyright Act, Section 53 Paragraph 2 of the German Copyright Act;). That means that the distribution of content via value-added services – on the basis of the limitation provision – is therefore possible within certain limits. Section 53a Paragraph 1, 2nd sentence of the draft bill for the 'second basket' ('zweiter Korb') of the German Copyright Act also provides for a relevant parallel regulation to the transmission of copies on order.[56] It is expected that the planned amendment of Section 53 (2) No. 2 will further limit the admissibility of electronic press archives to archives in the public interest.

c. Sanctions Under the Information Society Directive

In this respect, it is mainly the requirement of 'judicial order' for enforcing a right to information provided for in Article 8(3) that still needs to be clarified.[57] From the point of view of the rightholders it is desirable that rights to information also exist irrespective of an injunction issued by a judge so that they are also able to prosecute infringements of the law out-of-court. It has become evident, with regards to the enforcement of rights to information against access providers with respect to the data of persons infringing copyrights, that the interrelations among and demarcations of the secondary law provisions of the Information Society Directive, the E-Commerce Directive, the Enforcement Directive and the planned 'European Parliament and Council Directive on criminal measures aimed at ensuring the enforcement of intellectual property rights'[58] still require clarification.[59] The same is true with respect to data protection law and the protection of communication secrecy pursuant to national law.

3. Enforcement Directive

The very general wording of the provisions of the Directive grants the national legislator considerable freedom regarding the implementation of the Enforcement Directive. This does, however, also lead to problems and lack of clarity. This concerns, for instance, the modalities of the right to information[60] and the question as to whether universities become active as access providers 'on a

Medien und Recht, 385 (*Walter*); the same applies for the reworded Section 42, paragraph 1 of the Copyright Act, cf. M. Fallenböck/ S. Nitzl [2003] 102.

56. *See*, to this effect, also infra C.2.a), cf. also Federal Court of Justice BGH 25 February 1999, I ZR 118/96, [1999] *Gewerblicher Rechtsschutz und Urheberrecht*, 709.
57. Cf. A. Wiebe, 'Auskunftsverpflichtung der Access Provider' [2005] *Medien und Recht* Issue 4 Supplement.
58. Cf. COM(2005) 276.
59. *See*, to this effect, A. Wiebe [2005]
60. Cf. D. Frey/ M. Rudolph, 'EU-Richtlinie zur Durchsetzung der Rechte geistigen Eigentums' [2004] *Zeitschrift für Urheber- und Medienrecht*, 525.

commercial scale' and are thus under an obligation to provide information.[61] Furthermore, the enforcement instruments in the hands of the rightholders are comprehensive. It seems that the strongest instruments from all Member States have been included in this Directive. It will not always be possible to smoothly integrate these instruments into the national jurisdictions. Some are rather of a criminal law nature, such as seizure and search of premises, but are intended to be measures under civil law. This was caused by the uncertainty regarding the criminal law competencies of the EU at the time the Directive was issued. In the meantime, the ECJ has created a bit more clarity in this respect.[62] The decision to make a 'new start'[63] with the planned provisions for sanctions under criminal law was probably caused not least by the lack of clarity in this respect.

The success of the promotion of the production of content cannot be guaranteed by means of legal measures of enforcement alone. The use of swapping services for downloading pirate copies of films or pieces of music was one of the reasons for tightening the enforcement instruments. The increased use of such instruments in recent years also pursued the objective of creating awareness that these downloads are unlawful, because the works are protected goods that are not freely available. Given the conditions of online communications, a strategy which is solely based on the enforcement of legal rights will not however, be very promising as the development of the exchanges on the Internet has shown. Rather, it is also necessary to develop new business models which make a legal use acceptable.

4. Country-of-origin and Country-of-transmission Principles

a. Country-of-transmission Principle

In several Member States, the internal distribution of cross-border broadcasting programmes in hotel rooms is regarded as an activity of exploitation relevant under copyright law. The ECJ found that this issue is not governed by the Cable and Satellite Directive,[64] but considered such distribution to be an act of communication to the public.[65] To the extent the Austrian Supreme Court sees this as a copyright-free reception, the court's view is in violation of EU legislation, in particular with regard to Article 3 of the Information Society

61. Cf. D. Frey/ M. Rudolph [2004] 526.
62. *Commission of the European Communities v. Council of the European Union,* Case No. C-176/03 [2005] ECR, I-7879.
63. Cf. Heise online, 'Neustart bei EU-Gesetz zur Durchsetzung geistiger Eigentumsrechte', <www.heise.de> 30 November 2005.
64. Entidad de Gestión de Derechos de los Productores Audiovisuales (Egeda) v. Hostelería Asturiana SA (Hoasa), Case No. C-293/98, [2000] ECR, I-629.
65. So in ECJ Case C-293/98, *Egeda*, [2000] ECR, I-629, para. 28; F. Mahr, 'Interne Weiterleitung von grenzüberschreitenden Rundfunksendungen in die Hotelzimmer – Anmerkung zu EuGH 3 February 2000 (sechste Kammer) in der Rechtssache C-293/98' [2000] *Medien und Recht*, 157.

Directive,[66] and also in contradiction to the minimum standards laid down under the Revised Berne Convention with which the EU has committed itself to comply.[67]

b. Country-of-origin Principle

Following the decision regarding a Dutch Internet pharmacy, to which the E-Commerce Directive did not yet apply, it has to be assumed that mail order and advertising prohibitions according to Articles 28, 30 EC are admissible with regard to medicinal products subject to a doctor's prescription but not for non-prescription medicines. The latter are governed by the country-of-origin principle.[68] The application of this principle entails two problems: First, it causes discrimination against nationals in cases not covered by EU law,[69] which can only be counteracted in accordance with national law. Second, there is the risk of a so-called 'race to the bottom'. The resulting 'country shopping' or 'law shopping'[70] would hardly be accomplishable for small and medium-sized enterprises.[71] As a result, the economic laws would level off at a lower standard.[72]

The country-of-origin principle contributes to the realization of the single market by making cross-border business activities easier. On the other hand, the remaining fragmentation of the law in the Member States may result in distortions of competition. This increases the pressure for the Member States to take harmonization measures.[73] In addition, the companies concerned may use legally non-binding economic means of self-regulation to combat the 'race to the bottom', like, for instance, codes of conduct.[74]

---

66. OJ 2001 L 167/10.
67. F. Mahr, 'Interne Weiterleitung von grenzüberschreitenden Rundfunksendungen in die Hotelzimmer – Anmerkung zu EuGH 3 February 2000 (sechste Kammer) in der Rechtssache C-293/98', 159.
68. Cf. *Deutscher Apothekerverband eV v. 0800 DocMorris NV and Jacques Waterval*, Case No. C-322/01, [2003] ECR, I-14887; M. Nemetz, 'Internetapotheken – Post DocMorris' [2004] *ecolex*, 991.
69. M. Blasi, *Das Herkunftslandprinzip der Fernseh- und E-Commerce-Richtlinie* (Köln, Carl Heymanns, 2004), p. 418; cf. also *Konsumentombudsmannen (KO) v. De Agostini (Svenska) Förlag AB* (C-34/95) and TV-Shop i Sverige AB, Case No. C- 34/95 et al., [1997] ECR I -3843.
70. M. Blasi [2004] p. 416; T. Hoeren , 'Vorschlag für eine EU-Richtlinie über E-Commerce – Eine erste kritische Analyse' [1999] *MultiMedia und Recht*, 194.
71. M. Blasi [2004] p. 416; U. Fritze/C. Holzbach, 'Die Electronic-Commerce-Richtlinie' [2000] *Wettbewerb in Recht und Praxis*, 875; P. Mankowski, 'Internet und Internationales Wettbewerbsrecht' [1999] *Gewerblicher Rechtsschutz und Urheberrecht International*, 914.
72. M. Blasi [2004] p. 428; J. Micklitz/ H. Keßler, 'Europäisches Lauterkeitsrecht – Dogmatische und ökonomische Aspekte einer Harmonisierung des Wettbewerbsverhaltensrechts im europäischen Binnenmarkt' [2002] *Gewerblicher Rechtsschutz und Urheberrecht International*, 888; P. Mankowski [1999] 914.
73. M. Blasi [2004] p. 428.
74. Cf. Article 16 E-Commerce Directive, OJ 2000 L 178/1.

For copyright as a whole, the application of the country-of-origin principles has been excluded by the E-Commerce Directive. From a legal policy point of view the different treatment of this area is questionable. The transfer of the country-of-transmission and/or the country-of-origin principles to the Internet and/or the application of a universality principle are being discussed as alternatives to the principle of territoriality.[75] If, for instance, the 'country of reception' was determinative of the act of making available under the right of making available to the public, this would mean that, as a consequence, the legal status of a website under copyright law depends on the respective jurisdiction. If, however, the country-of-origin principle is applied, only one jurisdiction is decisive, so rights would have to be acquired for a single country only.[76] If the country-of-origin principle is applied, a 'race to the bottom', which has already taken place in other areas, is to be envisaged both regarding the emergence of the protection and the scope of the protection.[77]

5. Collective Exploitation of Rights and Collecting Societies

The transnational online exploitation of copyright and neighbouring rights is made extremely difficult by the distribution between the 450 different national collecting societies in the Member States. If, for instance, entrepreneurs want to operate an online music trading business or a web radio, they must enter into relevant agreements with the collecting societies in all of the Member States in which they intend to offer their services. The transaction costs are enormous and each agreement is only valid in the individual Member State. An author can only enter into exploitation agreements with the collecting societies in the Member State in which he or she is domiciled.

Because of the EU-wide distribution of the market between the collecting societies the system of license fees and tariffs is not transparent either. The distribution of the license fees discriminates against authors from other Member States since often there are no relevant agreements between the collecting societies. The agreements entered into between the collecting societies do not contain any provisions for the distribution of license fees to the respective collecting society in the State where the author resides.

As a consequence of the resulting limitations to the freedom of services, the turnover generated within the EU with copyright protected online content

75. Cf. H. Schack, *Urheber- und Urhebervertragsrecht* (2nd ed, Tübingen. Mohr Siebeck, 2001), margin No. 806 *et seq.*; S. Bechtold, 'Multimediarecht und Urheberrecht – einige grundsätzliche Anmerkungen' [1998] *Gewerblicher Rechtsschutz und Urheberrecht*, 23; M. Fallenböck, 'Internationales Urheberrecht und digitale Wirtschaft' in *Urheberrecht in der digitalen Wirtschaft – Beiträge zu Internet, Telekommunikation und Software*, M. Fallenböck/F. Galla/S. Stockinger (eds) (Wien, MANZ, 2005), p. 157; T. Dreier, 'Die Umsetzung der Urheberrechtsrichtlinie 2001/29/EG in deutsches Recht', 32.
76. Cf. T. Dreier, 'Die Umsetzung der Urheberrechtsrichtlinie 2001/29/EG in deutsches Recht', 33; *see,* to this effect, also Communication on copyrights, COM(2004) 261, 9.
77. There is a wide lack of harmonization in both areas, cf. SEC(2004) 995, 14, 16.

is so far comparatively small. In the year 2004, the income from online content in the USA was eight times (?) higher than in Western Europe.[78]

The Commission therefore concluded that there was an urgent need for action and has already prepared specific proposals for the adaptation of the collective exploitation of rights and the collecting societies.[79] According to these proposals, it is to be the authors' free choice as to which collecting societies within the EU they want to enter into a contract. This 'selected collecting society' would then represent the authors throughout Europe in the exploitation of their rights, e.g., for a certain type of exploitation. This would reduce the costs for the author, create competition and increase the efficiency of the collecting societies.[80]

In the opinion of the Commission, this solution[81] would encourage legal certainty and the transparency of the distribution of royalty payments. In addition, the collecting societies should publish their tariffs and design their license contracts in a reasonable and adequate manner. The users should also be given the opportunity to contest the license fees in or out of court.[82]

Increased income creates additional incentives for the author to produce content. The intra-Community trade in content would grow. Currently, there are a few collecting societies facing vertically integrated media companies with stronger bargaining power on the market. Increased competition would increase the bargaining power of the collecting societies. On the other hand, the collecting societies fear that their position might be weakened if the present structures are broken up.[83]

Finally the Commission Recommendation of 18 May 2005[84] on collective cross-border management of copyright and related rights for legitimate online music services was published. It invites Member States to take all necessary steps to facilitate the growth of online services by a suitable legislation for the management of rights without hindering EU-wide licensing. In addition, right holders should be able to choose the legal body for the management of online exploitation as well as the territorial scope of the management.

78. Cf. Commission Staff Working Document, Study on a Community initiative on the cross-border collective management of copyright, <ec.europa.eu/internal_market/copyright/docs/management/study-collectivemgmt_en.pdf> 19 June 2006.
79. Cf. Communication on copyrights, COM(2004) 261; Commission Staff Working Document, Study on a Community initiative on the cross-border collective management of copyright.
80. Commission Staff Working Document, Study on a Community initiative on the cross-border collective management of copyright 35 *et seq.*
81. Regarding the consequences cf. Commission Staff Working Document, Study on a Community Initiative on the Cross-Border Collective Management of Copyright, 36–48.
82. Cf. Communication on copyrights, COM(2004) 261, 18.
83. Financial Times Deutschland from 26 July 2005, 'GEMA warnt vor europaweiten Musiklizenzen' <www.ftd.de/tm/me/15786.html> 17 August 2005.
84. Commission Recommendation 2005/737/EC of 18 May 2005 on collective cross-border management of copyright and related rights for legitimate online music services, OJ 2005 L 276/54.

Recommendations regarding the rules for the relationship between rightholders and collecting societies are also part of the document.

6. Resale Rights Directive

It is uncertain whether the Resale Rights Directive may also be applied to sales transactions via the Internet. This is only definitely the case if an internet forum is to be regarded as a member of the art market,[85] such as, for instance, a trading platform specializing in the sale of works of art. The minimum selling price should, in any case, be below EUR 3,000 – so that in particular, young artists can also benefit from the resale right.[86] The exceptionally long implementation period expired in January 2006 but due to the low political consensus at the European level it has to be feared that some Member States have only implemented 'minimal versions' of the Resale Rights Directive.[87]

7. Harmonization of the Copyright Contract Law

In the area of copyright contract law the diverse interests clash. There are great differences between the regulations in the individual Member States which are also caused by differing dogmatic structures of civil law. In Germany, a reform was carried out in 2002 which was heavily debated politically.[88]

Today, many authors work under employment or services contracts or in principal-agent relationships so that a good portion of the income from protected works is paid for intermediary services and does not flow to the authors themselves. The bargaining position of the authors is usually rather weak, they can only choose between accepting the contractual provisions offered to them or refusing to enter into an agreement at all. The author is in a position of imbalance comparable to that of a consumer. An association of the free authors in order to strengthen their negotiating position would be critical under cartel law.[89] The control of the contracts by the court may also have adverse effects for the authors.[90]

---

85. H. Karl, 'Folgerecht-RL: Harmonisierung auf niedrigem Niveau? – Bericht von der Arbeitssitzung der ALAI-Landesgruppe Österreich vom 30 June 2005 [2005] *Medien und Recht*, 227.
86. H. Karl, 'Folgerecht-RL: Harmonisierung auf niedrigem Niveau? – Bericht von der Arbeitssitzung der ALAI-Landesgruppe Österreich vom 30 June 2005, 228.
87. Cf. also H. Karl, 'Folgerecht-RL: Harmonisierung auf niedrigem Niveau? – Bericht von der Arbeitssitzung der ALAI-Landesgruppe Österreich vom 30 June 2005, 228; M. Walter, 'Diskussionsentwurf für die Umsetzung der Folgerecht-RL in das österreichische Recht' [2005] *Medien und Recht*, 244.
88. German Act on the encouragement of author's right ('Urheberstärkungsrecht') 2002, German Law Gazette dBGBl I, 1155.
89. H. Schack, 'Neuregelung des Urhebervertragsrechts – Kritische Anmerkung zum Professorenentwurf' [2001] *Zeitschrift für Urheber- und Medienrecht*, 453; H. Schack, *Urheber- und Urhebervertragsrecht*, margin No. 993.

On the other hand, there is a demand for ensuring a certain minimum standard for the authors. Guaranteeing reasonable remuneration may be considered a very important element for creating incentives for creative activities. This view is also shared by the European legislator: 'Adequate legal protection of intellectual property rights is necessary in order to guarantee the availability of such a reward.'[91]

For these reasons, there is urgent need to strengthen the position of the authors.[92] This should include unwaivable claims for adequate compensation. The remuneration schemes for authors must be adapted to digital exploitation.[93] Further issues include the interpretation of contracts,[94] agreements concerning future types of use and distribution of works,[95] the duration of the contract, the termination of contracts[96] and the introduction of a 'best seller clause' and/or a 'fairness clause'.[97]

In this context, the issue of harmonization of the author's moral rights has to be dealt with. Because of the different approaches within Europe, this issue has so far always been excluded. With regard to the online exploitation of protected works, the issue of the scope and the possibility of waiving the relevant rights becomes increasingly important. In the medium-term, the growing relevance of these rights, also from an economic point of view, will require a certain degree of harmonization. For the time being, however, no feasible solution is in sight because of the large differences.

8. Consolidation of the European Copyright Law

After around 15 years of intensive regulatory activity in the area of copyright, a consolidation seems to make sense. One example of the lack of coherence is the different treatment of the reproduction right in the various directives.

---

90. H. Schack, 'Neuregelung des Urhebervertragsrechts – Kritische Anmerkung zum Professorenentwurf', 453.
91. Recital 10 of the Information Society Directive, OJ 2001 L 167/10.
92. Cf. in greater detail M. Walter, 'Die vier Säulen des Urheberrechts – Zugleich eine Standortbestimmung der österr Urheberrechtsreform nach der UrhGNov 1997' [1999] *Zeitschrift für Rechtsvergleichung, Internationales Privatrecht und Europarecht*, 88.
93. COM, 'Copyright at the Crossroads ?'[2005] *Single Market News*, Issue 37, 12; cf. Recital 10 of the Information Society Directive, OJ 2001 L 167/10.
94. Austrian Supreme Court OGH 2 June 1981, 4 Ob 347/81, [1982] *Österreichische Blätter für Gewerblichen Rechtsschutz*, 52; 23 March 1993, 4 Ob 121/92, MR 1993, 111 (*Walter*); 24 June 2003, 4 Ob 70/03b, [2003] *Medien und Recht*, 315; for Germany T. Dreier/G. Schulze, *Urheberrechtsgesetz*, Section 31, paragraph 5, margin No. 64–102.
95. Austrian Supreme Court OGH 18 October 1994, 4 Ob 93/94, [1995] *Medien und Recht*, 191 (*Walter*); for Germany T. Dreier/G. Schulze, *Urheberrechtsgesetz*, Section 31, paragraph 4, margin No. 103–149.
96. Cf. Austrian Supreme Court OGH 26 January 1999, 4 Ob 318/96p, [1999] *Medien und Recht*, 98 (*Walter*).
97. Cf. T. Dreier/G. Schulze, *Urheberrechtsgesetz*, Section 32a; C. Berger, 'Grundfragen der "weiteren Beteiligung" des Urhebers nach § 32a UrhG' [2003] *Gewerblicher Rechtsschutz und Urheberrecht*, 675.

The definition in Article 2 of Directive 2001/29/EC also includes direct and indirect reproductions and is based on Article 10 of the Rome Convention.[98] This provision was already repeated in Article 7(1) of the Rental Directive.[99] Two further directives deal with the right of reproduction without mentioning indirect reproduction.[100] Problems arise whenever the application of several directives is possible, for instance in the case of a DVD that contains both literary and artistic works and software. For this reason, the Working Paper also proposes the harmonization of the terminology used in the various directives.[101]

There is also some divergence with regard to transient and incidental reproductions as an exemption from the reproduction right: According to Article 5(1) in conjunction with Article 4 of the Software Directive this exemption does not apply to intermediaries, whereas this is the case according to Article 5(1) of the Information Society Directive. Here, the Software Directive should be adapted to the Information Society Directive.[102]

Further divergences refer to the right of communication/making available to the public for computer programmes, the scope of protection for music by several authors and a possible exception for disabled persons for the use of databases. In these areas, the Commission is planning legal adaptations in some points.[103] Furthermore, it is intended to analyze the economic consequences of the leeway that is left for arrangements as far as the criteria relevant for achieving protection (with regard to the 'points of attachment') under international copyright conventions is concerned.[104]

The EU is presently carrying out an estimate of the impact of the amendment of copyright law, which will probably be completed in the first half-year of 2006. The political debate on a reform of the copyright law will then be launched in autumn 2006.[105]

C. Summary

The main reason for starting a limited harmonization of the European copyright law was the development of the information technology which called for an adaptation of the existing regulations. This demand was met by the Information Society Directive. The exploitation rights under copyright law were defined broadly and limitation provisions were listed, most of which are, however, optional provisions. There is still lack of clarity regarding the scope

98. Federal Law Gazette BGBl 1973/413.
99. OJ 1992 L 346/61.
100. Article 4(a) Software Directive, OJ 1991 L 122/42 and Article 5 lit(a) Database Directive, OJ 1996 L 77/20.
101. SEC(2004) 995, 5 *et seq.*
102. SEC(2004) 995, 7 *et seq.*
103. SEC(2004) 995, 17.
104. SEC(2004) 995, 15 f, 17.
105. COM, 'Copyright at the Crossroads ?', 14.

of the online law with respect to e-learning, electronic press reviews and the operation of search engines. The application of the first sale doctrine to the distribution right in case of online transmission of works is mostly refused so that it remains subject to the control of the rightholders. The Enforcement Directive has harmonized and strengthened the instruments for the enforcement of claims under copyright law.

With regard to satellite and cable broadcasts and television broadcasts, the country-of-transmission or the country-of-origin principle was laid down according to which regulation may only take place in the country of origin. This principle serves the purpose of creating legal security and increases the pressure towards harmonization, but only indirectly contributes to the realization of the internal market. The application of the country-of-origin principle to copyright protection in the online area was, however, excluded by the E-Commerce Directive. The different treatment of this area must be questioned from a legal policy point of view.

The Commission has identified need for action regarding the cross-border activities performed by the collecting societies. Furthermore, the collective exploitation of rights has to be coordinated with the use of digital rights management systems as to which the Information Society Directive provides for strong legal protection. In addition, a consolidation of the secondary law provisions issued so far is required. From a legal policy point of view, the harmonization of the copyright contract law must also be put on the agenda.

Regarding the protection of databases, the European legislator, apart from harmonizing copyright protection, has introduced a new *sui generis* right which aims at the protection of investments in the creation and maintenance of databases. The broad protection approach pursued here has been considerably limited by the case law of the ECJ.

II. THE NECESSITY FOR EXCLUSIVITY – ENSURING FUNCTIONING MARKET STRUCTURES ON THE CONTENT MARKETS

According to the theory of dynamic competition, the interplay of proactive and reactive competition serves the purpose of innovation. The creation of new products and procedures, and their distribution by means of imitation, continuously elevates the service quality to a new level. Intellectual goods are basically available for everyone unless they are expressly protected by special laws (public domain principle).

Nevertheless, intangible goods show special characteristics of public goods in the economic sense that distinguish them from tangible objects.[106] Only if

106. Cf. A. Wiebe, 'Information als Schutzgegenstand im System des geistigen Eigentums' in *Information als Wirtschaftsgut*, H. Fiedler/H. Ullrich (eds), (Köln, Otto Schmidt Verlag, 1997), p. 103 with further reference.

the object to be protected is determined and defined by law, can these goods become tradable economic goods, as no one would be prepared to pay for them if they were freely available. The scope of the exploitation rights then controls the intensity of the distribution of such goods. Copyright and neighbouring rights thus form the basis for the economic operations performed in the content industry. [107]

The incentive to produce and/or create intangible goods is only created by conferring exclusive rights. If the economically relevant activities are divided into the three levels of innovation, production and consumption, the copyright, as a limitation on the production level, like the other industrial property rights, serves the purpose of creating incentives on the level of innovation.[108] The creation of exclusive rights thus encourages the promotion of competition.

Even advocates of the free distribution of content, that follow, for instance, the principles of Open Source and Open Content, are in favour of invoking the right of exclusivity under copyright law.[109] The recognition of the protection of content therefore is a prerequisite for the emergence of markets. The actual problem, from a legal and economic point of view, is the 'fine tuning' between the degree of protection (incentive) and the distribution.

III. CREATING A BALANCE – PROTECTION OF THIRD PARTIES AND FURTHER GENERAL INTERESTS

A. REVIEW OF THE STATUS QUO

The protection of creative production of information goods includes a balance of the partially diametrical interests of authors, exploiters, other creators, users and the general public. Copyright itself safeguards the various interests by defining the object of protection, formulating the exploitation rights and providing for a limited duration of protection. The protection of other creators and of science is, for instance, encouraged by the fact that doctrines and methodology are kept free from protection. In addition, the various interests are taken into account by means of the limitation provisions provided for by copyright law. Their scope is also founded in constitutional law, which on a European level has, for instance, been guaranteed by the application of Article 10 of the ECHR Convention.[110] The necessity of free access of the general public to information

107. Cf. T. Dreier, 'Urheberrecht an der Schwelle des 3. Jahrtausends – Einige Gedanken zur Zukunft des Urheberrechts' [2000] *Computer und Recht*, 45.
108. Cf. C. von Weizsäcker, 'Rechte und Verhältnisse in der modernen Wirtschaftslehre' (1981) 34 *KYKLOS*, 349 *et seq.*; A. Wiebe in H. Fiedler/H. Ullrich [1997] p. 105.
109. T. Dreier [2000] 45.
110. Cf. to this effect, Austrian Supreme Court OGH 24 June 2003, 4 Ob 105/03z, [2003] *Medien und Recht*, 317; Austrian Supreme Court OGH 20 May 2003, 4 Ob 100/03i, [2003] *Medien und Recht*, 387; Austrian Supreme Court OGH 3 October 2000, 4 Ob 224/00w, [2000] *Medien und Recht*, 373.

has also been affirmed by national courts according to national constitutional law.[111]

1. Information Society Directive

a. Limitations

The limitation on private copying is based on the fact that the reproduction for private use cannot be controlled and is not to be controlled by the copyright holder. Besides, less substantial material impairments of the primary market are to be feared if conventional media without the more advanced possibilities of copying works are being used.[112]

The limitation for educational, scientific or research purposes are particularly important with respect to the general interest in access to information and the freedom of information. An important case is the distribution of copies by libraries.[113] Furthermore, the scope of the use of archives and the possibilities to use the online medium are of importance. Finally, the scope of the provision of information in educational institutions, for instance in the course of e-learning programmes, is of relevance.

b. Technological Protection Measures/DRM

Article 6 provides for legal protection of technological measures against circumvention.[114] This includes devices whose primary purpose is circumvention. Article 6(4) provides for regulations in order to enforce the copyright limitations against technological protection.

c. Device and Media Charges, Double Remuneration

As the two systems of direct remuneration via DRM systems on the one hand and media and/or device charges on the other hand exist in parallel, there is the possibility of double remuneration, meaning that the rightholders might receive more than they are actually entitled to.

---

111. Cf. e.g., Federal Court of Justice 25 February 1999, Civil Law Case No. I ZR 118/96, [1999] *Gewerblicher Rechtschutz und Urheberrecht*, 707.
112. Cf. U. Decker, in *Urheberrechtsgesetz*, P. Möhring/K. Nicolini (eds), (2nd edn, München, Franz Vahlen, 2000), Section 53, margin No. 4.
113. Cf. Federal Court of Justice BGH 25 February 1999, I ZR 118/96, [1999] *Gewerblicher Rechtschutz und Urheberrecht*, 707.
114. Cf. B. Stickelbrock, 'Die Zukunft der Privatkopie im digitalen Zeitalter' [2004] *Gewerblicher Rechtschutz und Urheberrecht*, 742.

2. First Sale Doctrine Online

The principle of exhaustion or first sale doctrine is essential for the interests of the users and the general public in the merchantability of the protected works. The distribution of a copy that has been sold on the market can no longer be controlled by the holder of the right. The application of the first sale doctrine to the online transmission of protected works is disputed. In the three German-speaking countries alone considerable differences can be found in the legal positions in this respect. In Germany, the prevailing opinion is now denying an exhaustive effect of downloading. In Austria, there is strong opinion in favour of the exhaustion regarding the first permanent incorporation, provided that the copy must not be put online again and that the first user, in case of a resale, must not keep a copy of his own so that he is not a lawful user any more.[115] In Switzerland, application of the first sale doctrine to the intangible distribution is also predominantly supported and the latter is also regarded to be a 'sale'.[116]

On the level of European law, Article 3(3) of the Information Society Directive clearly demonstrates that the first sale doctrine does not apply to the online transmission of protected works.[117] This view has been expressly affirmed by the ECJ in its most recent decisions on database law.[118] Only the specific reasoning in Recital 29 appears somehow problematic, according to which the question of exhaustion does in no way arise in the case of online services.

3. Enforcement Directive

The strengthening of the enforcement of the rights of authors and holders of other rights as well as of licensees regarding their entitlement to receive information and the preservation of evidence according to the Enforcement Directive results in the emergence of conflicts with the legally protected interests of parties involved and third parties. These interests include data protection, the right to privacy and the protection of secrets.

---

115. Cf. M. Walter, *Urheberrechtsgesetz – UrhGNov 2003* (Wien, Medien und Recht, 2003), p. 26 *et seq.*
116. Cf. M. Widmer, *Open Source Software – Urheberrechtliche Aspekte freier Software* (Bern, Stämpfli, 2003), p. 93 *et seq.*, with further reference. According to this provision, the copy that remains with the seller is no longer deemed to be the same copy as the one sold to the seller.
117. Cf. also Recital 25 of the Information Society Directive, OJ 2001 L 167/10; critical opinion by T. Hoeren, 'Entwurf einer EU-Richtlinie zum Urheberrecht in der Informationsgesellschaft' [2000] *MultiMedia und Recht*, 517; C. Berger, 'Urheberrechtliche Erschöpfungslehre und digitale Informationstechnologie' [2002] *Gewerblicher Rechtsschutz und Urheberrecht*, 200 *et seq.*; G. Spindler, 'Europäisches Urheberrecht in der Informationsgesellschaft', 110.
118. ECJ Case C-203/02, *William Hill*, [2004] ECR I-10415.

4. Conditional Access Directive

With regard to the Conditional Access Directive[119] there are two main problematic issues: first, the question of the distinction from the protection of technological protection measures pursuant to the Information Society Directive,[120] and second, the question as to when a device as defined in Article 2(e) of Directive 98/84/EC[121] is 'designed' to give access to a protected service without authorization.

5. Obligations to Provide Information and Transparency in E-commerce

Online providers of content must observe the obligations to provide information pursuant to the E-Commerce Directive.[122] The obligation to make available the technical means for identifying and correcting input errors also serves the purpose of protecting the user. Further information obligations and a right of withdrawal are provided for by the Directive on Distance Selling.[123]

B. Problem Analysis

1. Information Society Directive

a. Limitations

From the point of view of the users of content, it is of importance whether the making of a private copy requires that this copy be reproduced from a 'legal source'. This problem occurs in particular in connection with downloads from private P2P networks. Here, there are still considerable uncertainties both from a legal point of view and regarding the factual assessment. The criterion of the existence of an 'evidently lawful original' according to Section 53 of the German Copyright Act is beneficial to the interests of the users, but in practice has proven to be too unspecific. Not least the inclusion of the 'three-step test' that – on the basis of Article 13 TRIPS, Article 10 WCT, Article 16(2) WPPT – is laid down in Article 5(5) of the Directive is alone in speaking for the requirement of a 'legal source'.[124] Apart from the lawful preparation of

119. OJ 1998 L 320/54.
120. Cf. O. Linnenborn, 'Update: Europäisches Urheberrecht in der Informationsgesellschaft' [2001] *Kommunikation & Recht*, 399.
121. Directive 98/84/EC on the legal protection of services based on, and consisting of, conditional access, OJ L 320/54, 1998.
122. OJ 2000 L 178/1.
123. OJ 1997 L 144/19.
124. M. Neubauer in A. Wiebe [2004] p. 78; in greater detail *see* F. Philapitsch, 'Zum Erfordernis einer legalen Quelle für die Digitale Privatkopie' [2004] *Medien und Recht*, 111.

the source used for copying, another criterion should still be whether the use of a work arose from lawful processes.[125] The problems that occur in practice show, however, that a need remains for clarification and harmonization in this area.

The exploitation interests of the authors are increasingly impaired because of the spreading of analogue and/or reprographic reproduction technologies and also because of the use of digital media. This changes the balance of interests that forms the basis of the limitation for private copying. Furthermore, a broad limitation for private copies can no longer be easily justified with reference to the freedom of information or a proprietary right to the data carrier acquired.[126] In addition, in the future private use will become measurable with the help of DRM systems. Although conflicts with data protection law are bound to arise in this context and will have to be solved, that means that one of the main arguments[127] for the copyright privilege of the private sector is then no longer available. Against this backdrop, the provision of Article 5(2)(b) of the Information Society Directive, according to which private copies are, in general, protected but the enforcement in case of the use of technological protection mechanisms may be banned, is therefore welcome. The prerequisite is, however that the use of such systems should not result in new barriers to access. Constitutional law guarantees access to information, this thus prompts the question whether current digital copying restrictions should be maintained. Having said this, further examination into the legal, political and economical aspects is also still required before a decision can be made. This is even more true for efforts regarding the abolition of private copying in the analogue area.

The scope of the limitation regarding archives – Article 5(2)(c) of the Information Society Directive – is of relevance to the distribution of electronic copies from libraries. The general question in this context is how far the technical process of the production can be left to a third party and whether the subsequent sending – be it by mail or electronically – is also covered by the respective limitation.[128] In the opinion of the Capital Market Group of German Book Trades ('Börsenverein des Deutschen Buchhandels') (and of other European associations), the electronic transmission of copies is in violation of European copyright so that it has filed a lawsuit with the Regional Court of Munich and a complaint with the European Commission (cf. also Section 53a of the draft

125. Cf. M. Walter, *Urheberrechtsgesetz – UrhG Nov 2003*, p. 54; cf. Section 53, paragraph 1 German Copyright Act ('dUrhG') draft bill on the 'second basket).
126. Cf. Federal Constitutional Court BVerfG 25 July 2005, 1 BvR 2182/04, [2005] *MultiMedia und Recht*, 751 (*Köcher/Kaufmann*); cf. to this effect, heise online, 'Verfassungsbeschwerde gegen, Un-CDs' abgewiesen', <www.heise.de> 7 September 2005.
127. Cf. U. Decker, in *Urheberrechtsgesetz*, P. Möhring/K. Nicolini (eds), Section 53, margin No. 1.
128. Cf. to this effect, Federal Court of Justice BGH 25 February 1999, Civil Law Case No. I ZR 118/96, [1999] *Gewerblicher Rechtsschutz und Urheberrecht*, 707; Section 53a of the German Copyright Act ('dUrhG') draft bill on the 'second basket'.

bill regarding the 'second basket' ('zweiter Korb') of the reform of the German Copyright Act).[129]

The scope of the archive limitation is also a question of relevance for new 'MP3 copy services'[130] and full-text 'libraries'[131] and full-text research options such as those planned by google[132] or amazon.[133] Even if these are private providers, the increasing level of digitization and the growing number of private databases have made the ensuring of access to information in this area an increasingly urgent concern. This has not been sufficiently taken into consideration in the formulation of the regulations. Their scope and the conclusions for the formulation of the copyright limitations therefore must be revised taking into consideration the new technological and economic conditions.

Like other limitations provided for by this Directive, the provision for private copying pursuant to Article 5(2)(b) states that the rightholders receive fair compensation. It must be noted in this respect that the amount of compensation paid for analogue and digital reproductions shall differ.[134] It must be examined in detail how far this has been taken into consideration by the regulations enacted by the individual Member States so far. Irrespective thereof, the amount of the compensation must be adapted in the case of technological protection measures being used. At least, however, the lump-sum remuneration through duty payment systems must be prevented in individual cases as, in case of widespread use of technological protection measures, this could lead to double remuneration. Suitable counter-measures must be taken to make sure that the rightholders do not receive more than a 'fair' or 'reasonable' compensation. This is preferably done on a European level, in order to prevent an impairment of the internal market, for instance on the basis of the already existing Austrian provision of Section 42b Paragraph 6 of the Austrian Copyright Act. Furthermore, the question as to whether remuneration schemes should continue to exist must be asked; the Directive does address this issue but fails to directly regulate it.[135]

The Directive provides for narrow limits for the online use of the knowledge contained in libraries. The limitation of Article 5(2)(c) does not apply to the making available to the public and according to Recital 40 it does not apply to other online deliveries either. Article 5(3)(n) therefore allows online use in very restricted manner only. According to this provision, even for registered

129. Cf. Spiegel online on 17 April 2004, Das bringt uns zurück ins Mittelalter <www.spiegel.de>, information also available at <www.boersenverein.de>.
130. Cf., e.g., http://www.ipodload.de (September 2005).
131. Cf., e.g., Die Zeit on 18 August 2005, p. 26, 'Google gebremst'.
132. Cf. heise online, 'Google wegen, massiver Copyright-Verletzungen verklagt' <www.golem.de/0312/28998.html> 21 September 2005.
133. <www.golem. de/0507/39365.html> 19 June 2006.
134. Cf. Recital 38 of the Information Society Directive, OJ 2001 L 167/10; *see* also Communication on copyrights, COM(2004) 261, 10.
135. Cf. C. Mayer, 'Die Privatkopie nach Umsetzung des Regierungsentwurfs zur Regelung des Urheberrechts in der Informationsgesellschaft' [2003] *Computer und Recht*, 278.

members the use is only admissible at dedicated terminals on the premises of the library. Again, private licensing models have priority in this context. In the age of the Internet, the libraries should also have the opportunity to access the new technological possibilities and to use the online full-text libraries. This is rendered difficult by the Information Society Directive. As information exhibits the characteristics of public goods, the supply of information cannot be sufficiently guaranteed by the market alone and on the basis of economic considerations only. For this reason, libraries will continue to play an important role in the supply of information in the future. The regulation does not sufficiently take this general interest into account.[136]

The same is true for the activities of other information intermediaries. An example in this connection would be search engines in respect of which it has not been fully clarified if they are covered by copyright, but which play an increasingly important role for the access to information. The situation is aggravated by the fact that even commercial providers of goods and services are using search engines in competition.

When it comes to online use, the question of who is to be regarded as a reproducer within the meaning of the Directive has to be asked with regard to many limitations. The activity of 'having a third party produce' included in some national provisions is not expressly addressed in the Directive. If the only criterion considered is the technological processes, this does not always lead to a clear result, especially not in a digital environment. Take, for instance, the process of downloading a file where technically one party requests a file, another party sends it and the result is a copy with the party having requested it. In a legal assessment, the reproduction is made by the party requesting the file. This point, which is not expressly regulated in the Directive, leads to a certain legal uncertainty both for rightholders and for third parties.

The implementation of limitations in favour of e-learning for the sole purpose of illustration is provided for in Article 5(3)(a) of the Information Society Directive. According to this provision, respective regulations on e-learning, such as Section 52a of the German Copyright Act, seem to be admissible for purposes of illustrations. However, any use beyond illustration is excluded and only possible on the basis of licensing models.

b. Technological Protection Measures

The safeguarding in the use of technological protection measures creates a uniform framework and also serves the objective of encouraging the development and distribution of such systems. The problem with this 'preventive' regulation is, however, that there is a lack of practical experience with the consequences of the use of such systems which could have been taken into account when drafting

136. Cf. to this effect, *privatkopie.net ua*, Submission to the Consultation on the review of EU legislation on copyright and related rights, p. 8, available in the materials at <ec.europa.eu/internal_market/copyright/review/consultation_en.htm> 19 June 2006.

the provisions. All in all, the provisions focus too one-sidedly on safeguarding the interests of the manufacturers. A revision of Articles 6, 7 of the Information Society Directive in the light of the practical use of such systems seems to be indispensable given the importance of a strong technological protection of the production and distribution of content.

According to the Information Society Directive there is strong protection against the circumvention of technological protection measures. The copyright limitations cannot be enforced by means of self-help (no 'right to hack'). Article 6(4) of the Information Society Directive provides that measures for circumvention by the rightholders must be made available in favour of certain limitations, which should be of special importance for the welfare of the general public.[137] These include the limitation for the reproduction on paper or similar data carriers, the limitations to the benefit of libraries, the press, education and scientific research. As a first step, provision is made for voluntary measures to be taken by the rightholders. If the manufacturers fail to fulfil their obligations, the Member States, as a second step, must take appropriate measures to ensure that they do meet their tasks.[138]

The Member States have implemented this provision into national law in different ways. In Austria, the legislator relies on voluntary measures. Whether this is in conformity with the Directive in the long run is, however, to be doubted.[139] In Germany, Section 95b of the German Copyright Act introduced a statutory entitlement to be provided with means of circumvention. This is also welcome from a user's point of view and a stronger harmonization in this area seems to be desirable.[140] In the area of communication of knowledge by libraries and universities, where the interests of the general public are concerned in a special way and where, because of the short life cycle of digital storage formats, the archiving of knowledge is threatened if measures of reproduction are prevented, a regulation seems to be indispensable. In this respect libraries are also left to the risk of insolvency of the information producer.[141]

---

137. Cf. J. Reinbothe, 'Die EG-Richtlinie zum Urheberrecht in der Informationsgesellschaft' [2001] *Gewerblicher Rechtsschutz und Urheberrecht International*, 741.
138. Cf. T. Dreier, 'Die Umsetzung der Urheberrechtsrichtlinie 2001/29/EG in deutsches Recht', 39; J. Reinbothe, 'Die Umsetzung der Urheberrechtsrichtlinie 2001/29/EG in deutsches Recht' [2002] *Zeitschrift für Urheber- und Medienrecht*, 51; M. Neubauer, 'Technische Schutzmaßnahmen und Recht' in *Internetrecht*, A. Wiebe (ed) (Wien, Spinger, 2004), p. 125; A. Wiebe [2003] 313.
139. Cf. Recitals 51 *et seq.* of the Information Society Directive, OJ L 167/10; on the whole, the provision of Article 6(4) is criticized as insufficient, for instance by *privatkopie.net ua*, Submission to the Consultation on the review of EU legislation on copyright and neighbouring rights, 9 and 11, available in the materials at <ec.europa.eu/internal_market/copyright/review/consultation_en.htm> 19 June 2006.
140. Regarding the aspects of consumer protection and DRM cf. also N. Helberger, 'Digital Rights Management aus der Sicht der Verbraucher', 1 *et seq.*
141. Cf. R. Kuhlen/T. Hoeren, 'Ein Dialog zwischen Ethik und Recht' in Heinrich-Böll-Stiftung (ed), *Digitales Urheberrecht*, 17, <www.boell.de/downloads/medien/Urheberrecht.pdf> 19 June 2006.

In this connection it also has to be noted that preparatory measures according to Article 6(2) are not affected by Paragraph 4.[142] That means, however, that the production and importation of devices for circumvention remains prohibited; thus, if the producer of the protective measure cannot deliver adequate software for circumvention to libraries, these might, under certain circumstances, no longer be in a position to meet their archiving tasks in the foreseeable future. Although there are contractual agreements – such as for instance between the IFPI and the Capital Market Group of German Book Trades on the one hand and the German Library on the other hand[143] – providing that a copy protection might be circumvented for archiving purposes, the question of where, under these circumstances, the means for circumvention should come from still needs to be clarified.[144]

No remedy is provided for the users according to Article 6(4) Subparagraph 4 of the Information Society Directive when it comes to online queries on the basis of contracts, which is an important scenario of online use of content. If the safeguarding of the protected interests for this increasingly important case remains exclusively subject to contractual agreement, this will fail to sufficiently take into account the users' interest in protection and the general public's interest in access. Problematic with respect to Recital 51 is that Article 6(4) Subparagraphs 1 and 2 can be contracted away.[145]

With regard to the scope of protection against circumvention it is unclear how high the requirements to be met by the solely protected 'effective' measures should be. The protection against circumvention is also subject to technological confinements. For the enjoyment of the work, for instance, a conversion from 'digital to analogue' is always necessary, as this is a prerequisite for human perception. For this reason, the analogue reproduction always remains possible ('analogue hole'). From a high-quality analogue copy which then is no longer protected – apart from the 'analogue copy proof' watermark – digital copies can be made without circumvention. This could also be reflected in the considerations regarding the copying protection of digital TV.[146]

According to Article 6(2) of the Information Society Directive devices for circumvention are prohibited if they have only a limited commercially significant purpose or use other than to circumvent. This should include programmes or programme patches whose primary purpose is circumvention.[147] What has not been clarified is whether this provision applies to computer programmes

142. Cf. J. Reinbothe [2002] 741.
143. Cf. heise online, 'Deutsche Bibliothek darf Kopierschutz knacken' <www.heise.de> 18 January 2005.
144. Regarding the problem of the 'technological lockup' *see also* Communication on copyrights, COM(2004) 261, 10.
145. Cf. T. Dreier [2002] 38; *see also* J. Reinbothe [2002] 742.
146. Heise online, 'EU-Kommission zeigt Interesse an Kopierschutz für Digital-TV' <www.heise.de> 25 August 2005.
147. Cf. heise online, 'Abmahnwelle der Musikindustrie rollt weiter' <www.heise.de> 23 February 2004.

for the copying of CDs which are capable of circumventing a copy protection by manipulating the error correction of the CDs but which may also be used for other, clearly admissible copying processes.[148] It is furthermore not clear how to determine whether a device for circumvention was 'primarily' produced for the purpose of circumvention. In addition, there is a lack of harmonization with the Software Directive which offers slightly weaker protection in this respect.[149]

The mere provision of descriptions of procedures for circumvention, whether in the form of abstract procedures or in the form of source codes, be it as scientific publications or as newspapers for the general public, may already suffice to meet the elements of that provision.[150] However, the Directive intends to cover only activities whose economic purpose is to circumvent and the research in the field of encryption technology is not to be obstructed either.[151]

An extensive interpretation of the characteristics of an inadmissible 'importation' and 'distribution' of devices facilitating circumvention may restrain communications on the Internet. The Higher Regional Court Munich and the Regional Court Munich I decided that the download of software for copying DVDs constituted an inadmissible importation and distribution of a device for the purpose of circumvention. According to the – arguable – opinion taken by the courts, a link to the Internet page where the programme is available for download was found to be a prohibited supporting activity that, even if it is carried out for the purposes of a news ticker, is not covered by the freedom of the press.[152]

Irrespective of whether this view is correct, this issue also shows that a European regulation regarding the liability of the party setting a link for third-party infringements of the law, which might, for instance, be modelled after the Austrian provision of Section 7 of the Austrian E-Commerce Act ('ECG'), is not only desirable but indeed required. Apart from that, the question of whether the mere indication of a URL in a news ticker can be considered an inadmissible contribution to a third-party violation of the law has to be answered.

According to Article 6(4) Subparagraph 2, the introduction of regulations for the realization of the limitation for private copying by the provision of devices facilitating circumvention is only optional. From the point of view of the content providers such a provision would be a heavy burden; content

148. Cf. to this effect, also B. Stickelbrock [2004] 741.
149. According to Article 7(1) Software Directive, OJ 1991 L 122/42, computer programmes are only protected against devices whose sole purpose is the elimination and circumvention of technological protection measures.
150. Cf. to this effect, M. Neubauer in A. Wiebe [2004] pp.121 *et seq.*
151. Cf. Recital 48 of the Information Society Directive, OJ 2001 L 167/10.
152. Higher Regional Court Munich OLG 28 July 2005, 29 U 2887/05, [2005] *Computer und Recht*, 821 (*Scheja*) = [2005] *MultiMedia und Recht*, 768 (*Hoeren*); Regional Court Munich I LG I, 7 March 2005, 21 O 32220/05, [2005] *Kommunikation & Recht*, 33; *see also heise online*, 'Heise legt Verfassungsbeschwerde gegen Link-Verbot ein' <www.heise.de> 1 September 2005.

providers therefore welcome the fact that there are no provisions to that effect, at least not in Austria and Germany.

The identification of the user may be a component of DRM systems and is possible via the use of the metadata that are related to the contents. Their protection according to Article 7 may get in conflict with data protection provisions. It will be of special importance to sufficiently guarantee compliance with the requirements under data protection law regarding the design and the operation of such systems. This should, if possible, be taken into consideration at a very early stage so that the concept of 'data protection through technology' can be realized.

2. First Sale Doctrine Online

What speaks against the application of the first sale doctrine to online transmissions is the increased risk to the interests of the authors. In networks, digital copy can no longer be controlled and its distribution is no longer traceable. It has been argued that the interests of the author do not materially differ from that of a buyer of digital copy on a tangible carrier, in which case the buyer benefits from the principle of exhaustion. Not only the clear wording but in particular also the special endangerment in the case of a first distribution via networks makes the exclusion of the first sale doctrine seem reasonable. The opposite interest in the merchantability of the contents must yield in favour of the protection interest of the rightholders.

3. Enforcement Directive

With respect to drafting enforcement instruments, the safeguarding of data protection interests and their relationship to the right to obtain information may pose an important problem from a third-party point of view.[153] Article 8(3)(c) expressly refers to the criterion of observance of the provisions under the data protection law, so that the priority of data protection law over the right of information must be assumed.[154] But even the possibilities for the preservation of evidence provided for in the Directive encroach upon the right to protection of privacy and other protected legal interests of the parties concerned. When implementing these provisions into national law, it must be ensured that this is taken into account. With its general wordings, the Directive does leave larger margins on the one hand, but also sets a relatively high minimum standard on the other hand. Provisions, such as the right to obtain information from a person named by a third party, seem to be problematic under constitutional law. Great importance must also be attributed to the principle of proportionality that is highlighted in the Directive itself.

---

153. Cf. to this effect, R. Schanda, 'Auskunftsanspruch gegen Access-Provider über die IP-Adressen von Urheberrechtsverletzern' [2005] *Medien und Recht*, 21.
154. Cf. A. Wiebe [2005] 13.

From the point of view of third-party interests, the planned Directive on the harmonization of criminal measures[155] is particularly problematic because of the planned installation of joint examination teams whose members shall be representatives of the public prosecutor's office, the police and the rightholders. This gives the rightholders a direct influence on the procedure and on the status of the investigators.

4. Conditional Access Directive

It is disputed whether the scope of application of the Information Society Directive, apart from use control, also covers access control. DRM systems contain both elements and may therefore be covered by both directives. This might result in legal uncertainties as the requirements and exceptions provided for by the Conditional Access Directive and by the Information Society Directive are different. Some take the view that the provisions of the Information Society Directive take precedence.[156] According to Recital 21 of the Conditional Access Directive this is without prejudice to the rules concerning the protection of intellectual property rights. This strongly suggests that the Conditional Access Services Act can, at least indirectly, also be made useable for the purpose of copyright protection.[157] If both the provisions for conditional access and those for DRM protection according to the Information Society Directive apply to the very same circumstances, there is, however, the risk that the access to information may be restricted excessively.

5. Information Obligations and Transparency in e-commerce

Service providers again and again complain about the scope and the complexity of the obligations to provide information in e-commerce. It is, however, clearly possible to meet these obligations with the help of technological measures. This has, in the meantime, been substantiated by many decisions.[158] In addition,

155. *See* Proposal for a Directive on criminal measures, COM(2005) 276; cf. also *heise online*, 'Neustart bei EU-Gesetz zur Durchsetzung geistiger Eigentumsrechte' <www.heise.de> 30 November 2005.
156. Cf. C. Arlt, 'Digital Rights Management-Systeme' [2004] *Gewerblicher Rechtsschutz und Urheberrecht*, 554.
157. Cf. M. Neubauer in A. Wiebe [2004] p. 117.
158. Austrian Supreme Court OGH 18 August 2004, 4 Ob 151/04s, [2005] *Medien und Recht*, 192; 18 November 2003, 4 Ob 219/03i, [2004] *Medien und Recht*, 46; Higher Regional Court Hamburg OLG 20 November 2002, 5 W 80/02, [2003] *MultiMedia und Recht*, 105; OLG Hamm 3 September 2003, 4 U 90/02, [2003] *MultiMedia und Recht*, 410; Higher Regional Court Cologne OLG 13 February 2004, 6 U 109/03, [2004] *MultiMedia und Recht*, 412 *et seq.* cf. also U. Schulte, 'Die Informationspflichten auf Internetseiten nach § 5 Abs 1 ECG. Zur österreichischen Rechtslage mit Blick auf Entscheidungen aus Deutschland' [2004] *Medien und Recht*, 444.

codes of conduct have been established which constitute an important means of self-regulation.[159]

C. Summary

The protection of the interests of other creators, users and the general public is imminently regulated under copyright law by means of definition of the rights of exploitation, in particular the limitation provisions. For this purpose, the European legislator has created a harmonized framework in the Information Society Directive while at the same time leaving latitude to take into account the various legal traditions and cultural differences between the Member States.

It must be said, however, that the limits provided for by the Directive are too narrow in some areas. This refers to the limited possibility of distribution of copies by libraries, the scope of the use of archives and the exclusion of an online offer without the consent of the rightholders. In these cases, the interest in access to science and the interest of the general public are concerned in a special manner. The Directive leaves hardly any latitude under copyright law for the use of protected materials in the field of e-learning.

The most important limitation to the benefit of the users of cultural goods is the freedom to make copies for private use. For the digital area, the increasing endangerment of the rightholders justifies that this limitation be no longer a mandatory one, as is also provided for by the Information Society Directive. With the use of DRM systems, the private use can be measured both technically and economically which is also beneficial for the user. That does not only mean that a material reason for the limitation of private copies ceases to exist, but rather that such limitation is in violation of the system. This assessment, however, is debatable. It is also possible to list legal, economic and societal reasons why the freedom of distribution – even if DRM systems are used – is to be maintained in the digital age.

The use of technological protection mechanisms in the content area will increase continuously in the future. The European legislator has already regulated the legal protection of such mechanisms in an anticipatory manner, but in doing so has one-sidedly taken into consideration the interests of the providers. This does not only refer to the wide scope of the protection against circumvention – which has not yet been clarified in detail. The main issue here is the question of the enforceability of the limitations regarding the technologically protected works in the general interest. The Information Society Directive relies primarily on voluntary measures taken by the rightholders. But a precise and

159. M. Nemetz, 'Verbraucherschutz im E-Commerce' in *Internetrecht*, A. Wiebe (ed), (Wien, Springer, 2004), p. 188; P. Burgstaller/G. Minichmayr, *E-Commerce-Gesetz – Praxiskommentar* (Wien, Medien und Recht, 2002), p. 86 f; W. Zankl, *Das E-Commerce-Gesetz – Kommentar und Handbuch* (Wien, Verlag Österreich, 2002), margin No. 384.

mandatory enforcement regulation seems to be required in particular for the purpose of protecting libraries, teaching and research. Neither must access to information in the online area be left exclusively to contractual agreements. Another issue that needs to be clarified is the relationship to the Conditional Access Directive. It is, however, of special importance to take into consideration the data protection provisions. If rights management systems are used it must be ensured that such systems do not result in a double remuneration of the rightholders under the system of collective rights management which exists in parallel.

The harmonization of the enforcement instruments seems to be excessively to the benefit of the rightholders. When it comes to enforcement or in case of a possible revision, the third-party interests concerned and their protection under constitutional law must be taken into consideration to a reasonable extent. Regarding the planned Directive on the harmonization of criminal enforcement measures, the direct participation of the rightholders in the criminal prosecution process must be observed critically. It also must be noted that the enforcement of legal powers cannot be a replacement for the development of new business models.

All of the above measures regarding copyright serve the purpose of preserving and promoting the internal market.

IV. MAKING ENDS MEET: SUMMARIZING EVALUATION – RECIPROCITY AND INTERCONNECTIONS BETWEEN THE OBJECTIVES PURSUED

The law on industrial property rights differs from other legal sectors by the special characteristics of the information goods which are to be protected. These goods can be perceived at many places at the same time and they are not diminished by being used. This is contrasted by the fact that the legal protection systems are strongly nationally bound and only apply to the respective national territory (principle of territoriality). For this reason, as early as the 19th century, international commercial transactions involving protected information goods were made easier by means of international agreements that contained certain minimum protection standards and were based on the principle of mutual recognition. This was once again affirmed and enhanced by the TRIPs Agreement of 1993 within the framework of the WTO.

The European regulation in the field of intellectual property rights must be seen against this backdrop. Its objectives include the elimination of trade barriers in the establishment of the internal market on the one hand and the strengthening of the position of European industry in global competition on the other hand. An important impetus for the regulation efforts was the development of information and communications technology which increasingly eliminates the need for information to be linked to carriers and media and allows its intangible character to emerge more and more. Insofar, another objective of European regulation is to adapt existing regulations to the technological and economic changes or even to lay down adequate provisions in an anticipatory manner.

The protection of industrial property has reached a high degree of harmonization on a European level. Three levels can be distinguished: On the basis of the primary EU legislation it is mainly the case law of the ECJ regarding Articles 28, 30 EC that has ensured that the biggest differences between the legal positions of the Member States were 'levelled off'. The instruments used to push forward the harmonization of the national intellectual property systems were the directives. Separate Europe-wide protection systems that meet the requirements of the internal market have been introduced by means of regulations. In the area of the industrial property rights (patents, trademarks, designs) the two latter instruments have been used almost ubiquitously.

Copyright, which is of primary importance for the production and distribution of content, has so far been harmonized only hesitantly. No Europe-wide protection system has yet been developed. An important reason for the differences to industrial property rights is the existence of different approaches to copyright. The continental approach that is strongly characterized by the moral rights faces the Anglo-American copyright approach that is designed as a purely economic right of exploitation. But even within the continental systems there are considerable differences. For the time being, neither a complete harmonization nor even a Europe-wide system is foreseeable because of these differences.

The main motive for the selective harmonization was the development of information technology which entailed a need for adaptation of existing provisions. At the same time, the economic importance of the content industry and thus also its importance for the internal market and for the competitive position of Europe was growing. Besides the required adaptation to the technological development, the objective of the directives issued in the area of copyright is also to ensure a high level of protection in order to encourage creative activities and cultural creation in Europe. Apart from supporting the authors themselves, these measures are also to the benefit of those who procure content or provide value-added services.

Initially, the regulation of the protection of information goods with special economic importance was the first priority. The most relevant measure for the content area was, apart from the protection of computer programmes in the year 1991, the protection of databases that was introduced by the Directive issued in 1996. In addition to harmonizing the limited copyright protection, the European legislator introduced a new *sui generis* right that was aimed at the protection of investments in the creation and maintenance of databases. This dual system showed an elegant way of bridging the different approaches of continental and British copyright systems. At the same time, the Directive also followed a broad protection approach. As a consequence, the legal protection of databases was expanded considerably, which did not cover the information contained in the database itself, but provided for the possibility to control access to databases.

Every protection system under the law on intellectual property is faced with the problem of ensuring an adequate balance between the incentive function by means of guaranteeing protection and a wide distribution by means of granting access. What is crucial here is the 'fine tuning', the exact formulation of the provisions regarding the object to be protected and the scope of the exploitation rights. Given the growing importance of databases for economy and science, there is the risk that large parts of the archived knowledge will be commercialized and that access to such knowledge will be limited. In several leading decisions handed down in the year 2004 the ECJ strongly restricted the scope of the *sui generis* right. While the limitation of the scope of protection was welcome, the strict requirements for evidencing the reasons for protection are excessive and in contrast to the broad legislative approach render the protective right partly void. Here, it is required, and also expected, that a certain loosening up will take place in the course of the further development of the case law.

Another problem concerns the ensuring of access to databases for which there is no alternative source, meaning where the protection of the database also results in a monopolization of the data contained therein ('sole source' databases). In this context, the more recent case law of the ECJ in competition matters provides certain guidelines for ensuring access. In addition, it remains to be examined whether the introduction of a compulsory licensing regulation is necessary. Given the often enormous demand for data in the scientific area, the substantiation by case law of the exception provided for research purposes will have to be monitored closely. Should the increasing application of the *sui generis* right in the area of research result in serious impediments, an intervention by the legislator in this respect will have to be considered.

Another focal point of the European regulatory activities concerns the exploitation rights regarding copyright and neighbouring rights. For satellite and cable broadcasts and for television programmes, the country-of-transmission or the country-of-origin principle has been laid down, according to which regulation may only take place in the country of origin. This serves the purpose of legal certainty and increases the pressure towards harmonization. For the online sector, the application of the country-of-origin principle is still excluded by the E-Commerce Directive. Under aspects of legal policy, the different treatment of this sector is debatable.

In the Information Society Directive the European legislator has harmonized the rights of exploitation in the digital area and created a framework for the copyright limitations. By clarifying the broad application of the copyright exploitation rights to the digital area legal certainty can be increased and the required incentives be created. What remains unclear, however, is the scope of protection in the downstream markets. The task of answering the questions arising in this respect may to a large extent be left to the courts.

The limitation provisions are in the interest of users, competitors and the general public. In this area, there are considerable differences between national legislations, which have been caused by different legal traditions and cultural differences. On the one hand, it is reasonable that the European legislator did not choose a general 'fair use' or 'fair dealing' clause in accordance with the Anglo-American tradition which must be substantiated by the courts on a case by case basis, but followed the continental tradition and provided for exactly defined exceptions. On the other hand, however, it is expedient that the European legislator left some latitude for the Member States. If the harmonization was too strong, this would run counter to these cultural differences and therefore be detrimental to the promotion and distribution of content.

It must be said, however, that the limits provided for by the Directive are too narrow in some areas. This refers to the limited possibility of distribution of copies by libraries, the scope of the use of archives and the exclusion of an online offer without the consent of the rightholders. In these cases, the interests in access to science and the interests of the general public are concerned in a special manner. The special characteristics of the information goods and the related market failure speak against leaving the supply of information solely to the market in a digital environment. Rather, an important function for libraries must also be ensured in a digital environment. The Directive leaves hardly any latitude under copyright law for the use of protected materials in the field of e-learning. Here, it will have to be monitored whether this will impair the development of respective offers and whether a greater amount of free uses must be provided for.

The most important limitation to the benefit of the users of cultural goods is the freedom to make copies for private use. In contrast to the opinion held by some commentators, there is no right to private copying. In the digital area, the increasing endangerment of the rightholders justifies that this limitation is no longer a mandatory one, as is also provided for by the Information Society Directive. With the use of DRM systems, the private use can be measured both technically and economically which is also beneficial for the user. That does not only mean that a material reason for the limitation regarding private copies ceases to exist, but rather that such limitation seems to be in violation of the system. This assessment, however, is debatable. It is also possible to list legal, economic and societal reasons why the freedom of private copying – even if DRM systems are used – is to be maintained in the digital age. In addition, the developments on the market in this respect will have to be observed.

The use of technological protection mechanism in the content area will increase continuously in the future. The European legislator has already regulated the legal protection of such mechanisms in an anticipatory manner, but in doing so has one-sidedly taken into consideration the interests of the providers. This, on the one hand, shows in the expansion of the protection to preparatory measures, whose scope still needs to be clarified. On the other hand, the question of the enforcement of these limitations in the general interest has to be asked even for technologically protected works. This is particularly important because the means of technological protection are even much more effective than the legal protection. The Information Society Directive fails to take this into account by relying primarily on voluntary measures taken by the rightholders and by leaving open the character of the measures to be taken as a second step. But in particular for the purpose of protecting libraries, teaching and research, a precise and mandatory enforcement regulation seems to be required in order not to jeopardize the balance of interests. In the online area, relying exclusively on contractual agreements is inappropriate. Here, the traditional civil law instruments such as the law on unfair contract terms and cartel law will not suffice for adequately taking into consideration the interests of the users and of the general public. The mandatory enforcement of important limitations is also required for the online area. All in all, the regulation should, in the light of the practical experience with the use of such systems, be reconsidered on a European level. Another issue that needs to be clarified is the relationship to the Conditional Access Directive. It is, however, of special importance to take notice of the data protection provisions. From a practical point of view, it is essential in this respect that the relevant requirements be already taken into consideration at the conceptual stage of such systems.

Given the increased use of rights management systems that is expected in the future and the individual charging that this will make possible, it must be ensured that there will be no double remuneration of the rightholders under the parallel system of collective exploitation of rights. For the time being, it is unclear whether the collecting societies, whose activities were indispensable in the area of the traditional media, will still play a role in the digital environment and what this role will be. Technological billing systems partly deprive the system of collective charging of its basis. In addition, a stronger competition among the collecting societies is required and may result in increased transparency and lower fees. This encourages the cross-border production and distribution of content and is also beneficial to the authors' interests. Here, European competition law may be made applicable. But in doing so, the interest in remuneration of the authors themselves must be kept in mind.

It is not sufficient to lay down criteria for protection, but the rights conferred must also be enforceable. The great differences between the national systems have induced the European legislator to achieve harmonization of the law on intellectual property rights. This is a welcome measure as it results in a reduction of transaction costs and increases the incentives for creating works. However, the Directive excessively favours the rightholders. It is required that the third-party interests concerned and their protection under constitutional law be also adequately taken into consideration. The Directive was adopted in great haste prior to the enlargement of the EU. Some of the provisions should again be reviewed (on a European level). This is particularly true with a view to the competencies regarding the harmonization of criminal enforcement measures that to a certain extent have been clarified in the meantime. With regard to the directive planned in this respect, the direct participation of the rightholders in the criminal prosecution process must be observed critically. It also must be noted that the enforcement of legal powers cannot be a replacement for the development of new business models.

In economic reality, the measures mentioned so far mainly benefit the intermediaries in the exploitation chain whereas the actual authors may profit only indirectly. Although the creation of incentives in the area of intermediaries and value-added services also encourages the creation and distribution of content, the authors themselves must not be neglected in their function as the creators of the works. A certain minimum protection both regarding the transfer of rights and remuneration must be introduced. In this respect, there are considerable differences between the individual Member States. As the introduction of such minimum standards in Germany has shown, there is strong opposition by the industry against the strengthening of the position of the authors. In the interest of the general public in the production of contents, this seems to be indispensable. Therefore, at least a limited harmonization of the copyright contract law with the constitution of minimum standards should be put on the agenda.

Copyright does not generally question the increased use of Open Source and Open Content models and the Open Access initiatives which propagate the free circulation of protected works, as even these models make use of the legal protection by means of license agreements. They may, however, be seen as indicators of the fact that the law in this field is no longer in a position to sustainably guarantee an adequate balance of interests.

The diametrical relationship between incentive and distribution that forms the basis of copyright law has changed because of the technological possibilities of exploitation, in particular the effects of digitization and networking. The increased vulnerability that goes along with easier distribution has resulted in a constant pressure towards increasing protection on the part of the rightholders. This has, however, increasingly restricted the interest in access to information by users, competitors and the general public. This development will once again be reinforced with the ubiquitous use of digital rights management systems. For this reason, the object of protection and the exclusive rights must be drafted in such a manner that these interests are also taken into consideration on a legislative level. In the long run, technological evolution might result in the development and discussion of new models, which put emphasis on use instead of exclusivity and thus may also be based on claims to remuneration to a greater extent.

The restoration of a reasonable balance has also summoned NGOs and consumer organizations to action. Within the framework of the 'A2K' initiative, a draft 'Treaty on Access to Knowledge' was prepared in May 2005, which contains a list of critical items and may form a good basis for further discussion.[160]

---

160. Cf. report by N. Helberger, A2K: Access to Knowledge – Make it happen; the draft contract is available for download at: <www.cptech.org/a2k/consolidatedtext-may9.pdf > 19 June 2006.

Consumers have an interest in the enjoyment of culture and in information. Competitors must rely on existing knowledge and cultural goods and develop them further. Libraries ensure free access to information. Science and research need the exchange of knowledge in the interest of the promotion of innovation. This also affects the fundamental right to freedom of information. Market failure that takes place in the area of information can well exist also in a digital environment. From a legal policy point of view, the information sector therefore must not be left entirely to the market. A complete commercialization without legal protection of the interests of the general public is incompatible with an institutional protection of fundamental rights.[161]

161. Federal Constitutional Court, 17 February 1998, 1 BvF 1/91, [1998] *Zeitschrift für Urheber- und Medienrecht*, 249.

Chapter 6
Regulation of the Content Industry through Tax Measures

Matthias Hofstätter

I. PROMOTING THE PRODUCTION AND DISTRIBUTION OF CONTENT THROUGH TAX MEASURES

A. THE FRAMEWORK CONDITIONS – EC LAW AND TAX LAW

One considers the promotion of the production and distribution of content through tax measures on the European level, one has to be aware of the fundamental distinction between two groups of taxes the EC Treaty provided for. On the one hand, Article 93 EC lists 'turnover taxes, excise duties and other forms of indirect taxation'. According to the list contained in Article 93 EC turnover taxes and excise duties fall under the heading of indirect taxation.[1] Then there are the direct taxes. This differentiation is of fundamental importance as the authorization to adopt harmonization measures provided for in Article 93 EC applies exclusively to indirect taxes.[2] Direct taxation is not covered by this harmonization authorization under Article 93 EC. In spite of the enormous significance of the distinction between indirect and direct taxes, the EC Treaty fails to provide legal definitions of these terms.[3]

1. A. Cordewener, *Europäische Grundfreiheiten und nationales Steuerrecht* (Colone, Schmidt Verlag, 2002), p. 6. Whether the term 'taxes' is used as a synonym for 'duties' is disputed. Favouring this view, for instance, R. Beiser and N. Zorn, 'Artikel 93' in *Kommentar zu EU- und EG-Vertrag*, H. Mayer (ed.) (Vienna, MANZ, 2003), margin No. 28; of a different opinion: Cordewener [2002] 7 fn. 6.
2. Cordewener [2002] 7.
3. Cf. regarding the concept of tax under Community law Kreibohm, *Der Begriff der Steuer im Europäischen Gemeinschaft* (Colone et al, Heymanns, 2004), pp. 5 *et seq.*

M. Holoubek, D. Damjanovic and M. Traimer (eds), *Regulating Content – European Regulatory Framework for the Media and Related Creative Sectors*, pp. 191–212

With regard to indirect taxation Article 93 EC provides that the Council shall, acting unanimously on a proposal from the Commission and after consulting the European Parliament and the Economic and Social Committee, must adopt provisions for the harmonization of legislation concerning turnover taxes, excise duties and other forms of indirect taxation to the extent that such harmonization is necessary to ensure the establishment and the functioning of the internal market. That means that for the harmonization remit under Article 93 EC to apply, the measures must be necessary for the internal market.[4] In the area of indirect taxation harmonization is typically achieved by means of directives.[5]

According to the present status of Community legislation the field of direct taxation does not fall within the responsibility of the Community. However, the Member States must exercise their taxation rights in compliance with Community law.[6] As direct tax law is the responsibility of the Member States, it is primarily up to them to enter into double tax treaties in order to prevent double taxation.[7] Article 293 EC contains a declaration of intent that the Member States shall, so far as is necessary, enter into negotiations with each other with a view to securing for the benefit of their nationals the abolition of double taxation within the Community. The lack of an explicit provision under Community law that requires the prevention of double taxation within the Community leads to an intense discussion in the literature whether the fundamental freedoms require the avoidance of double taxation.[8] As the ECJ has not yet decided on

4. Beiser/Zorn, in Mayer (ed.) [2003] Article 93, margin No. 5 *et seq.*
5. Beiser/Zorn, in Mayer (ed.) [2003] Article 93, margin No. 39. So far, the following directives have been adopted on the harmonization of indirect taxes: Directive 69/335/EEC, OJ 1969 L 249/25; Directive 77/388/EEC, OJ 1977 L 145/1; Directive 88/357/ECC, OJ 1988 L 172/1.
6. Cf. the case law of the ECJ regarding direct taxation. For instance, *Schumacker*, Case No. C-279/93 [1995] ECR I-225, para. 21; *Wielockx*, Case No. C-80/94 [1995] ECR I-2493, para. 16; *Asscher*, Case No. C-107/94 [1996] ECR I-3089, para. 36; *Royal Bank of Scotland*, Case No. C-311/97 [1999] ECR I-2651, para. 19; *Baars*, Case No. C-251/98 [2000] ECR I-2787, para. 17; *Metallgesellschaft & Hoechst*, Joined Cases No. C-397/98 and C-410/98 [2001] ECR I-1727, para. 37; *Lankhorst-Hohorst*, Case No. C-324/00 [2002] ECR I-11779, para. 26; *de Groot*, Case No. C-385/00 [2002] ECR I-11819, para. 75; recently *Schempp*, Case No. C-403/03 [2005] ECR I-6421, para. 19; *Marks & Spencer*, Case No. C-446/03, para. 29; OJ 2006 C 36/5.
7. Cf., in general, M. Lehner, 'EU-Recht und die Kompetenz zur Beseitigung der Doppelbesteuerung' in *Doppelbesteuerungsabkommen und EU-Recht*, W. Gassner, M. Lang and E. Lechner (eds) (Vienna, Linde Verlag, 1996), p. 13 *et. seq.* with further references; Geiger, *EUV/EGV-Kommentar des Vertrages über die Europäische Union und des Vertrages zur Gründung der Europäischen Gemeinschaft* (3rd edn, Munich, Beck, 2000) Article 293, margin No. 1 *et seq.*
8. Cf. M. Tumpel, 'Der Einfluss der Grundfreiheiten des EG-Rechts auf die Doppelbesteuerungsabkommen' [2003] *Österreichische Steuerzeitung*, 154 *et seq.* with further references; M. Lehner, 'Does the new Constitution for Europe disengage the Member States from their obligation to prevent double taxation?' [2005] *British Tax Review*, 337; with further references J. Schönfeld, 'Doppelbesteuerung und EG-Recht' [2006] *Steuer und Wirtschaft*, 80 fn. 12. Taking the view that juridical double taxation (on dividends) would not in itself be contrary to Articles 43 or 56 EC Opinion AG Geelhoed 6 April 2006, Case No. C-513/04 *Kerckhaert-Morres*, point 36.

this aspect, the problem of the avoidance of double taxation within the Community remains in dispute. However, it is undisputed that double taxation itself has a negative impact on the common market.[9] The elimination of double taxation within the Community is of particular interest for the content industry since otherwise the promotion of the production and distribution throughout Europe is hindered.

Despite the fact that direct taxes are the responsibility of the Member States according to the present status of Community legislation, there are a few directives promoting harmonization even in the area of direct taxation.[10] The primary basis for these directives in the area of direct taxation is Article 94 EC.[11] Article 94 EC provides that the Council shall, acting unanimously on a proposal from the Commission and after consulting the European Parliament and the Economic and Social Committee, issue directives for the approximation of such laws, regulations or administrative provisions of the Member States as directly affect the establishment or functioning of the common market. This means that in the area of direct taxation, the Member States of the European Union are entitled to act autonomously to a large extent. The national legislator is, however, bound by the provisions of Community law. This limits the scope of action of the national tax legislator. The legislators of the Member States are therefore not entitled to issue any tax provisions in the area of direct taxation to promote the production and distribution of content.

B. Promotion through Indirect Tax Measures

1. General Remarks

At the European level the promotion of content by indirect tax measures primarily takes place through measures taken in the area of VAT. The scope of VAT is constrained by provisions included in the Sixth VAT Directive.[12]

---

9. P. Pistone, *The Impact of Community Law on Tax Treaties: Issues and Solutions* (The Hague, Kluwer Law International, 2002), p. 74; EC Law and Tax Treaties, DOC (05) 2306, margin No. 14; J. Baßler, 'Zu den "Steuerspezifika" der Grundfreiheiten des EG-Vertrages' [2005] *Internationales Steuerrecht*, 825; J. Englisch, 'The European Treaties' Implications for Direct Taxes' [2005], *Intertax*, 323 with further reference; A. De Graaf, 'Avoidance of international double taxation: Community or joint policy?' [1998] *EC Tax Review*, 258; G. Fibbe and A. de Graaf, 'Is double taxation arising from autonomous tax classification of foreign entities incompatible with EC law?' in *A Tax Globalist – Essays in honour of Maarten J. Ellis*, H. van Arendonk, F. Engelen and S. Jansen (eds) (Amsterdam, IBFD, 2005), p. 238; Baßler, *Internationales Steuerrecht* 2005, 825; M. Lehner, *British Tax Review* 2005, 339; G. Kofler, *Doppelbesteuerungsabkommen und Gemeinschaftsrecht* (Linz, Habilitation, 2006), p. 50.
10. Cf., for instance, Directive 77/799/EEC, OJ 1977 L 336/15; Directive 90/434/EEC, OJ 1990 L 225/1; Directive 90/435/EEC, OJ 1990 L 225/6; Directive 2003/48/EC, OJ 2003 L 157/38; Directive 2003/49/EC, OJ 2003 L 157/49.
11. In contrast to Directive 77/799/EEC, OJ 1977 L 336/15, which is primarily based on Article 100 EC.
12. Directive 77/388/EEC, OJ 1977 L 145/1.

To promote European content one goal is that content from third countries is not given preferential tax treatment compared to European content. That was the reason why the Sixth VAT Directive was amended in 2002.[13] In particular, electronically supplied services supplied by enterprises of third countries were partly not subject to any VAT at all, whereas the same electronically supplied services supplied by intra Community enterprises were subject to VAT before the amendment of the Sixth VAT Directive in 2002. Therefore, before the 2002 amendment electronically supplied content from third countries was given a preferential tax treatment compared to content supplied by suppliers within the Community. Prior to the 2002 amendment of the Sixth VAT Directive it was advantageous for the final consumer to acquire electronically supplied content from third-country suppliers if the supplier established in the third-country was not subject to a tax similar to VAT in the third country.[14] However, after the 2002 amendment to the Sixth VAT Directive specific electronically supplied services are taxed at the place of consumption (in the EU). Therefore, European content is no longer discriminated against third-country content.

Additionally, the 2002 amendment of the Sixth VAT Directive ensures that the supply of electronically supplied services from suppliers within the EU is exempt from VAT if the electronically supplied services are provided for third country consumers.[15] Through this measure the promotion of European content is possible outside the European Union; especially when the country of consumption outside the European Union does not levy a tax similar to VAT. However, with respect to the 2002 amendment of the Sixth VAT Directive a point of critique is that the amendment does not cover every kind of electronically supplied service.[16]

2. Reduced Tax Rates Provided for by the Sixth VAT Directive

The Sixth VAT Directive authorizes the Member States to apply either one, or two, reduced tax rates. However, a Member State is not obliged to apply the reduced tax rates at all, or to include all categories, or all goods and services attributed to these categories, where a reduced tax rate may be introduced. 'These [reduced] rates shall be fixed as a percentage of the taxable amount, which may not be less than 5 per cent, and shall apply only to supplies of the categories of goods and services specified in Annex H.'[17] Annex H of the Sixth

13. Directive 2002/38/EC, OJ 2002 L 128/41.
14. S. Bernütz and C. Weinreich, 'Steuern' in *Rechtshandbuch Electronic Business*, G. Gounalakis (ed.) (Munich, Beck, 2003), p. 1167.
15. Bernütz/Weinreich, in Gounalakis [2003] 1167.
16. Bernütz/Weinreich, in Gounalakis [2003] 1168.
17. Article 12(3)(a) subpara. 3 of Directive 77/388/EEC, OJ 1977 L 145/1 as amended by Directive 1999/49/EC, OJ 1999 L 139/27.

VAT Directive[18] contains a list of supplies of goods and services which may be subject to a reduced rate of VAT. The list of goods and services in Annex H of the Sixth VAT Directive thus defines the maximum that may be subject to a reduced tax rate. According to category 6 of Annex H, the reduced VAT rate may be applied to the supply, including loans by libraries, of books (including brochures, leaflets and similar printed matter, children's picture, drawing or colouring books, music printed or in manuscript, maps and hydrographic or similar charts), newspapers and periodicals, other than material wholly or substantially devoted to advertising matter. In the same manner, the Member State may, according to category 7 of Annex H, apply the reduced VAT rate to admissions to shows, theatres, circuses, fairs, amusement parks, concerts, museums, zoos, cinemas, exhibitions and similar cultural events and facilities. The reception of broadcasting services may also be taxed at a reduced rate by the Member States. According to category 8 of Annex H the Member State may also opt to apply the reduced VAT rate to the supply of services by or royalties paid to writers, composers and performing artists. For this reason – provided that the Member State makes use of the possibility to apply the reduced VAT rates – all of the aforementioned goods and services may be 'promoted' by means of value added taxes. Not all of the Member States, for instance, exercise the option to apply the reduced VAT rate to the services listed under category 7 of Annex H of the Sixth VAT Directive.[19] Ultimately, a reduced VAT rate basically results in the consumption of the goods and services subject to the reduced tax rate being less burdened at the final consumer level.[20] This means that the distribution of European content may be promoted by utilizing the price elasticity to demand. The production of content is promoted indirectly when the demand for European content increases as a result of the lowered prices.[21] As, however, not all Member States exercise the option to apply the reduced VAT rate to some specified kind of content, it would even be possible to promote the production and distribution of content under the presently valid Sixth VAT Directive.

---

18. Directive 77/388/EEC, OJ 1977 L 145/1 as amended by Directive 92/77/EEC, OJ 1992 L 316/1.
19. B. Terra and J. Kajus identify six Member States that apply the reduced VAT rate: Austria, Belgium, France, Greece, Italy and Finland (only to royalties). The ten CEE Member States that joined the European Union in 2004 have not yet been considered in this survey. *See* B. Terra and J. Kajus, *European VAT Directives Volume I* (Amsterdam, IBFD, 2004), p. 665. As far as we know, no such survey has yet been made for the other categories of Annex H of the Sixth VAT Directive, OJ 1977 L 336/15.
20. Regarding the general influence of value added tax cf., for instance, W. Doralt, *Steuerrecht 2005* (Vienna, MANZ, 2005), pp. 109 *et seq.*; R. Beiser, *Steuern* (Vienna, WUV, 2001), pp. 234 *et seq.*; M. Lang, J. Schuch and C. Staringer, *Steuerrecht I+II* (4th edn, Vienna, WUV, 2005), margin No. 101 *et seq.*
21. The prerequisite is that the taxpayer does not increase the net sales price, i.e. passes the reduced tax rate on to the consumer and does not increase the sales price accordingly. Regarding tax incidence in general *see*, for instance, E. Nowotny, *Der öffentliche Sektor* (4th edn, Berlin et al, Springer, 1999), pp. 492 *et seq.*; H. Zimmermann and K.-D. Henke, *Finanzwissenschaft* (8th edn, Munich, Vahlen, 2001), pp. 239 *et seq.*

While the reduced VAT rate may be applied to the reception of radio and television broadcasting services as provided for in category 7 of Annex H to the Sixth VAT Directive, video and online services are not covered by Annex H. According to the prevailing view, this also means that the 'reception' of radio and television broadcasting services via the Internet may not be offered at a reduced VAT rate.[22] As a consequence, different tax rates apply to the reception of one and the same service, depending on the mode of transmission selected. This may lead to a distortion of competition because the 'traditional' reception of radio and television broadcasting services may be offered by the Member States at a reduced tax rate, whereas the reception via the Internet is taxed at the standard VAT rate. So far, the Commission has not observed any distortion of competition;[23] hence it has not yet proposed to abandon the reduced VAT rate for the reception of radio and television broadcasting services, or to expand it to include 'reception' via the Internet. In the year 2008, the Commission will present its next report, which will contain another review as to whether there is, in fact, any adverse effect on competition.[24] In order to determine whether competition is being distorted, it is always necessary to define the group of competitors. Should the products or services of a (potential) competitor be treated less favourably in terms of value added taxes than the products and services of another market participant, competition is deemed to be adversely affected.[25] If, however, the companies involved are not competitors, no competition exists between the two. In my opinion, equal treatment of non-competing companies is not mandatory in such cases.

Different tax rates not only apply for different modes of transmission for the reception of radio and television broadcasting services but also for the sale of books. Books sold in a traditional book shop are subject to a reduced VAT rate as provided for by Annex H of the Sixth VAT Directive. However, the selling of the same book online is subject to the standard VAT rate.[26]

Sound storage media are not listed in Annex H of the Sixth VAT Directive and may therefore not be taxed at a reduced VAT rate. Despite initiatives to put sound storage media carriers on the list of Annex H of the Sixth VAT Directive, the situation has not changed so far.[27]

22. *See*, for instance, Communication cinematographic and other audiovisual works, OJ 2002 C 43/6; Terra/Kajus [2004] 666.
23. *See*, without explicit reference to a Commission document, Terra/Kajus [2004] 666.
24. *See*, for instance, Terra/Kajus [2004] 666.
25. In my opinion, this conclusion could be drawn from Title VI (Articles 81 through 97) of the EC Treaty, which contains common regulations regarding competition, tax matters and approximation of legislation.
26. Article 1 (2) Directive 2002/38/EC, OJ 2002 L 128/41; With the same result Bernütz/ Weinreich, in Gounalakis [2003] 1168.
27. *See*, for instance, http://www.ifpi.org/site-content/library/vat-brochure-de.pdf. Downloaded on 1 December 2005.

Besides the fact that not all Member States exercise the option to apply the reduced VAT rate for the taxation of content, the list of goods and services taxable at a reduced rate with respect to Annex H of the Sixth VAT Directive does not cover content in general. In fact some kind of content has to be taxed at the regular rate. However, to enlarge the list of goods and services taxed at a reduced VAT rate, political initiatives have to be taken.

3. Exemptions under the Sixth VAT Directive

Article 13A(1) of the Sixth VAT Directive provides that, without prejudice to other Community provisions, the Member States shall generally exempt certain activities from value added tax. Only under very special circumstances, for instance if tax evasion or abuse could thereby be prevented, is it not mandatory to apply the exemptions from value added tax laid down in the Sixth VAT Directive. Under Article 13A(1)(n) of the Sixth VAT Directive certain cultural services (in the public interest)[28] and goods closely linked thereto supplied by bodies governed by public law or by other cultural bodies recognized by the Member State concerned are exempt from value added tax. The expression 'other [. . .] bodies recognized' is to be interpreted as meaning that it does not exclude soloists performing individually.[29] According to the principle of tax neutrality, it is prohibited that individual performers, as long as their services are recognized as cultural, may not be regarded, like cultural groups, as bodies similar to public-law bodies supplying certain cultural services mentioned in Article 13A(1)(n) of the Sixth VAT Directive.[30] In its judgment in the *Hoffmann* case the ECJ also decided that the heading of Article 13A of the Sixth VAT Directive[31] does not entail restrictions on the possibilities of tax exemption provided for by that provision.[32] Rather, Article 13A of the Sixth VAT Directive specifies in detail the activities that are to be exempted from value added tax, those which may be exempted by the Member States and those which may not.[33] That means that the fact that exemptions from value added tax are granted for certain activities in the public interest does not automatically exclude commercial activities from being exempt. A commercial activity may also be in the public interest.[34] Possible restrictions on the benefit of the exemptions provided for by Article 13A of the Sixth VAT Directive may be imposed only in the context of the application of Article 13A(2) of the Sixth VAT Directive.[35] Article 13A(2) of the Sixth VAT Directive entitles the Member States to

28. Cf. the heading of Article 13A of the Sixth VAT Directive.
29. *Hoffmann*, Case No. C-144/00 [2003] ECR I-2921, para. 30; regarding the term 'body' *see also Gregg*, Case No. C-216/97 [1999] ECR I-4947, para. 21.
30. *Hoffmann*, Case No. C-144/00 [2003] ECR I-2921, para. 27.
31. 'Exemptions for certain activities in the public interest'.
32. *Hoffmann*, Case No. C-144/00 [2003] ECR I-2921, para. 40.
33. *Hoffmann*, Case No. C-144/00 [2003] ECR I-2921, para. 38.
34. Terra/Kajus [2004] 709.

make the exemption from value added tax provided for in Article 13A(1)(n) subject to certain conditions if the bodies are not governed by public law. If one or more of the conditions are met, an exemption from value added tax on the basis of the Sixth VAT Directive is not mandatory. If, however, the body is governed by public law, the exemption from value added tax is mandatory, except in cases of abuse and evasion. The granting of an exemption from value added tax for bodies not governed by public law may be made subject to the condition that they do not systematically aim to make a profit. Any profits nevertheless arising may not be distributed, but may be assigned to the continuance or improvement of the services supplied.[36] Furthermore, the exemption from value added tax for bodies not governed by public law may also be dependent on the condition that they are managed and administered on an essentially voluntary basis.[37] The exemption from value added tax may also be linked to the condition that the prices charged by the bodies are subject to approval, or do not exceed such approved prices. If no price approval is required, the prices must be lower than those charged by commercial enterprises subject to value added tax.[38] In addition, exemptions may be made subject to the condition that the exemption from value added tax is not likely to create distortions of competition such as to place at a disadvantage commercial enterprises liable to value added tax.[39] Under Article 13A(2)(b) of the Sixth VAT Directive, an exemption from value added tax must be prohibited if it is not essential to the transactions exempted.[40] Furthermore, an exemption from value added tax may not be granted if 'its basic purpose is to obtain additional income for the organization by carrying out transactions which are in direct competition with those of commercial enterprises liable for value added tax.'[41]

While the Member States are entitled to exclude certain cultural services and goods closely linked thereto, within the meaning of Article 13A(1)(n) of the Sixth VAT Directive, supplied by bodies other than those governed by public law from the exemption from value added tax,[42] and under certain circumstances are even obliged to do so,[43] the Member States have no discretion regarding the activities of public radio and television bodies other than those of a commercial nature. The Member States must exempt such activities from value added tax.[44] The Sixth VAT Directive does not specify in detail what an activity of a commercial nature would be.

35. *Hoffmann*, Case No. C-144/00 [2003] ECR I-2921, para. 39.
36. Article 13A(2)(a) subpara. 1 of the Sixth VAT Directive, OJ 1977 L 145/1.
37. Article 13A(2)(a) subpara. 2 of the Sixth VAT Directive, OJ 1977 L 145/1.
38. Article 13A(2)(a) subpara. 3 of the Sixth VAT Directive, OJ 1977 L 145/1.
39. Article 13A(2)(a) subpara. 4 of the Sixth VAT Directive, OJ 1977 L 145/1.
40. Article 13A(2)(b) subpara. 1 of the Sixth VAT Directive, OJ 1977 L 145/1.
41. Article 13A(2)(b) subpara. 2 of the Sixth VAT Directive, OJ 1977 L 145/1.
42. Article 13A(2)(a) of the Sixth VAT Directive, OJ 1977 L 145/1.
43. Article 13A(2)(b) of the Sixth VAT Directive, OJ 1977 L 145/1.
44. Except for cases of abuse and evasion.

4. Subsidies Under the Sixth VAT Directive

Besides reduced VAT rates and an exemption from VAT, the production and distribution of content could be promoted by subsidies. Under Article 11A(1)(a) of the Sixth VAT Directive, the taxable amount may be everything which constitutes the consideration which has been or is to be obtained by the supplier from the purchaser, the customer or a third party for such supplies including subsidies directly linked to the price of such supplies. The term 'subsidy' is not defined in the Sixth VAT Directive,[45] but has been interpreted by the ECJ.[46] In the Court's interpretation, a subsidy is a payment in cash or in kind made in support of an undertaking other than the payment by the purchaser or consumer for the goods or services which it produces.[47] For a subsidy within the meaning of the definition by the ECJ to be included in the assessment base for value added tax, it must be directly linked to the price of the supplies. What this means has been made clearer by the case law of the ECJ.[48] 'However, the mere fact that a subsidy may affect the price of the goods or services supplied by the subsidized body is not enough to make that subsidy taxable. For the subsidy to be directly linked to the price of such supplies [. . .], it is also necessary [. . .] that it be paid specifically to the subsidized body to enable it to provide particular goods or services. Only in that case can the subsidy be regarded as consideration for the supply of goods or services, and therefore be taxable.'[49] It is immaterial whether or not the beneficiary of the subsidy has provided a distinct service to the body paying the subsidy, or to another party, for being granted the subsidy.[50]

If the production and distribution of content is to be promoted by means of subsidies, the decisive question is whether or not the subsidies are directly linked to the price of the supplies. If this is the case, the subsidy has to be included in the assessment base for the purposes of calculating value added tax. If there is no such connection, the subsidy does not form part of the assessment base. If the subsidy is included in the assessment basis, this increases the tax burden. It would, for instance, be possible to grant subsidies for cinema tickets in order to promote the European film industry if the relevant film was produced in Europe. In my opinion, the subsidy would have to be included in the value added tax assessment base in such a case since it was directly linked to the price of the ticket.

45. Terra/Kajus [2004] 609, fn. 587.
46. *De Gezamenlijke*, Case No. C-30/59 [1961] ECR, I-3.
47. *De Gezamenlijke*, Case No. C-30/59 [1961] ECR, I-3, 42.
48. Cf. *Office des Produits Wallons ASBL*, Case No. C-184/00 [2001] ECR I-9115; *Keeping Newcastle Warm Ltd.*, Case No. C-353/00 [2002] ECR I-5419.
49. *Office des Produits Wallons ASBL*, Case No. C-184/00 [2001] ECR I-9115, para. 12.
50. *Office des Produits Wallons ASBL*, Case No. C-184/00 [2001] ECR I-9115, para. 10.

C. Promotion through Direct Tax Measures

1. The Income Tax Treatment of Subsidies

As direct tax law is at the responsibility of the Member States[51] in the present status of Community law, and no directives have been issued in this field, the income tax treatment of subsidies for the promotion of the production and distribution of content has not been regulated at the European level. In general, the Member States are free to enact their respective legislation but they must comply with the provisions of primary and secondary Community law. Subsidies that are only granted to certain enterprises or business sectors must, in general, comply with the prohibition of state aid provided for in Article 87 EC.[52]

2. The Interest and Royalty Directive[53]

At the European level, the Interest and Royalty Directive was issued in 2003. The Directive governs the taxation of interest and royalty payments between associated companies from different Member States. The purpose of this Directive is to eliminate double taxation and to prevent cash-flow problems.[54] When it comes to the personal scope of the Interest and Royalty Directive, it only applies to associated companies provided that income, in the form of interest or royalties, accrues in one Member State while the beneficial owner of the interest or royalties is a company of another Member State, or has a permanent establishment situated in another Member State.[55] The term 'company of a Member State' means any company taking one of the legal forms listed in the Annex, which in accordance with the tax laws of a Member State is considered to be resident in that Member State and which is subject to the taxes included in the exhaustive list under Article 3(a)(iii) of the Interest and Royalty Directive. Companies are associated if one company has a direct minimum holding of 25 per cent in the capital of the other company. Interest as defined in Article 2(a) of the Directive and royalty payments fall within the material scope of the Interest and Royalty Directive. The term 'royalties' means payments of

---

51. Cf. the case law of the ECJ regarding direct taxation. For instance *Schumacker*, Case No. C-279/93 [1995] ECR I-225, para. 21; *Wielockx*, Case No. C-80/94 [1995] ECR I-2493, para. 16; *Asscher*, Case No. C-107/94 [1996] ECR I-3089, para. 36; *Royal Bank of Scotland*, Case No. C-311/97 [1999] ECR I-2651, para. 19; *Baars*, Case No. C-251/98 [2000] ECR I-2787, para. 17; *Metallgesellschaft & Hoechst*, Joined Cases No. C-397/98 and C-410/98 [2001] ECR I-1727, para. 37; *Lankhorst-Hohorst*, Case No. C-324/00 [2002] ECR I-11779, para. 26; *de Groot*, Case No. C-385/00 [2002] ECR I-11819, para. 75; recently *Schempp*, Case No. C-403/03 [2005] ECR I-6421, para. 19; *Marks & Spencer*, Case No. C-446/03, para. 29; OJ 2006 C 36/5.
52. Cf. Sections II and III *below*.
53. Directive 2003/49/EC, OJ 2003 L 157/49.
54. Recital 2 of Directive 2003/49/EG, OJ 2003 L 157/49.
55. Article 1(1) of Directive 2003/49/EC, OJ 2003 L 157/49.

any kind received as a consideration for the use of, or the right to use, any copyright of literary, artistic or scientific work, including cinematograph films and software, any patent, trade mark, design or model, plan, secret formula or process, or for information concerning industrial, commercial or scientific experience. Payments for the use of, or the right to use, industrial, commercial or scientific equipment are regarded as royalties.[56]

If the Interest and Royalty Directive applies both with respect to the personal and material scope, income in the form of interest or royalty payments arising in a Member State is exempt from the tax imposed on those payments in that Member State, irrespective of the form of tax assessment.[57] Under Article 4(1)(a) and Article 4(2) of the Interest and Royalty Directive the tax exemption applies only to the arm's length portion of the payment.

The Interest and Royalty Directive helps promote the distribution of content by providing that cross-border royalties between associated companies are not subject to double taxation. For instance, double taxation is avoided when a film production company domiciled in a Member State has associated companies in other Member States that commercialize the films of the film production company. The consideration paid to the production company is considered to be royalties within the meaning of the Interest and Royalty Directive, which are not subject to taxation in the Member State in which the film distribution company is domiciled.

D. SUMMARY

Content may be promoted by indirect taxation, on the one hand, and direct taxation on the other hand. This distinction is of fundamental importance for European tax law since only indirect tax law has been harmonized on the basis of Article 93 EC. The harmonization of indirect taxation has been made subject to the criterion of necessity for the internal market, under Article 93 EC. Direct tax law, however, is not harmonized but left the Member States. Their general freedom in legislation is, however, limited by provisions of primary and secondary Community law.

1. Indirect Taxation

The Sixth VAT Directive is of fundamental importance for the promotion of content by indirect taxation. This Directive provides that the Member States may apply a reduced tax rate to certain goods and services. The Member States are not obliged to apply a reduced VAT rate at all. If, however, they introduce a reduced VAT rate, its application must be limited to the goods and services listed in Annex H of the Sixth VAT Directive. The 'content relevant' list of

56. Article 2(b) of Directive 2003/49/EC, OJ 2003 L 157/49.
57. Article 1(1) of Directive 2003/49/EC, OJ 2003 L 157/49.

Annex H mentions the supply of books, including those lent by libraries. This also covers the supply of newspapers and periodicals. Printed material, either wholly or substantially devoted to advertising matter, is excluded. According to Annex H a reduced tax rate may also be applied to admission to shows, theatres, circuses, fairs, amusement parks, concerts, museums, zoos, cinemas, exhibitions and similar cultural events and facilities. The supply of services by, or royalties paid to writers, composers and performing artists may also be subject to the reduced VAT rate. While the reduced rate applies to the reception of radio and television broadcasting services, video and online services are not covered by the reduced VAT rate. This might result in a distortion of competition because the tax rate applied to radio and television broadcasting services depends on the transmission mode. The reduced tax rate is not available for radio and television broadcasting services that are 'received' via the Internet.

The Sixth VAT Directive also provides for certain exemptions from value added tax. These exemptions may only be avoided if very specific conditions are met. Certain cultural services (e.g. those in the public interest) and closely linked supplies of goods must be exempt from value added tax if they are provided by bodies governed by public law, or by other recognized bodies. Once the cultural nature of a service has been recognized, the term 'other recognized body' is to be interpreted in such manner that both groups and individuals are exempt. Possible limitations to these tax exemptions can only arise if covered by the exhaustive catalogue contained in Article 13A(2) of the Sixth VAT Directive. This list of exemptions eventually leads to the Member States not being obliged to provide for value added tax exemptions for certain cultural services and closely linked supplies. Activities performed by public radio and television broadcasting companies are, however, basically exempt from value added tax in all Member States.

If subsidies are provided in order to promote the content industry, these subsidies are subject to value added tax if they are directly linked to the price of the supplies. Such a direct link exists if the subsidies are paid for the supply of a specific good or the provision of a specific service, irrespective of the beneficiary of the subsidized supply.

2. Direct Taxation

The income tax treatment of subsidies is, in general, subject to regulation by the individual Member States. In doing so, however, the Member States must comply with the criteria set forth in the provisions of primary and secondary Community law.

The Interest and Royalty Directive governs taxation of interest and royalty payments between associated companies in different Member States. Companies are only associated if one company has a direct holding of at least 25 per cent in the capital of the other company. The Interest and Royalty Directive may contribute to the promotion of the content industry because it eliminates double taxation for royalties between associated companies. Royalties also include payments for the use, or the right to use, cinematographic films. That means that the Interest and Royalty Directive may also be applied where a company produces a film and then lends that film to associated performing rights companies in other Member States. Payments for the provision of the film rights are governed by the Interest and Royalty Directive. They must be exempt from tax in the Member State in which the associated performing rights company is domiciled.

II. ENSURING FUNCTIONING MARKET STRUCTURES ON THE CONTENT MARKETS

A. The Prohibition of State Aid in Tax Matters – An Overview

Article 87(1) of the EC Treaty incorporates the prohibition of state aid under Community law. The wording of the provision is as follows: 'Save as otherwise provided in this Treaty, any aid granted by a Member State or through State resources in any form whatsoever which distorts or threatens to distort competition by favouring certain undertakings or the production of certain goods shall, insofar as it affects trade between Member States, be incompatible with the common market.'

It has become the prevailing opinion that the prohibition of state aid under Article 87(1) EC may also cover taxes,[58] indirect taxes and direct taxes. The ECJ has also had to treat issues of state aid law in connection with taxes.[59] State aid by means of taxes may take various forms, as in general an entrepreneur or a certain group of entrepreneurs may be provided with a special advantage on

58. Cf., for instance, Communication on business taxation, OJ 1998, C 384/3, para. 2; F. Sutter, 'Beihilfen im materiellen Steuerrecht – Steuergesetze und Verwaltungshandeln der Steuerbehörden im Spannungsfeld zum EG-Beihilfenverbot' in *Beihilfenrecht*, Studiengesellschaft für Wirtschaft und Recht (ed.) (Vienna, Linde Verlag, 2004), p. 37; M. Lang, 'Rechtschutzfragen abgabenrechtlicher Beihilfengewährung' in *Beihilfenrecht*, Studiengesellschaft für Wirtschaft und Recht (ed.) (Vienna, Linde Verlag, 2004), p. 69; M. Lang, 'Die Besteuerung von Körperschaften des öffentlichen Rechts aus dem Blickwinkel des gemeinschaftsrechtlichen Beihilfenrechts' in *Körperschaften im Steuerrecht – Festschrift Wiesner*, E. König and W. Schwarzinger (eds) (Vienna, Linde Verlag, 2004), p. 237; F. Sutter, *Das EG-Beihilfenverbot und sein Durchführungsverbot in Steuersachen* (Vienna, Linde Verlag, 2005), pp. 21 *et seq.*; M. Lang, 'Die Aufhebung von Bescheiden wegen Widerspruchs zum Gemeinschaftsrecht gem § 302 Abs 2 lit c BAO' in *Abgabenverfahrensrecht und Gemeinschaftsrecht*, M. Holoubek and M. Lang (eds) (Vienna, Linde Verlag, 2006), p. 255 with further references; C. Staringer, 'Das Durchführungsverbot im Beihilfenrecht und das Abgabenverfahrensrecht' in *Abgabenverfahrensrecht und Gemeinschaftsrecht*, M. Holoubek and M. Lang (eds) (Vienna, Linde Verlag, 2006), p. 359 with further references.
59. *Adria-Wien Pipeline GmbH*, Case No. C-143/99 [2001] ECR I-8365; *Heiser*, Case No. C-172/03 [2005] ECR I-1627; Pending Case *Transalpine Ölleitung in Österreich*, Case No. C-368/04.

every level of the chargeable event. This may, for instance, be the case when defining the taxable person, the object to be taxed, the assessment base, the tax rates or the provisions regarding the creation of the tax liability.[60] The prohibition of state aid under Article 87(1) EC, however, not only governs direct state aid but also applies to indirect state aid.[61] In the field of tax law it is, for instance, possible that an investment incentive is granted in the form of a tax credit. If this investment incentive is linked to the investment in certain products or services, it may, under certain circumstances, be available for a selectively limited group of entrepreneurs only. If the other criteria for application are also met, this might be seen as an indirect state aid for the benefit of certain enterprises.

In its 'Communication on business taxation',[62] the Commission identified three different mechanisms for reducing the tax burden of an enterprise, that may amount to state aid. The list of possibilities is not exhaustive. This is based on the wording 'the advantage may be provided through a reduction in the firm's tax burden in various ways, including [...]'.[63] First of all, a reduction in the tax base is possible (such as special allowances, special or accelerated depreciation arrangements or the entering of reserves on the balance sheet). Secondly, the tax burden may be reduced by a total or partial reduction in the amount of tax paid (such as exemption or a tax credit). The third possibility for reducing the tax burden of an enterprise mentioned in the Commission report is deferment, cancellation of the tax burden or a special rescheduling agreement making the tax debt payable in instalments. The fact that the Commission also expressly addresses purely temporary tax relief makes it clear that an interest or liquidity advantage may also constitute state aid under Article 87(1) EC. The ECJ has already recognized in tax matters that a deferment advantage may constitute state aid.[64] For an advantage to qualify, in general, as state aid, it is even irrelevant whether the interest effect eventually has negative consequences in the individual case: By reducing the tax base early, taxable income in the succeeding year will increase and may even, in the case of a progressive tax scale, result in an overall disadvantageous effect.[65]

B. Legal Protection in Tax Matters – An Overview

If an actor in the content market identifies an aid granted only to a competitor, it is essential for the actor to question this aid by measures provided for by the

60. Sutter, in Studiengesellschaft für Wirtschaft und Recht (ed.) [2004] 38 *et seq.*
61. Sutter, in Studiengesellschaft für Wirtschaft und Recht (ed.) [2004] 39.
62. Commission notice on the application of the State aid rules to measures relating to direct business taxation, OJ 1998 C 384/3.
63. OJ 1998 C 384/3, para. 9.
64. *DM Transport*, Case No. C-256/97 [1999] ECR I-3913, para. 24.
65. Sutter, in Studiengesellschaft für Wirtschaft und Recht (ed.) [2004] 40 *et seq.*

legal system. It is not sufficient that the taxpayers or the competitors are granted rights on the basis of the substantive provisions, but rather, it is indispensable that they should also be able to enforce their rights through procedural provisions. As can be seen from settled case law of the ECJ, the principle of procedural autonomy applies.[66] That means that, when enforcing Community law, the Member States must, in the absence of relevant provisions under Community law, follow the procedural and substantive provisions of their national law. In doing so they must, however, comply with the requirements of the effectiveness imperative[67] and the equivalence imperative.[68] The imperative of effectiveness means that national proceedings must not render practically impossible, or disproportionately aggravate, the exercising of rights conferred on the basis of Community legislation.[69] The imperative of equivalence requires that national proceedings for the enforcement of claims under Community law must not be less favourable than proceedings in purely national matters.[70]

Community legislation on state aid is substantially based on the principle of protection of competitors.[71] Basically, state aid law makes a distinction between existing and new aid. This differentiation is of great relevance since Article 88 EC provides for completely different review systems on that basis.[72] In the case of existing state aid only a pro futuro monitoring procedure of the Commission under Article 88(1) EC takes place, whereas in the case of new state aid[73] the Commission has to be notified in advance. The purpose of this preventive review procedure for new state aid is to enable the Commission to evaluate planned state measures before they are implemented in order to prevent new undesirable burdens on the common market from the outset.[74] Under Article 88(3) EC, the

66. Cf., for instance, *Peterbroeck*, Case No. C-312/93 [1995] ECR I-4599, para. 12; *van Schijndel*, Joint Cases No. C-430/93 and C-431/93 [1995] ECR I-4705, para. 17; *Wells*, Case No. C-201/02 [2004] ECR I-723, para. 65 *et seq.*, T. Öhlinger and M. Potacs, *Gemeinschaftsrecht und staatliches Recht* (Vienna, LexisNexis, 2001), pp. 111 *et seq.*; M. Potacs, 'Gemeinschaftsrecht und Bestandskraft staatlicher Verwaltungsakte in *Internationale Gemeinschaft und Menschenrechte – Festschrift Ress*, J. Bröhmer, R. Bieber, C. Calliess, C. Langenfeld, S. Weber and J. Wolf (eds) (Colone, Heymanns, 2005) pp. 729 *et seq.*; Lang, in Holoubek/Lang (eds) [2006] 261.
67. Cf., most recently, V. Madner, 'Effektivitätsgebot und Abgabenverfahrensrecht' in *Abgabenverfahrensrecht und Gemeinschaftsrecht*, M. Holoubek and M. Lang (eds) (Vienna, Linde Verlag, 2006), p. 113.
68. Cf., most recently, T. Ehrke-Rabel, 'Äquivalenzgebot und Abgabenverfahrensrecht' in *Abgabenverfahrensrecht und Gemeinschaftsrecht*, M. Holoubek and M. Lang (eds) (Vienna, Linde Verlag, 2006), p. 127.
69. Madner, in Holoubek/Lang (eds) [2006] 115.
70. Madner, in Holoubek/Lang (eds) [2006] 115; Ehrke-Rabel, in Holoubek/Lang (eds) [2006] 130.
71. Sutter [2005] 130 with further references and 263; Staringer, in Holoubek/Lang (eds) [2006] 375.
72. Sutter [2005] 153 *et seq.*
73. Article 88(3) of the EC Treaty provides that any intended introduction or alteration of aid granted must be notified to the Commission.
74. Sutter [2005] 154.

Member State must not implement the intended measures (the new state aid) prior to the Commission issuing a final decision. Existing state aid is deemed lawful and may be granted without hesitation for as long as the Commission does not find it incompatible with the common market.[75]

C. Prohibition of State Aid in Tax Matters and the Promotion of Content

The central question concerning the prohibition of state aid in tax matters is when a measure actually qualifies as state aid within the meaning of Article 87(1) EC. With regard to the assessment of this question, a three-stage examination scheme has evolved in the literature, on the basis of which individual tax provisions are examined as to whether they qualify as state aid.[76] This examination scheme may also be used in assessing tax measures for the promotion of the European content industry.

(1) What is the common tax burden (the standard taxable event)?
(2) Is there any beneficial deviation from such a burden?
(3) May this deviation be justified by the nature or general scheme of the tax system?

It is impossible to distinguish clearly between examination steps one to three. The determination of the standard taxable event within the framework of question one requires an analysis of the nature and internal structure of the tax system. The question as to whether, or not, a tax provision is still covered by the standard taxable event, or constitutes a deviation which might be justified by the nature and internal structure of a tax system, follows the same pattern of argumentation.[77]

When it comes to answering the question whether a common tax burden is charged, formal arguments, such as the structure of a taxable event or the position of a legal rule as an exception to another rule, are not very helpful. Whether, for instance, a taxable event is formulated narrowly, or whether it is formulated broadly and its scope is then limited by means of exemptions, is just a question of legislative technique. This means that the mere fact that a legal rule constitutes an exception to another rule cannot make that rule a relief.[78] Rather, it is of importance whether a tax measure derives 'directly from the basic or guiding principles of the tax system in the Member State

75. Sutter [2005] 154.
76. Cf. Sutter, in Studiengesellschaft für Wirtschaft und Recht (ed.) [2004] 42; Sutter [2005] 94 *et seq.*; Staringer, in Holoubek/Lang (eds) [2006] 362.
77. Cf., for instance, Sutter, in Studiengesellschaft für Wirtschaft und Recht (ed.) [2004] 42.
78. F. Sutter, 'Artikel 87' in *Kommentar zu EU- und EG-Vertrag*, H. Mayer (ed.) (Vienna, MANZ, 2003), margin No. 105.

concerned'.[79] If this question is answered in the affirmative, the exception is part of a standard taxable event. If this question is answered in the negative the measure either constitutes a special burden to be paid or state aid to be received.[80] *Sutter* proposes, in order to find out whether a measure forms part of a standard taxable event, to always asking whether that measure is in line with the teleology of the legislator setting the legal standard or whether, on grounds of different motives, it challenges the legislator's original decision on the burden to be borne by a certain group of entrepreneurial taxpayers.[81] The evaluation of the internal logic of an existing legal system is difficult, and cannot be concluded without obtaining a Court's decision.[82]

In the area of content promotion the prohibition of state aid in tax matters means that every tax measure for the promotion of the content industry must be measured against Article 87(1) EC irrespective of the form the tax measure takes. For instance, tax investment incentives for the promotion of European films would have to be checked for their compatibility with the prohibition of state aid in tax matters, regardless of whether they were in the form of a shorter depreciation period (as compared to investment in 'non-European' films) or in the form of a different depreciation methods or depreciation beyond cost. The possible ways of promoting the European content industry by tax measures are manifold.

If a potential measure for the promotion of the content industry is classified as being generally worthy of promotion, the question of how to define the group of state aid beneficiaries has to be asked from a state aid law point of view. According to the prohibition of state aid provided for in Article 87(1) EC, state aid is incompatible if it distorts or threatens to distort competition by favouring certain undertakings or the production of certain goods. In order to be able to identify a distortion of competition, the group of market participants that is competing with each other has to be identified in advance. That means that the relevant market needs to be defined.[83] Only those who are in competition with each other must be treated equally. If, however, there is no competition, equal tax treatment is not required from a state aid law point of view. The definition of the group of competitors is not a trivial task. It is, for instance, obvious that print media are generally in competition with each other. But are radio media competitors of print media? If this question was answered in the affirmative, the preferential tax treatment of only one of these media sectors would be questionable under state aid law aspects. If this question was answered in the negative, the preferential tax treatment of one media sector would, in my opinion, be of no relevance under state aid law.

79. *Commission*, Communication on business taxation, OJ 1998 C 384/3, para. 16.
80. Cf. Sutter, in Studiengesellschaft für Wirtschaft und Recht (ed.) [2004] 43.
81. Sutter, in Studiengesellschaft für Wirtschaft und Recht (ed.) [2004] 43.
82. Sutter, in Studiengesellschaft für Wirtschaft und Recht (ed.) [2004] 43.
83. Sutter, in Mayer (ed.) [2003] Article 87, margin No. 105.

D. Summary

Taxes are subject to the prohibition of state aid in Article 87 (1) EC. The possible forms tax aid may take are manifold, since an entrepreneur or a certain group of enterprises may be granted a special advantage at any stage of the taxable event. Assessing whether a measure constitutes state aid within the meaning of Article 87(1) EC is complicated by the fact that not only direct but also indirect aid may be incompatible with the common market. The following examination scheme, the individual steps of which cannot be clearly separated, has been developed in order to establish whether a measure qualifies as state aid in tax matters:

(1) What is the common tax burden (the standard taxable event)?
(2) Is there any beneficial deviation from such burden?
(3) May this deviation be justified by the nature or general scheme of the tax system?

If the content industry is to be promoted, the question of how broadly to define the group of beneficiaries must be answered. Would it, for instance, be possible to promote the print media only, or would promotion of the radio media have to follow? Promotion is only defined as state aid if certain enterprises or lines of production are favoured and the advantage leads to (an imminent) distortion of competition. That means that the group of competitors has to be defined. Only those who are in competition with each other are required to be treated equally. If there is no situation of competition, equal treatment is not required from a state aid point of view.

III. THE PROMOTION OF THE CONTENT INDUSTRY AND ITS LIMITS

A. Interdependencies

In general, the tax promotion of the production and distribution of content and the prohibition of state aid provided for in Article 87(1) EC stand in opposition to each other. Every promotional measure must be checked for its compatibility with this prohibition of state aid. If a certain tax measure is identified as a state aid that does not mean per se that it is incompatible with the common market. Rather, this aid must be measured against the events described in Articles 87(2) and (3) EC.

If an aid measure is covered by any one of the events listed in Article 87(2) EC, it is definitely compatible with the common market.[84] State aid granted for the promotion of the production and distribution of content may, in my

84. Cf., for instance, Sutter, in Mayer (ed.) [2003] Article 87, margin No. 80 *et seq.*

opinion, not normally fall under Article 87(2) EC, since this Article only covers aid having a social character, aid to make good the damage caused by natural disasters and aid provided for the reunification of Germany.

Aid may also be compatible with the common market under Article 87(3) EC. Article 87 (3) EC contains different discretionary exemptions. In general, it would be possible to subsume the promotion of content in Europe under Article 87(3)(b) EC. Article 87(3)(b) EC provides that aid to promote the execution of an important project of common European interest may be compatible with the common market. With regard to Article 87(3)(b) of the EC Treaty[85] the ECJ has found in favour of the Commission's conclusion that a project may not be described as being of common European interest unless it forms part of a transnational European programme supported jointly by a number of governments of the Member States, or arises from concerted action by a number of the Member States to combat a common threat such as environmental pollution.[86] In the literature, there is also much decision or whether it would be sufficient if the project was at least in the direct interest of two Member States; where required, even political programmes should suffice for this purpose.[87] If one takes the view that a mere political programme of at least two Member States is sufficient for a discretionary exception under Article 87(3)(b) EC to apply, this might be of relevance for the area encompassing the promotion of the content industry. Even if Article 87(3)(b) EC has rarely been used as the basis for an exception,[88] it could be of importance, particularly for the area of the promotion of the production and distribution of content, as the Member States have entered into numerous 'political agreements' for the promotion of the content industry.[89] In the light of the Lisbon strategy the promotion of the content industry might qualify as an important project of European interest that might be subsumed under the exception of Article 87(3)(b) EC.

State aid for the promotion of the content industry could also be covered by the discretionary exception under Article 87(3)(c) EC. The provision states that aid to facilitate the development of certain economic activities or of certain economic areas may be regarded compatible with the common market where such aid does not adversely affect trading conditions to an extent contrary to the common interest. Due to this discretionary exception, the promotion of certain economic activities is deemed to be compatible with the common

---

85. Prior to the re-numbering: Article 92(3)(b).
86. *Executif regional wallon*, Joined Cases No. C-62/87 and C-72/87 [1988] ECR I-1573, para. 22 *et seq.*
87. Cf., for instance Sutter, in Mayer (ed.) [2003] Article 87, margin No. 101 with further references.
88. Cf. Sutter, in Mayer (ed.) [2003] Article 87, margin No. 101.
89. Cf., for instance, Decision of the European Parliament and of the Council of 14 February 2000, OJ 2000 L 63/1; Council Decision of 20 December 2000, OJ 2001 L 13/35; Council Decision of 22 December 2000, OJ 2001 L 14/32; Decision of the European Parliament and of the Council of 19 January 2001, OJ 2001 L 26/1; Decision of the European Parliament and of the Council of 29 April 2004, OJ 2004 L 157/4.

market under certain circumstances.[90] The content industry could be seen as such an economic activity which is thus worthy of promotion.

Aid granted for the promotion of the production and distribution of content may also be covered by the discretionary exception of Article 87(3)(d) EC. Article 87(3)(d) EC provides that aid to promote culture and heritage conservation where such aid does not affect trading conditions and competition in the Community to an extent that is contrary to the common interest may be considered compatible with the common market. That means that the distortion of trading conditions and competition must be compared to and measured against the cultural interest.[91] Whether the competition policy or goals in the common interest are to be given priority is disputed in the literature.[92] The ECJ speaks of a narrow interpretation of the exceptions under state aid law,[93] but also recognizes the broad discretionary freedom of the Commission.[94] *Sutter* concludes that the contracting parties of the EC Treaty want to 'balance' the strong position of competition which is manifested in Article 87(1) EC by a similarly strong corrective element in the hands of the Commission.[95] This opinion would also be supported by the fact that the exception of Article 87(3)(d) EC in conjunction with Article 151 EC was created by the Treaty of Maastricht. By expressly including culture as one of the Community policies in Article 151 EC, the promotion of culture was recognized for the first time as an important objective of the European Community and its Member States.[96] As cultural policy is on an equal footing with other policies such as competition, it is not acceptable that one of the two policies should be given more weight than the other in respect of the exception of Article 87(3)(d) EC. In my opinion, *Sutter's* view, that competition policy and cultural policy must be given equal standing when assessing the compatibility of a state aid with the common market is therefore correct.[97]

The fact that the European Commission does not subordinate cultural policy to competition policy becomes obvious if one takes a look at the 'Commission Communication on certain legal aspects relating to cinematographic and other audiovisual works'.[98] In this Communication, the Commission established four criteria for the compatibility of state aid with the common

90. Sutter, in Mayer (ed.) [2003] Article 87, margin No. 103 *et seq.*
91. Sutter [2005] 146.
92. Cf., for instance, T. Van Danwitz, 'Grundfragen der Beihilfenaufsicht' [2000] *Juristenzeitung*, 430; T. Oppermann, *Europarecht* (2nd edn, Munich, Beck, 1999), margin No. 1099; W. Mederer, 'Artikel 87' in *Kommentar zum Vertrag über die Europäische Union und zur Gründung der Europäischen Gemeinschaft*, H. von der Groeben and J. Schwarze (eds) (6th edn, Baden-Baden, Nomos, 2003), margin No. 3; U. Immenga, 'Wettbewerbspolitik contra Industriepolitik nach Maastricht' [1994] *Europäische Zeitschrift für Wirtschaftsrecht*, 17.
93. *Federal Republic of Germany v. Commission*, Case No. C-156/98 [2000] ECR I-6857, para. 49.
94. Cf., in extenso, Sutter [2005] 147.
95. Sutter [2005] 147.
96. Communication cinematographic and other audiovisual works, OJ 2002 C 43/6.
97. Sutter [2005] 147.
98. OJ 2002 C 43/6.

market (pursuant to the discretionary exception of Article 87 (3)(d) EC). *Inter alia*, the aid must be for the benefit of a cultural product. In the Commission's view, these four listed criteria strike a balance between the aims of the cultural creation and compliance with the EC rules on state aid.[99]

In addition to the restriction of the promotion of the content industry by means of the prohibition of state aid provided for in the EC Treaty, restrictions on a non-European level may also arise on the basis of WTO law.[100] This, however, will not be treated in greater detail in the course of this contribution.

B. SUMMARY

The tax promotion of content and the prohibition of state aid under Article 87(1) EC are in direct conflict with each other. This means that any promotional measure must be measured against the prohibition of state aid. If a certain tax measure is identified as state aid, this aid is not automatically incompatible with the common market. Rather, Articles 87(2) and (3) of the EC Treaty provide for events that (may) make aid compatible with the common market. Article 87(2) EC contains exceptions that must result in the compatibility of the aid with the common market, but these exceptions are of no primary relevance for the area of content promotion. Article 87(3) EC, however, contains discretionary exceptions. The Commission may consider aid compatible with the common market. These discretionary exceptions may also be applied in the area of content promotion. Aid may, for instance, be compatible with the common market if its purpose is to promote important projects of common European interest, to contribute to the development of certain economic activities or areas or to promote culture and heritage conservation, where it does not adversely affect the trading conditions and competition of the Community to an extent that is contrary to the common interest. The objective of promoting culture enjoys equal status to the goal of maintaining competitive conditions.

IV. EVALUATION

In the area of indirect taxation, harmonization at a European level has been widely achieved by means of directives. For the promotion of the content industry, the Sixth VAT Directive is of special importance. The individual Member

---

99. OJ 2002 C 43/6.
100. For the interaction of tax law and WTO law cf. S. van Thiel, 'General Report' in *WTO and Direct Taxation* M. Lang, J. Herdin and I. Hofbauer (eds) (Vienna, Linde Verlag, 2005), pp. 13 *et seq* with further references; for the interaction of Community law and WTO law cf. S. van Thiel and A. Steinbach, 'The Effect of WTO Law in the Legal Order of the European Community: a Judicial Protection Deficit or a Real-political Solution, or both?' in *WTO and Direct Taxation* M. Lang, J. Herdin and I. Hofbauer (eds) (Vienna, Linde Verlag, 2005), pp. 49 *et seq* with further references.

States do not make sufficient use of the existing possibilities for promoting content under the Sixth VAT Directive. Furthermore, by including 'content-relevant' activities in Annex H of the Sixth VAT Directive, a wider catalogue of 'content-relevant' activities could be made subject to a reduced value added tax rate. An exemption from value added tax for the promotion of content could be considered as well.

In the area of direct taxation, responsibility lies with the individual Member States who must, however, structure their tax systems in line with the provisions of primary and secondary Community law. That means that the Member States are basically free to formulate their provisions for the promotion of content but that any aid must be granted within the limits provided by the fundamental freedoms and the prohibition of state aid provided for in Article 87(1) EC. If a tax-promotional measure is identified as state aid, this does not necessarily mean that it is incompatible with the common market. Rather, the aid must be measured against the 'compatibility elements' of Articles 87(2) and (3) EC.

Part Three
Systematization, Evaluation and Conclusion – a Structural Analysis

Chapter 1

The 'System' of European Content Regulation – a Horizontal Analysis of the Individual Regulatory Areas

Michael Holoubek/Dragana Damjanovic

I. POINT OF DEPARTURE: 'CONTENT' AS A CROSS-SECTIONAL SUBJECT MATTER

'Content' cuts across a number of sectors: Unlike clearly definable products and services, 'content' as a part of culture comprises a multiplicity of products and services that cannot be assigned to one particular area of regulation. Rather, as the analysis in Part Two shows, the 'content industry' falls within a variety of political and thus regulatory efforts. In addition to funding programmes, primary-law requirements embodied in the EC Treaty (the cultural exemption clause and, in particular, the fundamental freedoms and general rules of competition), tax law and the law of intellectual property rights, the Community also provides important sector-specific provisions for the content industry, on the one hand for the electronic communications infrastructures, which are necessary to deliver eContent and are thus of crucial importance for the content industry as well, and on the other hand for the eContent itself.

Within the scope of these individual policy areas efforts to strengthen the European content industry are made in two essential directions: firstly, via the safeguarding of functioning market structures and secondly, by realizing certain social, democratic and cultural policy concerns in these markets. The former is pursued by protecting undistorted competition from interference by market players as well as by the Member States, and by maintaining the internal market by coordinating the Member States' regulatory efforts in the field of the content industry. The protection of intellectual property rights also serves this end as such rights form a prerequisite for making content a marketable product, i.e. a commodity that, in turn, forms the basis on which a content market can be established. The social, democratic and cultural policy objectives comprise

M. Holoubek, D. Damjanovic and M. Traimer (eds), *Regulating Content – European Regulatory Framework for the Media and Related Creative Sectors*, pp. 215–233

the direct support of the production and distribution of European content in the interest of fostering European identity; the guarantee of a basic supply of the public with content (and with the communications infrastructures required for the transmission of content); and the safeguarding of certain third-party interests in these markets, such as, in particular, the protection of human dignity, consumers and minors.

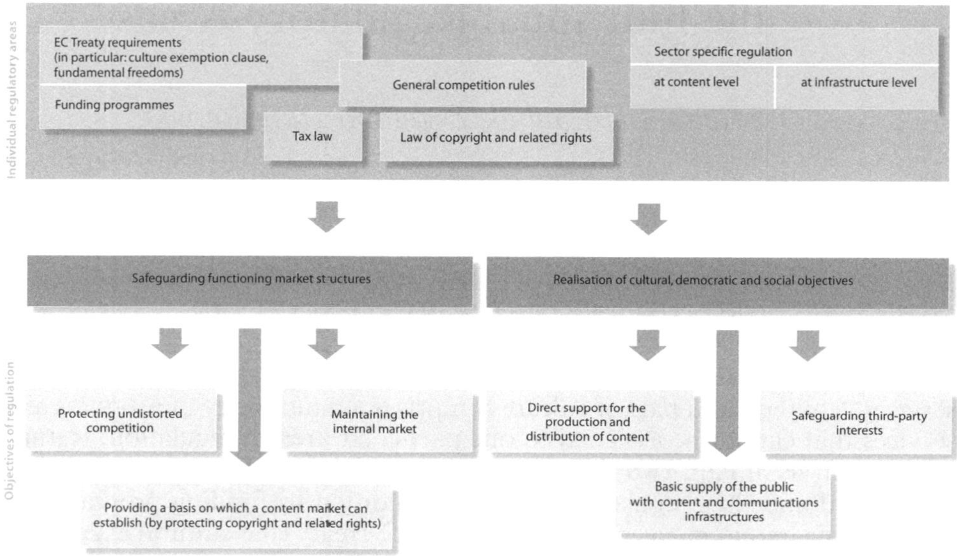

Figure 1: The individual regulatory areas and objectives of European content regulation

These two basic objectives of European content regulation, which are typical objectives of regulatory interventions into markets in general,[1] are not determined by uniform and clearly delineated regulatory areas. Rather, in line with the characteristic features of the content industry as a 'cross-sectional matter', they are both pursued within the different individual regulatory areas of European content regulation. The following will show, on the basis of the findings of the analysis in Part Two, where Community law contains provisions devoted in particular to social and cultural policy concerns, and which provisions of current Community law are primarily concerned with safeguarding the functioning of the content market, i.e. the media and related creative sectors.

1. On the different concepts of economic and public interest (or social) regulation in general, *see* G. Majone, 'Theories of regulation' in *Regulating Europe*, G. Majone (ed) (London and New York, Routeledge, 1995) p. 28 *et seq.*

II. SAFEGUARDING FUNCTIONING MARKET STRUCTURES IN THE CONTENT INDUSTRY

Functioning market structures in the content industry are primarily safeguarded by the general competition rules including, apart from their core provisions in Articles 81 and 82 EC Treaty, the state-aid law of the EC as well as the fundamental freedoms. As horizontal provisions, these regulations in principle apply to the content industry in the same way as to all other branches of industry. Their function is, by safeguarding individual economic freedom and equal treatment of all market players, to establish a system of an open market economy with fair and equal competition – or in other words the single market within the EC.[2]

In particular, with regard to the content industry, they can be categorized into the following groups:

- regulations dealing with the activities of the market players. They cover the prevention of practices by private entities that could inhibit competition and distort the marketplace, on the one hand, on a general basis referring to the entire content market (the 'antitrust rules')[3] and, on the other hand, on a sector-specific basis referring to a certain part of the content industry only, namely the online content markets.[4]
- regulations dealing with the activities of Member States and public enterprises, as well as other state-sponsored bodies. They cover the application of the fundamental freedoms, in particular the free movement of goods and services to the content markets,[5] the control of 'state aids' and the control of public enterprises and other state-sponsored bodies.[6] Furthermore, the harmonization measures of the EC in the field of copyrights and related rights[7] or the audiovisual media sector,[8] implemented in first instance to maintain a functioning single market, fall in this category as well.

---

2. On the role of competition policy within the single market program of the EC in general D. Dinan, *Ever closer union: An introduction to European intergration* (3rd edn, London, Lynne Rienner Publishers, 2005), p. 412 *et seq*, and on the development of the single market M. Egan, *Constructing a European Market: Standards, Regulation, and Governance* (Oxford University Press, Oxford, 2001).
3. For a detailed account of these rules with regard to the content industry cf. Part Two, Chapter 2, Section I.
4. The online content market is characterized by the fact that eContent (published content, games, audio/music and video/film in digitalized form) is transmitted via the three digital multiplatforms – the PC broadband platform, the digital TV platform and the mobile platform. In more detail cf. Part One, Chapter 3, Section II.
5. Cf. Part Two, Chapter 1, Section II.A.
6. Cf. Part Two, Chapter 2, Section VI.B.
7. Cf. Part Two, Chapter 5.
8. Cf. Part Two, Chapter 4, Section I.B.

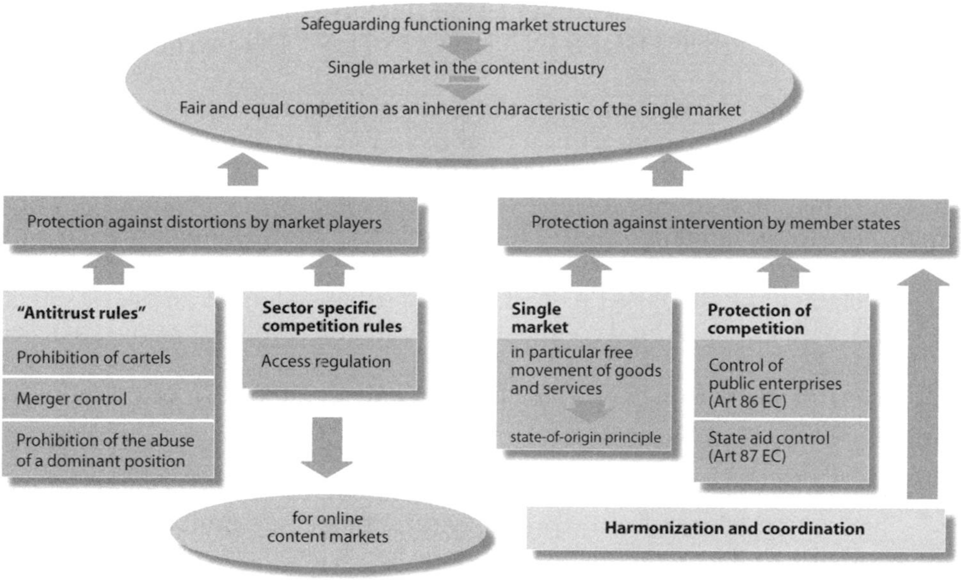

Figure 2: Safeguarding functioning market structures in the content industry

A. ANTITRUST RULES

The European single market is based on the principle of an open market economy with free competition (Articles 4 and 98 EC). Article 3 (1) (g) EC speaks of a system ensuring that competition within the Community is not distorted, thus establishing competition as an institution. EC competition policy and in particular the antitrust policy thus aim at an 'economic market model'. By safeguarding individual economic freedom and equal treatment, they serve to ensure functioning market structures as an inherent characteristic of the single market.

As horizontal measures, they are – without any differentiation to other sectors – also applicable to the content industry, which is therefore subject:

- to the 'general cartel prohibition' (Article 81 EC), which generally prohibits agreements between two of more undertakings which may affect trade between Member States and which have as their object or effect the prevention, restriction or distortion of competition within the common market. Therefore, the production and distribution of content by way of cooperation between undertakings must be assessed primarily on the basis of Article 81 EC and any secondary legislation and soft law instruments deriving from it.

  Particular importance attaches with regard to the content industry to the assessment of exclusive agreements. Even though such agreements usually serve justified objectives, e.g. the amortization of past or future investments, they can nevertheless cause considerable foreclosure problems *vis-à-vis* downstream markets. Therefore, agreements concerning the purchase and sale of goods in combination with conferring exclusive rights must always be assessed in the light of Article 81 EC.[9] The assessment of exclusive rights in the light of Article 81 EC plays also a role in the context of the collective exploitation of rights by copyright collecting societies. The cooperation between European collecting societies in order to introduce a global licence has been judged as admissible under Article 81 EC, because this agreement also enables competition among the copyright collecting societies themselves.[10]

- to merger control under the Merger Regulation, which aims at preventing ex ante distortions of effective competition in the common market, in particular as a result of the creation or strengthening of a dominant position. The recent decision of the European Commission in favour of the merger between Sony Music and BMG, in which the Commission failed to bring sufficient proof of the creation of a market-dominating position and therefore unconditionally approved the merger, is a case in point.[11]
- to the prohibition of any abuse of a dominant position within the common market pursuant to Article 82 EC. Exclusive agreements, e.g., have to be examined also in the light of this provision (not only of Article 81) – a fact that clearly shows the connection between these two antitrust rules. The denial of access to high-value 'premium' contents may, for instance, constitute an abuse of a dominant position.[12]

Even though, in principal, these antitrust rules only subject the private entities, they may play an essential role with regard to the activities of the Member States as well, insofar as they also ensure that the national single market barriers that were eliminated by the fundamental freedoms, and related secondary legislation, are not replaced by measures set up by undertakings to foreclosure the markets.[13] The ruling of the ECJ in context with the territorial monopolies of copyright collecting societies may serve as an example of this function of the antitrust rules.[14]

---

9. *See*, e.g., *Coditel / Ciné-Vog Films*, Case No. 262/81 [1982] ECR 3381. For further references in this context cf. Part Two, Chapter 2, Section I.D.1.
10. *IFPI Simulcasting*, Commission Decision 2003/300/EC, OJ 2003 L 107/58; in detail *see* Part Two, Chapter 2, Section I.D.1.
11. *Sony/BMG*, Commission Decision COMP/M.3333 of 19 July 2004; cf. Part Two, Chapter 2, Section I.C.3.
12. *Vivendi/Canal+/Seagram*, Commission Decision IV/M.2050, OJ 2000 C 311/3; cf. Part Two, Chapter 2, Section II.B.
13. In detail on this function of the EC competition rules cf. Part Two, Chapter 2, Section VI.A.
14. *Ministère Public v. Jean-Louis Tournier (SACEM I)*, Case No. 395/87 [1989] ECR, 2521; *Lucazeau v. SACEM (SACEM II)*, Case No. 110/88, 241/88 and 242/88 [1989] ECR 2811.

B. Sector-specific Competition Regulation

Due to the economic specificities of the online content markets as network-based industries, their functioning is also ensured by sector-specific competition rules laid down in the 2002 regulatory package for the electronic communications infrastructure markets.[15] The most important regulatory instrument within this sector-specific market regulation framework is the so-called access regime, which aims at ensuring open platforms in the electronic communication markets beyond the provisions of general competition law.[16]

C. Fundamental Freedoms

Of the various policies and regulatory instruments that aim at the creation and maintenance of a single market, the fundamental freedoms are by far the most important. They aim at the protection against restrictions on the single market imposed by the Member States. As regards the content industry the free movement of goods and the freedom to provide services are of particular importance. They prohibit discriminatory national measures, which hinder the market entry for goods and services from other Member States to a greater extent than for domestic goods and services. Beyond this, they prohibit also restrictive non-discriminatory national measures, i.e. measures which are indistinctly applicable to both domestic and imported goods and services and which are liable to hinder or make less attractive the exercise of the fundamental freedoms unless they are not justified by imperative requirements in the general interest.[17] The European Court of Justice has identified a number of such imperative requirements in the general interest with regard to the content industry, which enable the Member States to intervene in the content industry on the ground of other than mere economic policy aspects, i.e. to pursue certain cultural, democratic and social policy aspects. These content-specific imperative requirements include, e.g., the protection of consumers from excessive commercial advertising, the maintenance of a certain standard of programme quality as an aim of cultural policy or the protection of media pluralism by maintaining the diversity of programmes.[18] In addition, there are a number of other imperative requirements in the general interest, which may also play a role with regard to regulations affecting the content industry, such as the protection of human dignity, fair trade or consumer protection in general, as well as justifications explicitly mentioned in the Treaty such as the protection of the national

15. The measures are for download available <http://europa.eu.int/information_society/policy/ecomm/index_en.htm>, 23 June 2006.
16. For a detailed analysis on these provisions *see* Part Two, Chapter 3, Section II.C.
17. In detail *see* Part Two, Chapter 1, Section II.A.
18. For a detailed account on the ruling of the ECJ in this context *see* Part Two, Chapter 1, Section II.A.

cultural heritage.[19] This is to say that the fundamental freedoms, as interpreted by the European Court of Justice, recognize regulatory interventions into the content industry, taken by Member States for reasons of cultural, media or consumer policy concerns, provided they meet, in each individual case, the often strict criteria of proportionality and are non-discriminatory in nature. National rules fixing the retail selling price of books in the interest of cultural diversity have thus been considered by the ECJ only then to violate the free movement of goods if they treat imported books differently or if they provide obstacles for the sale of re-imported books that have not been exported solely for the purpose of circumventing said restrictions.[20] Otherwise, as the uncontested practices of several Member States show, book price fixing is apparently seen as being compatible with the principles governing the free movement of goods.[21]

Discussions like the one about the compatibility of a system of 'fixed book prices' with Community law again show the connection between competition law and fundamental freedoms, as such national measures are examined not only with a view to their restrictive effect on fundamental freedoms but also in terms of EC general competition rules. The question is whether a Member State, by requiring anticompetitive arrangements, does not violate the principle of allegiance to the Community laid down in Article 10 EC with regard to the competition rules stipulated in Articles 3(g) and 81 EC.[22]

D. Harmonization and Coordination of Member States' Interventions into the Content Industry

Since the fundamental freedoms essentially establish the country-of-origin principle in order to realize the internal market, Member States' regulations of the content industry for the protection of general public interests – such as, for instance, the protection of cultural policy concerns – are under considerable pressure in terms of economic competition amongst national governments within the European economy. Apart from this, Member States' interventions into the content industry justified as imperative requirements in the general interest according to the ruling of the ECJ in terms of fundamental freedoms may impose different requirements with regard to, e.g., the market entry or the activities of the private entities within the content industry, and thus form restrictions on the single market. These problems can only be successfully

19. In general to the approach of the ECJ to the four freedoms *see* P. Craig/G. de Burca (eds) *EU-Law – Text, Cases and Materials*, (3rd edn, Oxford, 2003), p. 784 *et seq.*
20. *See Leclerc*, Case No. 229/83 [1985] ECR, 1, as well as the resolution on fixed book-price systems, OJ 2001 C 73/5.
21. Cf. Part Two, Chapter 1, Section II.A.1.
22. *Ministère public v. Asjes*, Case No. 209/84–213/84 [1986], 1425 (paragraph 72). Cf. Part Two, Chapter 2, Section VI.

resolved by a, at least partial, harmonization of the national provisions at Community level.

Among the secondary instruments passed specifically for the content industry as harmonization measures are the TWF Directive[23] (which will in future be extended to all audiovisual media services)[24] and the E-Commerce Directive[25] and the sector-specific regulations for the communication markets,[26] which provide in particular the basis for standardization, i.e. the fixing of uniform technical standards within the online content markets.[27] If the Commission draft proposal for amending the TWF Directive and for expanding its scope towards an Audiovisual Media Service Directive[28] currently under discussion will come into force, significant changes will take place regarding the regulatory approach towards audiovisual media services on Community level. As far as they are 'transferred' from the scope of the E-Commerce Directive[29] to the scope of the Audiovisual Media Service Directive, they will on the one hand be subject to a combined 'economic-cultural' approach. On the other hand – as audiovisual media services are currently excluded from the strict country-of-origin principle of the E-Commerce Directive[30] – they will be subjected to the country-of-origin principle of the Audiovisual Media Services Directive, which narrows the margin for Member States to intervene with transboundary services significantly.[31] Furthermore, the planned horizontally effective Service Directive[32] might have some implications for the content industry as well.[33]

In this context, considerable importance also attaches to the harmonization measures under Community law in the field of intellectual property rights, in particular copyright and related rights.[34] By granting such rights, i.e. creating intangible assets and thereby making content an economic commodity, the law creates a system of incentives for the production and distribution of content, which forms the very basis for economic activity in the content markets. In so doing, these provisions make a significant contribution to the functioning of the 'single content market'. At the same time, by protecting those who

23. Directive 97/36/EC, OJ 1997 L 202/60.
24. Cf. the proposal for a directive amending the TWF Directive 89/552/EEC, COM (2005) 646 final.
25. Directive 2000/31/EC, OJ 2000 L 178/1.
26. For an account on these provisions cf. Part Two, Chapter 3, Section II.
27. In more detail on the standardization activities within the online content markets, *see* Part Two, Chapter 3, Section IV.
28. Proposal for a directive amending the TWF Directive 89/552/EEC, COM (2005) 646 final.
29. Directive 2000/31/EC, OJ 2000 L 178/1.
30. Cf. Art. 1(6) and especially Art. 3(6) E-Commerce Directive 2000/31/EC, OJ 2000 L 178/1.
31. Member States may adopt measures only 'to prevent abuse or fraudulent conduct', cf. Art. 2 (7)-(10) of the proposal for a directive amending the TWF Directive 89/552/EEC, COM (2005) 646 final.
32. Proposal for a directive on services in the internal market, COM (2006) 160 final.
33. To these implications, *see* Part Two, Chapter 1, Section IV.B.
34. For an account on these rights relevant to the content industry cf. Part Two, Chapter 5.

produce content, they guarantee also the preservation and development of creative activities and therefore the required resources for cultural creation in Europe. The most important regulatory instruments in this field at EC level are the Information Society Directive,[35] the Database Directive,[36] the Satellite and Cable Directive,[37] the Artists' Resale Rights Directive,[38] the Enforcement Directive,[39] and the Rental Directive.[40] These instruments basically harmonize the provisions concerning the scope of exploitations rights and admissible restrictions thereof and establish as a central rule the state-of-origin principle for satellite and cable broadcasts as well as terrestrial TV broadcasts. As regards copyright protection in online operations, however, the territoriality principle still holds, since copyright and related rights are expressly exempted from the country-of-origin principle embodied in the E-Commerce Directive.[41]

Finally, in context with the harmonization measures within the content industry the Commission's proposal for a directive on services in the internal market,[42] which in a horizontal way establishes general provisions facilitating the exercise of the freedom of establishment for service providers and the free movement of services, has to be mentioned as well. According to the original draft[43] it should, due to its horizontal approach, in principle also apply to the audiovisual sector and thus to a full range of undertakings in the content industry. This led to heated debates at EC level and finally to the exclusion of 'audiovisual services, whatever their mode of production, distribution and transmission, including radio broadcasting and the cinema' from the scope of the directive.[44] The electronic communication services and networks governed by the sector-specific provisions of the '2002 Telecommunications Regulatory Package'[45] were already exempted pursuant to the original draft.[46] Thus, the Service Directive does not apply (according to its current state) in principle to most of the activities of the online content markets. Merely the eContent services, which neither fall under the definition of audiovisual media services nor under the definition of the communication services[47] are subject of the

35. Directive 2001/29/EC, OJ 2001 L 167/10.
36. Directive 96/9/EC, OJ 1996 L 77/20.
37. Directive 93/83/EEC, OJ 1993 L 248/15.
38. Directive 2001/84/EC, OJ 2001 L 272/32.
39. Directive 2004/48/EC, OJ 2004 L 195/16.
40. Directive 92/100/EEC, OJ 1992 L 346/61.
41. In detail on the state-of-origin and territorial principle with regard to copyright and related rights, *see* Part Two, Chapter 5, Section I.4.
42. Proposal for a directive on services in the internal market, COM (2006) 160 final.
43. Cf. the proposal for a directive on services in the internal market, COM (2004) 2 final/2.
44. *See* Art. 2(2)(cd) of the proposal for a directive on services in the internal market, COM (2006) 160 final.
45. Cf. fn. 15.
46. Cf. Art. 2(2)(b) of the proposal for a directive on services in the internal market, COM (2006) 160 final.
47. For a definition of the audiovisual media services and of communication services, *see* Part One, Chapter 3, Section III.

Service Directive. This concerns only a small section of the 'information society services'[48] governed by the E-Commerce directive,[49] as for example online newspapers or online music stores. In addition, the Service Directive is in principle also applicable to all services within the content industry provided offline. But for these services of the content industry, not already *ex ante* excluded from the scope of the Service Directive, the general exemption clause in Article 1(5) of the current proposal can be invoked, according to which measures taken at Community level or at national level, in conformity with Community law, in order to protect or promote cultural or linguistic diversity or media pluralism shall not be affected. Thus, all in all, it can be said that the planned directive on services in the internal market will only be of minor importance for the content industry.

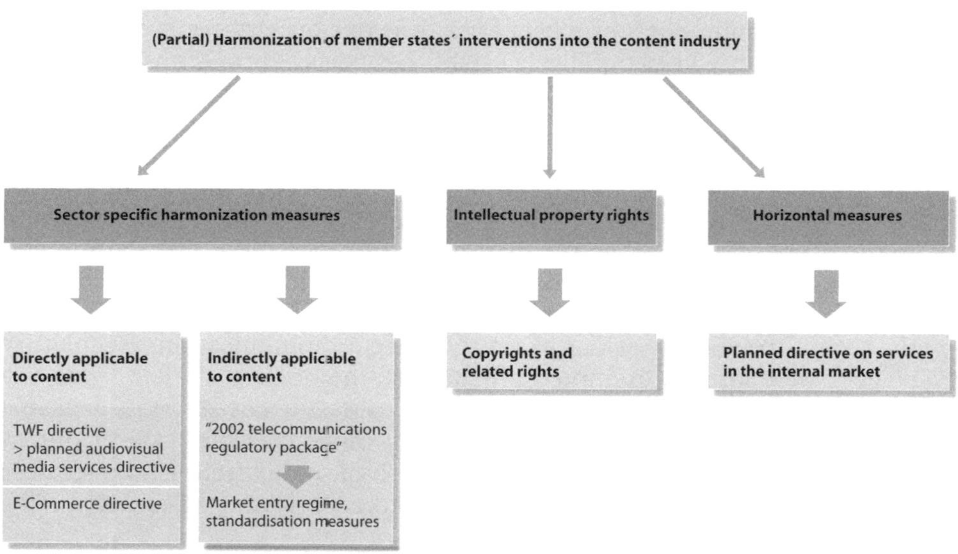

Figure 3: Harmonization measures

E. PROTECTION OF COMPETITION FROM MEMBER STATES' INTERVENTIONS

Control of European state aid under Article 87 EC and the limitations imposed on Member States by Article 86 EC with regard to their public enterprises are to protect undistorted competition in the content markets from interventions by Member States. European state aid law provides protection from state

48. For a definition cf. Part One, Chapter 3, Section III.
49. Directive 2000/31/EC, OJ 2000 L 178/1.

aid distorting competitive structures.[50] With regard to the content industry it establishes important limitations on the subsidization of content by Member States.[51]

On the basis of state aid law and Article 86 EC the European Commission has in recent years introduced a number of state aid review procedures by which it has examined the financing systems in particular of public broadcasters in various European Member States. In so doing it has mainly focused on their activities in the field of the new media (digital interactive television and Internet), and in particular on the question of, in how far these activities are part of the respective broadcasters' public mandate and can therefore be seen as services of general economic interest, which may as such be financed from public funds.[52] The Commission has furthermore taken action on account of financial aid provided by Member States for the development of a new technical infrastructure and has, in one concrete case – the state aid for the Berlin/Brandenburg DVB-T Project[53] – found that such state aid is in violation of Community law.

However, European state aid law also contains special provisions which in principle allow targeted aid by the Member States for the benefit of the content industry according to the cultural exemption clause of Article 87(3)(d)EC.[54] One important example is the possibility to promote films shown in cinemas and TV productions by the Member States.[55]

III. THE REALIZATION OF CULTURAL, DEMOCRATIC AND SOCIAL POLICY CONCERNS

The cultural, democratic and social policy concerns with regard to the content industry include a) the direct support for the production and distribution of European content in order to foster European identity, b) the guarantee of a basic supply of the public with content (and with communications infrastructures required for the transmission of content) and c) the safeguarding of certain

50. Within the scope of the Lisbon Strategy these rules are to be revised – in terms of both substantive and procedural law – by the State Aid Action Plan 'Less and better targeted state aid: a roadmap for state aid reform 2005–2009' <http://ec.europa.eu/comm/competition/state_aid/others/action_plan/>, 23 June 2006.
51. Cf. Part Two, Chapter 2, Section V.
52. *See* in this context the preliminary views of the European Commission on state financing of the public service broadcasters in Germany, D/51650 (Brussels, 3.3.2005) and of RTÉ and TnaG (TG4), Ireland, D/51652 (Brussels, 3.3.2005).
53. *See* IP/05/1394 (Brussels, 9 November 2005).
54. Article 87(3)(d) EC holds that 'aid to promote culture and heritage conservation where such aid does not affect trading conditions and competition in the community to an extent that is contrary to the common interest is compatible with the Common Market'. Cf. Part Two, Chapter 1, Section II.C and Chapter 2, Section V.
55. Here the Commission has established criteria to specify the exception in Article 87(3)(d)EC. *See* the Communication on cinematographic and other audiovisual works, COM(2001) 534 final, OJ 2002 C 43/6.

third party interests in these markets, such as, in particular, the protection of human dignity, consumers and minors.

A. Direct Support for the Production and Distribution of European Content

The European Community to a considerable extent provides direct support for the production and distribution of content with the objective to strengthen the content industry both as an economic factor and as a factor of social integration and in so doing to foster both the cultural heritage of Europe as well as European identity. Direct support is primarily provided in the form of funding programmes, i.e. subsidies, as for example by the well known programme MEDIA Plus[56] and MEDIA Training.[57] In addition, Community law also contains regulatory measures which directly support the content industry by creating incentives for the production and distribution of content, as for example the aforementioned cultural exemption clause of state aid law, laid down in Article 87(3)(d) EC.

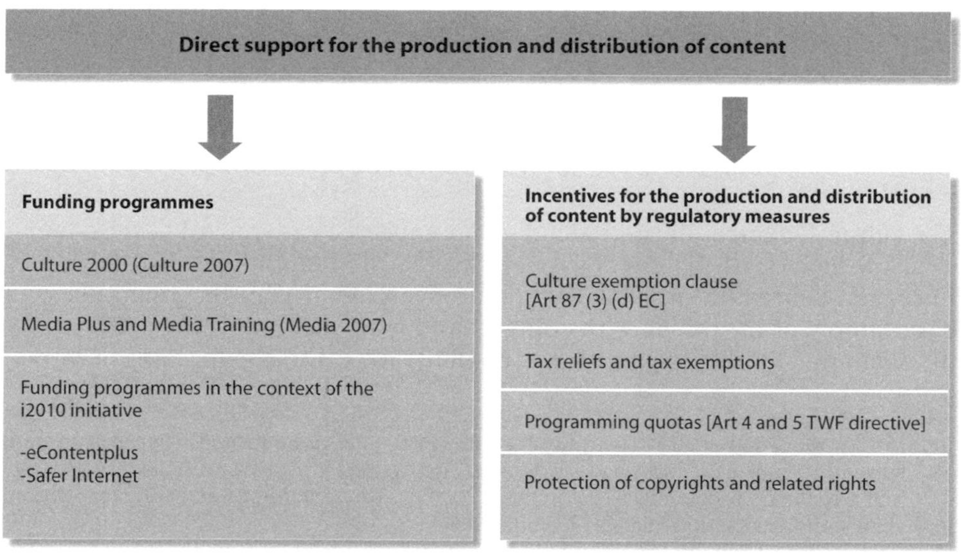

Figure 4: Direct support for the production and distribution of content

56. Council Decision 821/2000/EC on the implementation of a programme to encourage the development, distribution and promotion of European audiovisual works (MEDIA Plus – Development, Distribution and Promotion) (2001–2005), OJ 2000 L 336/82.
57. Decision 163/2001/EC on the implementation of a training programme for professionals in the European audiovisual programme industry (MEDIA-Training) (2001–2005), OJ 2001 L 26/1.

1. Funding Programmes

Based on Article 151 (5) EC (culture), Article 157 (4) EC (industry) and Article 150 (4) EC (vocational training) as well as in the context of the initiative 'i2010 – A European Information Society for growth and employment' a number of funding programmes related to 'content' have already been started at Community level. The number of such programmes is steadily increasing, which reflects the significance attached to the content industry and its expected high growth potential by the European Community.

The most important funding programmes directly relevant to the content industry include:[58]

- the Culture 2000 Programme (and its successor, Culture 2007)[59] which deals with the fostering of cultural projects with a Community-wide dimension extending across the entire content industry in all areas of culture.
- the MEDIA Plus programme and MEDIA Training, which are to be consolidated into a single instrument, the new MEDIA 2007 programme.[60] These programmes serve the purpose of strengthening the competitiveness of the European audiovisual industry, including the development, distribution and promotion of European audiovisual works within and outside the Community by promoting the continuous vocational training of the respective professionals in the audiovisual field.
- the programmes established in connection with and within the framework of the i2010 Initiative for the creation of a European information society for growth and employment.[61] Of particular importance for the content industry – or the online content market – are those funding programmes which aim at the expansion of digital distribution technologies, at the creation, utilization and dissemination of digital content and at ensuring the safety of the information society. Special mention has to be made of the funding programme eContentplus, which is to facilitate access to digital content and its use and exploitation in Europe, as well as the programme 'Safer Internet plus', which aims to promote the safer use of the Internet and new online technologies, particularly for children, and to fight against illegal content and content unwanted by the end user. Another stimulating effect on the content industry can be expected from a number of measures within the framework of the third pillar of i2010 with regard to an 'inclusive' information society (eInclusion), as e.g. suggested in the

58. For a detailed account on these programmes cf. Part Two, Chapter 1, Section III.B-E.
59. Decision 508/2000/EC establishing the Culture 2000 Programme, OJ 2000 L 63/1 as well as Decision 626/2004/EC amending Decision 508/2004/EC, OJ 2004 L 99/3.
60. *See* the Proposal for a Decision MEDIA 2007, COM(2004) 470.
61. Communication i2010, COM(2005) 229. Also *see* the relevant Communication on the information society, COM(2005) 757.

Communication of the Commission 'eAccessibility' for the promotion of a barrier-free access to information and communication technologies, since these initiatives indirectly also ensure the basic supply of content.

2. Incentives for the Production and Distribution of Content by Regulatory Measures

The most important regulatory measures at Community level which, by providing incentives, directly aim at promoting the production and distribution of content are:

- the special cultural exemption clause of European state-aid law – Article 87 (3) (d) EC – which permits in principle the promotion of the content industry by the Member States in that it considers as compatible with the common market the granting of aid for the promotion of culture and the preservation of the cultural heritage. So far this principle has mostly been applied to films shown in cinemas and TV productions, for which the Commission has formulated detailed compatibility criteria.[62]
- tax measures, such as tax reliefs and tax exemptions for certain content-relevant services that indirectly provide incentives for the production and distribution of content. Compared with the funding policy of the Member States these measures are of minor importance since the Community's scope of action in this respect is limited to the harmonization of indirect taxes. Under Community law in its present form direct taxation of funding measures continues to fall within the competence of the Member States.[63]
- the programming quotas under Articles 4 and 5 of the TWF Directive,[64] which, designed as an obligation concerning content, makes it binding on European broadcasters to reserve at least 10 per cent of their transmission time or 10 per cent of their programming budget for European works.[65]
- by providing a fundamental incentive for the production and distribution of content, the EC copyright and related rights regime also has a direct supporting effect on the content industry side by side with its function to establish and safeguard market structures in the content markets.[66]

62. Cf. fn. 54 and 55.
63. For details *see* Part Two, Chapter 6.
64. Directive 97/36/EC, OJ 1997 L 202/60.
65. Cf. Part Two, Chapter 4, Section III.A.1.
66. Cf. Part Two, Chapter 5, Section I.

B. SAFEGUARDING THE BASIC SUPPLY OF THE PUBLIC WITH CONTENT (AND WITH COMMUNICATIONS INFRASTRUCTURE)

In the interest of the 'free flow of information' and 'diversity of opinion' one essential sociopolitical concern in the field of content is the adequate supply of the public with certain content services. Due to the development of modern technologies – digital television, third-generation mobile systems and broadband communication systems – and the danger associated with these developments, that parts of the population might be excluded from full participation in the digital society, this issue will play an even greater role in future, not least because the markets created by these new technologies are also becoming economically increasingly important.

- Safeguarding this basic supply at the level of Community law is, at least initially, largely a matter of 'soft-law' measures. Such measures aim, on the one hand, at self-regulation on the part of the industry ('eAccessibility' and 'eInclusion')[67]. On the other hand, they operate in the form of financial support for the development of communication platforms in remote and rural areas in order to give everybody access to the necessary infrastructure and the content transmitted by it,[68] or in the form of financing special initiatives such as 'digital libraries', by means of which Europe's written and audiovisual heritage is to be digitalized, stored and made available via the Internet.[69]
- In addition, the basic supply of content is also guaranteed by special provisions within the scope of sector-specific regulation of the electronic communication markets.[70] The individual provisions can be found a) in the Universal Service Directive,[71] which guarantees on the basis of the so-called universal service regime the transmission of content via a simple internet connection, on the one hand, and provides for the imposition of 'must-carry' obligations on certain network operators with regard to certain radio and television programmes by the Member States, on the other hand; and b) in the TWF Directive[72] which in Article 3a provides a legal basis that enables the Member States to guarantee a basic supply with 'major events' on television broadcast.

67. For more information on these initiatives, *see* <http://europa.eu.int/information_society/policy/accessibility/index_en.htm>, 23 June 2006.
68. As regards these soft law measures cf. the Communication: National Broadband Strategies, COM(2004) 369 and the criteria and modalities for the use of Structural Funds for electronic communications according to the guidelines on Structural Funds, SEC(2003) 895.
69. For more information on the initiative digital libraries, *see* <http://europa.eu.int/information_society/activities/digital_libraries/index_en.htm.>, 23 June 2006.
70. For an account on these provisions *see* Part Two, Chapter 3, Section III.
71. Directive 2002/22/EC, OJ 2002 L 108/51.
72. Directive 97/36/EC, OJ 1997 L 202/60.

- The basic supply of the public, particularly with high-quality content, is also ensured by the Amsterdam Protocol, which recognizes the significant role of public service broadcasting and permits the establishment of a dual broadcasting system, meaning the parallel provision of services on the broadcasting markets by private entities as well as by partially funded public service broadcasters.

In the context of the aforementioned provisions – the universal service regime, the 'must-carry' provisions, and the recognition of the special importance and role of public service broadcasting – it should, however, be noted that for the most part Community law as such does not provide substantive regulations but merely allows Member States to pass such regulations and at the same time imposes limitations in the interest of preserving the single market as well as fair and equal competition. It is only in the context of the universal service regime that secondary Community law states minimum requirements which contain both restrictions and guarantees.

Lastly, the basic supply of the EC public with content is also ensured by the fundamental freedom to receive and impart information. This fundamental right is in large part implemented through the limitations in the law on copyrights and related rights which limit exclusiveness claims on the part of rights holders and in this way stipulate free access to content and its use and distribution for the public.[73] The Information Society Directive,[74] e.g., permits the production of private copies for educational, scientific and research purposes, for example via the transmission of copies by libraries or in the course of archive studies. Similarly, the Commission's proposal for an Audiovisual Media Services Directive[75] envisages a 'short reporting regime' that would enable television broadcasters to report on events of considerable public interest in the form of 'short news extracts' that can be freely selected from the transmission signal of the transmitting TV broadcaster. The objectives of this planned provision are to ensure both the information of the public, and, quite importantly, a diversifying effect on competition among the broadcasters, since it enables smaller television stations to include at least short information about the events in question in their programmes. It should also be noted that the planned regulations would possibly also cover 'mediators', i.e. in particular news agencies, which would also be authorized to claim access to 'short news extracts'.[76]

73. For details *see* Part Two, Chapter 5, Section III.
74. Directive 2001/29/EC, OJ 2001 L 167/10.
75. COM (2005) 646 final.
76. In detail N. Helberger, 'The 'Right to Information' and Digital Broadcasting: About Monsters, Invisible Men and the Future of European Broadcasting Regulation' (2006) 2 *Entertainment Law Review*, 70 *et seq.*

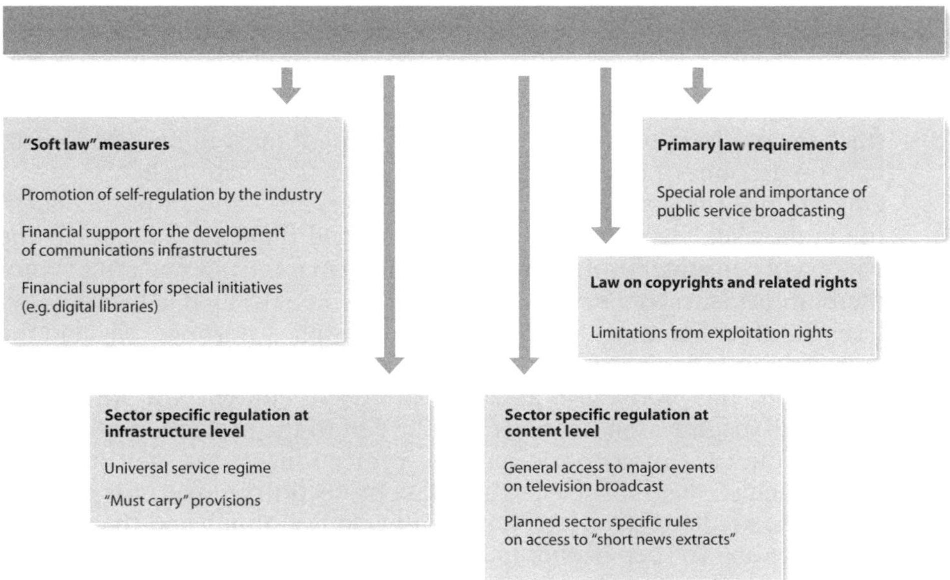

Figure 5: Safeguarding basic supply of the public with content

C. SAFEGUARDING CERTAIN THIRD-PARTY INTERESTS

Finally, European Content Regulation contains provisions motivated by social and sociopolitical concerns, which may be subsumed in the category 'consumer protection in the content markets'.[77] The term consumer is to be understood in a very broad sense and stands for the general public as users of content. On account of the specific characteristics of content as a product that is not only an economic commodity but in particular also a cultural one, and on account of its usually strong mass-media effect which may be detrimental to individuals, 'consumer protection in the content markets' is not confined to regulations focusing on the classic aspects of consumer protection, such as the protection from misleading advertising, but comprises a wide range of consumer interests which may be presented in rough outline as follows:

- First, the regulations focus on the classic consumer interests, i.e. the protection of consumers against misleading and excessive advertising, that is to say against being 'swamped' by advertising. Where misleading advertising may have detrimental effects on the individual's health, as in the

77. Part Two, Chapter 4 primarily deals with these provisions.

case of medicinal products, tobacco and alcohol, health aspects are also an important consideration.[78]

- Secondly, the regulations aim at safeguarding human dignity and other fundamental values cherished by democratic societies. According to these rules the production and distribution of content must in no case foment hate on account of race, gender, religious beliefs or nationality.[79]
- One group of consumers in the content markets – and in particular in the audiovisual sector – is exposed to special dangers: minors. In the context of consumer protection in the content markets, special importance therefore attaches to the protection of minors, in particular at Community level. The focal point is the protection from explicit pornography and the glorification of violence.[80]
- Ultimately, the production and distribution of content also affects the personality rights of individuals. In addition to the protection of privacy and, in the case of corporations, the protection of classified information, which is essentially covered by data protection regulations, mention should be made of the protection of a person's honour and the right of the individual to keep his/her image from being exploited by others.[81]

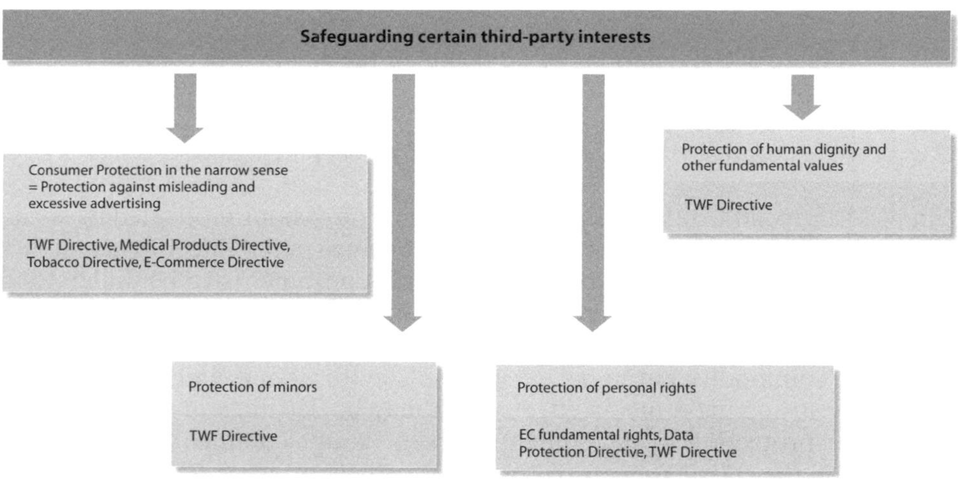

Figure 6: Safeguarding certain third-party interests

At Community level, these 'consumer protection' concerns are recognized first and foremost in the form of ECJ case law according to which Member

78. In detail Part Two, Chapter 4, Section II.A.4.
79. Cf. Part Two, Chapter 4, Section II.A.1.
80. *See* Part Two, Chapter 4, Section II.A.2.
81. For an overview of the protection of personality rights at EC level cf. Part Two, Chapter 4, Section II.A.5.

States' regulations in this field are seen as justified restrictions of fundamental freedoms, on condition that they are proportional. In principle, however, the competence to safeguard consumer protection is left to a large extent to the Member States. Community law lacks genuine competence to regulate, for instance, the protection of personality rights, human dignity or comparable fundamental values of a democratic society. Harmonizing regulation at Community level is only called for if there is some sort of linkage with Community competences and in particular with matters affecting the functioning of the single market, i.e. in the case of the regulation of cross-frontier commerce.[82] In this context, 'consumer protection' is also an object of sector-specific regulations at Community level. To date, such specific provisions have by and large been passed in respect of the television sector and – to a lesser extent – the so-called 'information society services'. They are laid down in the TWF Directive[83] and the E-Commerce Directive.[84] As the TWF Directive is reviewed, these provisions are to be extended – though with different degrees of intensity – to all audiovisual media services.[85] It is worth mentioning that the Commission's draft proposal also invokes media pluralism as a reason why certain harmonizations (e.g. in respect of the independence of national regulatory authorities) are necessary.[86] In addition, Community law contains some isolated product-related regulations, which take the specific properties or modes of action of a given product as a basis for also regulating advertising for said product. Specific examples are the relevant provisions in the Tobacco Advertising Directive[87] and the Medicinal Products Directive.[88]

What most of these regulations have in common is that they restrict the presentation of content and thus the artistic and economic freedom of content providers. As such they are largely determined by fundamental law, particularly by Article 10 ECHR and the intervention provisions and the proportionality requirement of Article 10 (2) ECHR, a position that is confirmed by Article 6 (2) EU and Article 11 of the Charter of Fundamental Rights.[89]

82. This is for example the case with the EC regulations on advertising in broadcast programmes at EC level as advertising is a central economic factor within the audiovisual sector and thus for the development of a single market with regard to this sector of crucial importance. For an account on these provisions, *see* Part Two, Chapter 4, Section IV.
83. Directive 97/36/EC, OJ 1997 L 202/60.
84. Directive 2000/31/EC, OJ 2000 L 178/1.
85. For this revision process, the scope of application of the new directive and the envisaged two-tier system of regulation, *see* Part Two, Chapter 4, Section I.B; as well as the various papers on this issue available at <http://ec.europa.eu/comm/avpolicy/reg/tvwf/modernisation/liverpool_2005/index_en.htm>, 23 June 2006.
86. Cf. Recital 47 proposal for a directive amending the TWF Directive 89/552/EEC, COM (2005) 646 final.
87. Directive 2003/33/EC, OJ 2003 L 152/16.
88. Directive 2001/83/EC, OJ 2001 L 311/67.
89. In general to the application of Article 10 ECHR with regard to the production and distribution of content *see*, C. Ovey and R.C.A. White, *European Convention on Human Rights* (3rd edn, Oxford, Oxford University Press, 2002), p. 276 *et seq.*

Chapter 2
Evaluation and Conclusions: Basic Principles and Structural Elements of European Content Regulation

Michael Holoubek/Dragana Damjanovic

I. EUROPEAN CONTENT REGULATION – A NETWORK OF REGULATION SYSTEMS

As this survey of European content regulation shows, content and the content industry are in many respects subject to Community level policy-making. There are a number of interconnected regulation areas. Together they form a network of regulation systems that determines the framework under which the content industry has to act.[1]

It follows that there is no such thing as a uniform European 'content policy'. Rather, the content industry forms the point of reference for a variety of policy areas, and thus diverse regulatory activities. The individual regulatory areas look at content from different angles and with different degrees of intensity, either as a primary focus of policy-making[2] or with the objective to establish conditions for the European economy in general, in which the content industry (and others) find an adequate basis for performing the services expected of them.[3] To put it in other words, the individual areas of European content regulation seek to set up rules, to provide solutions for the various problems within the European content industry, and thus merely refer to individual parts of the conglomerate of products and services called 'content', or regulate the content industry just in a specific way.

1. For an overview of the various regulatory areas relevant to the content industry *see* in this Part, Chapter 1, figure 1 above.
2. As for example the TWF Directive 97/36/EC, OJ 1997 L 144/19.
3. An example of such a regulatory area is the EC general competition law. For a detailed account on this regulatory area with regard to the content industry, *see* Part Two, Chapter 2.

M. Holoubek, D. Damjanovic and M. Traimer (eds), *Regulating Content – European Regulatory Framework for the Media and Related Creative Sectors*, pp. 235–249

The law of copyrights and related rights for example plays a significant role in the attempt to come to grips with the problem of piracy. In so doing, it focuses on the entire area of 'content', since due to technological developments piracy has affected all areas of online distribution of content: What used to be a problem only for the music industry until recently has by now become a problem for the film industry and may soon affect the book content market, once the projected developments in the field of digital libraries[4] have become reality. This does not mean, however, that copyright and related rights law is about to become the area of regulation which develops an integrative, comprehensive regulation approach regarding content. Its objective is 'merely' to find a solution for the specific problem 'piracy'. In this context it should be noted that, as far as we can *see*, there is no tendency for any major alliance to be formed between copyright law and, say, sector-specific market regulation. It might be worthwhile to consider laying down – in the field of infrastructure regulation[5] – market entry or market operating conditions imposing obligations on the infrastructure providers in support of the particular copyright obligations incumbent on service providers. On the other hand, it has to be noted that such an approach would inevitably give rise to all those difficulties we are all too familiar with from the discussions about the network service provider's liability for content (e.g. the discussion in connection with pornographic content or content glorifying violence).[6] Accordingly, it may well be that an across-the -board approach to the solution of the problems in hand is not due to a lack of insight into the way in which things are connected, but lies in the nature of the subject matter.

This is not to say that the experience and insights gained in one area of regulation cannot be used profitably in another one as well. Thus, the discussion about the adequate extent to which infrastructure providers should be subjected to sector-specific regulation in order to safeguard open communication platforms has shown how difficult it is to draw a line between safeguarding these undeniably important third-party concerns and ensuring the equally important economic freedom of action of infrastructure providers, which is at the same time protected by fundamental rights.[7] This problem has also to be faced in the field of copyright when it comes to effectively monitoring the safeguarding of

4. Cf. fn. 69 in Chapter 1 *above*.
5. For sector-specific regulation at infrastructure level, *see* Part Two, Chapter 3.
6. *See* Green Paper on the protection of minors and human dignity, COM (96) 483 final; and for the latest developments in this field at EC level the proposal for a Recommendation on the Protection of Minors and Human Dignity and the Right of Reply in relation to the Competitiveness of the European Audiovisual and Information Services Industry on 20 January 2006, COM(2006)31 final.
7. On this discussion *see*, *e.g.*, the Commission Communication on Barriers to widespread access to new services and applications of the information society through open platforms in digital television and third generation mobile communications, COM(2003) 410 final.

rights and their exploitation. 'Informational self-determination' also sets limits to 'copyright control'.[8]

What is important is to understand that the different policy areas and areas of regulation in most cases cover content 'only' partially, i.e. in certain segments and aspects, and, secondly, that policy-making is necessarily based on specifically delineated objectives but will never aim at a comprehensive and definitive regulation of the cross-sectional matter content.

The statement that there is no comprehensive European content policy and no area of regulation that would comprise all aspects of content and the content industry is simply an empirical statement without qualitative evaluation. In particular, it does not claim that such a comprehensive and uniform content policy is missing or would be necessary and desirable in the interest of effective political and regulatory conditions for the content industry in line with the Lisbon strategy.[9] Nor does it advocate competences regarding the political and regulatory conditions governing content and the content industry to be largely, or even exclusively, assigned to the Member States.

In view of these considerations one might even ask whether it is at all useful to make content and the content industry the subject of a horizontal investigation into individual areas of regulation,[10] as is done in this book.[11] Are there any common features of the content industry that justify the attempt to look for a uniform approach to the regulation of the content industry? Could it be that, like other areas of industrial activity, the content industry, or more exactly the individual content categories, have just a few problems in common,[12] while otherwise these distinct branches of the content industry share no common features that would justify, speak for or require a uniform regulatory approach?

This view is countered by the well-reasoned argument that the content industry always deals with cultural products and services, i.e. with commodities that should also be considered from a cultural and not only from a purely economic angle. It is this very argument, which is valid for a number of areas, that calls for more stringent regulatory interventions: this is the case in the field of copyrights and related rights just as in that of sector-specific market regulation or (particularly with regard to the scope for Member States' interventions)

8. Cf. Part Two, Chapter 5, Section III.
9. For a brief insight to the Lisbon strategy, *see* Part Two, Chapter 1, Section III.A.
10. In principle the approach to content in the individual areas of regulation is also a horizontal one, in that the arguments used to justify regulation are most of the time drawn from the fields of culture and the promotion of democracy, without any strict distinction between the individual content categories or branches of the content industry. This is only different with regard to the sector-specific regulations, where the subject to be regulated is, at the infrastructure level, limited to the area of eContent, and at the content level, mainly to television broadcasting, respectively in the future to audiovisual media services.
11. On the objective and the methods of this book, *see* Part One, Chapters 1 and 2.
12. As an example we might cite electronic financial services and goods purchases, which just share certain 'security problems', such as payment transactions, but do not show other substantive similarities.

fundamental freedoms. The second common feature of the individual content areas, particularly the ones in the field of eContent, which is predominant in the European context, is their reliance on networks. Digitalization and technological convergence have not failed to affect the 'cultural condition' of the eContent areas.[13] This common feature, the convergence of electronic distribution platforms, also justifies, speaks for or requires – at least for the online content market – a form of regulation that pays attention to the overall situation and the effects regulations of individual parts might have on other parts of the system.

Thus, first and foremost the two aspects 'culture' and 'convergence' militate for the usefulness of an overall, integrative consideration of the European content industry, but they do not automatically also call for an overall and integrative regulation of it. There appear to be some valid arguments suggesting that while it is important to adopt an integrative point of view, it is at the same time important to make sure that the solutions, and in particular the regulatory instruments used, are specific to the areas in question. This means, in other words, that the regulatory response to the commonality engendered by the above-mentioned aspects should consist, first and foremost, in a coordinated regulation rather than a single, closed-in-itself regulatory framework into which the individual partial areas and systems are integrated. Or, to put it differently, that there is no such thing as an overall solution but there can only be area-specific solutions that must, however, not lose sight of a common perspective of the content industry and of an integrated approach to it.

This, in turn, means that the individual areas will have to find the necessary area-specific balance between an 'economic' regulatory approach and interventions motivated by cultural and democratic policy concerns. Thus, an adequate balance of interests between the holders of copyrights, the claims of the exploitation industry and the access needs of the general public to copyrighted content has to be found in copyright law.[14] The balance between the innovative development of new audiovisual content services in a climate of free competition on the one hand and the safeguarding of justified third-party concerns, cultural policy objectives and goals pursued in the interest of the promotion of democracy in connection with these services on the other will have to be sought in sector-specific regulations of the audiovisual media services.[15] And the balance between the potential of innovative developments

13. On the convergence developments in the communications markets, *see* Green Paper on the Convergence of the Telecommunications, Media and Information Technology Sectors and the Implications for Regulation. Towards an Information Society Approach, COM (1997) 623 final; *see also* IP/97/1073 <http://europa.eu.int/ISPO/convergencegp/greenp.html>, 23 June 2006.
14. For a critical appraisal on an adequate balance between these interests within the field of copyright law, *see* Part Two, Chapter 5, Section III.
15. This is a main objective of the future audiovisual media service directive. *See* the proposal for a directive amending the TWF Directive 89/552/EEC, COM(2005) 646 final. The question of how to adequately balance economic and other interests within the content industry also

in the market and the special protection of the diversity of structures in the content industry in the interest of cultural policy concerns must be sought in competition law and in particular merger control legislation. The ever-present need for the balancing of interests cannot be achieved in a meaningful way by applying a uniform, 'content-specific' yardstick but only on the basis of area-specific criteria of copyright law, sector-specific market regulation or general competition law.

However, the absence of a uniform, content-specific yardstick does not mean that 'content-specific' criteria, i.e. criteria that take into account cultural policy concerns, cannot, or should not, be developed in all these areas. If such criteria are to be binding they will have to be enshrined in legal norms. Otherwise the resulting regulation will be a purely economic one which focuses only on the economic conditions of the market in question. Giving such criteria the form of legal norms, however, is subject to multiple tensions: In the context of merger control, for instance, a 'content-specific' evaluation criterion will have to give an answer to the question of whether it satisfies the need for a strengthening of the European content industry with European market players capable of standing up to 'global players', and in how far it takes account of special cultural (and language) policy criteria and the multiplicity of European languages. The decisions here must be based on careful evaluation.

If there is consensus on the above, the individual sub-areas will have to continue to develop their specific criteria, adapt those to new developments and in particular take political decisions as to how in concrete cases divergent interests should be balanced or the weight attributed to them shifted. On the other hand, common coordinating guiding principles will be needed, and will have to be embodied in legal norms, to ensure that the overall content-specific perspective is not lost and that the commonalities derived from the shared aspects of 'culture' and 'convergence' are given due consideration. In this regard, primary Community law still appears to be wanting. In particular, the 'Culture Article' appears to be lacking force, the cross-sectional clause of Article 151 (4) EC notwithstanding, since the – rare – references to that article are only of a declaratory character rather than being pronouncements from which concrete legal effects might be deduced.

That things can be done differently is proved by 'guiding principles' couched in the form of general clauses, such as the one on Community loyalty[16] or the guarantees of fundamental rights. If one wants to embody such a guiding principle in law and thus to enforce compliance with it in the individual fields of regulation, one will inevitably have to accept that there must be a

---

plays a role within the definition of the scope of application of the planned directive on services in the internal market, cf. proposal for a directive on services in the internal market, COM (2006) 160 final. For this debate, *see also* in this Part, Chapter 1, Section II.D. above.

16. On this guiding principle of EC law, laid down in Article 10 EC, in general: A Hatje, *Loyalität als Rechtsprinzip in der Europäischen Union* (Baden-Baden, Nomos: 2001); A. Bogdandy, 'The case for unity: The European Union as a single organization with a single legal system' 36 *Common Market Law Review* (1999), 887.

regulatory competence at European level for such matters. If the cultural policy model regarding content is to become a European concern and thus effective in Community law, acceptance of the regulatory competence at Community level is the inevitable consequence. Cultural diversity and a 'common' strategy are not mutually exclusive objectives. In fact, cultural diversity should be seen, and established, as an essential element of the European model. This is a political view of the matter, but there are valid reasons to believe that in the face of global competition Europe's cultural diversity can be more effectively defended by accepting a common European model and regulation strategies designed to achieve it than by the individual countries 'going it alone'.

A. 'Economic' Market Structure Regulations and External 'Cultural Policy' Goals

As is the case with all kinds of market interventions, interventions into the content markets and the content industry aim at safeguarding the further development of these markets and thus of the content industry as an economic factor as well as at asserting certain general interests intended above all to promote the content industry and the content markets as a cultural and at the same social factor of European integration.[17] If we look at Community law in its present form we will *see* that, generally speaking, objectives motivated by social and cultural policy are mainly sought to be achieved by direct or indirect funding instruments, with particular emphasis being placed on funding programmes at Community level.[18] Structural regulatory interventions aimed at giving the 'market model' a certain cultural or social policy direction are found only in isolated cases. As can be seen in the case of the cultural exemption clause in state-aid law[19] or the regulation of matters concerning the protection of third-party interests,[20] Community law regulations are for the most part limited to a minimum and are intended to leave the Member States sufficient margin for the realization of such external objectives. By and large, Community law only influences these aspects by way of funding programmes. It can only be assessed from a political point of view whether – if we look at the funding volume provided for content in relation to the funding of other areas and the overall budget available[21] – the verbal commitment to certain focal points contained

17. In detail on these two essential directions of European content regulation cf. the systematic overview in this Part, Chapter 1, Section II and III *above*.
18. For an overview of these funding instruments, cf. in this Part, Chapter 1, Section III.A.1.
19. Article 87(3)(d)EC.
20. Cf. Chapter 1, Section III *above*.
21. For some figures which can only give rough estimates of how much the EU spends for the content industry, *see, e.g.*, the framework 7 budget lines [< http://www.ist-ec.org/news>, 23 June 2006], which contain the draft budget for 2007–13 and figures on how much the EU spends for the information sector (of which the online content market forms a major

in the funding regulations is also adequately reflected in the amount of funds actually made available.

As a result of the lively ongoing discussion about competencies in cultural matters and the restriction of the competence of the Community to the funding of content as a cultural asset, which has been upheld despite various revisions of the Community Constitution in the last few years, the European model of the content market and of the content industry and thus of a European content policy can still by and large only be influenced via financial incentives. At the same time, however, this means that efforts at regulating European content mainly focus on the establishment of an economic market model for the content industry. Objectives of a cultural and social nature are merely seen as external objectives largely left to the discretion of the Member States.

To give an example: According to the market entry regime within the sector-specific regulations for the electronic communications markets[22] the Member States are limited to requiring just a notification of the relevant economic activities. Prior licences are only admissible in cases where the efficient use of scarce resources, in particular of broadcast frequencies, is to be ensured. The principle applying in such cases is that resources are assigned in accordance with economic efficiency criteria. In the case of the allocation of broadcast frequencies to be used for the provision of audiovisual content, however, still other specific criteria may apply, if they meet the requirement of proportionality. Thus, media or cultural policy aspects may be taken into consideration when broadcast frequencies are allocated for the purpose of transmitting audiovisual content services. This enables the Member States to use 'licensing' as a regulatory instrument to pursue the aim of 'safeguarding a functioning media landscape'. However, EC law does not harmonize these selection criteria based upon media or cultural policy considerations (e.g. the selection criteria for the admissibility of the multiplex platform).[23]

The fact that Community law enables the Member States – via specific exceptions and authorizations – to lay down structural rules of a cultural and democratic policy nature, but fails to define them even in the form of minimum standards, has one consequence well-known from the application of the dogma of fundamental freedoms: due to the country-of-origin principle governing large parts of the market structure regulations embodied in Community law, regulations laid down by the Member States give rise to competition within the single market. The consequence may be that uncoordinated structural regulations on the part of Member States and the relevant political decisions will finally either have no effect at all or may become subject to such pressure that any such attempt at regulation loses its persuasiveness. There is the rub, because

---

part) or the information at the Media Programme (cf. fn. 56 in this Part, Chapter 1 *above*) available at <http://ec.europa.eu/comm/avpolicy/media/index_en.html>, 23 June 2006.

22. For an account on these provisions, *see* Part Two, Chapter 3, Section II.B.
23. On this function of the market entry regime within the sector-specific regulatory framework of the electronic communication markets, *see also* in Part Two, Chapter 3, Section II.B.2.

any regulating approach in particular in the field of culture, which is coordinated at a European-wide level will have an entirely different and much more promising effect than isolated steps taken by individual Member States. In particular in areas such as the eContent sector, which is per se of a transboundary nature, a European content policy may be more efficient than measures taken by the Member States alone.

It must, of course, not be overlooked that these two approaches to regulation – the safeguarding of functioning market structures and the realization of, above all, cultural concerns of general interest – need not necessarily be conflicting objectives, but may in fact largely move in the same direction. It is via the allocation function of the market that the efficient and adequate production and distribution of content, and thus its variety and adequate supply, are to be safeguarded. It can only be assessed from a political point of view whether or in how far such models of economic variety and the production and distribution of content governed by an economic market model can ensure the desired content and the extent of supply of such content that is considered to be sufficient also from a cultural and democratic policy point of view. If we assume, however, that in addition to 'economically' oriented structural measures further interventions are required to ensure the desired efficiency of the content markets – an approach by and large followed by the content policies of the Member States as well as the European content policy – the question arises which instruments should be used to implement these objectives in a meaningful way.

The reason why such specific objectives of a content policy nature are at EC level largely reflected in 'soft' funding activities rather than in 'hard' structural regulation that would modify the economic principles of the content market is, in all likelihood, not merely a question of selecting the efficient regulatory instruments but rather the as yet unresolved question of competencies.

Under primary law, cultural policy matters fall in principle within the competencies of the Member States, and Article 151 EC merely provides for a specific and limited 'subsidiary competence' of the Community, in particular for the promotion of specific cultural objectives of the EC Treaty while explicitly excluding competencies in the field of the harmonization of laws and regulations. Article 151 (2) EC reiterates the importance of the subsidiarity principle, particularly in this area.[24]

This does not say much, since, as has been outlined, content is a cross-sectional matter, which in many ways and respects falls within the competence of the Community legislators to enact harmonizing secondary law. Suffice it in this context to recall the rules governing sector-specific market regulation,[25]

24. In detail *see* Part Two, Chapter 1, Section II.D.3.
25. Including, in particular, the sector-specific provisions for electronic communications infrastructures (cf. Part Two, Chapter 3, Section II.), for audiovisual media services (cf. Part Two, Chapter 4) and for the other eContent services that fall in the category of 'information society services' (cf. the E-Commerce Directive 2000/31/EC, OJ 2000 L 178/1).

relevant tax harmonization in the field of indirect taxes[26] or the rules of European copyright and related rights law.[27] In particular where economic interest in a low regulation intensity coincides with Member States' interest in safeguarding their regulatory scope, arguments in favour of Community-level regulations in the interest of democracy and cultural policy are likely to fall on barren ground. Two conclusions may be drawn from this state of affairs:

For one thing, horizontal rules – as the example of general competition law shows – for the most part merely follow the regulatory logic inherent in the system. Even the cross-sectional clause of Article 151 (4) EC has so far failed to establish itself as a general horizontal objective capable of impacting on the individual regulatory areas of Community law. Accordingly, general competition law relies on the same regulatory instruments to achieve its effects on the content industry as it employs with regard to other economic sectors. Apart from the fact that competition law has to take note of and, when interpreting the rules of competition, consider the actual conditions prevailing in the respective sectors under investigation and the rules of functioning specific to them, European competition law has not developed any distinct 'content-specific' competition rules, but has remained – as in other economic sectors – 'general competition law'. Thus, no references to Article 151 (4) EC are found in any of the recent decisions of the Commission on merger control in the content sector. Article 151 (4) EC does not deploy any interpretive effect nor does it supply any modified yardsticks or criteria that would introduce a special 'culture-specific perspective' into the examination from the angle of competition law. The effects that the principle of Community loyalty in Article 10 has had on the decisions of the ECJ,[28] to quote but one example, shows that this is not due to the fact that such effects could not be derived from such general principles; Article 151 (4) EC simply seems to lack the 'visionary force' it would need to have a model function in this context.

Before this background we *see* all the more clearly the special importance that attaches to the Commission's initiative embodied in its proposal to amend the TWF Directive[29] and to include all audiovisual media services in the sector-specific market regulation approach of that Directive.[30] The proposal for a more stringent regulation, which is backed up by arguments in favour of the promotion of democracy and cultural policy, including the explicitly laid down authorization of Member States to provide for further measures in regard of

26. Cf., in particular, the VAT Directive 77/799/EC, OJ 1977 L 336/15 and the survey on these provisions in Part Two, Chapter 6, Section I.B.
27. For an account on these EC provisions, *see* Part Two, Chapter 5.
28. On these effects, *see, e.g.*, A. Hatje [2001].
29. OJ 1997 L 202/60.
30. *See* the Proposal for a directive amending the TWF Directive 89/552/EEC, COM(2005) 646 final; and for a critical appraisal on this proposal (with further references) Part Two, Chapter 4, I.B.

media service providers subject to their jurisdiction,[31] attributes a position to the entire sector that is separate and distinct from the multiplicity of other services and constitutes a specific regulatory approach which, according to the proposal currently under discussion, will be capable of asserting itself against the regulatory approach of the planned Directive on services in the internal market.[32]

However, apart from the planned audiovisual media services directive, Community market structure law usually considers special cultural policy objectives in the content sector merely as exemptions, which are accepted either on grounds of expressly formulated provisions in positive law, such as the culture exemptions clause within state aid law[33] or the various socio-politically motivated provisions within the sector-specific regulation framework for the electronic communication markets,[34] or through the interpretation of general EC regulatory mechanisms by the ECJ, as for example the fundamental freedoms;[35] in either case, the way in which these exemptions are handled is, however, left to the Member States. Or more precisely: Faced with such objectives, Community law first and foremost lays down limitations designed to safeguard functioning market structures and a functioning internal market, but usually the rules passed at Community level will not pursue a course of action aimed at genuine structural modification for cultural, democratic or social policy reasons.[36]

Before this background it will depend on one's perspective whether one sees this state of affairs as one safeguarding cultural diversity in Europe and preserving the Member States' role in influencing developments or expects that, in the longer term, the existing rules governing market structures will, owing to their inherent strength, assert themselves against incentive systems (particularly in view of the growing scarcity of public funds) and will ultimately result in a particular 'market model' the substance of which the Member States might have wished to shape differently.

One might say that under globalized competitive conditions only a European structural model, but not individual rules developed by the individual states, will stand a chance of success and assert itself in global competition. This line of thought might also provide an answer to the question of whether

---

31. *See* recital 24 of the Proposal for a directive amending the TWF Directive 89/552/EEC, COM(2005) 646 final.
32. Proposal for a directive on services in the internal market, COM (2006) 160 final.
33. Article 87(3)(d) EC. Cf. Part Two, Chapter 1, Section II.C and Chapter 2, Section V.
34. For these provisions *see* Part Two, Chapter 3, Section II.C.
35. Cf. in this Part, Chapter 1, Section II.C.
36. Usually the exemptions clauses formulate that the Member States may pursue other than economic objectives, if they are necessary to meet clearly defined general interest objectives and if they are proportionate and transparent. *See, e.g.*, the conditions to impose must-carry provisions (cf. Part Two, Chapter 3, Section III.C) or the conditions under which the Member States may deviate from the fundamental freedoms (cf. Part Two, Chapter 1, Section II.A.).

in view of changing global competitive conditions the idea of 'regional' European integration had not become obsolete, at least insofar as the safeguarding of competitive conditions in the single market or in a globalized market is concerned, and whether the relevant decisions and regulatory principles should not be negotiated at the global level within the framework of the WTO. The formulation of specific European market structure models for certain areas such as essential parts of the content industry might actually greatly strengthen a self-contained European content industry in the struggle between competing systems.

On the other hand, we ought to bear in mind that there are very few cases in which such European structural decisions on cultural matters or the promotion of democracy in the field of content have actually worked. That this is a most arduous task is demonstrated, amongst other things, by the cumbersome and reluctant efforts to harmonize copyright, where finding a common denominator for the different substantive approaches in the various Member States has proved difficult.[37] Here again, the comparatively well functioning harmonization of industrial property rights shows that a much larger degree of agreement might be achieved provided that the parties concerned confine themselves to an economic market model.

Before this backdrop the Commission's proposal for an amendment of the TWF Directive[38] and its approach, which is explicitly directed at promoting democracy and cultural policy,[39] once again emphasizes the special significance of this initiative. We should not underestimate the importance of this effort to integrate these concerns, so far largely considered mere 'external' concerns at EC level, into European law governing the market structures within the content industry, since it would create a specifically European market model, for the time being at least for the audiovisual media services.

B. THE ONLINE CONTENT MARKET AS A FOCAL POINT

European content regulation, i.e. European policies and thus also regulatory efforts, generally tend to focus on the online content market. This applies to both funding programmes[40] and 'hard' regulatory interventions[41] into the content industry as well in terms of both economic and cultural policy making at

37. For a critical account on this debate, *see* Part Two, Chapter 5, Section V.
38. Proposal for a directive amending the TWF Directive 89/552/EEC, COM(2005) 646 final.
39. Recital 3 of the proposal states: 'The importance of audiovisual media services for societies, democracy and culture justifies the application of specific rules to these services'.
40. Except from the Culture programme, the European funding programmes relevant for the content industry refer to the audiovisual media industry, eContent and the communications infrastructures. *See* the overview in this Part, Chapter 1, Section III.A.1. *above*.
41. Especially the sector-specific provisions, both at infrastructure (for these *see* Part Two, Chapter 3) and at content level (for these *see* Part Two, Chapter 4) refer merely to the online content market.

EC level. This fact has been underscored by the Commission's i2010 Initiative[42] adopted within the scope of the EU's renewed Lisbon Strategy.

That this area should be focused on is a logical conclusion, since it is one of the European Union's most promising economic sectors which also plays a significant role in developing the future model of society in the Union and in particular in creating the information society for all. The eContentplus funding programme[43] and in its wake the major initiatives 'digital libraries'[44] and 'eAccessibility'[45] are just a few examples of such efforts to influence the content industry.

Promotion in this area is guided by the general premise that these technologies are per se of a transboundary nature. In other fields of content promotion Community policies more or less concentrate on establishing cultural services as specifically European services in the single market with particular emphasis on the exchange of such services within Europe.

The concentration of the European Community on this area is also illustrated by the fact that sector-specific provisions, i.e. provisions specially developed for the content industry, so far exist only for the online content markets and here they apply primarily – the transboundary aspect again comes into play – to the infrastructure level, i.e. the distribution platforms for eContent. On account of the convergence developments they became subject to uniform technology neutral regulations with the 2002 regulatory package for communications markets.[46] With regards to the sector-specific regulations at content level such a step towards a 'convergent' regulation (at least of the audiovisual content) by the development of a common concept for linear services (TV broadcasts) and non-linear media services (basically on-demand services) has yet to be taken.[47] The same holds for the essential political decision as to whether and in how far classic principles governing the regulation of television broadcasting – with all necessary modifications – should also be applied to non-linear services. Thus, regulatory interventions like programming quotas will in future have to consider the public reach of such services, in particular in view of the increasing competition between linear and non-linear media services.[48] Similarly, the specific conditions of converging technological distribution platforms

42. Communication i2010, COM(2005) 229. Also *see* the relevant Communication on the information society, COM(2005) 757.
43. Decision 456/2005/EC of the European Parliament and of the Council establishing a multiannual Community programme to make digital content in Europe more accessible, usable and exploitable, OJ 2005 L 79/1.
44. Cf. fn. 69 in this Part, Chapter 1 *above*.
45. Cf. fn. 67 in this Part, Chapter 1 *above*.
46. In detail on these provisions *see* Part Two, Chapter 3.
47. To the revision workings in this direction at EC level *see* Part Two, Chapter 4, Section I.B.
48. *See* Impact Study of Measures (Community and National) Concerning the Promotion of Distribution and Production of TV Programmes Provided for Under Article 25(a) of the TV Without Frontiers Directive – Final Report, prepared by David Graham and Associated Limited for the Audiovisual, Media and Internet Unit Directorate-General Information Society and Media European Commission (24 May 2005).

(such as Internet and digital television) are known to have given rise to extensive discussions on adequate regulatory approaches in the field of the protection of minors,[49] where in particular new approaches such as regulated self-regulation or co-regulation[50] have raised hopes among the regulators although a final and consensual evaluation is yet outstanding.[51]

Finally, the focus of European content regulation on the online content market is also reflected in the field of copyright law. A close look will show that harmonization at Community level is predominantly found in areas where problems arise from the new distribution technologies. This is where sector-specific rules of particular significance to the eContent sector are likely to be developed (e.g. a 'Digital Rights Management').[52] Increased recourse to, and the further extension of, Community competencies will, however, have to compete with Member States' efforts to coordinate their regulations to fit the global environment. To date it is probably an open question whether the integration of international efforts and arrangements will pass through Community organs or the Member States.

II. SOME THESES FOR FURTHER DISCUSSION

European content regulation is not a uniform policy field and has not been codified in a homogeneous set of rules. Much rather it consists of a network of regulating systems which set rules concerning segments or special aspects of the cross-sectional matter 'content' from specific angles. Thus, legislative regulating systems react to a highly complex subject to be regulated with a complicated network of regulations in which the individual subsystems retain a relatively wide scope of action. Whether this is an advantage or a drawback is subject to interpretation, though there are valid arguments for the view that only such

49. Cf. fn. 6.
50. For these measures, *see* Study on Co-Regulation Measures in the Media Sector, prepared by The Hans-Bredow-Institute and the Institute of European Media Law for the European Commission, Directorate Information Society and Media Unit A1 Audiovisual and Media Policies (19 January 2006).
51. The development of convergence may also suggest regulatory consequences in more remote fields. To give one example, the 'catalogue of options' left by the 6th VAT Directive 77/779/EC, OJ 1997 L 336/15, for tax relief in its current form still contains some inconsistencies: unlike the reception of radio and television programmes, video and online services are not covered by Annex H of the 6th VAT Directive. This means that the 'reception' of radio and TV programmes via the Internet cannot be offered at a reduced value-added tax rate. As a result, different rates operate for the reception of one and the same programme depending on which transmission mode has been chosen. To date, the Commission has not seen this as a distortion of competition, and has therefore not yet proposed either to abandon the reduced rate for the reception of radio and TV programmes or to extend it to the reception via the Internet. The Commission's report on the 6th VAT Directive, which will be due in 2008, might well present an opportunity for reconsideration.
52. Cf. Part Two, Chapter 5, Section I.B.5.

network systems have the necessary flexibility, openness to new developments and innovative capacity to meet the regulatory challenges. To put it simply: There is not, and there cannot be, a 'super-legislator' who would be able to finally regulate the cross-sectional matter 'content' in a comprehensive and uniform way. Only 'partial legislators' who confine themselves to their special fields will be in a position to reduce the complexity to such an extent that adequate regulation becomes possible.

If one accepts this premise and bears in mind that under current European constitutional law the cross-sectional matter 'content' falls within the competences of partial legislators at both European level and that of the Member States, it follows that the first and foremost task confronting European content policy and content regulation is one of 'coordinating networks'. This means that common guiding principles should be developed and that the individual segments, including the rule-setting at the level of Member States, should be coordinated to such an extent as to avoid inconsistencies and conflicting interpretations. This, in turn, will require general framework regulations at European level – such as the existing horizontal ones which aim at preserving the market structure – as well as focused sector-specific harmonization.

Where, as in the case with eContent, material conditions are largely of a transboundary nature (also in a cultural sense and with regard to languages), there are valid reasons for aiming at a tighter coordination of harmonization measures in terms of improvements of the European market structure law for essential areas of content. It is the two aspects 'culture' and 'convergence' that militate in particular for a common and integrative approach to the European content industry. The regulatory consequence would certainly not be a 'uniform content regulation', but specific regulations for individual areas that would, however, be held together by a common guiding principle. The stronger this guiding principle, the more effective will be the linkage between these areas. It is therefore essential to adopt an integrative stance but at the same time to develop solutions for these problems, and in particular adequate instruments, with a view to the specific conditions of the area concerned. To what extent the catchword 'European culture' is to be endowed with an authentic profile and the relevant policies are predominantly to be entrusted to the Community level, is in itself a political decision. In this light, the Commission's proposal to extend the application of the TWF Directive and thus to opt for a special approach to the regulation of audiovisual media services is a highly remarkable and most significant step. The same thing can be said about cultural-policy-motivated measures and projects regarding harmonization in the field of intellectual property, and in particular copyright law.

A European content policy that is more than the sum total of the individual Member States' policies must be clearly identifiable as such. European primary law would be the right place for embodying democratic and cultural-policy guiding principles for a special European market model covering important parts of the content sector. The 'Culture Article' in its present form, which expresses scepticism regarding European efforts rather than propounding a

European vision for the cultural aspects of the content industry, does not appear to live up to this challenge. A set of rules characterized by mistrust can neither form a sound basis for developing guiding principles nor inspire positive action in the individual areas of Community policy. Such common guiding principles at EC level, on the one hand, will have to define – adjusted to each regulatory area – criteria for an appropriate balance between economic and cultural aspects to be followed Europe-wide (while leaving at the same time an adequate margin of appreciation to the Member States). On the other hand it is also important to establish on a general primary level of Community law a 'mission' for the European content policy that fosters the cultural approach within this common European strategy (e.g. 'common diversity for a multi-cultural community'). If, in an open and proactive approach, a culture-oriented European content policy is sought that preserves and promotes the global competitiveness of Europe's content industry, the Community must be equipped with the necessary regulatory competencies in the field of cultural policy.

In line with the subsidiarity principle and on account of the specific cultural and social conditions of the individual regions, it would be appropriate to leave, wherever possible in the light of material conditions, the formulation of exemption clauses or limitations, particularly in regulating third-party concerns (personality rights, protection of minors etc.), to the Member States, which would have to build on a European (minimum) standard. In concrete individual cases, the balancing of interests between the 'free flow of information' and 'freedom of opinion' on the one hand and legitimate third-party interests on the other, cannot be determined at European level.

However, where the form and characteristics of market structures are involved, a sustainable European content policy ought to be reflected in European market structure regulations. If European content markets are to be seen, and to function, not only along the lines of an economic market model but also on one concerned with the promotion of cultural matters and democracy, there may be legitimate doubts as to whether these objectives can be effectively reached merely through European funding programmes and market structure regulations on the part of Member States within the scope of exemption clauses granted by the Community. It might very well be a more promising and future-oriented approach to adopt a (partial) harmonization formula also for a 'structural policy for content' at European level.

Bibliography

Altes in *Beck'scher Kommentar zum Rundfunkrecht,* Hahn/Vesting (eds) (Munich, CH Beck, 2003).

Apel J. / Grapperhaus T., 'Das Offline-Online-Chaos oder wie die Europäische Kommission den grenzüberschreitenden Werbemarkt zu harmonisieren droht' [1999] *Wettbewerb in Recht und Praxis,* 1253.

Arlt C., 'Digital Rights Management-Systeme' [2004] *Gewerblicher Rechtsschutz und Urheberrecht,* 554.

Bartosch A., 'The Relationship between Public Procurement and State Aid Surveillance – The Toughest Standard Applies?' (2002) 39 *Common Market Law Review*, 551.

Baßler J., 'Zu den "Steuerspezifika" der Grundfreiheiten des EG-Vertrages' [2005] *Internationales Steuerrecht,* 825.

Bechtold S., 'Multimediarecht und Urheberrecht – einige grundsätzliche Anmerkungen' [1998] *Gewerblicher Rechtsschutz und Urheberrecht,* 23.

Beck D. et al, *Service Public unter Druck? Die Auswirkungen der EU-Transparenzrichtlinie auf den öffentlichen Rundfunk* (Zurich, Rüegger, 2004).

Beiser R. and Zorn N. 'Art. 93' in *Kommentar zu EU- und EG-Vertrag,* Mayer H. (ed) (Vienna, Manz, 2003).

Beiser R., *Steuern* (Vienna, WUV, 2001).

Berger, C., 'Elektronische Pressespiegel und Informationsrichtlinie' [2004] *Computer und Recht,* 360.

Berger C., 'Grundfragen der 'weiteren Beteiligung' des Urhebers nach § 32a UrhG' [2003] *Gewerblicher Rechtsschutz und Urheberrecht,* 675.

Berger C., 'Urheberrechtliche Erschöpfungslehre und digitale Informationstechnologie' [2002] *Gewerblicher Rechtsschutz und Urheberrecht,* 200.

Berka W., 'Content-Regulation im Lichte der Konvergenz' [2000] *Journal für Rechtspolitik*, 197.

Bernütz S. and Weinreich C., 'Steuern' in *Rechtshandbuch Electronic Business,* Gounalakis G. (ed) (Munich, Beck, 2003).

Blanke H.-J., 'Art. 151 EG' in *Kommentar zu EU-Vertrag und EG-Vertrag* C. Calliess/ H.-J. Ruffert (eds) (Neuwied 2002).

Blasi M., *Das Herkunftslandprinzip der Fernseh- und E-Commerce-Richtlinie* (Colone, Carl Heymanns, 2004).

von Bogdandy A., 'Europäischer Protektionismus im Medienbereich' (1992) 1 *Europäische Zeitschrift für Wirtschaftsrecht,* 14.

von Bogdandy A., 'The case for unity: The European Union as a single organization with a single legal system' (1999), 36 *Common Market Law Review*, 887.

Brenn C., *Das ECG – E-Commerce-Gesetz* (Vienna, Manz, 2002).

Burgstaller P. and Minichmayr G., *E-Commerce-Gesetz – Praxiskommentar* (Vienna, Medien und Recht, 2002).

Capobianco A., 'Licensing of Music Rights: Media Convergence, Technological Developments and EV Competition Law' [2004] *European Intellectual Property Review,* 113.

Castendyk O., 'Förderung der audiovisuellen Produktion in Europa' in *Die Zukunft der Fernsehrichtlinie,* EMR (eds) (Nomos, 2005), p. 99.

Craig P. and de Burca G. (eds) *EU-Law – Text, Cases and Materials,* (3rd edn, Oxford, 2003).

Cordewener A., *Europäische Grundfreiheiten und nationales Steuerrecht* (Colone, O. Schmidt, 2002).

Damjanovic D. and Holoubek M. and Lehofer H.P. and Kassai K. and Urbantschitsch W., *Handbuch des Telekommunikationsrechts* (Vienna, Springer, 2006).

Damjanovic D., *Regulierung der Kommunikationsmärkte unter Konvergenzbedingungen* (Vienna, Springer, 2002).

Damjanovic D., 'Öffentlich-rechtliche Aspekte des E-Commerce' in *Handbuch Öffentliches WirtschaftsrechtI,* M. Holoubek and M. Potacs (eds.) (Vienna, Springer, 2002) p. 1143.

Decker U., in *Urheberrechtsgesetz,* P. Möhring/K. Nicolini (eds) (2nd edn, Munich, Franz Vahlen, 2000), Section 53.

De Graaf A., 'Avoidance of international double taxation: Community or joint policy?' [1998] *EC Tax Review,* 258.

Deselaers W., 'Sportverbände und Europäisches Kartellrecht' [1998] *Wirtschaft und Wettbewerb,* 946.

Dethloff N., 'Europäisches Kollissionsrecht des unlauteren Wettbewerbs' (2000) 4 *Juristenzeitung,* 181.

Dillenz W., *Urheberrecht* (Vienna, Springer, 2004).

Dinan D., *Ever closer union: An introduction to European intergration* (3rd edn, London, Lynne Rienner Publishers, 2005), p. 412.

Dirksen D., 'Article 82', in *Kommentar zum deutschen und europäischen Kartellrecht,* E. Langen and H. Bunte (eds) (Neuwied, Luchterhand, 2001).

Doralt W., *Steuerrecht* (Vienna, Manz, 2005).

Dreier T., 'Die Umsetzung der Urheberrechtsrichtlinie 2001/29/EG in deutsches Recht' [2002] *Zeitschrift für Urheber- und Medienrecht,* 30.

Dreier T. and Schulze G., *Urheberrechtsgesetz* (Munic, C.H.Beck, 2004).

Dreier T. in *Europäisches Urheberrecht,* M. Walter et al. (eds) (Wien, Springer, 2001).

T. Dreier, 'Urheberrecht an der Schwelle des 3 Jahrtausends – Einige Gedanken zur Zukunft des Urheberrechts' [2000] *Computer und Recht,* 45.

Eilmansberger T., 'How to distinguish good from bad competition under Article 82 EC: In search of clearer and more coherent standards for anti-competitive abuses' (2005) 42 *Common Market Law Review,* 129.

Eilmansberger T., Herzig G., Jaeger T. and Thyri P., *Materielles Europarecht* (Vienna, LexisNexis, 2005).

Egan M., *Constructing a European Market: Standards, Regulation, and Governance* (Oxford, Oxford University Press, 2001).

Ehrke-Rabel T, 'Äquivalenzgebot und Abgabenverfahrensrecht' in *Abgabenverfahrensrecht und Gemeinschaftsrecht,* Holoubek M. and Lang M.(eds) (Vienna, Linde Verlag, 2006).

Englisch J., 'The European Treaties' Implications for Direct Taxes' [2005] *Intertax,* 323.

Ennöckl D. and Windhager M., "Paparazzi-Fotos" von Prominenten' [2004] *Medien & Recht,* 246.

Fallenböck M., 'Urheberrecht in der digitalen Ökonomie: Die EG-Urheberrechtsrichtlinie und ihre Umsetzung' [2002] *ecolex,* 104.

Fallenböck M. and Nitzl S., 'Urheberrechtliche Rahmenbedingungen für elektronische Pressespiegel' [2003] *Medien und Recht,* 102.

Fallenböck M., 'Internationales Urheberrecht und digitale Wirtschaft' in *Urheberrecht in der digitalen Wirtschaft – Beiträge zu Internet, Telekommunikation und Software,* in Fallenböck M. and Galla F. and Stockinger S. (eds) (Vienna, Manz, 2005), p. 157.

Faull J. and Nikpay A., *The EC Law of Competition,* (Oxford, OUP, 1999).

Fibbe G. and de Graaf A., Is double taxation arising from autonomous tax classification of foreign entities incompatible with EC law? in *A Tax Globalist – Essays in honour of Maarten J. Ellis,* van Arendonk H. et al (eds) (Amsterdam, IBDF, 2005), p. 237.

Flechsig N., 'Grundlagen des Europäischen Urheberrechts' [2002] *Zeitschrift für Urheber- und Medienrecht,* 9.

Fox E., 'We Protect Competition, You Protect Competitors' [2003] *World Competition,* 149.

Frey D. and Rudolph M., 'EU-Richtlinie zur Durchsetzung der Rechte geistigen Eigentums' [2004] *Zeitschrift für Urheber- und Medienrecht,* 525.

Fritze U. and Holzbach C., 'Die Electronic-Commerce-Richtlinie' [2000] *Wettbewerb in Recht und Praxis,* 875.

Garzaniti L., *Telecommunications, broadcasting and the Internet – EU Competition Law and Regulation* (2nd edn, London, Sweet & Maxwell, 2003).

Geiger R., *EUV/EGV-Kommentar des Vertrages über die Europäische Union und des Vertrages zur Gründung der Europäischen Gemeinschaft* (3rd edn, Munich, Beck, 2000).

Geradin D., 'Access to Content by New Media Platforms: A Review of the Competition Law Problems' (2005) 30 *European Law Review,* 68.

Gersdorf H., *Grundzüge des Rundfunkrechts* (Munich, Beck, 2003).

Grabenwarter C., *Europäische Menschenrechtskonvention* (2nd ed, Vienna, Manz, 2005).

Griller S., 'Der Anwendungsbereich der Grundrechtscharta' in *Gundrechte für Europa – Die Europäische Union nach Nizza,* Griller S. and Duschanek A. (eds) (Vienna, Springer, 2002) p. 158.

Hailbronner K. and Weber C., 'Möglichkeiten zur Förderung der europäischen Kultur in Rundfunk und Fernsehen anhand der Fernsehrichtlinie der EG' (1997) 14 *Die Öffentliche Verwaltung,* 565.

Haller J., *Urheberrechtsschutz in der Musikindustrie* (Lohmar, Josef Eul, 2005).

Hatje A, *Loyalität als Rechtsprinzip in der Europäischen Union* (Baden-Baden, Nomos: 2001).

Hatzopoulos V., 'Recent Developments of the Case Law of the ECJ in the Field of Services' (2000) 37 *Common Market Law Review* 2000, 43.

Heidenhain M., *Handbuch des Europäischen Beihilfenrechts* (Munich, Beck, 2003).
Heinemann A., 'Schutzrechte in der Informationsgesellschaft und ihr Verhältnis zum Kartellrecht', in *Stand und Perspektiven des Schutzes Geistigen Eigentums in Europa,* Behrens P. (ed) (Baden-Baden, Nomos, 2004).
Helberger N., *Controlling Access to Content. Regulating Conditional Access in Digital Broadcasting* (The Hague, Kluwer Law International, 2005).
Helberger N., 'The "Right to Information" and Digital Broadcasting: About Monsters, Invisible Men and the Future of European Broadcasting Regulation' (2006) *2 Entertainment Law Review,* 70.
Helberger N., 'Digital Rights Management aus der Sicht der Verbraucher' [2005] IRIS plus, Supplement IRIS Issue 2005–08, 1–8.
Henry C. and Matheu M., 'New regulations for public services in competition' in *Regulation of Network Utilities. The European Experience,* Henry C., Matheu M. and Jeunemaître A. (eds) (Oxford, Oxford University Press, 2001).
Himberger S., 'Digitales terrestrisches Fernsehen in Österreich' (2005) *Medien & Recht,* 159.
Hoeren T., 'Vorschlag für eine EU-Richtlinie über E-Commerce – Eine erste kritische Analyse' [1999] *MultiMedia und Recht,* 194.
Hoeren T., 'Entwurf einer EU-Richtlinie zum Urheberrecht in der Informationsgesellschaft' [2000] *MultiMedia und Recht,* 517.
Hoffmann-Riem W., *Regulierung der dualen Rundfunkordnung* (Baden-Baden, Nomos, 2000).
Holoubek M. 'Normung' in *Handbuch Öffentliche Wirtschaftrecht II,* Holoubek/Potacs (eds) (Vienna, Springer, 2002], p. 23.
Holznagel B., 'Der Zugang zu Premium-Inhalten: Grenzen einer Exklusivvermarktung nach Europäischen Recht' [2005] *Kommunikation & Recht,* 385.
Immenga, 'Wettbewerbspolitik contra Industriepolitik nach Maastricht' [1994] *Europäische Zeitschrift für Wirtschaftsrecht,* 14.
Jones A. and Sufrin B., *EC Competition Law* (2nd edn, Oxford, OUP, 2004).
Karl H., 'Folgerecht-RL: Harmonisierung auf niedrigem Niveau? – Bericht von der Arbeitssitzung der ALAI-Landesgruppe Österreich vom 30.06.05' [2005] *Medien und Recht,* 227.
Kleist T. and Scheuer A., 'Audiovisuelle Mediendienste ohne Grenzen' [2006] *MultiMedia und Recht,* 128.
Kleist T. and Scheuer A., 'Neue Regelungen für audiovisuelle Mediendienste' [2006] *MultiMedia und Recht,* 206.
Kofler G., *Doppelbesteuerungsabkommen und Gemeinschaftsrecht* (Linz, Habilitation, 2006).
Köhntopp K. and Köhntopp M. and Seeger M., 'Sperrungen im Internet' [1998] *Kommunikation & Recht,* 25.
Koutrakos P., 'On Groceries, Alcohol, and Olive Oil: More on Free Movement of Goods after Keck?' (2001) 26 *European Law Review,* 391.
Kreibohm F., *Der Begriff der Steuer im Europäischen Gemeinschaftsrecht* (Colone, Heymann, 2004).
Kröger D., *Informationsfreiheit und Urheberrecht* (Munich, C. H. Beck, 2002).
Kröger D., 'Die Urheberrechtsrichtlinie für die Informationsgesellschaft – Bestandsaufnahme und kritische Bewertung' [2001] *Computer und Recht,* 318.
Kühling J., *Sektorspezifische Regulierung in den Netzwirtschaften* (Munich, Beck, 2004).
Kucsko G., *Geistiges Eigentum* (Vienna, Manz, 2004).

Ladeur K.H., *Das Werberecht der elektronischen Medien* (Vienna, Verlag Recht und Wirtschaft, 2004).
Ladeur K.H., 'Rundfunkaufsicht im Multimediazeitalter' [2000] *Kommunikation & Recht,* 176.
Lang M. and Schuch J. and Staringer C., Steuerrecht I + II (4th ed, Vienna, WUV, 2005).
Lang M.,' Rechtsschutzfragen abgabenrechtlicher Beihilfengewährung' in *Beihilfenrecht,* Studiengesellschaft Wirtschaft und Recht (ed) (Vienna, Linde Verlag, 2004).
Lang M., 'Die Besteuerung von Körperschaften des öffentlichen Rechts aus dem Blickwinkel des gemeinschaftsrechtlichen Beihilfenrechts' in *Körperschaften im Steuerrecht – Festschrift Wiesner,* König E. and Schwarzinger W. (eds) (Vienna, Linde Verlag, 2004).
Lang M., 'Die Aufhebung von Bescheiden wegen Widerspruchs zum Gemeinschaftsrecht gem § 302 Abs 2 lit c BAO' in *Abgabenverfahrensrecht und Gemeinschaftsrecht,* Holoubek M. and Lang M.(eds) (Vienna, Linde Verlag, 2006).
Larouche P., *Competition Law and Regulation in European Telecommunication* (Oregon, Hart Publishing, 2000).
Lehner M. 'EU-Recht und die Kompetenz zur Beseitigung der Doppelbesteuerung' in *Doppelbesteuerungsabkommen und EU-Recht,* Gassner W. and Lang M. and Lechner E. (eds) (Vienna, Linde Verlag, 1996) p. 11.
Lehner M. 'Does the new Constitution for Europe disengage the Member States from their obligation to prevent double taxation?' [2005] *British Tax Review,* 337.
Linnenborn O., 'Update: Europäisches Urheberrecht in der Informationsgesellschaft' [2001] *Kommunikation & Recht,* 399.
Madner V., 'Effektivitätsgebot und Abgabenverfahrensrecht' in *Abgabenverfahrensrecht und Gemeinschaftsrecht,* Holoubek M. and Lang M.(eds) (Vienna, Linde Verlag, 2006).
Mahr F., 'Interne Weiterleitung von grenzüberschreitenden Rundfunksendungen in die Hotelzimmer – Anmerkung zu EuGH 3.2.2000 (sechste Kammer) in der Rechtssache C-293/98' [2000] *Medien und Recht,* 157.
Majone G., 'Theories of regulation' in *Regulating Europe,* G. Majone (ed) (London and New York, Routeledge, 1996) p. 28.
Mankowski P., 'Internet und Internationales Wettbewerbsrecht' [1999] *Gewerblicher Rechtsschutz und Urheberrecht International,* 914.
Mayer C., 'Die Privatkopie nach Umsetzung des Regierungsentwurfs zur Regelung des Urheberrechts in der Informationsgesellschaft' [2003] *Computer und Recht,* 278.
Mederer W., 'Artikel 87' in *Kommentar zum Vertrag über die Europäische Union und zur Gründung der Europäischen Gemeinschaft,* von der Groeben H. and Schwarze J. (eds) (6th edn, Baden-Baden, Nomos, 2003).
Mestmäcker E.-J. and Schweitzer H., *Europäisches Wettbewerbsrecht* (2nd edn, Munich, Beck, 2004).
Micklitz J. and Keßler H., 'Europäisches Lauterkeitsrecht – Dogmatische und ökonomische Aspekte einer Harmonisierung des Wettbewerbsverhaltensrechts im europäischen Binnenmarkt' [2002] *Gewerblicher Rechtsschutz und Urheberrecht International,* 888.
Möschel W., 'Article 86' in *EG-Wettbewerbsrecht,* U. Immenga and E.-J. Mestmäcker (eds) (Munich, Beck, 1997).
Nemetz M., 'Internetapotheken – Post DocMorris' [2004] *ecolex,* 991.

Nemetz M., 'Verbraucherschutz im E-Commerce' in *Internetrecht,* Wiebe A.(ed) (Vienna, Springer, 2004), p. 188.
Neubauer M., 'Urheberrecht und digitale Netze' in *Internetrecht,* Wiebe A.(ed), (Vienna, Springer, 2004), p. 74.
Nowotny E., Der öffentliche Sektor (Berlin et al, Springer, 1999).
Öhlinger T and Potacs M., *Gemeinschaftsrecht und staatliches Recht* (Vienna, Lexis-Nexis, 2001).
Oppermann T., *Europarecht* (2 nd edn, Munich, Beck, 2005).
Osserbühl T., *RundFunk zwischen nationalem Verfassungsrecht und Europäischem Gemeinschaftsrecht* (Frankfurt, Alfred Metzner Verlag, 1986).
Ovey C. and White R.C.A., *European Convention on Human Rights* (3rd edn, Oxford, Oxford University Press, 2002).
Philapitsch F., 'Zum Erfordernis einer legalen Quelle für die Digitale Privatkopie' [2004] *Medien und Recht,* 111.
Phillips C.F., *The Regulation of Public Utilities. Theory and Practice* (Virginia, Public Utilities Reports, Inc, 1985).
Pierce, Jr., R.J. and Gellhorn E., *Regulated Industries in a nutshell* (4th edn, St. Paul, Minn, West Group, 1999).
Pistone P., *The Impact of Community Law on Tax Treaties: Issues and Solutions* (The Hague, Kluwer Law International, 2002).
Potacs M., 'Gemeinschaftsrecht und Bestandkraftstaatlicher Verwaltungsakte' in *Internationale Gemeinschaft und Menschenrechte – Festschrift Ress,* Bröhmer J. et al (eds) (Colone, Heymanns, 2005).
Rehbinder M., *Urheberrecht* (12 edn, Munich, C. H.Beck, 2002).
Reinbothe J., 'Die EG-Richtlinie zum Urheberrecht in der Informationsgesellschaft' [2001] *Gewerblicher Rechtsschutz und Urheberrecht International,* 741.
Reinbothe J., 'Die Umsetzung der Urheberrechtsrichtlinie 2001/29/EG in deutsches Recht' [2002] *Zeitschrift für Urheber- und Medienrecht,* 51.
Ress G. and Ukrow J., 'Art. 151 EC' in *Das Recht der Europäischen Union,* E. Grabitz/M. Hilf (eds) (Munich, 2000).
Schack H., *Urheber- und Urhebervertragsrecht* (2nd ed, Tübingen, Mohr Siebeck, 2001).
Schack H., 'Neuregelung des Urhebervertragsrechts – Kritische Anmerkung zum Professorenentwurf' [2001] *Zeitschrift für Urheber- und Medienrecht,* 453.
Schanda R., 'Auskunftsanspruch gegen Access-Provider über die IP-Adressen von Urheberrechtsverletzern' [2005] *Medien und Recht,* 21.
Schmidt-Preuß M., 'Verwaltung und Verwaltungsrecht zwischen gesellschaftlicher Selbstregulierung und staatlicher Steuerung' in *Veröffentlichungen der Vereinigung der deutschen Staatsrechtslehrer,* vol. 56 (De Gruyter, 1997) p 162.
Schoenthal M., 'Major Events and Reporting Rights' (2006) 04, Iris Plus, Legal Observations of the European Audiovisual Observatory.
Schönfeld J., 'Doppelbesteuerung und EG-Recht' [2006] *Steuer und Wirtschaft,* 80.
Schröter H., 'Article 81 to 89' in *Kommentar zum Europäischen Wettbewerbsrecht,* Schröter H., Jakob T. and Mederer W. (eds) (Baden-Baden, Nomos, 2003).
Schröter H., 'Article 82', in *Kommentar zum Vertrag über die Europäische Union und zur Gründung der Europäischen Gemeinschaft,* H.v.d. Groeben and J. Schwarze (eds) (Baden-Baden, Nomos, 2003).
Schweitzer H., *Daseinsvorsorge, 'service public', Universaldienst* (Baden-Baden, Nomos, 2002).

Schuhmacher F., 'Kollektive Marktbeherrschung und koordinierte Effekte im EG-Wettbewerbsrecht' [2005] *wirtschaftsrechtliche blätter,* 245.
Schulte U., 'Die Informationspflichten auf Internetseiten nach § 5 Abs 1 ECG. Zur österreichischen Rechtslage mit Blick auf Entscheidungen aus Deutschland' [2004] *Medien und Recht,* 444.
Schulz W. and Seufert W. and Holznagel B., *Digitales Fernsehen. Regulierungskonzepte und – perspektiven* (Leske & Budrich, 1999).
Seifert M., 'Rechtliche Grundlagen des Bologna-Prozesses und der Lissabon-Strategie – Europaweite Vereinheitlichung der Studienstrukturen und Maßnahmen zur Erleichterung der Anerkennung von Diplomen', *Working Paper of the Europainstitut No. 56,* Vienna 2004, <www.fgr.wu-wien.ac.at/institut/ef/wplist.html>, 16 June 2006.
Shy O., *The economics of network industries* (Cambridge, Cambridge University Press, 2001).
Sparr J., 'Art. 151' in *EU-Kommentar,* Schwarze J. (eds) (Baden-Baden, Nomos, 2000).
Spaventa E., 'From Gebhard to Carpenter: Towards a (non-)economic European Constitution' (2004) 41 *Common Market Law Review,* 743.
Spindler G., 'Europäisches Urheberrecht in der Informationsgesellschaft' [2002] *Gewerblicher Rechtsschutz und Urheberrecht,* 112.
Spindler G. and Fallenböck M., 'Das Herkunftslandprinzip der E-Commerce-Richtlinie' [2002] *Zeitschrift für Rechtsvergleichung, internationales Privatrecht und Europarecht,* 214.
Spoerr W. and Sellmann C., 'Informations- und Kommunikationsfreiheit im Internet' [2004] *Kommunikation & Recht,* 372.
Staringer C., 'Das Durchführungsverbot im Beihilfenrecht und das Abgabenverfahrensrecht', in Abgabenverfahrensrecht und Gemeinschaftsrecht, Holoubek M. and Lang M.(eds) (Vienna, Linde Verlag, 2006).
Steiner J., 'Drawing the Line: Uses and Abuses of Art 30 EEC' (1992) 29 *Common Market Law Review,* 749.
Stickelbrock B., 'Die Zukunft der Privatkopie im digitalen Zeitalter' [2004] *Gewerblicher Rechtschutz und Urheberrecht,* 742.
Sutter F.P., *Das EG-Beihilfenverbot und sein Durchführungsverbot in Steuersachen* (Vienna, Linde Verlag, 2005).
Sutter F.P., 'Art. 87' in *Kommentar zu EU- und EG-Vertrag,* Mayer H. (ed) (Vienna, Manz, 2003).
Sutter F.P 'Beihilfen im materiellen Steuerrecht – Steuergesetze und Verwaltungshandeln der Steuerbehörden im Spannungsfeld zum EG-Beihilfenverbot' in *Beihilfenrecht,* Studiengesellschaft Wirtschaft und Recht (ed) (Vienna, Linde Verlag, 2004).
Terra B. and Kajus J., *European VAT Directives Volume I* (Amsterdam, IBFD, 2004).
Thyri P., 'Immaterialgüterrechte und Zugang zu wesentlichen Einrichtung' [2005] *Wirtschaft und Wettbewerb,* 388.
Thyri P., 'Gemeinwirtschaftliche Dienstleistungsaufträge zwischen Beihilfenanmeldung und Vergabeverfahren' [2003] *Österreichische Zeitschrift für Wirtschaftsrecht,* 126.
Traimer M., 'Neufassung der EU-Richtlinie Fernsehen ohne Grenzen verabschiedet' [1997] *Medien und Recht,* 128.
Traimer M., 'Europäische Rahmenbedingungen staatlicher Medienregulierung im Lichte der Konvergenz' [2000] *Journal für Rechtspolitik,* 137.

Tumpel M. 'Der Einfluss der Grundfreiheiten des EG-Rechts auf die Doppelbesteuerungsabkommen' [2003] *Österreichische Steuerzeitung,* 154.
von Ungern-Sternberg J., in *Urheberrecht Kommentar,* G. Schricker and et al (eds) (2nd edn, München, C.H.Beck, 1999).
Van Danwitz F., 'Grundfragen der Beihilfenaufsicht' [2000] *Juristenzeitung,* 429.
Van Thiel S., 'General Report' in *WTO and Direct Taxation,* Lang M and Heradin J. and Hofbauer I. (eds) (Vienna, Linde Verlag, 2005), p. 13.
Van Thiel S. and Steinbach A., 'The Effect of WTO Law in the Legal Order of the European Community: a Judicial Protection Deficit or a Real-political Solution, or both' in *WTO and DirecTaxation,* Lang M. and Heradin J. and Hofbauer I. (eds) (Vienna, Linde Verlag, 2005), p. 49.
Walter M., 'Diskussionsentwurf für die Umsetzung der Folgerecht-RL in das österreichische Recht' [2005] Medien und Recht, 244.
Walter M., *Urheberrechtsgesetz – UrhGNov 2003* (Vienna, Medien und Recht, 2003).
Walter M., 'Ministerialentwurf einer UrhGNov 2002 – Ausgewählte Aspekte' [2002] *Medien und Recht,* 218.
Walter M., 'Die vier Säulen des Urheberrechts – Zugleich eine Standortbestimmung der österr Urheberrechtsreform nach der UrhGNov 1997' [1999] *Zeitschrift für Rechtsvergleichung, Internationales Privatrecht und Europarecht,* 88.
Weatherill S., 'After Keck: Some Thoughts on how to Clarify the Clarification' (1996) 33 *Common Market Law Review,* 885.
Weiser Ch., *Preismissbrauch nach Artikel 86 EWG-Vertrag* (Köln, Heymann, 1987).
von Weizsäcker C., 'Rechte und Verhältnisse in der modernen Wirtschaftslehre' (1981) 34 *KYKLOS,* 349.
Wiebe A., 'Auskunftsverpflichtung der Access Provider' [2005] *Medien und Recht* Issue 4 Supplement.
Wiebe A., 'Europäischer Datenbankschutz nach 'William Hill' – Kehrtwende zur Informationsfreiheit?' [2005] *Computer und Recht,* 169.
Wiebe A., 'Das neue 'digitale' Urheberrecht – Eine erste Bewertung' [2003] *Medien und Recht,* 311.
Wiebe A., 'Abwehr unerwünschter Links' in *Hyperlinks,* Ernst S. and Vassilaki I. and Wiebe A. (eds) (Colone, Verlag Otto Schmidt, 2002).
Wiebe A., 'Information als Schutzgegenstand im System des geistigen Eigentums' in *Information als Wirtschaftsgut,* Fiedler H. and Ullrich H. (eds) (Colone, Otto Schmidt Verlag, 1997), p. 103.
Widmer M., *Open Source Software – Urheberrechtliche Aspekte freier Software* (Bern, Stämpfli, 2003).
Wilbert S., 'Joint Selling of Bundesliga media rights – first Commission decision pursuant to Article 9 of Regulation 1/2003' [2005] *Competition Policy Newsletter* 2, 44.
Wittmann H., 'Die EU-Urheberrechts-Richtlinie – ein Überblick' [2001] *Medien und Recht,* 144.
Wolff Ch., *Zwangslizenzen im Immaterialgüterrecht* (Göttingen, V & R Unipress, 2005).
Zankl W., *Das E-Commerce-Gesetz – Kommentar und Handbuch* (Vienna, Verlag Österreich, 2002).
Zimmermann H. and Henke K-D., *Finanzwissenschaft* (8th edn, Munich, Vahlen, 2001).

Table of EU Legislation

DIRECTIVES

Directive 2005/36/EC on the recognition of professional qualifications, OJ 2005 L 255/22

Directive 2005/29/EC concerning unfair business-to-consumer commercial practices in the internal market and amending Council Directive 84/450/EEC, Directives 97/7/EC, 98/27/EC and 2002/65/EC and of the Council and Regulation (EC) No 2006/2004, OJ 2005 L 149/22

Directive 2004/48/EC on the enforcement of intellectual property rights, OJ 2004 L 195/16 [Enforcement Directive]

Directive 2003/49/EC in regards to the possibility for certain Member States to apply transitional periods for the application of a common system of taxation applicable to interest and royalty payments made between associated companies of different Member States, OJ 2003 L 157/49

Directive 2003/48/EC on taxation of savings income in the form of interest payments, OJ 2003 L 157/38

Directive 2003/33/EC on the approximation of the laws, regulations and administrative provisions of the Member States relating to the advertising and sponsorship of tobacco products, OJ 2003 L 152/16 [Tobbaco Directive]

Directive 2002/58/EC concerning the processing of personal data and the protection of privacy in the electronic communications sector, OJ 2002 L 201/37 [Directive on privacy and electronic communications]

Directive 2002/38/EC amending and amending temporarily Directive 77/388/EEC in regards to the value added tax arrangements applicable to radio and television broadcasting services and certain electronically supplied services, OJ 2002 L 128/41

Directive 2002/22/EC on universal service and users' rights relating to electronic communications networks and services, OJ 2002 L 108/51 [Universal Service Directive]

Directive 2002/21/EC on a common regulatory framework for electronic communications networks and services, OJ 2002 L 108/33 [Framework Directive]

Directive 2002/20/EC on the authorization of electronic communications networks and services, OJ 2002 L 108/21 [Authorization Directive]

Directive 2002/19/EC on access to, and interconnection of, electronic communications networks and associated facilities, OJ 2002 L 108/7 [Access Directive]

Directive 2001/83/EC on the Community code relating to medicinal products for human use, OJ 2001 L 311/67

Directive 2001/84/EC on the resale right for the benefit of the author of an original work of art, OJ 2001 L 272/32 [Artist's Resale Right Directive]

Directive 2001/29/EC on the harmonization of certain aspects of copyright and related rights in the information society, OJ 2001 L 167/10 [Information Society Directive]

Directive 2000/31/EC on certain legal aspects of information society services, in particular electronic commerce, in the Internal Market, OJ 2000 L 178/1 [E-Commerce Directive]

Directive 1999/49/EC amending, with regard to the level of the standard rate, Directive 77/388/EEC on the common system of value added tax, OJ 1999 L 139/27

Directive 98/84/EC on the legal protection of services based on, and consisting of, conditional access, OJ 1998 L 320/54 [Conditional Access Directive]

Directive 98/48/EC amending Directive 98/34/EC laying down a procedure for the provision of information in the field of technical standards and regulations, OJ 1998 L 217/18

Directive 98/34/EC laying down a procedure for the provision of information in the field of technical standards and regulations and of rules on Information Society services, OJ 1998 L 204/37

Directive 97/55/EC amending Directive 84/450/EEC concerning misleading advertising so as to include comparative advertising, OJ 1997 L 290/18

Directive 97/38/EC Annex C to Council Directive 92/51/EEC on a second general system for the recognition of professional education and training to supplement Council Directive 89/48/EEC, OJ 1997 L 184/31

Directive 97/36/EC amending Council Directive 89/552/EEC on the coordination of certain provisions laid down by law, regulation or administrative action in Member States concerning the pursuit of television broadcasting activities, OJ 1997 L 202/60 [TWF Directive]

Directive 97/7/EC on the protection of consumers in respect of distance contracts, OJ 1997 L 144/19

Directive 96/71/EC concerning the posting of workers in the framework of the provision of services, OJ 1997 L 18/1

Directive 96/9/EC on the legal protection of databases, OJ 1996 L 77/20 [Databases Directive]

Directive 95/46/EC on the protection of individuals with regard to the processing of personal data and on the free movement of such data, OJ 1995 L 281/31

Directive 93/98/EEC harmonizing the term of protection of copyright and certain related rights, OJ 1993 L 290/9

Directive 93/83/EEC on the coordination of certain rules concerning copyright and rights related to copyright applicable to satellite broadcasting and cable retransmission, OJ 1993 L 248/15 [Satellite and Cable Directive]

Directive 93/39/EEC concerning the placing of biocidal products on the market, OJ 1993 L 214/22

Directive 93/7/EEC on the return of cultural objects unlawfully removed from the territory of a Member State, OJ L 1993 74/74

Directive 92/100/EEC on rental right and lending right and on certain rights related to copyright in the field of intellectual property, OJ 1992 L 346/61 [Rental Directive]

Directive 92/77/EEC supplementing the common system of value added tax and amending Directive 77/388/EEC, OJ 1992 L 316/1

Directive 92/51/EEC on a second general system for the recognition of professional education and training to supplement Directive 89/48/EEC, OJ 1992 L 209/25

Directive 91/250/EEC on the legal protection of computer programs, OJ 1991 L 122/42 [Software Directive]

Directive 90/435/EEC on the common system of taxation applicable in the case of parent companies and subsidiaries of different Member States, OJ 1990 L 225/6

Directive 90/434/EEC 1990 on the common system of taxation applicable to mergers, divisions, transfers of assets and exchanges of shares concerning companies of different Member States, OJ 1990 L 225/1

Directive 89/48/EEC on a general system for the recognition of higher-education diplomas awarded on completion of professional education and training of at least three years' duration, OJ 1989 L 19/16

Directive 88/357/EEC on the coordination of laws, regulations and administrative provisions relating to direct insurance other than life assurance and laying down provisions to facilitate the effective exercise of freedom to provide services and amending Directive 73/239/EEC, OJ 1988 L 172/1

Directive 84/450/EEC relating to the approximation of the laws, regulations and administrative provisions of the Member States concerning misleading advertising, OJ 1984 L 250/17

Directive 77/799/EEC concerning mutual assistance by the competent authorities of the Member States in the field of direct taxation, OJ 1977 L 336/15 [VAT Directive]

Directive 77/388/EEC on the harmonization of the laws of the Member States relating to turnover taxes – Common system of value added tax: uniform basis of assessment, OJ 1977 L 145/1

Directive 69/335/EEC concerning indirect taxes on the raising of capital, OJ 1969 L 249/25

Directive 65/65/EEC the approximation of provisions laid down by law, regulation or administrative action relating to medicinal products, OJ 1965 L 22/369

Proposal for a Directive of the European Parliament and of the Council on services in the internal market, COM(2006) 160.

Proposal for a directive amending council directive 89/552/EEC on the coordination of certain provisions laid down by law, regulation or administrative action in Member States concerning the pursuit of television broadcasting activities, of 13 December 2005 [Proposal for a directive amending the TWF Directive 89/552/EEC]

Proposal for a directive on criminal measures aimed at ensuring the enforcement of intellectual property rights, COM(2005)276 final [Proposal for a Directive on criminal measures]

REGULATIONS

Regulation (EC) No. 139/2004 on the control of concentrations between undertakings (OJ 2004 L 24/1

Regulation (EC) No. 1/2003 on the implementation of the rules on competition laid down in Articles 81 and 82 of the Treaty, OJ 2003 L1/1

Regulation (EC) No. 2790/1999 on the application of Article 81(3) of the Treaty to categories of vertical agreements and concerted practices, OJ 1999 L 336/21

Regulation (EEC) No. 3911/92 of 9 December 1992 on the export of cultural goods, OJ 1992 L 395/1

Regulation (EEC) No. 1612/68 of the Council on freedom of movement for workers within the Community, OJ 1968 L 257/12

Regulation No. 17 First Regulation implementing Articles 85 and 86 of the Treaty, OJ 1962 L 13/204

Proposal for a Regulation of the European Parliament and the Council on the law applicable to non-contractual obligations, COM(2003) 427 final.

DECISIONS

Decision No 854/2005/EC of the European Parliament and of the Council establishing a multiannual Community Programme on promoting safer use of the Internet and new online technologies, OJ C 2005 17/6 [Decision promoting safer use of the Internet]

Decision No 456/2005/EC of the European Parliament and of the Council establishing a multiannual Community programme to make digital content in Europe more accessible, usable and exploitable, OJ 2005 L 79/1 [Decision establishing a Community programme to make digital content more accessible]

Decision No 846/2004/EC of the European Parliament and of the Council amending Council Decision 2000/821/EC on the implementation of a programme to encourage the development, distribution and promotion of European audiovisual works (MEDIA Plus – Development, Distribution and Promotion) (2001–2005), OJ 2004 L 157/4 [Desicion 846/2004/EC MEDIA Plus]

Decision No 845/2004/EC of the European Parliament and of the Council amending Decision No 163/2001/EC on the implementation of a training programme for professionals in the European audiovisual programme industry (MEDIA-Training) (2001–2005), OJ 2004 L 157/1 [Desicion 845/2004/EC MEDIA-Training]

Decision No 508/2000/EC of the European Parliament and of the Council establishing the Culture 2000 Programme, OJ 2000 L 63/1 [Desicion Culture 2000]

Decision No 276/1999/EC of the European Parliament and of the Council adopting a multiannual Community action plan on promoting safer use of the Internet by combating illegal and harmful content on global networks, OJ 2003 L 162/1 [Decision combating illegal and harmful content on global networks]

Council Decision 163/2001/EC of the European Parliament and of the Council on the implementation of a training programme for professionals in the European audiovisual programme industry (MEDIA-Training) (2001–2005), OJ 2001 L 26/1 [Desicion 163/2001/EC MEDIA-Training]

Council Decision 48/2001/EC adopting a multiannual Community programme to stimulate the development and use of European digital content on the global networks and to promote linguistic diversity in the information society, OJ 2001 L 14/32 [Decision development and use of European digital content]

Council Decision 821/2000/EC on the implementation of a programme to encourage the development, distribution and promotion of European audiovisual works (MEDIA Plus – Development, Distribution and Promotion) (2001–2005), OJ 2000 L 336/82 [Desicion 821/2000/EC MEDIA Plus]

Commission Decision 56/2005/EC setting up the Education, Audiovisual and Culture Executive Agency for the management of Community action in the fields of education, audiovisual and culture in application of Council Regulation (EC) No 58/2003, OJ 2005 L 24/35 [Decision setting up the Education, Audiovisual and Culture Executive Agency]

Commission Decision 622/2002/EC establishing a Radio Spectrum Policy Group, OJ 2002 L 198/49

Proposal for a Decision of the European Parliament and the Council concerning the implementation of a programme of support for the European audiovisual sector (MEDIA 2007), COM(2004) 470 final [Proposal for a Decision Media 2007]

Proposal for a Decision of the European Parliament and the Council establishing the Culture 2007 programme (2007–2013), COM(2004) 469 [Proposal for a Decision Culture 2007]

Table of EU Cases

EUROPEAN COURT OF JUSTICE

Adria-Wien Pipeline GmbH, Case No. C-143/99 [2001] ECR I-8365

Alpine Investments BV, Case No. C-384/93 [1995] ECR I-1141

Altmark-Trans, Case No. C-280/00 [2003] ECR I-7747

Ambulanz Glöckner, Case No. C-475/99 [2001] ECR I-8089

Arbeitsgemeinschaft Deutscher Rundfunkanstalten (ARD), Case No. C-6/98 [1999] ECR I-7599

ARD/Pro Sieben, Case No. C-6/98 [1999] ECR I-07599

Asscher, Case No. C-107/94 [1996] ECR I-3089

Baars, Case No. C-251/98 [2000] ECR I-2787

Bacardi France, Case No. C-429/02 [2004] ECR I-6613

Brasserie de Haecht v. Consorts Wilkin-Janssen, Case No. 23/67 [1967] ECR 544

British American Tobacco, Case No. C-491/01 [2002] ECR I-11453

British Horseracing Board Ltd and Others v. William Hill Organization Ltd, Case No. C-203/02 [2004] ECR I-10415

BRT v. SABAM I, Case No. 127/73 [1974] ECR 51

Bodson, Case No. 30/87 [1988] ECR 2479

Cassis de Dijon, Case No. 120/78 [1979] ECR 649

Centre Belge d'Etudes de Marché Télémarketing v. SA Compagnie luxembourgeoise de télédiffusion, Case No. 311/84 [1985] ECR 3261

Centros, Case No. C-212/97 [1999] ECR I-1459

CNSD v. Commission, Case No. T-513/93 [2000] ECR II-1807

Coditel v. Ciné-Vog Films SA (Coditel II), Case No. 262/81 [1982] 3381

Commission v. Belgium, Case No. C- 11/95 [1996] ECR I-4115

Commission v. France, Case No. C-154/89 [1991] ECR I-659

Commission v. Great Britain, Case No. C-222/94 [1996] ECR I-4025

Commission v. Netherlands, Case No. C-353/89 [1991] ECR I-4069

Commission v. Netherlands, Case No. C-350/02 [2004] ECR I-6213

Commission v. Italy (customs agents), Case No. 118/85 [1987] ECR 2599

Commission v. Italy (customs agents), Case No. C-35/96 [1998] ECR I-3851

Dassonville, Case No. 8/74 [1974] ECR 837b

De Agostini, Cases No. C-34/95, C-35/95 and C-36/95 [1997] ECR I-3843

De Gezamenlijke, Case No. C-30/59 [1961] ECR I-3

De Groot, Case No. C-385/00 [2002] ECR I-11819

Debauve, Case No. 52/7 [1980] ECR 833

Deliège v. Ligue francophone de judo, Case No. C-51/96 and C-191/97 [2000] ECR I-2549

Delimitis, Case No. C-234/89 [1991] ECR I-935

Denuit, Case No. C-14/96 [1997] ECR I-2785

Deutscher Apothekerverband eV v. 0800 DocMorris NV and Jacques Waterval, Case No. C-322/01 [2003] ECR I-14887*DocMorris*, Case No. 322/01 [2003] ECR I-14887

DM Transport, Case No. C-256/97 [1999] ECR I-3913

Entidad de Gestión de Derechos de los Productores Audiovisuales (Egeda) v. Hostelería Asturiana SA (Hoasa), Case No. C-293/98 [2000] ECR I-629

ERT, Case No. C-260/89 [1991] ECR I-2925

Evans Medical Ltd, Case No. C-324/93 [1995] ECR I-563

Executif regional wallon, Cases No. C-62/87 and C-72/87 [1988] ECR I-1573

Federal Republic of Germany v. Commission, Case No. C-156/98 [2000] ECR I-6857

Ferring, Case No. C-53/00 [2001] ECR I-9067

Fixtures Marketing Ltd v. Organismos prognostikon agonon podosfairou AE, Case No. C-338/02 [2004] ECR I-10549

Gebhard, Case No. C-55/94 [1995] ECR I-4165

Gourmet, Case No. 405/98 [2001] ECR I-1795

Gregg, Case No. C-216/97 [1999] ECR I-4947

Heiser, Case No. C-172/03, OJ 2005 C 106/5.

Hoffmann, Case No. C-144/00 [2003] ECR I-2921

Hoffmann-La Roche v. Commission, Case No. 85/76 [1979] ECR 461

Imperial Chemical Industries, Case No. 48/69 [1972] ECR 619

IMS Health, Case No. C-418/01 [2004] ECR I-5039

Italy v. Council and Commission, Case No. 32/65 [1966] ECR 458

J. C. J. Wouters et al. v. Algemene Raad van de Nederlandse Orde van Advocaten, Case No. C-309/99 [2002] ECR I-1577

Keck and Mithouard, Cases No. C-267 and 268/91 [1993] ECR I-6097

Keeping Newcastle Warm Ltd., Case No. C-353/00 [2002] ECR I-5419

Konsumentombudsmannen (KO) v. De Agostini (Svenska) Förlag AB) and TV-Shop i Sverige AB, Case No. C- 34/95 et al [1997] ECR I -3843

Kerckhaert-Morres, Case No. C-513/04, OJ 2005 C 57/14

KPN Telekom, Case No. C-109/03 [2004] ECR I-11273

Ladbroke Racing, Case No. C-359/95 P und C-379/95 P [1997] ECR I-6265

Lankhorst-Hohorst, Case No. C-324/00 [2002] ECR I-11779

Lasteyrie du Saillant, Case No. C-9/02 [2004] ECR I-2409

Leclerc, Case No. 229/83 [1985] ECR 1

Leclerc-Siplec, Case No. C-412/93 [1995] ECR I-179

Lucazeau v. SACEM (SACEM II), Case No. 110/88, 241/88 and 242/88 [1989] ECR 2811

Luisi and Carbone, Case No. 286/82 and 26/83 [1984] ECR 377

Marks & Spencer, Case No. C-446/03, OJ 2006C 36/5

Metallgesellschaft & Hoechst, Cases No. C-397/98 and C-410/98 [2001] ECR I-1727

Ministère Public v. Jean-Louis Tournier (SACEM I), Case No. 395/87 [1989] ECR 2521

Ministère public v. Asjes, Case No. 209/84 – 213/84 [1986] 1425

Neste Markkinointi Oy v. Yötuuli Ky and Others, Case No. C-214/99 [2000] ECR I-11121

Office des Produits Wallons ASBL, Case No. C-184/00 [2001] ECR I-9115

Omega Spielhallen- und Automatenaufstellungs-GmbH, Case No. C-36/02 [2004] ECR I-9609

Pavlov et al., Cases No. C-180/98 to C-184/98 [2000] ECR I-6451

Peterbroeck, Case No. C-312/93 [1995] ECR I-4599

Poucet and Pistre, Cases No. C-159/91 and C-160/91 [1993] ECR I-637

Radio Telefis Eireann (RTE) and Independent Television Publications LTD (ITP) v. Commission ('Magill'), Cases No. C-241/91 P & C-242/91 P [1995] ECR I-743.

Raymond Vander Elst, Case No. C-43/92 [1994] ECR I-3803

Royal Bank of Scotland, Case No. C-311/97 [1999] ECR I-2651

RTI, Cases No. C-320-94, C-328-94, C-329-94, V-337/94 [1996] ECR I-06471.

RTL, Case No. C-245/01 [2003] ECR I-12489

Sacchi, Case No.155/73 [1974] ECR 428

Schempp, Case No. C-403/03, OJ 2005 C 217/12

Schröder, Case No. 40/72 [1973] ECR 142

Schumacker, Case No. C-279/93 [1995] ECR I-225

Stergios Delimitis v. Henninger Bräu AG, Case No. C-234/89 [1991] ECR I-935

Stichting Collective Antennevoorziening Gouda and others v. Commissariaat vor de Media ('Mediawet I'), Case No. C-288/89 [1991] ECR I-4007

Suiker Unie et al. v. Commission, Case No. 40–48, 50, 54–56, 111, 113 and 114/73 [1975] 1663

Transalpine Ölleitung in Österreich, Case No. C-368/04, OJ 2004 C 273/13

TV10, Case No. C-23/93 [1994] ECR I-4795

Überseering, Case No. C-208/00 [2002] ECR I-9919

United Brands v. Commission, Case No. 27/76 [1978] ECR 207

Van Binsenberg, Case No. 33/74 [1974] ECR I-1299

van Schijndel, Cases No. C-430/93 and C-431/93 [1995] ECR I-4705

Veronica, Case No. C-148/91 [1993] ECR I-487

VT4 Ltd, Case No. C-56/96 [1997] ECR I-3143

Wells, Case No. C-201/02 [2004] ECR I-723

Wielockx, Case No. C-80/94 [1995] ECR I-2493

William Hill, Case No. C-203/02 [2004] ECR I-10415

Wouters et al., Case No. C-309/99 [2002] ECR I-1577

EUROPEAN COURT OF FIRST INSTANCE

Aéroports de Paris, Case No. T-128/98 [2000] ECR II-3929

Airtours v. Commission, Case T-342/99 [2002] ECR II-2585

BPB Industries, Case No. T-65/89 [1993] ECR II-389

Endemol Entertainment Holding v. Commission, Case No. T-221/95 [1999] ECR II-1299

Hilti, Case No. T-30/89 [1991] ECR II-1439

IMPALA v. Commission, Case No. T-464/04 (application published in OJ 2005 C 6/46).

Infront WM AG v. Commission of the European Communities, Case No. T/33/01 (application published in OJ 2006 C 48/25)

Tiercé Ladbroke SA v. Commission ('Ladbroke II'), Case No. T-504/93 [1997] ECR II-923

Michelin II, Case No. T-203/01 [2003] ECR II-4071

M6 et. al., Cases No. T-185/00, T-216/00, T-299/00 and T-300/00 [2002] ECR II-3805

Schneider Electric v. Commission, Case No. T-310/01 [2002] ECR II-4071

Tetra Laval v. Commission, Case No. T-5/02 [2002] ECR II-4381

Tetra Pak II, Case No. T-83/91 [1994] ECR II-755

Tokai Carbon v. Commission, Case No. T-236/01 [2004] ECR II-1181

EUROPEAN COMMISSION DECISIONS ON INDIVIDUAL CASES

Barcelona Agreement, COMP/C2/38.377, OJ 2002 C 132/18

Canal+/RTL/GJCD – JV, Commission Decision Comp/M.2483 (Press release of the Commission of 12 November 2001, IP/01/1579)

Deutsche Bundesliga, Commission Decision COMP/C-2/37.214 of 19 July 2005

Eco-Emballages, Commission Decision 2001/663/EC, OJ 2001 L 233/37

Eurovision, Commission Decision 2000/400/EC, OJ 2000 L 151/18

IFPI Simulcasting, Commission Decision 2003/300/EC, OJ 2003 L 107/58

Ilmailulaitos/Luftfartsverket, Commission Decision 1999/198/EC, OJ 1999 L 69/24

ISAB Energy, Case No. IV/E-3.35.698, OJ 1996 C 138/3

Newscorp/Telepiu, Commission Decision 2004/311/EC, OJ 2004 L 110/73.

RAI/UNITEL, Commission Decision 78/516/EEC, OJ 1978 L 157/39, 40

REN/Turbogas, Case No. IV/E-2/35.485, OJ 1996 C 118/7

RTL/Veronica/Endemol, Commission Decision 96/649/EG, OJ 1996 L 294/14

Santiago Agreement, COMP/C2/38.126, OJ 2001 C 145/2

Scottish Nuclear, Commission Decision 91/329/EEC, OJ 1991 L 178/31

Sony/BMG, Commission Decision COMP/M.3333 of 19 July 2004

UEFA Champions League, Commission Decision 2003/778/EC, OJ 2003 L 291/25

Universal International Music BV/MCPS and other (The Cannes Extension Agreement), COMP/C2/38.681, OJ 2006 C 122/2

Vivendi/Canal+/Seagram, Commission Decision IV/M.2050, OJ 2000 C 311/3

EUROPEAN COMMISSION STATE AID DECISIONS

(all decisions available at <http://ec.europa.eu/comm/competition/state_aid/register/ii/#by_case_number>, 7 July 2006).

Commission Decision N 411/2004 of 14 December 2004

Commission Decision N 496/2004 of 3 November 2004

Commission Decision N 224/2004 of 30 June 2004

Commission Decision N 181/2004 of 16 June 2004

Commission Decision N 530/2003 of 16 December 2003

Commission Decision N 513/2003 of 16 December 2003

Commission Decision N 353/2003 of 10 December 2003

Commission Decision N 261/2003 of 15 October 2003

Commission Decision N 313/2004 of 6 December 2004

Commission Decision N 37/2003 of 1 October 2003

EUROPEAN COURT OF HUMAN RIGHTS

ECHR *Barthold*, Series A Case No. 90
ECHR *Groppera Radio AG* et al, Series A Case No. 173
ECHR *Handyside* Series A Case No. 24
ECHR *Lingens*, Series A Case No. 103
ECHR *Informationsverein Lentia*, Series A Case No. 276
ECHR *Markt Intern*, Series A Case No. 165
ECHR *Tele 1 PrivatfernsehgesellschaftmbH*, Case No. 32240/96 [2000]
ECHR *Sunday Times*, Series A Case No. 30
ECHR *Von Hannover*, Case No. 59320/00 [2004]

Index

EUROPEAN MONOGRAPHS

1. Lammy Betten (ed.), *The Future of European Social Policy* (second and revised edition, 1991).
2. J.M.E. Loman, K.J.M. Mortelmans, H.H.G. Post, J.S. Watson, *Culture and Community Law: Before and after Maastricht* (1992).
3. Prof. Dr. J.A.E. Vervaele, *Fraud Against the Community: The Need for European Fraud Legislation* (1992).
4. P. Rawortli, *The Legislative Process in the European Community* (1993).
5. J. Stuyck, *Financial and Monetary Integration in the European Economic Community* (1993).
6. J.H.V. Stuyck, A.J. Vossestein (eds.), *State Entrepreneurship, National Monopolies and European Community Law* (1993).
7. J. Stuyck, A. Looijestijn-Clearie (eds.), *The European Area EC-EFTA* (1994).
8. R.B. Bouterse, *Competition and Integration – What Goals Count?* (1994).
9. R. Barents, *The Agricultural Law of the EC* (1994).
10. Nicholas Emiliou, *The Principle of Proportionality in European Law: A Comparative Study* (1996).
11. Eivind Smith, *National Parliaments as Cornerstones of European Integration* (1996).
12. Jan H. Jans, *European Environmental Law* (1996).
13. Siofra O'Leary, *The Evolving Concept of Community Citizenship: From the Free Movement of Persons to Union Citizenship* (1996).
14. Laurence Gormley (ed.), *Current and Future Perspectives on EC Competition Law* (1997).
15. Simone White, *Protection of the Financial Interests of the European Communities: The Fight against Fraud and Corruption* (1998).
16. Morten P. Broberg, *The European Commission's Jurisdiction to Scrutinise Mergers*, Third Edition (2006).
17. Doris Hildebrand, *The Role of Economic Analysis in the EC Competition Rules: The European School*, Second Edition (2002).
18. Christof R.A. Swaak, *European Community Law and the Automobile Industry* (1999).
19. Dorthe Dahlgaard Dingel, *Public Procurement. A Harmonization of the National Judicial Review of the Application of European Community Law* (1999).
20. J.A.E. Vervaele (ed.), *Compliance and Enforcement of European Community Law* (1999).
21. Martin Trybus, *European Defence Procurement Law: International and National Procurement Systems as Models for a Liberalised Defence Procurement Market in Europe* (1999).

KLUWER LAW INTERNATIONAL

22. Helen Staples, *The Legal Status of Third Country Nationals Resident in the European Union* (1999).
23. Damien Geradin (ed.), *The Liberalization of State Monopolies in the European Union and Beyond* (2000).
24. Katja Heede, *European Ombudsman: Redress and Control at Union Level* (2000).
25. Ulf Bernitz, Joakim Nergelius (eds.), *General Principles of European Community Law* (2000).
26. Michaela Drahos, *Convergence of Competition Laws and Policies in the European Community* (2001).
27. Damien Geradin (ed.), *The Liberalization of Electricity and Natural Gas in the European Union* (2001).
28. Gisella Gori, *Towards an EU Right to Education* (2001).
29. Brendan Smith, *Constitution Building in the European Union* (2001).
30. Freidl Weiss and Frank Wooldridge, *Free Movement of Persons within the European Community* (2002).
31. Ingrid Boccardi, *Europe and Refugees: Towards an EU Asylum Policy* (2002).
32. John A.E. Vervaele, André Klip (eds.), *European Cooperation Between Tax, Customs and Judicial Authorities* (2001).
33. Wouter P.J. Wils, *The Optimal Enforcement of EC Antitrust Law: Essays in Law and Economics* (2002).
34. Damien Geradin (ed.), *The Liberalization of Postal Services in the European Union* (2002).
35. Nick Bernard, *Multilevel Governance in the European Union* (2002).
36. Jill Wakefield, *Judicial Protection through the Use of Article 288(2)EC* (2002).
37. Sebastiaan Princen, *EU Regulation and Transatlantic Trade* (2002).
38. Amaryllis Verhoeven, *The European Union in Search of a Democratic and Constitutional Theory* (2002).
39. Paul Torremans, *Cross Border Insolvencies in EU English and Belgian Law* (2002).
40. Malcolm Anderson, Joanna Apap (eds.), *Police and Justice Co-operation and the New European Borders* (2002).
41. Christine M. Forstinger, *Takeover Law in the EU and the USA: A Comparative Analysis* (2002).
42. Antonio Bavasso, *Communications in EU Antitrust Law: Market Power and Public Interest* (2003).
43. Fiona Wishlade, *Regional State Aid and Competition Policy* (2003).
44. Gareth Davies, *Nationality Discrimination in the European Internal Market* (2003).

EUROPEAN MONOGRAPHS

45. René Barents, *The Autonomy of Community Law* (2004).
46. Gerhard Dannecker, Oswald Jansen (eds.), *Competition Law Sanctioning in the European Union. The EU-Law Influence on the National System of Sanctions in the European Area* (2004).
47. NautaDutilh (ed.), *Dealing with Dominance. The Experience of National Competition Authorities* (2004).
48. Stefaan Van den Bogaert, *Practical Regulation of the Mobility of Sportsmen in the EU Post Bosman* (2005).
49. Katalin Judit Cseres, *Competition Law and Consumer Protection* (2005).
50. Philipp Kiiver, *The National Parliament, in the European Union* (2006).
51. Alexander Heinrich Türk, *The Concept of Legislation in European Community Law: A Comparative Perspective* (2006).
52. Dimitrios Sinaniotis, *The Interim Protection of Individuals before the European and National Courts* (2006).
53. Michael Holoubek, Dragana Damjanovic, Matthias Traimer (eds.), *Regulating Content – European Regulatory Framework for the Media and Related Creative Sectors* (2007).

KLUWER LAW INTERNATIONAL